W9-BBK-584

How Wars End

WITHDRAWN

WITHDRAWN

How Wars End

Dan Reiter

PRINCETON UNIVERSITY PRESS

PRINCETON AND OXFORD

CARL A. RUDISILL LIBRARY
LENOIR-RHYNE UNIVERSITY

February 2011

Copyright © 2009 by Princeton University Press
Requests for permission to reproduce material from this work should
be sent to Permissions, Princeton University Press
Published by Princeton University Press, 41 William Street,
Princeton, New Jersey 08540
In the United Kingdom: Princeton University Press, 6 Oxford Street,
Woodstock, Oxfordshire OX20 1TW

All Rights Reserved

Library of Congress Cataloging-in-Publication Data

Reiter, Dan, 1967–
    How wars end / Dan Reiter.
        p.   cm.
    Includes bibliographical references and index.
    ISBN 978-0-691-14060-5 (paper : alk. paper) —
    ISBN 978-0-691-14059-9 (cloth : alk. paper)
    1. Peace—History—20th century. 2. Peace—History—19th century.
    3. War"History—20th century. 4. War—History—19th century. I. Title.
    JZ5560.R45 2009
      355.02—dc22   2009008556

British Library Cataloging-in-Publication Data is available

This book has been composed in Sabon

Printed on acid-free paper. ∞

press.princeton.edu

Printed in the United States of America

10   9   8   7   6   5   4   3   2   1

JZ
5560
.R45
2009

CARL A. RUDISILL LIBRARY
LENOIR-RHYNE UNIVERSITY
OCLC # 311311031Y
924.95

DEDICATED WITH LOVE

To Noah Charen Reiter and Zev Franklin Reiter

Every war must end.

 —*Fred Iklé*

Contents

Figures and Tables

Acknowledgments

I FIRST STARTED THINKING about how wars are fought and ended in the mid-1990s. Allan Stam and I were hard at work on our project explaining why democracies win wars, and in 1997 we presented one of the early papers from that project at a special conference on the conduct of war organized by Scott Gartner at the University of California, Davis. Several important papers on the prosecution and termination of war appeared at that conference, including a paper by Hein Goemans (a precursor to his major war-termination book *War and Punishment*), the first in a string of papers connecting wartime casualties to public opinion by Scott Gartner and Gary Segura, a quantitative paper by Suzanne Werner explaining why wars end in absolute or limited outcomes, a quantitative paper by Allan Stam and Scott Bennett on the duration of wars, and one of the earliest theoretical papers explaining bargaining during war by Alastair Smith, among others. Donald Wittman, author of a critical and often underappreciated 1979 *Journal of Conflict* article on war termination, appropriately served as discussant. This collection of papers helped establish and advance the developing theoretical and empirical agenda for understanding how wars are fought, won, and ended.

Around this time, the field was just beginning to realize how powerful the bargaining metaphor is for describing war. Harrison Wagner's 2000 *American Journal of Political Science* article, which built on James Fearon's seminal 1995 *International Organization* article, really opened my eyes to the power of thinking about war as a bargaining process. I was invited to a 2001 conference organized by Alastair Smith at Yale on the bargaining model of war, for which I wrote a paper that reviewed the bargaining model of war literature. That conference included a number of important papers by scholars that pushed the boundaries in this area. Some of the same people who were at the 1997 Davis conference attended, plus others such as Robert Powell, Barbara Walter, and William Reed. The 2001 Yale conference produced a number of important papers that went on to be published in top journals and to shape the field. My review paper was probably the least ambitious in the group, and eventually was published in *Perspectives on Politics* in 2003.

It struck me around this time that although the bargaining model of war was enjoying extensive theoretical development, the empirical side was lagging. Do wars actually play out as the bargaining model portrays? My first inclination was to construct a gigantic quantitative dataset of intrawar behavior, collecting data in particular on the outcomes of battles within wars. I knew that such a project would likely consume hundreds of thousands of dollars in grant money and take several years. However, two problems soon appeared. First, my initial grant requests were rejected. Second, the more I thought about applying quantitative/statistical techniques to tackle this issue, the more I concluded that the applications of such techniques faced serious problems. Most importantly, the data were too messy and wars were too heterogeneous. I recount some of my thinking on these issues in chapter 4 of this book.

I also started to think about the theoretical structure of the bargaining model of war. I scratched out one or two ideas in a paper I presented at a 2003 special conference on military effectiveness hosted by Risa Brooks at Northwestern University. That paper received what can kindly be described as a lukewarm reception, and I switched topics for the next conference in the Northwestern project (I ending up writing a paper on Japanese military effectiveness in World War II; working on that paper helped prepare me to write chapter 10 in this book).

But I kept thinking about the theoretical side of the bargaining model. I went back to the drawing board on theory, and sketched out a few more ideas. I wrote another paper laying out those ideas and then illustrating them with a case study of the American Civil War. I presented that paper at the 2005 meeting of the Peace Science Society (that paper provided some of the foundations for chapter 8 in this book). This paper also attracted little interest, and I began to have doubts about what to do next.

After the Peace Science meeting, I decided that another way to go might be to develop at least one of my theoretical insights within the structure of a formal model. I selected one of the half dozen or so theoretical ideas I had been batting around, and roped a colleague and a graduate student (Cliff Carrubba and Scott Wolford) into coauthoring a paper with me presenting a formal model of the basic theoretical point that fear of a belligerent reneging on a war-ending agreement may affect wartime bargaining behavior (this insight is presented informally in chapter 3 of this book). We presented this paper at the 2006 Midwest Political Science Association meeting and a few other places and spent the next couple of years getting feedback and revising it (as of this writing, the paper is under review for publication). I began to have faith there was an important theoretical point to be made.

However, I could not let go of the empirical side. I was torn. I had long believed that quantitative analysis was the most productive way to test scientific propositions, but my doubts about executing quantitative tests in this area remained substantial. To my great luck, I had coincidentally agreed to teach summer school at Dartmouth College in 2006. While in Hanover, I had several discussions with various members of the faculty in Dartmouth's government department about the project, both the theoretical and empirical sides. From my Dartmouth colleagues, I received useful feedback and general encouragement that a case study approach would make a contribution. As is often the case, the most useful advice came here and there, while shooting the breeze in someone's office, grabbing a hamburger for lunch, or strolling to Fenway Park in Boston. Reinvigorated, I returned to Atlanta that August ready to tear into the project.

The bulk of the book gushed out in the 2006–7 academic year. Once I was ready to let go of quantitative tests and really embrace case studies, the pieces quickly fell together. My colleagues at Dartmouth did me another great favor, agreeing to attend a small conference on the first draft of the book manuscript, offering me feedback. The conference took place in summer 2007, and I was again blessed with considerable encouragement, constructive feedback, and ideas for new directions. Around this time, I finished a somewhat related quantitative empirical paper, coauthored with two Emory graduate students, Nigel Lo and Barry Hashimoto. This paper provided quantitative empirical support for the model's empirical assumption that the imposition of foreign-imposed regime change would significantly decrease the likelihood of war between two former belligerents. We presented this paper at the 2007 annual meeting of the American Political Science Association. It was published in *International Organization* in 2008.

As is likely evident, I have accumulated substantial personal debts in writing this book. Thanks to Virginia Lewick of the Roosevelt Presidential Library in Hyde Park, New York. David Clark and the rest of the staff at the Truman Presidential Library in Independence, Missouri were extremely helpful. For research assistance of all types, my thanks to Rochdi Alloui, Barry Hashimoto, Aryeh Reiter, Chana Reiter, John Reuter, Emily Hencken Ritter, Phil Fuerst, Jakub Kakietek, Maryann Gallagher, Matthew Payne, Michiyo Sakai, Goran Peic, and Terry Chapman. I received helpful comments when portions of this project were presented at the 2005 Peace Science Society (International) meeting, the 2006 Midwest Political Science Association meeting, the University of Chicago, the University of South Carolina, Emory University, Yale University, Duke University, and Princeton University. For comments on various stages of this project, I'd also like to thank Ashley Leeds, James Morrow, Hein Goemans, and Bumba Mukherjee. Thanks as well to Bill Wohlforth and the Dickey Center at Dartmouth and the Institute for Comparative and International Studies at Emory for supporting a small conference at Dartmouth on the book project. Participants at the book conference, including Allan Stam, Ben Valentino, Bridget Coggins, Daryl Press, Jenny Lind, and Stephen Brooks all provided tremendously useful feedback. Thanks to Amy Benson Brown for her feedback on the writing and style of the manuscript. Thanks to Randy Strahan, Kyle Beardsley, Jack Snyder, and Tanisha Fazal for graciously reading the entire manuscript and providing feedback. Thanks to my coauthors, Cliff Carrubba, Barry Hashimoto, Nigel Lo, and Scott Wolford, for working with me on papers that served as pieces for various parts of the book. Thanks to Shane Kelley for drawing such useful maps. Thanks once again to Chuck Myers of Princeton University Press for his always helpful editorial guidance. This research was supported in part by the University Research Committee and the Bill and Carol Fox Center for Humanistic Inquiry, both of Emory University. All opinions and any remaining errors are of course exclusively my own. My deepest gratitude, however, is saved, as always, for my wife Carolann, for all her patient support.

I left out various exhortations, notions, original and hortatory allusions, notes, denials; zeal exceeded volume. Such omissions notwithstanding, I dedicate this book with love to my sons, Noah Charen Reiter and Zev Franklin Reiter. When writing this book, I often thought of them and John Adams' famous remark, "I must study politics and war that my sons may have liberty to study mathematics and philosophy. My sons ought to study mathematics and philosophy, geography, natural history, naval architecture, navigation, commerce, and agriculture in order to give their children a right to study painting, poetry, music, architecture, statuary, tapestry, and porcelain." I must confess that unlike John Adams I find the study of politics and war as joyful as the study of poetry, music, or anything else. I wish my sons great luck in finding their own paths to joy.

How Wars End

CHAPTER ONE

Ending Wars

> Love is like war; easy to begin but very hard to stop.
> —H. L. Mencken

HOW, WHEN, AND WHY do belligerents end wars? Why do some losing belligerents, such as the United States in the early months of the Korean War, the Confederacy in the twilight of the American Civil War, Britain during the dark night of May 1940, and the United States in the first months of World War II, refuse to consider negotiating to end their wars on acceptable terms and instead fight on in pursuit of victory? Why do some winning belligerents, such as the Soviet Union in the latter months of its 1939–40 and 1941–44 wars against Finland, elect to stop fighting and accepted limited gains rather than fight onward in pursuit of the total defeat of the adversary?

This book seeks to solve these and other puzzles regarding the termination of wars. Why are some belligerents willing to end wars on limited terms? Why do some belligerents refuse to end war short of total victory? What factors push belligerents to demand more or less of the adversary at the negotiating table while war is raging? We know relatively little about how wars end, in contrast to the mountain ranges of ideas and scholarship we have about how wars start. Indeed, there has been something of an aversion to the study of war termination over the past several decades. The total nature of World War II seemed a denial of the political significance of war termination since in an era of total war the belligerents fight with all their resources until one side is utterly crushed. This neglect of war termination persisted through the Cold War, when most assumed that any major war would quickly escalate to nuclear attacks and Armageddon, making the topic of war termination a grim joke. Interest in war termination received little boost by the Vietnam War, as the bad taste left by that conflict encouraged thinking about stopping wars from happening rather than stopping wars once they have started. Beyond work of purely historical interest, such as the voluminous literature on why Japan surrendered in 1945, relatively few works exist that consider the question of war termination more generally.[1]

War termination must receive closer attention. The end of the Cold War did not bring the "end of history" and the end of war as some had forecast and fervently hoped for. In the twenty-first century, policymakers must understand how to end the wars that their nations have become involved in, and they must have better tools to help end wars being fought by other nations. On the scholarly side, a full understanding of war, if not international relations more broadly, requires developing theoretical structures that provide integrated accounts of all aspects of war, its duration, outcome, termination, and post-war phase, as well as initiation. The theory of war termination provided here is developed in the context of comprehensive ideas about the nature of war and politics, and offers progress towards developing a grand unified theory of war that would provide an integrated account of all of war's phases.

The Nature of War, The Nature of War Termination

War termination, war, and even international relations itself can be usefully conceived as a bargaining process, following Thomas Schelling's famous insight that "most conflict situations are essentially *bargaining* situations."[2] States clash over issues such as the placement of international borders and the composition of national governments, and bargain with each over how these issues should be settled (for example, where an international border should lie). War is part of this bargaining process, since states start wars to get more of what they want on disputed issues, and the ends of wars are literally bargains struck to create new settlements of the disputed issues. Underlying this notion of war as bargaining is the assumption that war is fought for political goals. As the Prussian military thinker Carl von Clausewitz memorably put it, *"war is nothing but the continuation of policy with other means."*[3]

This book presents a bargaining theory of war termination. A central advantage of using a bargaining approach to war termination is that it nicely incorporates two of our most profound and powerful insights about international relations: that uncertainty about the power and intentions of states pervades the international system, and that states cannot make binding commitments to each other. The bargaining approach proposes that the problems of uncertainty and unenforceable commitments cause war, fighting war serves to alleviate these problems, and war ends when these problems have been reduced sufficiently or eliminated.

Uncertainty and incomplete information comprise a long-standing account of how wars break out. Specifically, when two states in dispute disagree about the balance of power or the relative steadfastness of each side to prevail, war may result, especially if each side is confident it can prevail in a clash of arms. The outcomes of combat and the decisions of states to make concessions or hold fast help reduce disagreement between the two sides about the balances of power and resolve. Eventually, when enough disagreement has been reduced and the two sides are in sufficient accord about the true balances of power and resolve, then war-ending agreement becomes possible. In short, uncertainty causes war, combat provides information and reduces uncertainty, and war ends when enough information has been provided. A central information-based war-termination hypothesis is that a belligerent will be more likely to make concessions to its adversary in pursuit of war termination following combat defeats, and following combat successes it is less likely to make concessions and may even present new demands of its adversary. This well-established insight is described and developed in chapter 2.

The exposition of a commitment-based explanation of war termination, the heart of chapter 3, is this book's greatest theoretical contribution. The chapter considers a core problem with war-termination settlements. Even if two combatants sign an agreement to end their war, the commitment of each not to attack the other after war's end is not enforceable. There is no world government with the authority or power to compel two former belligerents to comply with the terms of a war-ending agreement. The lack of such a government is the central difference between international politics and national politics. Of course, scholars as far back as the ancient Greek Thucydides have used the commitment insight to explain the causes of war, proposing in particular that a changing balance of power between two states can make war more likely, because the nation growing in relative power cannot credibly commit not to attack in the future.[4] The commitment insight has been fruitfully applied to explain the dynamics of civil wars, because civil war belligerents, governments, and rebel groups gravely fear that the other side will violate a war-ending agreement, especially if the deal calls for one side to lay down its arms. This commitment fear explains why civil wars last so long, and also why third-party intervention is so important for helping achieve a negotiated settlement.[5]

Although the existing commitments scholarship has provided some very useful insights and advances, it leaves essentially unasked questions of how war (and specifically war outcomes) can solve commitment compliance problems. This book pushes these core insights about commitments and war termination in new directions, examining interstate as well as civil wars and moving beyond viewing commitment noncompliance fears as simply barriers to war termination. Specifically, this book explores how these noncompliance fears shape war-termination decision-making during wartime, and relatedly how states pursue certain war outcomes in order to solve these noncompliance problems.

One central point is that total victory can solve commitment problems. Sometimes a belligerent can achieve what Clausewitz called an "absolute" war outcome, utterly vanquishing the adversary. In application, this can mean the victor installing a new leadership in the defeated state, occupying or annexing the adversary's territory, or at worst annihilating the adversary's entire population. All of these outcomes permit the belligerent to impose essentially whatever war outcome it wishes. These outcomes also permit the belligerent to remove in effect or in fact the adversary's ability to violate the agreement, thereby solving the compliance commitment problem. Liquidating the adversary through annexation or genocide, of course, directly prevents breaking the commitment to peace. Foreign imposed regime change, a more frequent war outcome, substantially decreases the likelihood that the war-ending agreement will be broken, since an installed puppet is generally unlikely to deviate from the demands of the puppet-master victor. The central proposition in chapter 3 is that the more a belligerent fears its adversary may violate the war-ending terms of an agreement, the more likely the belligerent will be to pursue an absolute victory.

War can also solve the commitment problem with more limited outcomes that fall short of absolute victory. Sometimes the terms of a limited war outcome directly alter the balance of power, as when a peace treaty transfers strategic territory from one side to another, or when a peace treaty demands that one side abandon or eschew a powerful weapon. A belligerent, fearful that its adversary may reattack in the future, may be willing to accept such a limited war outcome that shifts the balance of power and makes a future attack less appealing to the adversary.

This book integrates the information and commitment perspectives on war termination into a single theory, towards understanding how information and commitment dynamics interact in affecting war-termination decision-making. Importantly, these two dynamics sometimes operate in tension with each other. For example, credible commitment fears may delay war termination, even as uncertainty and disagreement are being reduced. Specifically, under some conditions severe credible commitment fears may cause a state to seek absolute victory over its opponent even in the face of battlefield defeat. This prediction runs counter to an information-only view of war termination, that battlefield defeats should always make a belligerent consider making diplomatic concessions as a means of hastening war's end. Conversely, the reduction of uncertainty may make war termination possible, despite a belligerent's enduring concerns about commitment credibility. As a belligerent comes to learn that continuing the war will pose escalating costs and dangers, it may become willing to accept a peace settlement, even if such a settlement leaves standing an untrustworthy adversary.

The theoretical portion of this book provides a structure for understanding when information dynamics are likely to determine war-termination behavior, and when commitment dynamics are likely to determine war-termination behavior. Specifically, belligerents fearful of a credible commitment problem are more likely to fight on to solve the commitment problem when the costs of continuing to fight are acceptable, when the dangers of a broken war-ending agreement grow, and/or when there is at least some hope of eventual victory. Conversely, belligerents fearful of a credible commitment problem are more likely to accept war termination short of total victory and a completely satisfying solution to the commitment problem when the costs of continuing to fight threaten to escalate significantly, when the dangers one side will break a war-ending agreement are lower, when the chances of eventual victory approach zero, and/or when the belligerent is able to reduce the commitment problem through limited means, such as acquiring strategic territory.

The Termination of Actual Wars

Any understanding of war must be grounded in the empirical. How have wars actually ended? How well does actual behavior square with our theoretical expectations?

I provide some of the first empirical evidence that directly assesses how belligerents try to end wars, and whether and how war-termination behavior is shaped by information and commitment dynamics. Specifically, a belligerent who loses battles is supposed to downgrade its estimates of its own military power, and be more willing to offer concessions. Is this what actually happens? Does war-termination diplomacy tend to follow battlefield outcomes in this manner? If not, are there conditions under which this pattern is observed, and conditions under which it is not? While there is a small body of research that looks for empirical patterns indirectly implied by the growing theoretical scholarship on bargaining and war, almost no work exists that attempts to assess more directly whether the exact processes forecast by these and other models, such as battlefield defeat causing pessimism and thus diplomatic concessions, actually occur during wartime.

This book examines war-termination decisions and dynamics in an array of wars, including the Korean War, the Allies in World War II, Japan during World War II, Germany during World War I, the Union and Confederacy during the American Civil War, and Finland and the Soviet Union during both the Winter War and the Continuation War. These cases are neither a complete sample of all belligerents during wars nor are they a random sample. However, they do represent a wide range of historical/political/military contexts since they include long wars and short wars, both civil and international wars, wars between equal powers and between unequal powers, wars fought to the finish of unconditional surrender and wars fought to more limited outcomes, wars fought in a variety of regions including North America, Europe, and East Asia, and wars fought across nearly a century of time, from the 1860s to the 1950s.

Analysis of these wars permits exploration of a number of specific historical war-termination puzzles, beyond those enumerated at the beginning of this chapter. Some of these puzzles include:

- How did the Soviet Union react to the December 1939 battlefield disasters it faced against Finland during the Winter War?
- How did the Soviet Union react in the first few months after the June 1941 German invasion, when the capture of Moscow appeared likely and imminent?
- How did President Lincoln react to the apparent collapse of support for the Union war effort in summer 1864, when continuation of the war seemed to ensure his electoral defeat that November?
- Why did Lincoln embrace the emancipation of the slaves, an act that raised the Union's war aims, in autumn 1862?
- Why did Germany, as it was defeating Russia in the East, reject Allied peace overtures in the winter of 1917–18 and instead choose to continue the war by renewing its offensive in the West?
- How did Japan react to the steady slide in its military fortunes from 1943 to 1945, and why did it eventually accept near unconditional surrender in August 1945?

The empirical results in this book are complex and nuanced. Both commitment and information dynamics play important roles in determining war-termination behavior. The results provide support for the most novel theoretical proposition of the model, that credible commitment fears help determine war-termination behavior. Belligerents sometimes press for absolute victory because they fear this is the only true solution to an enduring credible commitment problem. The results also indicate that information dynamics play an important role in determining war-termination behavior, although perhaps in contrast to some conventional thinking, information cannot provide a complete account of how states end wars. Sometimes belligerents pursue absolute victory to solve commitment problems, even in the face of combat setbacks. Conversely, though, not all belligerents who fear that the adversary will break a war-ending agreement decide to pursue absolute victory. Belligerents are less likely to pursue absolute victory if they fear the costs of war will escalate gravely (perhaps because of third-party intervention) if such an outcome is pursued, if breaking the war-ending commitment has less than catastrophic consequences, if they see the chances of eventual victory as approaching zero, and/or if the vagaries of geography or military technology make a limited war outcome an acceptable if partial solution to a credible commitment problem.

There are other findings as well. The fog of war and the patience of leaders also sometimes sever the connection between battle outcomes and war-termination behavior. Additionally, the cases indicate the curious insignificance of domestic politics in war-termination decision-making, in contrast to existing theoretical and empirical research on how democracies fight wars. There is little evidence that democratic leaders are especially casualty-sensitive, and hence are more likely than other kinds of leaders to consider concessions as casualties mount. There is also little evidence for the specialized hypothesis that leaders of semirepressive, moderately exclusionary regimes are likely to raise their war aims when their states are losing in order to avoid facing the severe personal punishment that awaits them in the event of defeat in war. That being said, there is some evidence for a perhaps related pattern of behavior, that belligerents with weak civilian control of the military may fight longer wars.

OUTLINE OF THE BOOK

The structure of the book is as follows. The theory of war termination is developed in chapters 2 and 3. Chapter 2 lays out the main ideas and propositions of the information approach. Chapter 3 develops a number of ideas about how commitment concerns shape war-termination behavior. Chapter 4 addresses a number of issues regarding research design and methodology. Chapters 5 through 10 present the historical case studies.

Chapter 11 seeks to accomplish two tasks. First, it offers a summary of the book's empirical findings, relating them back to the theoretical ideas laid out in chapters 2 and 3, and to the study of international relations more broadly. Second, it applies the empirical findings to problems of American foreign policy in the twenty-first century. After 9/11, the George W. Bush Administration thought about wars in the context of commitment problems, that rogue states like Iraq could not be trusted to adhere to their international commitments, meaning that war culminating in absolute victory, such as foreign imposed regime change, may be the only way of assuring American national security. Some have also suggested lesser means of solving commitment problems faced by the United States, including launching air strikes against rogue states' weapons of mass destruction production facilities. Chapter 11 discusses and evaluates both the regime change and airstrikes strategies, framing them within the book's general theory.

CHAPTER TWO

Bargaining, Information, and Ending Wars

The battlefield is the most honest place on Earth.
—Retired U.S. Lieutenant Colonel Bo Gritz

WAR IS FUNDAMENTALLY POLITICAL. It is launched, fought, and ended in pursuit of political goals. This was the fundamental insight of nineteenth-century Prussian thinker Carl von Clausewitz. He opposed the more traditional view that war is an exercise in military engineering, a fulfillment of one nineteenth-century German general's wish that, "The politician should fall silent the moment that mobilization begins."[1]

War is about politics, and politics, especially in this context, is essentially about the allocation of scarce goods. Goods are phenomena valued by political actors. Goods are scarce if there is not an optimal or infinite supply of the good, meaning that all actors cannot simultaneously consume or possess an optimal or infinite amount of the good. Territory, natural resources, and the composition of a national government are all examples of phenomena viewed by international actors as scarce goods. Even nonmaterial phenomena like reputation can be viewed as scarce goods, as in a confrontation where a state best proves its toughness by coercing the other side to retreat and concede its weakness.

A useful metaphor for thinking about how states interact with each other and attempt to maintain or expand their possessions of scarce goods is *bargaining*, the process by which two actors strive to divide a disputed good.[2] Buyers and sellers bargain over price, labor and management bargain over wages, and nations bargain over goods like the placement of an international border. Scholars have also used bargaining models to shed light on how wars start, focusing in particular on the role of information and uncertainty. This chapter advances the application of the bargaining metaphor, going beyond using it to understand how wars start, and applying it to also understand how wars end. It presents the first half of this book's theory.

A WAR INITIATION PUZZLE

Imagine that two states dispute the allocation of a scarce good, such as the placement of a territorial border, and war looms. Assume that war is costly for both sides, since both the winner and loser must pay war costs in blood and treasure. If both sides knew who would win the war, and how the disputed good would be (re)divided at war's end, wouldn't each side be better off not fighting and just dividing the good to reflect how the good would have been divided if the war had occurred? Each would get the same amount of the good it would have gotten had the war occurred, and neither has to pay the unavoidable war costs of money wasted and lives lost. This insight is also demonstrated by a "divide the dollar" game, where two players pay a referee five cents each to roll a one-hundred-sided die, and the number turned up by the die roll determines how a dollar is divided between the two players (for example, a roll of seventy-five gives one player seventy-five cents, and one player twenty-five cents), and the payoff is the die roll minus the nickel fee (seventy-five cents minus five cents equals seventy cents). But, if each player knew ahead of time what number the die would turn up, the two of them could just divide the dollar according to what that die roll would have been, each saving the five cents that the referee would have collected as a fee for rolling the die. So the puzzle is: Why would these two players ever roll the die? Why do states ever go to war?

Importantly, the assumption that wars are always on balance costly for each side is not uncontroversial. Some feminist approaches contend that states may fight for the sake of fighting, as wars serve patriarchy by reinforcing gender identity.[3] A more mainstream critique is that leaders go to war for domestic political reasons, such that a war-avoiding bargain might not be reachable even when both sides knew who would win, as fighting itself provides domestic political benefits from a war to both winner and loser.[4] Under some conditions, especially if a state is undergoing democratization or if a national leader is experiencing domestic political problems such as unrest or economic downturn, a state may see war as a way to rally the public around the leader and stave off domestic political challenges.[5] The proposition that leaders go to war when facing domestic difficulties is often called the "diversionary" hypothesis.

However, the evidence that leaders choose war to solve internal political problems is thin. The underlying assumption is that going to war engenders a rally round the flag effect that boosts the popularity of leaders, but leaders reap this benefit only under very narrow conditions (which often cannot be controlled by the attacking state), and even the biggest rallies are short-lived.[6] Importantly, there is almost no smoking gun historical evidence of a leader launching a war primarily as a means of solving domestic political problems. At most, politicians have occasionally speculated about diversionary action, such as Secretary of State William Seward's (ignored) April 1861 suggestion to President Abraham Lincoln that the United States provoke crises with European powers as a means of staving off civil war between the Union and the seceding southern states.[7] A Russian minister is famously thought to have declared just after the outbreak of the 1904–05 Russo-Japanese War that, "We need a little, victorious war to stem the tide of revolution," but the story is likely too good to be true.[8] Leaders sometimes see indirect relationships between starting war and reaping domestic political benefits, such as the possibility that Lyndon Johnson escalated the Vietnam War in 1965 to protect his Great Society program from domestic political attack.[9] Some quantitative studies have found that the presence of internal problems like declining economic growth, rising inflation, partial democratization, or declining leader popularity are correlated with an (often slightly) increased likelihood in the use of force. However, these relationships are often limited in scope, occurring only under certain economic or political conditions.[10] Any possible diversionary effects might in turn be moderated by the tendency of states to avoid provoking other states that might have diversionary incentives.[11]

AN INFORMATION-BASED SOLUTION TO THE WAR INITIATION PUZZLE

One long-standing solution to the war initiation puzzle of "Why do states ever fight?" is to relax the assumption that the two states agree on what the outcome of the war would be, and allow for the two sides to disagree. For example, if each side thinks it will win, that constitutes disagreement about how the war will end. If each side thinks it will win, then prior to war each will demand a victor's share of the disputed good as the price for avoiding war. However, the scarcity of the good makes such an arrangement impossible, as one cannot give simultaneously to each side the majority of a finite good. At least one state will prefer to take its chances with war rather than take an unacceptably low share of the good, encouraged by confidence in its own war-making abilities and faced with an adversary who is unwilling to make a sufficient concession because it in turn also thinks it will win.

This argument received formal treatment in a famous 1995 article by James Fearon.[12] He developed a formal model of two states bargaining over a disputed good, culminating with this same puzzle that when two states agree on how a war will unfold, they should be able to avoid war and (re)divide the good to reflect how the good would be divided if the war were fought. Fearon developed three answers to the puzzle of why war happens. First, war may occur if the two sides do not agree on how the war will unfold on the battlefield.[13] Second, war may occur if the good under dispute does not lend itself to division. This argument is discussed at the end of chapter 3. Third, war may occur if at least one side fears the willingness of the other side to comply with a war-ending bargain. This argument is closely related to the commitment propositions developed in chapter 3.

The focus in this chapter is on the first solution to the puzzle, disagreement between states about how the war will unfold. More specifically, there may be war-causing disagreement between states over five different phenomena, each of which affects war outcomes. The first is aggregate military power, which is a combination of size of standing army, the industrial capacity to produce munitions, the size of the population that can be mobilized into military service, and the political capacity to mobilize. Aggregate military power is one of the single biggest factors determining war outcomes, and if states disagree about the comparative ability of each side to field and arm troops, they may not agree on who will ultimately win, and will not be able to reach a war-avoiding agreement.[14]

More concretely, many wars have begun because of disagreement over aggregate military power. The core flaw behind Germany's ultimately doomed decision to invade the Soviet Union in June 1941 was the overestimation of its military strength in relation to Soviet military power.[15] Commenting in August 1941 on General Heinz Guderian's 1937 estimates of Soviet tank strength, Hitler told Guderian, "If I had known that the figures for Russian tank strength which you gave in your book were in fact the true ones, I would not—I believe—ever have started this war."[16] Conversely, when the asymmetry in power is unavoidably apparent, both sides may agree on the likely outcome of conflict, and avoid war. For instance, when the USSR made severe demands on Estonia in late September 1939 following the German invasion of Poland, the Estonians considered putting up a fight, but decided instead to make concessions, recognizing that their military of 15,000 would be no match for even the limited detachment of 160,000 Soviet soldiers deployed to the Soviet–Estonian border earlier that month.[17] Interestingly, however, there are some examples of leaders of clearly overmatched states nonetheless deciding to fight (examples include Belgian resistance to Germany in 1914 and 1940), often motivated by a variety of reasons including honor, domestic politics, and international reputation.[18]

The second area of potential war-causing disagreement is military technology, defined as machines or tools that contribute to aggregate firepower, accuracy of firepower, mobility, logistics, force protection, command and control, and/or intelligence gathering. There may be disagreement either about what technology each side has available to it, or how untested technology will play out during war. For example, in 1990–91 Iraq's military strategy rested on the assumption that it would be able to impose significant casualties on American and coalition forces, and that American and other democratic publics would be unwilling to absorb casualties to liberate Kuwait. However, Iraq underestimated the ability of American technology to protect coalition forces, specifically American air superiority and the longer firing range of American tanks, the latter of which permitted American tanks to destroy Iraqi tanks before entering the firing range of Iraqi tanks.[19] Serbia made a similar miscalculation in 1999, resting its strategy in the conflict with NATO over Kosovo on the hope it would be able to shoot down NATO aircraft. However, NATO forces, such as the American B-2 bomber, were able to execute bombing sorties from altitudes high enough to be out of range of some Serb air defense assets, thereby providing perfect force protection (no NATO personnel were lost during the war), and undermining Serb strategy.[20] A last example is the 1973 Yom Kippur War. Egypt secretly acquired advanced surface-to-air missiles (SAMs) from the Soviet Union after the debacle of the 1967 Six-Day War, which enabled Egyptian forces (at least initially) to improve the balance of power by neutralizing Israeli air assets.[21] Their confidence in their secret weapon helped encourage Egypt to launch the attack.

Third, there may be disagreement about the comparative interactions and effectiveness of the two sides' military strategies.[22] As with military technology, strategy—the plans for the employment of military forces during war—may be unknown and/or untested. In 1940, Germany and France disagreed about what military strategy Germany would employ in the event of a German invasion. France expected Germany to repeat its World War I strategy and move through Belgium en route to Paris. Germany instead planned a feint at Belgium to draw Allied forces forward, making their real attack through the Ardennes forest. Because France misunderstood Germany's strategy, France substantially overestimated its chances of victory, the "Phony War" of autumn 1939–spring 1940 blew up into a real war in Western Europe in May, and Germany conquered France, Belgium, Luxembourg, and the Netherlands with shocking speed.[23]

Secret strategy also played a role in the outbreak of the 1967 Six-Day War. Egypt maintained a substantial air force to bolster its ground power. Israel devised a strategy to neutralize the entire Egyptian air force before it could be used in battle. Israeli defense planners knew that essentially the entire Egyptian air force was on the ground at a particular time every morning, making it vulnerable to Israeli airstrikes. At the outset of the Six-Day War, the Israeli aircraft struck Egyptian aircraft on the ground at just this moment in the morning, destroying the bulk of the Egyptian air force and swinging the balance of power decisively in Israel's favor.[24]

Fourth, there may be disagreement about resolve, which is how a state values the stakes of the war in relation to the costs it must pay to win. Levels of resolve are an integral part of war outcomes, as the decision to continue fighting is a function of the costs of continued fighting as well as what benefits a side expects to get by continued fighting. Even if both belligerents knew how many casualties each would suffer if the war continued, they might disagree on the relative willingness of the two sides to suffer casualties. More generally, if both sides agreed on who would back down first and when, they could avoid war and settle on the outcome that would have happened had they fought.[25] If the two sides disagree about the balance of resolve and who would back down first and when, then war may ensue or endure if already begun. Iraq invaded Kuwait in 1990 falsely confident that the United States did not have the will to go to war to liberate Kuwait. Saddam Hussein blustered to an American diplomat before the invasion of Kuwait that America "is a society which cannot accept ten thousand dead in one battle."[26] Conversely, America underestimated North Vietnamese resolve in the 1960s. The United States assumed that North Vietnam had a "breaking point," and that all it needed to do was wield its considerable military superiority sufficiently to impose (or threaten to impose) enough losses on North Vietnam to pass that breaking point, and North Vietnam would make concessions to end the war. Secretary of State Henry Kissinger often remarked that, "North Vietnam could not be the only country in the world without a breaking point."[27] This strategy was half successful, in that the U.S. did impose staggering losses on North Vietnam during the war, in the range of 500,000 to 600,000 deaths, amounting to almost as much as 3 percent of its prewar population. And yet, North Vietnam never reached its breaking point in terms of civilian deaths. It made concessions only after American airpower had inflicted significant damage on North Vietnamese military assets in 1972.[28] As former Secretary of State Dean Rusk commented in 1971, "I personally underestimated the resistance and the determination of the North Vietnamese. They've taken over 700,000 killed which in relation to population is almost the equivalent of—what? Ten million Americans? And they continue to come."[29]

Fifth, there may be disagreement about the likelihood and/or impact of third-party intervention. This point can be related to the first four points since disagreement over third-party intervention means disagreement over the capabilities, technology, strategy, and/or resolve of the third party. An otherwise overmatched side may prefer war to concession if it thinks a third party may rescue it.[30] The Southern states of the U.S. were very confident up to 1861 that European dependence on the import of Southern cotton would force European intervention on the Southern side in the event of war. This "King Cotton" theory encouraged the Southern provocation and obstinacy that culminated in the outbreak of the American Civil War.[31]

Belief that a third party will not intervene to rescue its ally may inspire an aggressor to attack. Hitler ordered the September 1939 German attack on Poland confident that neither Britain nor France would uphold their treaty obligations to defend Poland.[32] Third-party intervention was also a critical factor in the escalation of the Korean War. In early September 1950, President Truman committed the United States to conquering North Korea as well as liberating the entirety of South Korea, "provided that at the time of such operations there has been no entry into [that area of]...major Soviet or Communist Chinese forces, no announcement of intended entry, nor a threat to counter our operations [there] militarily."[33] This assumption of Chinese neutrality proved, of course, to be wrong, and Chinese intervention that autumn turned the course of the war dramatically against South Korea and the United States.[34]

Disagreement between states about these five factors is endemic to the international system, and is created and maintained by a variety of conditions. There is, of course, no central clearinghouse of information on warmaking capacity or resolve. Making matters worse, states have incentives to misrepresent their capabilities and resolve to each other. Many states maintain their military and even industrial capacities as state secrets, forcing their adversaries to make rough estimates of actual fighting ability. Moreover, states are likely to be especially secretive about military strategy and technology since the power offered by military strategy and technology can be substantially reduced if it loses its surprise value. The German strategy of attacking through the Ardennes in 1940 worked only because France guessed wrong and placed the bulk of its military forces elsewhere. The Israeli strategy of launching a preventive airstrike against the Egyptian air force at the outset of the 1967 Six-Day War worked only because Egypt did not know the timing of the attack, and hence most of its aircraft were caught on the ground. Egyptian SAMs in 1973 made an impact initially because Israel was unprepared. Indeed, war becomes especially likely when states mobilize their forces secretly, hoping to capture a surprise attack advantage.[35]

INFORMATION AND WAR TERMINATION

The focus in this book is on war termination rather than war initiation. Some existing bargaining model scholarship often has a very simple, essentially mechanical, view of war as a "costly lottery."[36] That is, once war starts, its outcome is determined by some fixed probability, such as one side having a 70 percent chance of winning, and the other side having a 30 percent chance of winning.

A more nuanced approach rejects the assumption that war is an apolitical mechanical process, instead allowing for political actors to change their beliefs during wartime and bargain towards reaching a war-ending deal. This approach sees fighting as having a very specific political function: to reduce the war-causing disagreement between the two sides.[37] The point was perhaps first made in 1904 by the prominent German sociologist Georg Simmel, who wrote that "the most effective presupposition for preventing struggle, the exact knowledge of the comparative strength of the two parties, is very often only to be attained by the actual fighting out of the conflict." This idea was occasionally restated in the literature on war termination from the 1950s through the 1970s, perhaps most famously by Geoffrey Blainey in his classic 1973 book on war.[38]

In recent years, scholars have applied formal analysis towards understanding the relationship between combat, information, and war. There is an array of different models of bargaining during war, but they often describe a fundamentally similar dynamic, that fighting battles provides information to the belligerents, which in turn affects war-termination decisions.[39] This current of scholarship describes two states in disagreement over the distribution of a particular good, such as the placement of a border. There is a fixed balance of power between the two states, and more narrowly a fixed probability that one side will win any given battle between them.[40] At least one side does not know the true balance of power, and instead can only speculate about the true balance.[41] The offers to divide the good reflect each side's assessment of the balance of power, such that a side demands more of the good as it becomes more confident in its own strength. War can be avoided when the two sides agree on the balance of power, as the side seeing itself as stronger demands more, and the side seeing itself as weaker demands less. However, if each side sees itself as stronger, then the two sides will make ambitious, ultimately irreconcilable offers (such as each demanding seventy-five cents of a single dollar, or both France and Germany each demanding exclusive control of Alsace and Lorraine). In the face of irreconcilable offers, one side may choose to attack as a means of proving its military power, pushing the other side to change its understanding of the balance of power, and demand less of the good. If one side attacks, war erupts, and battles occur. The belligerents observe battle outcomes, taking note of things like territory gained or lost, and casualties suffered by each side. On the basis of the observed battle outcomes, belligerents update their beliefs about the likelihood of winning future battles—in other words, the true balance of power.

Critically, each side's war-termination offer is inextricably tied to its views of the balance of power: more confident belligerents demand more as a condition of ending the war, and less confident belligerents demand less. After a state wins a battle and updates its estimate of the balance of power, it changes its war-termination offer, that is, it demands more of the disputed good as a condition of ending the war. Therefore, *following a combat success, a belligerent will raise its war-termination offer (demand more); however, following a combat defeat, a belligerent will lower its war-termination offer (demand less).* I refer to this as the "information proposition." Note that it bears directly on Clausewitz's ideas about the relationship between "real" or limited war and absolute war. Clausewitz proposed that a war is "real" or limited if it ends short of the utter defeat of one side's military, and is absolute if it ends with the complete defeat of one side's military. Clausewitz proposed that wars often end in limited outcomes because, by fighting, belligerents learn about who would win if the war was fought to the finish. Better informed, the belligerents are able to end the war short of an absolute outcome and curb the costs of fighting.[42]

The preceding proposition begs the question, what is combat success? As discussed in greater detail in chapter 4, combat success is a highly contextual concept, as sometimes belligerents want to gain territory irrespective of casualties, sometimes they want to inflict casualties irrespective of territory, and so on. Success needs to be defined on a case by case basis, in the context of the political-military strategy of the belligerent, rather than using a one-size-fits-all rule like territorial loss or gain.

The information proposition emerges from a more purely mathematical vision of this updating process, such that even if a belligerent has a strong belief in its relative power, a battlefield victory will encourage the belligerent to increase incrementally its estimate of the balance of power, and then increase incrementally its demands of the other side. In practice, the process may not be so precise. A belligerent may expect to win battles, and then when it does win those battles it will see this as evidence supporting its general beliefs about the balance of power, thereby encouraging the belligerent to maintain (rather than increase) its (high) war-termination demands. This possibility produces a slight modification of the information proposition, that *changes in war-termination demands are most likely when battle outcomes are surprising.*

Besides the capability of the armed forces of the primary belligerents, another important factor affecting the balance of power is the potential contribution of third-party interveners. If another country decides to intervene in the war, this will change each side's estimate of the balance of power and its eventual likelihood of winning. Therefore, another form of the more general information proposition is that *if a third party intervenes on behalf of a belligerent, that belligerent becomes less likely to lower its war aims and more likely to raise its war aims. If a third party intervenes on behalf of a belligerent's opponent, that belligerent becomes more likely to lower its war aims and less likely to raise its war aims.*

The focus so far has been on how factors more or less outside the control of the belligerents, such as battle outcomes and the decisions of third-party interveners, affect the war-termination process.[43] However, war-termination offers may be both a cause and effect in this process, since if a belligerent's adversary makes a new war-termination offer, the offer itself sends information about the true balance of power or balance of resolve, which in turn may cause the belligerent to change its war-termination offer.[44] Specifically, if a belligerent's adversary sends a new offer that demands fewer concessions, this may be seen by the belligerent as a sign of weakness, and may in turn cause the belligerent to stiffen its own negotiating position. Conversely, demanding more concessions can send a signal of resolve and power. Further, even if a bargainer makes no changes in its settlement offer, the very act of deciding to continue the costly conflict without making concessions sends a credible signal of resolve.[45]

INFORMATION AND CHANGING EXPECTATIONS

The discussion thus far has assumed a certain evenness in war. Belligerents' beliefs about the likely costs and outcome change across the war, but the assumption is that the likely casualties and outcome probability of all battles is the same for all battles across the war. As states fight, they observe battle outcomes, and eventually both come to agree sufficiently on the true and unchanging balance of power and end the war.

This assumption that casualties and outcomes are determined by a constant probability across the span of a war is not trivial. Consider instead the possibility that belligerents recognize that in the future the costs of fighting will change, and/or the likelihood of winning any battle will change. This could occur for several reasons. Future combat may take place on terrain more favorable to the adversary. A third party may be on the verge of intervening on behalf of the defender. Conversely, one's own ally may be close to exiting the war. Third parties may threaten to impose economic sanctions or other diplomatic costs if the war continues. One's own military power may soon collapse if one's standing stocks of munitions approach exhaustion.

Figure 2.1 displays these two separate assumptions, that the per battle costs of war (or, the likelihood of victory in any given battle) remain constant throughout the war, and that the per battle costs of war promise to escalate midway through the war. The x axis reflects time, starting at the beginning of the war. The y axis reflects expected costs per unit of time (that is, not cumulative costs). The solid line reflects the assumption that

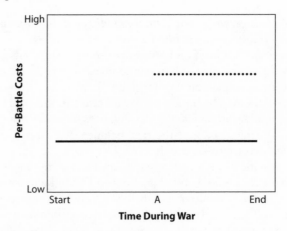

Figure 2.1 Per-Battle Costs during War

per-battle costs are constant for all battles throughout the war. The dotted line shows a different assumption, that at time A, the per-battle costs of fighting jump up significantly, and remain at a high level for the rest of the war.

Relaxing the assumption of constant probabilities of combat outcomes affects our forecasts for war-termination behavior. If a belligerent is doing well in combat, then the information propositions developed in this chapter would forecast that that belligerent should prefer to keep fighting and would not be likely to lower its war-termination demands, and might even raise them. However, a belligerent may believe that despite past and present successes, future combat might bear significantly higher costs, and/or the likelihood of success in future combat might be significantly lower. In such cases, even a winning belligerent may move to end the war before costs escalate and/or achieving combat success becomes much more difficult, accepting a limited outcome which might seem excessively generous given its past combat successes. Therefore, *a belligerent is more likely to make concessions if it believes that the costs of war promise to escalate significantly, and/or if the likelihood of combat success promises to drop significantly.* Chapter 3 will return to the topic of interactive effects of changing expectations about costs and victory.

War Termination and Domestic Politics

The discussion thus far has black-boxed the state as a single actor. In a major work of scholarship, Hein Goemans developed a war-termination theory that fused domestic politics with war-termination bargaining.[46] He (almost incidentally) laid out the core bargaining dynamics of the information proposition, that battles serve to reduce uncertainty, and that if a state wins a battle it will demand more of an adversary, and if it loses a battle it will offer concessions. Goemans' real objective, however, was to present an entirely novel theory of war termination based on domestic politics. He proposed that leaders in more repressive states were less likely to lose power following defeat in war than leaders in less repressive or moderately repressive states. He further proposed that leaders in more repressive and moderately repressive states had a greater fear of losing political power than leaders of less repressive states, because more repressive and moderately repressive leaders were likely to suffer severe political punishment, namely prison, exile, or death. He combined these two propositions to hypothesize that leaders of moderately repressive states, that is states with mixed political institutions, are especially fearful of suffering even moderate defeat. In contrast, highly repressive leaders are less fearful of facing moderate defeat because they can effectively use the tools of repression to stay in power. Democratic leaders are also less fearful of facing moderate defeat because a democratic leader thrown from power does not suffer severe personal consequences. As a result, when such mixed regimes are losing wars, Goemans predicted that rather than offer concessions, as the information dynamic would forecast, such regimes should instead raise their war aims, hoping that doing so will make available greater spoils of war, which can be distributed to the regime supporters, thereby keeping the regime in power. Leaders in such circumstances may "gamble for resurrection," adopting risky military strategies that increase the chances of ultimate victory while simultaneously increasing the chances of exposing the state to disastrous military defeat. Goemans presented impressive case studies of belligerents in World War I to test his arguments, as well as some quantitative analyses that tested more indirect implications of his theory. In this book, Goemans' theory receives empirical attention in chapters 9 and 10.

Other scholars have also described unusual decision-making behaviors for regimes with both autocratic and democratic qualities, so-called mixed regimes. Some have argued that such regimes are prone to overexpansion, as the tendency for such regimes to be ruled by cartelized oligarchies makes pro-imperial log-rolling politics more likely. Further, such regimes are especially prone to imperial myth-making, falling victim to false confidence in one's own power and being unable to analyze objectively the likelihood of victory in a potential war. Although this theory has been applied to the initiation of war, it could also be applied to the termination of war. The core propositions might be that such mixed regimes are especially averse to making concessions during war, and also that such regimes are especially unlikely to assess accurately the information provided by battle outcomes.

Our last domestic politics perspective on war termination focuses on public opinion.[47] The basic idea is that democratic leaders are more politically sensitive to casualties than non-democratic leaders. This notion emerges from the democratic peace proposition that democracies are especially unlikely to fight (each other) because democratic leaders must beware popular discontent, which is likely to grow as casualties mount. However, there is no scholarly consensus as to whether and how the accumulation of American casualties in war has eroded popular support for presidents.[48] Some studies, however, propose that democracies fight shorter wars because, as casualties mount, democratic governments become more likely to offer concessions in reaction to the sliding popularity of the war.[49] This book engages this casualty-sensitivity argument empirically, exploring in its empirical chapters whether democratic leaders were especially likely to make concessions as casualties mounted.

THE TRUTH OF COMBAT?

Otto von Bismarck once declared that, "People never lie so as much as after a hunt, during a war, or before an election."[50] However, the information proposition declares that, public statements aside, combat bears unavoidable truth. Although some see the battlefield as the most "honest place on earth" because it mercilessly reveals the character of the soldier, it also bears this moniker because it provides unmanipulable information about the true balance of power between two belligerents. As horrible as combat is, it does serve the critical function of providing real information to the belligerents. That information may be the critical resource belligerents need to reach an agreement ending the war. The reliability of such war-ending agreements, and the effect of (un)reliability on war-termination behavior is the subject of the next chapter, to which we now turn.

Returning to the simple costs/benefits framework presented at the beginning of this chapter, the information environment affects a belligerent's belief about the shape of the cost curve. Poor battlefield performance will cause a belligerent to raise its estimates of the costs of continued conflict, making the belligerent more likely to consider crafting concessions to seek an end to the war. If the enemy's military is faring well, it will take longer and/or be more costly to destroy the enemy's willingness to resist, or take longer to convince the adversary that eventually its military will be destroyed if the war continues to a fight to the finish. If the belligerent receives information that a third party is likely to intervene on behalf of the adversary, then this also raises the belligerent's estimates of the costs of continuing conflict, making the belligerent more likely to consider concessions.

CHAPTER THREE

Credible Commitments and War Termination

Promises like pie crusts are leaven to be broken.
—Vladimir Lenin

THERE IS NO WORLD GOVERNMENT to enforce laws, treaties, or promises. Conspiracy theories notwithstanding, there is no fleet of black helicopters or blue-helmeted stormtroopers at the ready to carry out the rulings of institutions like the United Nations (UN) or the World Trade Organization (WTO). Without such support, state-to-state promises can be as fragile as Lenin's pie crusts. This absence of government, literally anarchy, has severe and often tragic consequences, as it makes the maintenance of international order and the prevention of crimes against humanity such as genocide much more difficult. More generally, anarchy is perhaps the single most important factor that distinguishes global politics from national politics, as only in the latter are there governments that use monopolies of force to maintain law and order.

Scholars in the realist theoretical tradition have used the anarchy insight to propose that the inability of states to make enforceable commitments is an important cause of war. Peace and international order rest, according to realists, on a stable balance of power. If the balance of power is changing, declining states may fear that rising states will eventually demand changes in the international order reflecting the rising states' emerging strength. Declining states would like some commitment from the rising states not to demand concessions or attack as they grow in power, but because of anarchy such guarantees would not be enforceable and hence not credible. Declining states may become motivated to attack, thinking that war now would be preferable to concessions or war later. This logic was behind the initiation of several wars, including the German attack on Russia in 1914, the Japanese attack on Pearl Harbor in 1941, the Israeli attack on Egypt in 1956, and the American attack on Iraq in 2003.

Although the credible commitment insight has long been applied to international relations theory and to the causes of conflict, it has almost never been applied to war termination, and to interstate war termination in particular.[1] Specifically, although classics in the post-1945 realist canon meticulously draw out the implications of the information and commitment insights for the causes of war, they say almost nothing about applying these insights to the termination of wars.[2] This chapter takes this very conventional realist insight about commitment credibility and applies it to the area of war termination.[3] Doing so completes the development of the war-termination theory begun in the previous chapter, demonstrating that a comprehensive understanding of war termination requires incorporating the dimensions of both information and commitments. Information and commitment dynamics sometimes work in contrast, but can also work in complement. Chapter 2 demonstrated that information dynamics often shape a belligerent's expectations about future costs, specifically, the costs of continuing to fight and pursue victory. This chapter will demonstrate that commitment dynamics are often about shaping a belligerent's expectations regarding future benefits, specifically that commitment problems can serve to make some war-termination settlements more valuable than others.

Enforcing War-Ending Bargains

The theory employed in the bargaining model of war was imported from economics. Economists are most interested in understanding phenomena such as how buyers and sellers set prices and how labor and management settle on long-term wage contracts. However, economic actors (especially those interacting within a mature national economy) enjoy one important advantage over states: they know their contracts will be enforced. If a party violates the terms of a business or labor contract, the other party can resort to the legal system to enforce the terms of the contract, receive financial compensation, and even have the violator jailed. Most of the bargaining literature in economics assumes compliance with bargains reached.[4] Much of the bargaining model of war literature imports this enforcement assumption, that the terms of any war-ending bargain will enjoy automatic compliance.[5]

This assumption of automatic compliance, as applied to international relations, deserves further examination. A war-ending settlement is of course an international agreement, as the belligerents agree to stop fighting and perhaps to reallocate the disputed good. However, there is no world government to enforce the war-ending contract. Different international relations theories offer varying perspectives on the likelihood of state compliance with international agreements, but critically all theories agree that the degree of compliance varies, and must not be assumed. Realism famously proposes that compliance with international agreements is likely to be rare, as lack of enforcement, fear of adversarial defection, and relative gains concerns all push states to ignore such agreements. Realism proposes that the only agreements that enjoy compliance are those that are trivial, either calling for cooperation on peripheral issues, or demanding behavior that states would have engaged in even absent an agreement.[6] Institutionalism is more optimistic, forecasting that the presence of appropriately designed international institutions can facilitate interstate cooperation.[7] Constructivism proposes that cooperation is most likely when the states share a collective identity, and/or possess other-interest as well as self-interest.[8] But centrally, realism, institutionalism, and constructivism all agree that state compliance with international agreements is not automatic.

Falsely assuming that compliance with international agreements is automatic can be dangerous, as the possibility of non-compliance affects both the existence and character of international agreements. States are less likely to sign an agreement that is unlikely to enjoy satisfactory compliance. For example, American suspicion about possible Soviet cheating on arms control agreements kept progress in that area slow, and was the basis of President Ronald Reagan's famous declaration, "Trust, but verify." Neglecting how decision makers think about the risks of non-compliance warps our understanding of how treaties are crafted.[9]

Assuming automatic compliance with war-ending agreements is especially suspect. Clausewitz recognized that states break peace treaties: "Lastly, even the ultimate outcome of a war is not always to be regarded as final. The defeated state often considers the outcome merely as a transitory evil, for which a remedy may still be found in political conditions at some later date."[10] It is not difficult to imagine why states would break ceasefire agreements.[11] The benefits to breaking such agreements can be great since restarting a war can offer the possibility of capturing even more of the valuable disputed good, or recapturing whatever was lost in the last war. Egypt and Syria attacked Israel in 1973 in the hopes of recapturing territories they had each lost in the 1967 Six-Day War. World War I gave France the chance to recapture the provinces of Alsace and Lorraine, lost to Germany in the Franco-Prussian War, and the 1940 German attack on France gave Germany the chance to get Alsace and Lorraine back after France reacquired these lands in the Versailles agreement that ended World War I. Conversely, there are dangers if one side fears the other may unilaterally defect to capture more of the disputed good. Israel preemptively attacked Egypt in 1967, fearing Egyptian defection on the cease fire agreements ending the 1948–49 and 1956 wars. Perhaps not surprisingly, the rate of compliance with war-ending agreements is far from perfect. Over the 1914–2001 period, nearly one third of all interstate war ceasefires (56 out of 188) eventually broke down into renewed war.[12]

This is of course a grim picture, that the international order is a jungle, and states can never fully trust each other. Some might reply that trust can emerge in international relations, that states can come to trust each other and cooperate.[13] However, belligerents consumed by the heat of war are especially unlikely to trust each other. Two states cannot build much trust while fighting. Making matters worse, there is likely a history of broken trust between two belligerents, as an attacker often breaks a neutrality or border agreement when it decides to launch a war.

TOTAL VICTORY, TOTAL PEACE: ABSOLUTE WAR AS A SOLUTION TO CREDIBLE COMMITMENT PROBLEMS

If a wartime belligerent fears its adversary might break a war-ending agreement and reattack after war ends, one possible solution to this noncompliance problem is the imposition of an absolute war outcome. Rivals sometimes continue to break ceasefire agreements and attack each other. This cycle can end when one side suffers total military defeat, enabling the victor to impose terms that would directly prevent the adversary from breaking the peace treaty and reattacking in the future.[14] Clausewitz summarized this logic at its most brutal: "So long as I have not overthrown my opponent, I am bound to fear he may overthrow me."[15]

An absolute war outcome can, perhaps paradoxically, take many forms. The most severe peace terms would be the annihilation of the adversary's population. This outcome is thankfully mostly theoretical, with the possible exception of Athens' slaughter of all of the Melian men and enslavement of its women and children during the Peloponnesian Wars.[16] Lesser versions of the annihilationist strategy have been considered and sometimes put into action. Half of Paraguay's total population and most of its adult male population were killed in the War of the Triple Alliance in the 1860s, although within less than a century Paraguay had recovered sufficiently to fight another war, although with different adversaries.[17] World War II saw several examples of annihilationist behavior, including Hitler's elimination of twelve million Jews and other minorities as imagined threats to the Nazi state, and the 1940 Soviet execution of nearly 22,000 Polish military officers and policemen in the infamous Katyn massacre to eliminate possible future threats to Soviet power.[18] More generally, combatants sometimes engage in annihilationist strategies during wartime to defeat guerrilla forces.[19]

Extinguishing the adversary's sovereignty and annexing its territory is a more common though still severe solution to the commitment problem. This approach means dismantling the adversary's government and military, thereby eliminating its ability to launch a new war. Some have referred to such an outcome as "state death."[20] After such an action, adversarial defection would be possible only after the recovery of sovereignty, which in turn might occur through an internal regime change causing the conquering government to disgorge its conquests (such as the Baltic states exiting the Soviet Union following the collapse of Communism), secession by the conquered state (such as Ireland's successful twentieth-century fight for independence, throwing off more than eight centuries of British rule), or rescue by the military action of a third party (such as the Allied liberation of France in 1944 or the UN liberation of Kuwait in 1991).

A third means by which a war outcome can prevent defection is through foreign imposed regime change. A belligerent may impose a puppet regime, install democratic institutions, and/or hardwire pacifism into a nation's laws and constitution as a means of preventing postwar defection.[21] Foreign imposed regime change cripples a state's foreign policy sovereignty and renders compliance with war-ending agreements far more likely by changing the target state's preferences for war and its political institutions. Regarding preferences, the architect of a foreign-imposed regime change executes, exiles, imprisons, or at least permanently removes from power militarist leaders and their subordinates, dismantles pro-war industrial complexes, and empowers or imports leaders with more compliant and pacific preferences. The Soviet Union eliminated non-Communist Hungarian leaderships in 1945 and 1956, replacing them with more pliable Communists each time. The Allies held war crimes trials in Germany and Japan after World War II, purging these countries of militarists.[22] Saddam Hussein was thrown from power and captured in 2003, and then executed in 2006.

Foreign-imposed regime change also means overhauling the political institutions of the target country. Some democratic belligerents may see the installation of democratic governance as a promising means of preventing an adversary's future aggression. The proposition that democracy is a cure for war and militarism has recurred in American foreign policy over the past century. In his April 2, 1917 speech asking for a congressional declaration of war on the Central Powers, Woodrow Wilson proposed that the taproot cause of the war in Europe was Prussian militarism, and that peace required the democratic transformation of Germany. He famously declared that, "The world must be made safe for democracy. Its peace must be planted upon the tested foundations of political liberty."[23] During World War II, Roosevelt and then Truman saw Japanese, Italian, and German authoritarianism as intertwined with militarism, and that democratization of these societies would cure them of their warlike tendencies. The 2001 war in Afghanistan was intended to rid that country of the anti-American Taliban, and democracy was seen as a long-term inoculation against the Taliban's return. The goal of the 2003 Iraq War was the overthrow of Saddam Hussein, and the Bush administration saw the installation of democracy there as the best way to prevent Iraq from reemerging as a threat. As Bush remarked in a critical October 2002 speech, "regime change in Iraq is the only certain means of removing a great danger to our nation."[24] Of course, regime change need not culminate in democratization, as governments sometimes install nondemocratic puppet regimes. After conquering France in 1940, Nazi Germany installed the undemocratic Vichy regime. After World War II ended, the Soviet Union helped put in place a number of friendly Communist regimes, both in former foes (such as [East] Germany, Hungary, and Romania) and former victims of Nazi aggression (such as Poland and Czechoslovakia).

As part of a foreign-imposed regime change, a target is also often forced to hardwire pacifism—resulting in restrictions on the size, deployment, and/or weaponry of the national military—into its new political institutions. One severe (although unimplemented) proposal was Secretary of the Treasury Henry Morgenthau's 1944 plan for Germany after World War II. Morgenthau recommended that all Germany be deindustrialized as well as demilitarized, with the intent of removing the very foundations of German military power.[25] Morgenthau's proposal was rejected, but Germany was forced to accept constraints on the use of its armed forces, as expressed in the 1949 German Basic Law.[26] American occupation forces also wrote the 1946 Japanese constitution, which declares in Article Nine: "Aspiring sincerely to an international peace based on justice and order, the Japanese people forever renounce war as a sovereign right of the nation and the threat or use of force as means of settling international disputes. . . . In order to accomplish the aim of the preceding paragraph, land, sea, and air forces, as well as other war potential, will never be maintained. The right of belligerency of the state will not be recognized."[27] Article 11 of the 1947 Italian constitution "repudiates war as an instrument offending the liberty of the peoples and as a means for settling international disputes."[28] Afghanistan's post-Taliban 2004 constitution explicitly declares that, "The state prevents all types of terrorist activities."[29] Iraq's 2005 constitution also commits it to fighting terrorism, and not acquiring weapons of mass destruction.[30] These institutional changes can affect societal preferences by eradicating militarist culture, through means such as altering the educational system.[31]

Each of these outcomes—annihilation, annexation, and foreign-imposed regime change—solves or at least substantially ameliorates the peace settlement compliance problem by de jure or de facto revoking of the adversary's sovereignty, thereby directly preventing the defeated state from violating a war-ending agreement. I classify these war outcomes as absolute. As to whether this definition overlaps exactly with Clausewitz's definition of absolute war, Clausewitz himself is a bit imprecise on this point. He talks about forcing the defeated state "to do your bidding" as descriptive of an absolute outcome, and that absolute war means to render the defeated state "politically helpless or militarily impotent, thus forcing him to sign whatever peace we please." He also describes absolute war as "completely governed and saturated by the urge for a decision."[32]

Some may prefer a narrower definition of an absolute war outcome, that it represents zero concessions by the victorious side, and/or the utter annihilation of the defeated state. The narrow definition would arguably offer some advantages. Most generally, it would accurately demonstrate that essentially every war outcome involves choice by both the victor and the defeated. On the victor's side, in nearly all wars the victor makes at least some concessions. For example, even as part of the "unconditional" surrender of Japan in 1945, the Allies allowed that the Emperor could remain as the spiritual head of the Japanese government. On the side of the defeated state, in nearly all wars the loser must decide to stop fighting. Even those suffering state death or foreign-imposed regime change have the opportunity to continue resistance at some level, perhaps in post-defeat guerrilla warfare. Such insurgencies have occurred. Violent acts of resistance arose in Nazi-occupied Europe after official government surrenders to German forces. Although Nazi Germany surrendered formally and unconditionally to the Allies in May 1945, there persisted after the surrender some guerrilla activity of the Nazi *Werwolf* underground against Allied occupation forces. The underground was not a completely renegade movement, and had received support and direction from the Nazi government prior to the surrender.[33] The Japanese government in August 1945 made deliberate efforts to ensure that members of the military complied with the terms of the surrender. The government required high-level military leaders to sign an agreement of compliance with the surrender terms, and to disarm and defuel aircraft to prevent their use for kamikaze attacks. These efforts were not completely successful, as there was a coup attempt before the surrender terms were announced to the Japanese public, and a navy captain did independently organize a post-surrender insurrection lasting several days calling for defiance of the surrender terms.[34] More recently, although American conventional forces achieved foreign-imposed regime change in Afghanistan in 2001 and Iraq in 2003, in both states enduring and extensive armed resistance against American forces in the form of irregular insurgencies has continued.

Again, some might claim that the presence either of any victor's concessions or of any post-surrender violence is sufficient to disqualify a war outcome from being absolute. Under these conditions, absolute outcomes have essentially never occurred, and become purely theoretical. However, the utter non-existence of absolute wars is a position to which even

Clausewitz, who proposed that absolute wars are uncommon, would disagree. Clausewitz thought of Napoleon's wars as absolute. He also allowed that conditions sometimes demand absolute war, such that a leader pursues absolute war *"when he can* or *when he must."*[35]

In this book, absolute war means removing the defeated state's ability to organize resistance. As noted, in practice this can take the form of annihilation, but more commonly means state death, occupation, or foreign-imposed regime change. This definition is consistent with Clausewitz's conception of absolute war, summarized earlier. This definition matches the heart of the commitment component of the theory described later in this chapter, as a war outcome that essentially removes the possibility of the defeated state reneging on a war-ending settlement.

Some may object that because this broad definition would mean that some war outcomes would be inaccurately described as including no victors' concessions, it would underestimate the role played by information dynamics in determining war termination and war outcomes. However, it is not necessarily the case that the termination of a particular war was dominated by information dynamics if the victor enjoyed a decisive battlefield victory and still offered tiny concessions. Often, if a victor achieves decisive victory on the battlefield and intends to annex its adversary or impose a new regime, it may make concessions in relatively trivial areas in order to facilitate postwar stability. That is, the concessions do not detract from the victor's ability to accomplish its aims of permanently removing the (interstate) threat posed by its adversary, and in fact may further this goal by providing for greater political stability within the nation of the defeated. For example, under the terms of surrender ending the American Civil War, the Confederacy as a political entity was extinguished but Confederate soldiers and officers were allowed to keep their horses, permitting them to plant crops more easily and feed their families, thereby reducing the likelihood of widespread famine in the southern states in the coming year. Lincoln and his leading commanders recognized that allowing Confederate soldiers to return to their farms with their horses and even their guns would help move the country towards economic and social normalcy, and would improve the chances that these ex-rebels would accept the Union and its laws as their own.[36]

The case of World War II Japan also demonstrates this point. The historical argument made by some is that because the Allies conceded to Japan's summer 1945 demand that the Emperor not be tried as a war criminal, the terms of Japan's August 1945 surrender constitute a limited rather than absolute outcome. However, the concession over the Emperor was allowed in part because the United States (correctly) decided that doing so would increase the likelihood of its acceptance by the Japanese military.[37] Further, the Emperor concession itself was extremely limited, and merely implied by the language that "the ultimate form of government in Japan shall . . . be established by the freely expressed will of the Japanese people." It was severely curtailed by the additional statement that "From the moment of surrender the authority of the emperor and the Japanese Government to rule the state shall be subject to the Supreme Commander of the Allied Powers."[38] Certainly, the concession did not in intention or effect prevent the United States from accomplishing its central aims of demilitarizing Japan and completely refashioning the Japanese political landscape. In implementation, the Emperor became a politically irrelevant and powerless figure in the postwar period.

A limitation of this definition is that it may code wars as absolute even when violent insurgency emerged after the formal surrender. This is especially important as a policy issue since from a belligerent's perspective sometimes the benefit of breaking an adversary's ability to launch state-to-state violence is outweighed by the cost of creating an enduring insurgency. Many have made this point in the context of the 2003 Iraq War, that the interstate threat from Saddam Hussein's Iraq could have been contained without war through deterrence, but the postwar insurgency has been gigantically costly in human, financial, and geopolitical terms.[39]

Assessing the causes of postwar insurgency is an important question, but such a task is beyond the scope of this book. More relevant to this work are the causes of postwar interstate violence, which are mostly different from the causes of postwar insurgency. Regarding postwar interstate violence, the assumption is that annihilation, state death, or foreign-imposed regime change virtually eliminate the possibility that the defeated state will launch interstate violence against the victorious state. The empirical basis of this assumption is discussed in further detail later in these pages. Regarding postwar insurgency, several factors affect the likelihood of insurgency. A general point is that the "actor" that would decide to launch an insurgency—the population at large or some subgroup(s) of the population—is often different from the actor that would decide to launch an interstate war: the government. So, the victorious state is often not bargaining directly with the potential insurgent, meaning there is no opportunity for the potential insurgent to commit to *not* launching a postwar insurgency. The victorious state can attempt to offer concessions to the defeated state in an attempt to encourage the defeated state to discourage postwar insurgency, as was the case with postwar Japan. However, several other factors are perhaps more important in understanding the causes of postwar insurgencies. Sometimes leaders, such as Confederate General Robert E. Lee at the close of the American Civil War, reject postwar insurgency not because of some concession offered by the victory, but simply because insurgency would be pointlessly destructive.[40] Structural factors, such as the geographic terrain in the country, and postwar occupation policy choices are likely to be critical. Studies have found that "work or starve" threats are effective in managing populations in occupied areas. The provision of domestic security is critical. Perhaps the single biggest mistake of the post-2003 Iraq War, for example, was the early dismissal of the Iraqi Army.[41] That being said, the prospect of fighting a costly counterinsurgency campaign in the wake of the absolute defeat of a state's conventional forces may be enough to dissuade a state from pursuing absolute victory (see the following).

In sum, the ability of an absolute war outcome such as annihilation, occupation, annexation, or foreign-imposed regime change to eliminate the compliance problem offers real temptations to belligerents who fear the other side will not adhere to its war-ending commitments. A belligerent may worry that any war-ending agreement that leaves intact the adversary's sovereignty may allow the adversary to reinitiate war, and that this problem can be solved by achieving absolute victory and eliminating the other side's sovereignty. As Immanuel Kant noted, "For some confidence in the character of the enemy must remain even in the midst of war, as otherwise no peace could be concluded and the hostilities would degenerate into a war of extermination."[42] The central hypothesis emerging from the credible commitment logic is that *the more a belligerent fears its adversary will violate war-ending commitments, the more likely that belligerent will be to pursue absolute victory.* This is the "commitment proposition." When compliance fears dominate, belligerents may doggedly pursue an absolute war outcome, not seeking a limited war outcome to divide the disputed good and leave the other side's sovereignty intact. The logic is that a belligerent is relatively uninterested in a limited settlement if the adversary is unlikely to abide by its terms. In comparison, achieving an absolute war outcome would solve the compliance problem by eliminating the adversary's sovereignty, so the belligerent becomes motivated to ignore the possibility of a limited settlement and pursue an absolute outcome.

One way to frame the commitment proposition is to understand that it affects the expectations about the *benefits* of continuing to fight: How much utility or welfare does a belligerent gain for each added increment of the good it might obtain in a possible war-ending settlement? The relationship of increments of the good to increments of utility can be illustrated graphically, in which the x axis represents increments of the good obtained in the postwar settlement, and the y axis represents increments of overall utility. A common assumption is that the shape of the benefits curve is linear since each increment of the disputed good is as valuable as every other increment. However, if a belligerent perceives that the adversary will defect on a war-ending agreement and reattack, then this means the belligerent will get much less welfare out of any outcome short of

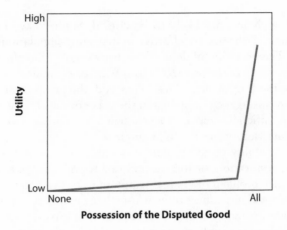

Figure 3.1 Increments of the Good and Utility with Noncompliance Fears

absolute victory, because the belligerent will not be able to enjoy the sub-absolute allocation of the good for long before war resumes. However, if the belligerent is able to achieve absolute victory, it will be able to consume the good without fear of losing its gains in a new war. Hence, under such conditions the shape of the benefits curve should be relatively flat for most increments of the good, meaning that acquiring additional increments of the good provides little extra utility, but that the curve should jump up for the possession of all of the good, as possession of all of the good reflects absolute victory and the solution of the postwar commitment problem. This step function relationship of good increments to utility under conditions of fears about postwar non-compliance is represented in figure 3.1.

The step function in figure 3.1 introduces the possibility of divergence between the predictions of the information and commitment propositions. A belligerent that is both losing battles and fears postwar commitment problems may elect not to make concessions to the adversary in the hopes of achieving a limited war outcome, as the information proposition forecasts. A limited outcome deal in which a belligerent gets part of the good may hold relative value to the belligerent, because if the adversary breaks the deal and reattacks, the belligerent may not be able to consume the portion of the good it received under the limited outcome settlement. Hence, the belligerent gathers few benefits from stopping the fighting to reach a limited outcome settlement. The belligerent instead may fight on in the hopes of achieving an absolute victory, which would solve the postwar commitment problem, as the commitment proposition would predict. Achieving an absolute victory would permit the unthreatened consumption of the entire good because of the solution of the commitment problem, a prize that may encourage belligerents to fight on, sometimes even in the face of discouraging combat outcomes. Formal theoretical analysis confirms that the more severe the credible commitment fears, the less likely that combat outcomes are to affect war-termination behavior and discourage an adversary from pursuing absolute victory. Under some conditions of severe credible commitment fears, a belligerent may make an initial, moderate offer, and if the offer is rejected and the belligerent loses a battle, the belligerent may actually raise its demands (contra the information proposition), viewing the rejection of the first offer as evidence of the adversary's true power, and so encouraging the pursuit of absolute victory.[43] In sum, *when commitment concerns are severe, discouraging information coming from the battlefield may not cause a belligerent to abandon its pursuit of absolute victory.*

This process of commitment fears attenuating the effects of information revelation is illustrated by French war-termination behavior during the 1870–71 Franco-Prussian War. The war began in July 1870, after Otto von Bismarck of Prussia maneuvered France into war over a diplomatic slight. The war proceeded well for Prussia, with a string of important victories at Metz, Sedan, and elsewhere. As the information proposition forecasts, Prussia began to raise its war aims as it achieved early victories, especially towards seeking territorial gains from France.[44] By early December, a Prussian victory in arms seemed at hand. However, contrary to the expectations of the information hypothesis, the French refused to budge on making the territorial concessions that Prussia demanded. The historian Michael Howard commented in his classic study of the war, "By all the normal customs of warfare observed by the regular armies and the traditional statesmen of Europe, the defeats suffered by the French armies between 30th November and 5th December should have made the [French] Government of National Defence sue for peace; and it was assumed by the Germans and by Europe that they would do so. . . . In military logic there now seemed no prospect of defeating the Germans, nor was there any reason to suppose that a prolongation of the war would secure a more favorable peace. The struggle was kept alive only by the will and the energy of a few men at the centre of power, who inflexibly refused to admit defeat."[45]

Part of the French motivation in rejecting a negotiated peace was the desire to inflict absolute defeat on Prussia in order to solve the enduring problem of incredible Prussian commitments, and thereby achieve a solution to the Prussian threat that did not rely on an incredible Prussian commitment not to attack. French Minister of War Léon Gambetta wrote in a private letter in early January 1871, "The whole country understands and wants a war to the end, without mercy, even after the fall of Paris. . . . The simplest clearly understand that since the war has become a war of extermination covertly prepared by Prussia for thirty years past, we must, for the honour of France and for our security in the future, finish for good this odious power. . . . We shall prolong the struggle to extermination."[46]

THE EMPIRICAL RECORD: THE FREQUENCY AND EFFECTIVENESS
OF ABSOLUTE WAR OUTCOMES

Some scholars declare the frequency of absolute war outcomes to be very low, interpreting this as evidence of the centrality of information in the process of war termination, as combat and intrawar diplomacy usually eventually provide enough information to permit war termination short of an absolute outcome.[47] This assumption deserves closer examination. To discern the frequency of absolute war outcomes, I first combine two datasets on war outcomes.[48] The first dataset is a list of all state deaths from 1816–1992.[49] A total of thirty-five violent state deaths occurred during this time period, some (but not all) of which occurred in the context of interstate wars. A second dataset is of all foreign-imposed regime changes occurring at the close of interstate wars from 1816–1980. A total of twenty-six such events occurred during this period, although some wars (such as World War II) experienced more than one foreign-imposed regime change (note that most foreign-imposed regime changes are not violent state deaths). As noted, for the purposes of this book, both state death and foreign-imposed regime change constitute absolute war outcomes.

There is no universally accepted list of wars or war participants, although most recognize that wars are generally violent conflicts between states that result in at least 1,000 combat deaths. Scholars differ over, for example, whether and how complex multilateral wars like World War II should be broken up into several wars. The Correlates of War (COW) project provides a commonly used dataset on interstate wars.[50] It lists seventy-nine interstate wars from 1816–1997, and within this set there are eighteen wars (23 percent) in which at least one belligerent experienced state death and/or foreign-imposed regime change. Allan Stam and I made some modest changes to the COW dataset, breaking up some large multilateral wars into component conflicts, and updating the list to 2001.[51] In our dataset of ninety-eight wars, there are twenty-five absolute war outcomes (26 percent). Beyond these groupings, in some wars that ended in limited outcomes at least one belligerent sought at least at one point during the war the absolute defeat of its adversary. Such wars include the Korean War, the Iran–Iraq War, the Winter War, the Finnish–Soviet Continuation War, the War of Israeli Independence, and others.

Overall, absolute war outcomes have occurred in roughly one quarter of interstate wars. This is certainly a higher frequency than the extreme rarity predicted by the view that the information provided by combat is sufficient for efficient war termination. It better fits the perspective of the theory presented here, that sometimes information dynamics dominate, allowing wars to end prior to an absolute outcome, and sometimes states pursue absolute victory, perhaps seeking lasting solutions to credible commitment problems.

Knowing that absolute war outcomes occur with minor to moderate frequency, the next question is, do such outcomes in fact prevent states from violating their war-ending commitments not to reinitiate war? Here, the historical record is quite clear, that absolute war outcomes very significantly decrease the likelihood that war will reerupt between two states. Since 1816, when a war has ended in state death, the defeated state almost never itself comes back to life to attack the victor, except in the circumstance when it is "rescued" by a third party, as Britain and the United States rescued European states "killed" by Nazi Germany in World War II, and the UN Coalition rescued Kuwait from Iraqi annexation in 1991. But, these episodes are not examples of noncompliance by the dead state, but rather of third-party action.

Foreign-imposed regime change is also a very effective means of reducing the chances of war reerupting between two former belligerents. Systematic studies examining conflicts from 1816 to 2001 have produced strong support to this effect, as there are virtually no examples of a state suffering foreign-imposed regime change and then after war's end attacking its former adversary. Generally, war is very significantly less likely to reerupt between former belligerents when it ends with foreign-imposed regime change compared to when war does not end in foreign-imposed regime change.[52] Indeed, perhaps the greatest foreign policy success of the twentieth century, the transformation of the Nazi German, Fascist Italian, and Imperial Japanese war machines into prosperous, pacific, internationally engaged democracies is largely attributable to foreign-imposed regime change.

INFORMATION AND COMMITMENT FACTORS IN INTERACTION: WHEN DO WARS REMAIN LIMITED?

If former belligerents at least sometimes break war-ending agreements, states cannot effectively bind themselves to comply with war-ending agreements, and absolute war outcomes promise to reduce very substantially the likelihood of noncompliance, then why don't states *always* pursue absolute war outcomes? The information proposition offers one answer to this question. Recall from the previous chapter that the information approach sees war as breaking out because of disagreement over the balance of power. War ends when disagreement is reduced sufficiently such that bargaining space between the two sides opens, and the war-ending settlement reflects the new understanding the two sides have about the true balance of power between them. That is, if the battles fought during the war reveal that one side is stronger than was thought before war began, then the war-ending settlement will provide more of the disputed good to that stronger side then it possessed before the war began.[53] For example, the U.S.–Mexico War of 1846–48 clearly demonstrated American military superiority, and common knowledge of this superiority dissuaded Mexico from reattacking after war's end to reacquire the substantial territories it had lost in the war-ending Treaty of Guadalupe Hidalgo. When both sides agree on the military balance and that the distribution of the good reflects the military balance, the war-ending agreement is a self-enforcing equilibrium. Both sides agree on the balance of power, and that if the war restarted, it would end with the same outcome. As a result, neither side has an incentive to break the commitment, pay the sunk costs of fighting, and not end up receiving more of the disputed good.

However, this self-enforcing peace equilibrium may break down if after the war one side comes to believe it can reinitiate the war with better chances of acquiring more of the disputed good. Three sets of factors might cause a belligerent to think it might enjoy better chances of winning.[54] First, there might be a postwar shift in the aggregate balance of power. Most simply, there might be a change in the balance of military power between the two former belligerents, if one belligerent enjoys faster demographic or economic growth than the other, decides to devote a greater fraction of its economy to defense spending than the other, or acquires some new military technology or strategy that enhances its military power. The core theoretical insight is that a rising state cannot commit to adhere to a goods-dividing agreement with the declining state, and such circumstances can make war more likely, even when all agree on the balance of power and its rate of change.[55] As noted at the outset of this chapter, when the balance of power is changing, the state growing stronger may go to war to expand its share of the disputed good. The acquisition of advanced Soviet SAMs encouraged Egypt to attack Israel in 1973 in the hopes of recapturing the Sinai desert, breaking its 1967 ceasefire agreement with Israel. Or, the state facing relative decline may launch a war while conditions are more favorable, fearing that as the adversary grows stronger it will demand more or even launch a new attack. As noted, a number of wars have been started by fearful states in relative decline. Systematic studies exploring whether postwar changes in the balance of power make the reeruption of war more likely have produced mixed results.[56]

Second, even if the aggregate balance of power is stable, one side may conclude at some point that it will enjoy advantages from attacking first, temporarily tipping the balance in its favor, enough to allow it to make important military gains. The primary source of such a faith in surprise attack would be that after peace is concluded, the adversary might demobilize or redeploy its forces, creating a window of opportunity allowing an attacker to remobilize its own forces secretly and enjoy a passing military advantage as the target slowly remobilized. International crises are more likely to escalate to war when one side mobilizes its forces secretly, perhaps because the secret mobilizer is genuinely bent on war, and is trying to create a temporary military advantage.[57] Differences in mobilization speeds may create windows of opportunity, tempting one side to strike first. However, the evidence that (perceived) first strike advantages make war more likely is mixed.[58]

Third, war might reerupt if a new leadership came to power in one country, with either a higher or lower resolve for fighting. If a higher resolve leadership came to power, that country might be willing to restart the war, hoping to make greater gains because of its greater willingness to bear costs. If a lower resolve leadership came to power, that country might be attacked, as the other side might seek to exploit the new low resolve leadership and extract greater concessions.[59] Perhaps most famously, Germany became much less willing to accept the settlement ending World War I, even at the risk of war with Britain and France, after Adolf Hitler and the Nazi party took power in 1933. If a regime change in a former belligerent occurs through revolution, renewed conflict may be especially likely, as revolutionary regimes such as fundamentalist Iran in the late 1970s and France in the 1790s are especially likely to launch wars of liberation and to attract attacks from fearful neighbors.[60] Notably, though, postwar regime change can have the opposite effect and improve relations if a new, less hawkish leader takes power. Anglo-Argentinian relations improved dramatically when the ruling Argentinian junta was thrown from power after the 1982 Falklands War. More generally, enduring rivalries between states are significantly more likely to end when there is internal political change within one of the adversaries.[61]

Any of these three developments, change in the aggregate balance of power, the appearance of a first-strike advantage, or change in leadership, might be sufficient to cause a postwar peace to break down. The key issue is whether states fighting wars forecast that any of these developments might occur after war's end. Unfortunately, states can never be certain that such future changes in power or leadership will not happen. Adverse shifts in the balance of power are always possible, the enemy may develop new and supremely effective weaponry first, and/or the enemy may discover some way to carry out an effective surprise attack. An adversary's leadership may be replaced by more hawkish individuals, or one's own successors may be more dovish, inviting challenge. Therefore, states are to some degree always fearful that adversaries may violate war-ending agreements. Further, the very fact that war has broken out between these states helps create suspicions between them. Given these problems, the question then becomes, why do not belligerents *always* pursue absolute war outcomes as a means of solving the compliance problem? Why do we *ever* observe limited war outcomes? Addressing these questions is critical since the answers to them in turn constitute hypotheses as to when we should observe states accepting limited outcomes, and when states pursue absolute outcomes. These questions have four answers.[62]

Vanished Hopes for Victory

Rejecting negotiations for a limited war outcome to fight on for better terms and perhaps an absolute war outcome presumes there is some possibility, however distant, of eventually prevailing. A belligerent will ignore bad news from the front and fight on only if it has some hope of turning the tide in the future. It may be willing to fight on even with only a slim chance of eventual victory, rather than accept war termination now and an unstable peace settlement. It may be encouraged to fight on if it thinks its probability of victory may rise in the future, since perhaps in the future the balance of power will shift when the belligerent fully mobilizes its economy, if it can deploy a new wonder-weapon against the adversary, or if a third party intervenes on its behalf.

Conversely, a state with essentially no hope of turning the tide faces a different calculus. Assuming that the costs of continuing the war are nontrivial (see the following), a belligerent may be willing to accept defeat now, even if it means a limited war settlement susceptible to being violated or even an absolute defeat, rather than fight on, suffer costs, and likely suffer the same fate. Therefore, *a belligerent, even if it doubts the credibility of an adversary's commitment to a war-ending settlement, becomes more likely to lower its war aims and seek war termination as its chances for improving its military prospects in the future approach zero.* This hypothesis has been derived formally.[63]

The information environment may or may not affect whether a belligerent reaches this conclusion. A belligerent will resist the grim conclusion that things are utterly hopeless, even in the face of combat setbacks, if its long-term strategy for victory has not been discredited. Combat setbacks may not discredit a belligerent's long-term strategy for victory if the combat setbacks do not cast doubt on factors the belligerent is counting on.

For example, if a belligerent is expecting a powerful ally to eventually enter the war and turn the tide, the belligerent will not become excessively discouraged if its own forces perform poorly. Or, if a belligerent is counting on a future strategic or technological innovation to change the balance of power on the battlefield, it will not be discouraged by battlefield losses. Indeed, some have postulated that bad combat performance may cause a belligerent to change military strategy rather than reduce its war-termination offer.[64] However, if combat or international events cause a belligerent to lose faith in its strategy for victory, if a potential ally joins the other side, if the belligerent was counting on victory through economic mobilization and the adversary captures wide swaths of its economy, if no strategic or technological innovations present themselves, or if a belligerent was counting on exacting enemy concessions through coercion and combat outcomes cause it to lose faith in its ability to inflict cost on the enemy, the belligerent may become sufficiently discouraged to accept defeat, even an absolute defeat.

Escalating Costs

Belligerents may be unwilling to reject absolute war outcomes and pursue limited war settlements if the costs of continued fighting promise to escalate significantly (this dynamic parallels the discussion surrounding figure 2.1 in chapter 2). Absolute war outcome as a solution to credible commitment problems is in some sense a luxury that a state can purchase, and states may elect not to purchase the luxury if the cost becomes too high. Small states facing more powerful adversaries, such as Finland confronting the Soviet Union in 1940, Japan facing the United States during World War II, and Iraq facing the United States in 1991, would certainly like to pursue absolute military victory to eliminate the large threat of the adversary, but doing so is seen to be prohibitively costly because of the unfavorable military imbalance.

High costs dissuade states from pursuing absolute war outcomes in other circumstances as well. A large belligerent with the military capacity to crush a small foe at acceptable human and financial costs may decide not to do so for other reasons. The belligerent may fear that the small foe will escalate to the use of weapons of mass destruction (WMD), as Iraq considered doing in 1991 if the UN Coalition had marched on Baghdad.[65] Alternatively, although the larger belligerent may feel confident in its ability to defeat its adversary at reasonable cost, if the larger belligerent is worried about the possibility of a third power soon intervening on behalf of its smaller adversary, the prospective escalation in the costs of fighting may be sufficient to push the more powerful country to accept a limited outcome.[66] In the 1973 Yom Kippur War, Israel eventually achieved decisive military superiority over Egypt and Syria. The combined external pressures of the United States and the Soviet Union, including the threatened withdrawal of military support by the former and the possibility of military intervention on the Arab states' behalf by the latter, pushed Israel to accept a limited war outcome, and in particular spare the Egyptian army from complete annihilation.[67]

Some belligerents may view the post-victory costs of administering an absolutely defeated foe to be prohibitive. At the outset of the 1846–48 U.S.–Mexico War, the United States hoped to acquire California, New Mexico, and perhaps other territories, although the unexpected success of American military forces, including the capture of Mexico City, opened the door for increased American war aims.[68] The war-ending Treaty of Guadelupe Hidalgo provided the U.S. with more substantial territorial gains than it had originally hoped for, but it stopped short of demanding the annexation of the entire country. This is puzzling from the perspective of the commitment proposition, as a "common expansionist objection [to the Treaty] was that it would be foolish to expect the treacherous Mexican government to carry out the terms of any treaty."[69] However, the majority in the U.S. Congress viewed the ingestion of all of Mexico to engender too many costs and dangers, including the difficulties of annexing an alien and hostile people, the risks that maintaining a large American army would undermine American democracy, and concern that annexation would incite European opposition. Underlying these issues were even more complicated debates about the effects of slavery, as advocates took different positions as to whether annexation would support or undermine slavery in America.[70] A century later, President Dwight Eisenhower worried about the costs of absolute victory in discussions about the possibility of nuclear war with the Soviet Union. He argued that occupying the Soviet Union "would be far beyond the resources of the United States," and fretted about the hollowness of a nuclear victory: "Here would be a great area from the Elbe to the Vladivostok . . . torn up and destroyed, without government, without its communications, just an area of starvation and disaster. I ask you what would the civilized world do about it? I repeat there is no victory except through our imaginations."[71] The George H. W. Bush administration was also dissuaded from marching on Baghdad in 1991 partly because of the costs of such a total victory, especially the escalation of anti-American insurgency warfare and international diplomatic backlash.[72] Conversely, the George W. Bush administration decided in 2002–3 to overthrow Saddam's regime under the flawed assumptions that the financial costs would be low and that Iraq would quickly enjoy stability, prosperity, and democracy.[73]

Costs of fighting aside, the perceived consequences of a broken agreement may push a belligerent to accept a limited outcome. Would a new war following a breach of the war-ending agreement threaten the conquest of the belligerent? Such an outcome might be more likely if the adversary is at least as powerful as the belligerent or contiguous to the belligerent. Conversely, if the enemy is far away and/or less powerful, a breach of the war-ending agreement may be seen as being less costly, making a limited (if unstable) outcome more acceptable.

In sum, *a belligerent, even if it is fearful that its adversary might break a war-ending agreement, will be more likely to accept a limited war outcome if it believes the costs of continuing the war promise to escalate significantly.* Note that accepting a limited war outcome may mean making concessions, or it may mean accepting the adversary's standing war-termination offer.

Postwar Peacekeeping Tools

Postwar peacekeeping tools might also reduce commitment fears and thereby affect the interplay of commitment and information dynamics. One possibility would be to create international institutions as a means of helping peace endure, such as inviting third parties to monitor and keep the peace, establishing demilitarized zones, signing arms control agreements, pursuing confidence building measures, and so forth.[74] However, such institutions are unlikely to provide comprehensive solutions to the postwar commitment problem. Not all of these tools, such as third-party peacekeepers, are always available. Usually, the former belligerents need to agree to allow the entry of peacekeepers, and of course a third party needs to be willing to supply them. Peacekeepers have been more commonly available after 1945 than before, and even in the post-1945 period are not always available or employed when available.[75] Further, the evidence that these tools help keep the peace between states is mixed, with some studies casting doubt on the ability of such tools to help peace endure.[76] Lastly, many of these tools are designed most directly to help prevent the accidental escalation of conflict. They are not necessarily intended to prevent the deliberate reignition of conflict. For example, UN peacekeepers were sent to the Sinai peninsula after the 1956 Suez War. As tensions mounted between Egypt and Israel in late spring 1967, Egypt simply ordered the peacekeepers to leave, and war broke out in June.[77] Nevertheless, this existing scholarship implies that *a belligerent, even one fearful that its adversary will break a war-ending commitment, will be more likely to accept a limited war outcome if a third party promises to deploy peacekeeping troops or related measures.*

International institutions aside, another way to reduce the commitment problem, thereby permitting war termination short of an absolute outcome, is to pre-deploy forces to reduce the possible mobilization advantages an adversary might try to gather. A belligerent might be defending a geographically far-flung ally, and it might fear that following a limited war outcome, if the belligerent brought its forces home from the ally's territory, the adversary might reattack sometime in the future, hoping to conquer the ally before the belligerent could remobilize and redeploy its forces to the ally's territory. One possible solution to this is the permanent forward deployment of forces by the belligerent, which would reduce the mobilization speed advantage, and also possibly serve as a tripwire automatically engaging the belligerent.[78] This was part of the American defense strategy in Western Europe especially after Eisenhower adopted the New Look defense policy, by which pre-deployment of American conventional forces guaranteed American involvement in the event of a Soviet invasion of Western Europe.[79]

However, the pre-deployment strategy is designed to address only a very specific kind of commitment problem, a possible short-term shift in the balance of power gained by mobilization advantages. It also assumes that the belligerent is willing to deploy standing forces to the ally in question for years if not decades on end, a policy that may not be economically or politically sustainable.

Capturing Goods that Reduce the Commitment Problem

Under some conditions, a belligerent may be willing to forgo an absolute war outcome because a limited war outcome may offer at least a partial solution to a credible commitment problem. Most centrally, seizure of at least part of the disputed good may decrease the likelihood that the adversary will defect on a war-ending agreement by making the prospect of a future attack by the adversary prohibitively costly or unlikely to succeed. Even a state fearful of an adversary's incredible commitment may be willing to accept a limited outcome, if that outcome provides a partial solution to the credible commitment problem and pursuing absolute war as a complete solution of the credible commitment problem promises to be prohibitively costly.

How exactly might acquisition of part of the disputed good decrease the chances the war-ending commitment would be broken? Most straightforwardly, if acquiring a specific component of the good makes a future attack less attractive to an adversary, then this may help alleviate the commitment problem. Specifically, possessing a specific increment of the good may make it easier to repel a future attack by the adversary, thereby decreasing (though not eliminating) the adversary's incentive to renege on the war-ending commitment and launch a future attack. Most commonly, this occurs when the attacker can seize a strategically critical piece of territory that makes national defense easier. Examples include mountain ranges, all the territory up to a body of water such that the national boundary becomes the shore of the water body, thick forests, and so forth. Empirical studies have shown the importance of geographic terrain on war outcomes, and other work has found that a state is less likely to attack if territorial features such as mountains or water bodies promise to make attack difficult.[80]

The Franco-Prussian War of 1870–71 demonstrates this dynamic. Prussia's desire for territorial gains was driven by credible commitment concerns. It perceived France as an enduring threat, and saw territorial acquisition as one means of making the French commitment not to attack in the future more credible by making the execution of such an attack more difficult. As Prussian Prime Minister Otto von Bismarck told a French representative, "Over the past 200 years, France has declared war on Prussia thirty times and . . . you will do so again; for that we must prepared, with . . . a territorial *glacis* between you and us."[81] Elsewhere, Bismarck stated that the French border city of Strasbourg would become Prussia's "Gibraltar," and that Strasbourg was "the key to our house."[82] The outcome of the war reflected Prussia's needs, since in the peace settlement France handed over to Prussia the provinces of Alsace and Lorraine, and the city of Strasbourg.

An increment of the good can make future defense easier if the increment contributes to military-industrial power. Two belligerents may be in dispute over a large territorial area, but key economic resources (such as coal mines, oil fields, or factories) may be concentrated in one small portion of the area, meaning that possession of that small portion may increase a belligerent's military power and make it less likely that its adversary will renege on a war-ending agreement and attack in the future. The idea that military conquest can mean the capture of resources, which in turn fuels military power and makes future victory easier, has been called by some the "cumulativity of resources."[83] In the twentieth century, military victors have been able to convert captured economic resources into future military power, as a conquered foe yields roughly half the economic resources that an ally of similar size provides.[84] Germany certainly reaped tremendous gains from its March 1939 seizure of Czechoslovakia. Czechoslovakia possessed tremendous supplies of arms and world-class munitions factories. In April 1939, twenty-three trains filled with ammunition and weapons were sent from Czechoslovakia to Germany *per day*.[85]

The theoretical point that the capture of increments of the disputed good can affect the balance of power has been explored in some bargaining models.[86] Notably, the existing work generally maintains the assumption that each increment of the good is equally valuable—that is, acquiring each increment offers a similar change to the balance of power. This work has produced several results, including that as each

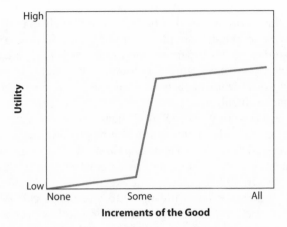

Figure 3.2 Utilities with a Supervaluable Increment of the Good

increment of the good is captured and the balance of power shifts, the side gaining the increment may have an incentive to demand even more of the opponent, reflecting its recognition that the balance of power is shifting, and that when the good contributes to the balance of power, war is more likely.[87]

Here, I relax some important assumptions of this past work. I first relax the assumption that all increments of the good are equally valuable. Some increments of the good, such as some portions of territory, may be more valuable than others. Put another way, oil fields, coal mines, mountains, and munitions factories may not be equally distributed throughout the entirety of a territorial area.[88] I term an increment as "supervaluable" if it contains more value than other increments of the good. For example, a portion of territory might be supervaluable if it contains the only oil reserves in the entire country. Note that if the disputed good is territory, then the supervaluable increment could be the first, last, or any intervening increment of territory. If it lies in the middle of the disputed area, then the relationship between possession of the good and utility is illustrated in figure 3.2.

Like the curve in figure 3.1, the curve in figure 3.2 is not linear, but rather at one point spikes up (a "step function"). In figure 3.1, the last increment of the good is supervaluable since it represents the absolute defeat of the adversary's military. In figure 3.2, the middle increment of the good is supervaluable, representing the possibility that any increment of the good can be supervaluable in its contribution to the military balance since, for example, the oil fields or a critical mountain range may rest in the center of the country.

If the utility return on the good is nonlinear as described in figure 3.2, some important implications follow. If the marginal return to fighting drops off after the belligerent seizes the supervaluable increment of the good, that belligerent may be more likely to accept war termination on limited terms, especially if the costs of war promise to escalate, even if its armed forces were performing well in combat. Therefore, *after a belligerent has captured an increment of the good that alleviates its postwar commitment problem, it will become more likely to accept war termination on limited terms, even if it is enjoying success on the battlefield.*

One critique might be that if the increment of the good is so valuable, then a war-ending settlement that allows for the exchange of the good from loser to winner may be difficult to reach, because the loser will be especially averse to abandoning that part of the good. However, the supervaluable increment of the good may make defense easier, but not make attack easier. This is most likely the case for geographic features such as mountain ranges and bodies of water, which facilitate defense but do not necessarily facilitate the attack. So, the capture of a supervaluable increment may not necessarily increase the offensive power of the victor, pushing it to continue fighting and raise its demands.

Two belligerents are especially likely to settle on a war-termination agreement in which one side gives up a supervaluable increment of a good short of suffering absolute military defeat when one side has proven its decisive military superiority, but the costs of pursuing future military operations threaten to escalate for that side. The winning side has the military advantage such that it could push further, but it does not because the costs of going further threaten to escalate the conflict, and it is less motivated to keep going because additional increments of the good are not as valuable. The losing side is willing to accept the loss of the supervaluable increment, because it recognizes that continuing to fight is unlikely to allow it to keep the supervaluable increment, and also continuing to fight introduces the dangers of suffering greater losses, including absolute defeat.

An example of these dynamics is the termination of the 1967 Six-Day War between Israel and its Arab adversaries. Israel achieved tremendous success on the battlefield, capturing in short order the Gaza Strip and Sinai from Egypt, the Golan Heights from Syria, and East Jerusalem and the West Bank from Jordan. A historical puzzle is why Israel decided to stop when it did. After achieving such great and unexpected success on the battlefield, perhaps the growth in Israeli confidence should have encouraged Israel to consider raising its war aims, in pursuit of overthrowing the Arab regimes. Indeed, Israel did have contingency plans for going farther, including a 1964 plan called Hatchet that envisioned two Israeli divisions swiftly conquering the Syrian capital city of Damascus. During the war, one Israeli newspaper had as a huge headline on its front page,

"Mission: Damascus!" However, Israel accepted war termination on limited terms even in the wake of battlefield victory, in part because its limited territorial gains had substantially increased its security and helped solve its credible commitment problem by making any future Arab attack on Israel more difficult, and in part because continued military operations would engender growing diplomatic costs, especially regarding relations with the United States. The acquisition of a substantial territorial buffer in Sinai and the high ground up to and including Mount Hermon in the Golan were especially important in reassuring Israeli security concerns.[89] Arab states accepted the loss of these territories because the shocking wave of Israeli military successes left them unconfident they could recapture their lost lands. Syria and Egypt did eventually reattack in 1973, their self-confidence restored by the acquisition of advanced Soviet military technologies.

The 1991 Iraq War provides a further example of a winning military from a country concerned with postwar agreement compliance deciding to accept a limited outcome that shifted the balance of power. The George H. W. Bush administration was deeply concerned about the long-term military threat posed by Saddam Hussein's Iraq, based on Iraq's allegedly battle-tested conventional forces, touted as the third biggest in the world, and its WMD programs, the details of which emerged after Iraq's August 1990 invasion of Kuwait. The United Nations coalition stopped its advance after liberating Kuwait, foregoing the opportunity to conquer Baghdad and impose an absolute outcome. Some have speculated that the decision to do so reflected both domestic and international political constraints, specifically that although the public strongly supported the use of military force to liberate Kuwait, it would not support a longer war that promised higher casualties, and that the supporting coalition would break apart if the United States exceeded its UN mandate and marched on Baghdad.[90] For its part, Iraq accepted the loss of Kuwait as a limited outcome of the war, clearly recognizing that the UN coalition had demonstrated its military superiority.

The United States and UN accepted the limited outcome of the 1991 Gulf War because they believed this outcome substantially ameliorated the commitment problem, by significantly reducing Iraqi conventional and unconventional military power. Regarding Iraqi conventional forces, a central aim of the war was to smash the Iraqi army, beyond the liberation of Kuwait. This was expressed most clearly in a January 1991 meeting with Bush and his advisers. Bush and his national security adviser Brent Scowcroft argued against the acceptability of a peaceful Iraqi withdrawal from Kuwait. The problem, they pointed out, is that it would have been politically impossible for American forces to remain in the region indefinitely as a deterrent to further Iraqi aggression, and when the American forces eventually left, Iraq could exploit the shift in the immediate balance of forces and reinvade Kuwait.[91] As a result, the good in dispute was not just the sovereignty of Kuwait, but also the strength of the Iraqi army, and achieving the American preference on the latter (destroying Iraqi conventional military power) would be necessary to make the Iraqi commitment to respect the war-ending settlement on the former (recognize Kuwait's sovereignty) more credible. At the January 1991 meeting, Bush explicitly argued that the U.S. desired both Kuwaiti liberation *and* the destruction of the Iraqi army, remarking, "If they crack under force, it is better than withdrawal."[92] In February, Soviet General Secretary Mikhail Gorbachev floated the possibility of an Iraqi withdrawal from Kuwait over a period of weeks. The U.S. viewed this proposal as flawed in part because it would have allowed the Iraqi military to withdraw intact, giving Saddam the ability to reattack Kuwait in the future.[93] The Bush administration's counterproposal (rejected by Iraq) of a seven-day withdrawal would have forced Iraq to abandon a sizable fraction of its heavy forces in Kuwait, because many units were disabled or dug in.[94]

The UN had similar views about Iraqi WMD. Absent the overthrow of Saddam's regime, the concern remained that Iraq might in the future use WMD against its neighbors, and like the degradation of Iraq's conventional military forces, the destruction of Iraq's WMD infrastructure was part of the good that constituted coalition war aims. The U.S. perceived that even with a limited outcome, it could reduce the WMD credible commitment problem. The UN coalition conducted extensive airstrikes against known Iraqi WMD facilities during the war, and the operational success of these strikes gave the coalition confidence that Iraq's WMD capacity had been gutted. Further, the deal ending the war required Iraq to comply with UN Security Council resolutions on WMD disarmament, and to allow UN inspectors to visit suspected WMD sites. At war's end, all were confident that these two measures crippled the Iraqi WMD threat, and that the inspectors would be able to wrap up their work within six months at the most.[95] The reality was different, as the world quickly learned that there were wide secret swaths of the Iraqi WMD program left untargeted during the war. Iraq's ongoing resistance to UN inspectors in the 1990s further raised fears that Iraq was defying the terms of the 1991 settlement. Perhaps ironically, it became evident in 2004 that Iraq had abandoned its WMD programs in the late 1990s.[96]

ISSUE INDIVISIBILITY

The previous discussion of commitments has framed commitment effects in the context of the relationship between increments of the good and utility—that is, the benefits curve of continued fighting. Another factor that could shape the benefits curve is so-called "issue indivisibility," the claim that some issues cannot be divided in a bargain between two disputants, and that the presence of issue indivisibility can make war more likely even between two rational, fully informed states.[97] Indivisibility is easiest to think of as physical indivisibility, a good that cannot materially be divided, or would be destroyed if division is attempted. The biblical story of King Solomon provides the classic example, in which two women are in dispute over a child, and Solomon's offer to cut the child in two as a solution to the dispute is rejected by one of the women because doing so would of course kill the child. International relations are commonly much more about easily physically divisible goods like territory and natural resources. Even settling on political control within a national government is subject to divisibility, through institutionalized power-sharing in the parliament or even the office of the president, the latter exemplified by Bosnia's three-headed presidency since the middle 1990s. Probably the best example of a literally physically indivisible good in international relations might be a state's possession of a first nuclear weapon. However, even the possession of a nuclear weapon can be divided somewhat. The dual key system in NATO during the Cold War allowed the United States to own nuclear weapons based abroad, while the host nation controlled the missile used to deliver the nuclear weapon. Further, nuclear possession is functionally divisible through side payments, as American promises of extended nuclear deterrence have persuaded states like (West) Germany, Japan, South Korea, and Taiwan to forgo national nuclear programs.

A number of scholars have maintained that states treat some goods in international relations as if they were indivisible, even if they can be physically divided. Some scholars have posited that cultural and social forces sometimes push a belligerent to frame a good, especially a territorial area, as having value only if its entirety is possessed, perhaps because the territory is seen as "sacred space."[98] Another, more rationalist theory proposes that reputation effects may create indivisibility effects. An actor may perceive that making concessions to split a good may encourage the other actor to make more challenges in the future (also known as "salami tactics"), or encourage other actors to make challenges, a dynamic related to what economists call the "chain store paradox."[99]

Issue indivisibility fits into the theoretical framework envisioned here. Specifically, because the issue pertains to the benefits side of the calculus, issue indivisibility is a factor that shapes the relationship between increments of the disputed good and a belligerent's utility. The curves in figures 3.1 and 3.2 describe two possible relationships between these factors. If a belligerent genuinely thinks an issue is indivisible, this would mean that that side would receive no welfare from any increment of the good except when all of the good is acquired, meaning the benefits curve ought to look something like figure 3.1, a line with a near zero slope, but then a step function at the right-hand side jumping up if the belligerent can capture the entire good. The war-termination prediction might be that if a war is fought over an indivisible issue, then belligerents are less likely to negotiate for a limited outcome to split the good, and are more likely to fight to the finish.

In practice, issue indivisibility is unlikely to play a central role in war initiation or war termination. Some have proposed that issue indivisibility can at least in theory be overcome through side payments or lotteries, although such mechanisms may be infeasible because states cannot credibly commit to carrying out the terms of such a deal—that is, giving up claim on an indivisible issue on the basis of the outcome of a random number draw.[100] A more aggressive claim is that no issue is ever literally indivisible, either physically or perceptually. Even when an actor places a very high value on possession of a good such that it appears to treat the issue as indivisible, the actor will almost never be completely indifferent between possessing none of the good and some of the good (true indivisibility requires this indifference). Pakistan would not be indifferent to acquiring an extra 10 percent of Kashmir, and the Palestinians would not be indifferent to reacquiring the 50 percent of Jerusalem they controlled before the Six-Day War.

As an empirical matter, scholars have been unable to point to many episodes of war-causing indivisibility. Note that even with the two leading examples, Kashmir and Jerusalem, the parties possessing less than 100 percent of the good go years without attacking. Pakistan and India have fought some wars over Kashmir, although the vast majority of their fifty years since independence have been without conflict. Regarding Jerusalem, the Arab states have not attacked with the aim of recapturing Jerusalem since Israel took control of all of it in 1967. Interpretation problems arise with other alleged episodes of issue indivisibility.[101] More generally, public statements alone are insufficient to prove indivisibility, as actors are motivated to claim that an issue under dispute is indivisible in order to provide increased bargaining leverage.[102] For example, in the 1944 war-termination negotiations between Finland and the Soviet Union, the former claimed that the pre–Winter War 1939 borders must be restored, because of the indivisibility of all of Finnish territory. One Finnish delegate argued that the portion of Finland lost at the end of the Winter War in 1940 "constitutes in the economical as well as in the national sense so to speak an organic part of our nation's body, and it affects our total existence in a most decisive way. . . . I repeat once more that the ceded part of Karelia belongs organically to Finland, and that our people cannot conceive that this frontier will be a final one."[103] Yet the Finns gave up this territory as part of the 1944 peace treaty with the Soviet Union, accepting a division of this allegedly indivisible territory peacefully for the more than six decades that have elapsed since. Similarly, regarding whether Germany would give up the Alsace-Lorraine territories acquired in the 1870–71 Franco-Prussian War in any peace deal to end World War I, the German foreign minister Richard von Kühlmann declared to the German Reichstag in 1917, "We have but one answer to the question of whether Germany will make any concessions in the matter of Alsace-Lorraine. That answer is no, no, never! So long as a single German can still lift a gun, the integrity of the Reich territory, handed down to us by our fathers as a glorious heritage, shall never be the subject of any negotiations or concessions. Alsace-Lorraine is Germany's shield, the symbol of German unity." Kühlmann admitted in his memoirs that the speech was intended to restore patriotic unity in the Reichstag, and Germany of course returned the territories to France as part of the Versailles Treaty.[104]

AN INTEGRATED RATIONALIST THEORY OF WAR TERMINATION

The past two chapters have laid out ideas about war termination that share some common assumptions: the state is the primary actor, states are rational, anarchy is unavoidable, and uncertainty is quite common. The two chapters together have presented a rationalist theory of war termination that contains as its two principal strands information and commitment dynamics. These two dynamics sometimes work in complement, and they sometimes pull in opposite directions. This chapter has laid out some of these tensions as well as conditions under which we should expect information or commitment dynamics to predominate. The following several chapters address the next task, assessing the power of this theory by applying it to wars that have actually occurred.

CHAPTER FOUR

Conducting Empirical Tests

> The world can never be well known by theory: practice is
> absolutely necessary.
>
> —Lord Chesterfield

> In theory there is no difference between theory and practice.
> In practice there is.
>
> —Yogi Berra

CHAPTERS 2 AND 3 DEVELOPED these central hypotheses: battle outcomes affect war-termination offers; third-party activities affect war-termination offers; severe postwar commitment fears encourage a state to ignore combat outcomes and pursue absolute victory; fears of escalating costs can push a fearful state to accept a limited outcome; if a fearful state sees almost no chance of eventual victory, it will make concessions to end the war; capture of a good that reduces the commitment problem can encourage a belligerent to accept a limited war outcome. This book tests these central hypotheses (the cases did not lend themselves to testing the peacekeeping hypothesis presented in chapter 3). This chapter describes how these hypotheses were tested. The first section describes the principal mode of analysis employed, qualitative case study techniques. The second section explores the possibility of executing quantitative tests, explaining why conducting such tests with satisfactory validity is difficult.

A QUALITATIVE APPROACH

In this book, the dependent variable is the decision of a wartime belligerent at a particular point in a war to demand more concessions, offer more concessions, or make no change in its war-termination offer. A war-termination offer is a belligerent's proposal to end the war under certain described conditions, such as redrawing an international territorial border or the change in the national leadership of the adversary. Note that there can be several cases (decisions) per belligerent per war. To test the hypotheses, an empirical sample needs to include cases of intrawar behavior in which belligerents made decisions about war-termination behavior, namely whether to raise, lower, or leave unchanged their war-termination offers.

The central empirical approach here is qualitative, the in-depth examination of war-termination behavior in a small number of wars. The specific strategy taken, especially within the individual empirical chapters, is within-case analysis, employing process tracing. Within-case analysis "focuses not on the analysis of variables across cases, but on the causal path in a single case."[1] Process tracing, "a procedure for identifying steps in a causal process leading to the outcome of a given dependent variable of a particular case in a particular historical context,"[2] is almost by definition an integral part of within-case analysis.

Process tracing enjoys some important advantages over a pure congruence method, in which the covariation between independent and dependent variables is observed. Establishing universal rules for combat success and combat failure is difficult, because interpreting battle outcomes is highly context-dependent. Sometimes, capturing territory constitutes combat success, and sometimes it does not. The only way to assess with high confidence whether the hypothesized information proposition relationship of combat failure making concessions more likely is to assess directly how a particular combat outcome was interpreted by the national political leadership, and then whether and how that interpretation was translated into a change in war-termination demands.

This book analyzes the war-termination behavior of belligerents in several wars. An array of wars and their belligerents have been included in the sample, including the American Civil War, the Korean War, World War II in both Europe and the Pacific, World War I, the Winter War, and the Continuation War. Although this sample is not large or random, it does have several important virtues. First, each war contains several different war-termination decisions, meaning that the size of the sample of decisions exceeds twenty, providing more information with which to test the theory. Second, and relatedly, there is variance in the dependent variable. For the variety of war-termination decisions, in some instances greater concessions were demanded (as after the Union victory at Gettysburg, after the Soviets broke the Mannerheim line in Finland in 1940, and on the U.S. side of the Korean War in September 1950), in some instances greater concessions were offered (as on the Soviet side in the Continuation War, on the Finnish side towards the end of the Winter War, and on the Japanese side in August 1945), and in some instances there was no change in war-termination demands (such as Japan during almost all of the Pacific War, Britain in 1940, and the Confederacy during almost all of the American Civil War). Relatedly, some belligerents maintained limited war aims (such as the Soviet Union in the second half of the Winter War, the U.S. in the Korean War after the Chinese intervention, and Japan during World War II), and some pursued absolute war aims (such as the Allies during World War II, the Soviet Union at the outset of the Winter War, and the U.S. in the Korean War in September 1950).

Third, there is variation in the independent variables, and there is variation in information received on combat capabilities. Belligerents received favorable and unfavorable information from the battlefield, since sometimes belligerents got encouraging information (such as the Union at the end of the Civil War and the Soviet Union in February–March 1940), sometimes belligerents received discouraging information (such as the U.S. in summer 1950, the Soviet Union in 1941, and the Soviet Union in December 1939–January 1940), sometimes the information the belligerent received was expected (such as Japanese successes up through middle 1942), and sometimes it was unexpected (such as the Red Army's setbacks against Finland in December 1939 and the poor performance of South Korean and American forces in summer 1950). There is also variation in third-party behavior, as sometimes third parties do intervene, which in turn changes belligerents' calculations (such as China's intervention in the Korean War in October 1950 and Soviet intervention against Japan in August 1945), sometimes third-party intervention seems possible but never arrives (such as plans for Anglo-French intervention in the Winter War), sometimes there is the hope for long-term third-party intervention that does eventually arrive (British recognition in 1940 that American intervention was not imminent, though possible in the medium or long term), sometimes third parties consider but then dismiss intervention (such as the European powers eventually declining to intervene on behalf of the Confederacy during the Civil War), and sometimes there is no variation in the role of third parties (Germany remained a Finnish ally throughout the Continuation War).

There is variation on some of the commitment-related variables. Generally, there is little consequential variation on the central commitment variable, fear that the adversary might renege on a war-ending deal. The theoretical discussion in chapter 3 explains this minimal variation. Anarchy means that a state is always fearful of the possibility of another state violating the terms of an agreement. The temptation to break an agreement is high, both because of greed and fear. Although trust can be a basis for making cooperation between states possible, belligerents have especially low levels of trust, both because of the ongoing violence between them, and because the initiation of the war likely broke a neutrality or border agreement.

There is variation on other variables which mediate the effect of credible commitment concerns on war-termination behavior. The theory predicts that belligerents' fears about adversaries breaking postwar agreements should be more intense when the postwar balance of power changes, when first strike advantages might appear, and/or when the preferences of the adversary change, perhaps because of a change in leadership. Some belligerents were fearful that troop demobilizations following war's end would shift the balance of power and create a temporary window of opportunity for the adversary (the U.S. in 1950 fearing that troop withdrawal would encourage a North Korean reattack). Sometimes belligerents' fear shifts in the material balance of power (such as U.S. fears about the growing power of the Communist bloc in 1950, as well as belligerents such as Britain 1940 and the Union in the Civil War, which worried that the terms of the peace deal would cause a shift in the balance of power; see next paragraph). Some belligerents feared that possible domestic political changes might encourage the adversary to renege on an agreement (the Confederacy feared that laying down its arms and rejoining the Union would tempt Northern politicians to ignore moderate reconstruction terms,[3] and Roosevelt in 1942 feared that less than absolute victory might permit a repetition of the collapse of the 1919 Versailles agreement, which was caused by the rise of Hitler and the Nazi Party). Some feared that the adversary might in the future attract a powerful ally (the Soviet Union feared in 1939 that Finland would join Germany or Britain in a future war). Fear existed among some belligerents that in the future conditions favorable to a new war would present themselves, and the adversary would reattack (such as general German paranoia of Britain and France in World War I). This last set of belligerents understood that a change in the balance of power can make war more likely, but also projected that variations in the balance of power are inevitable, and sooner or later an attractive opportunity for a new war will reappear. In other words, fear of an unfavorable shift in the balance of power is endemic, and such belligerents maintained these fears without necessarily deep consideration of the structural determinants of the balance of power (e.g., the comparative growth in each side's population).

Variance occurred across the cases to the extent that the good itself affected the intensity of the commitment problem. Sometimes belligerents perceived that capture of some increment of the good would reduce the commitment problem (such as German capture of Belgium in World War I and Soviet capture of bits of Finnish territory in the Winter and Continuation Wars), sometimes they feared that making concessions on the good exacerbated the commitment problem (such as Churchill's fear that a peace deal with Hitler in summer 1940 would require the sacrifice of British naval power, Lincoln's concerns about the dangers of giving up on the emancipation issue, and American fears in the Korean War that concessions on the prisoners of war issue would swing the balance of power), and sometimes they perceived that the good had no effect on the balance of power (Japan felt confident that abandoning its colonial claims would not affect the balance of power or the likelihood of American compliance with a peace deal).

Variance also occurred in belligerents' perceptions about the costs of continuing to fight, and the chances for eventual victory if fighting continued. Some fearful belligerents receiving discouraging information still maintained some hope of eventual victory (such as Britain in 1940 hoping for eventual American intervention to turn the tide, the U.S. in 1942 counting on long-term economic mobilization, and Japan up to August 1945 hoping that it could eventually force the U.S. to make concessions if it could inflict on the U.S. a decisive battle defeat), and some fearful belligerents had almost no hope of eventually winning (such as Japan in August 1945 and perhaps the Soviet Union in 1941). Some belligerents feared that the costs of continuing to fight the war and/or pursue absolute victory promised to escalate steeply (such as Japan in August 1945, the Soviet Union in February–March 1940, and the United States after Chinese intervention) and some belligerents saw the costs of continuing to fight the war as being acceptable (such as the U.S. in World War II and the Union in the Civil War). There is virtually no variation in the promise of postwar peacekeeping (with the arguable exception of U.S. discussion from 1951 forward of postwar troop deployments in Korea), so that hypothesis was not tested.

The main hypotheses aside, the cases vary along other potentially relevant dimensions. There are wars with roughly symmetric power relationships (World Wars I and II) and wars with more asymmetric power relationships (Korea, the Winter War, and the Continuation War). The sample includes wars taking place in Asia, Europe, and North America. The wars take place across a wide temporal range, from the mid-nineteenth to the mid-twentieth century. The duration of the wars varies from months (such as the Winter War) to years (such as the Civil War and Korean War). The belligerents include democracies (the U.S., Britain, and Finland), dictatorships (the Soviet Union), and mixed regimes having characteristics of both (Germany in World War I and Japan).

The analysis in each empirical chapter usually focuses on a handful of key decisions in each war, rather than evaluating all war-termination decisions throughout the war. The chapters are designed to test the variety of propositions presented in chapters 2 and 3. One goal is to test the information propositions of chapter 2 as being themselves sufficient explanations of war-termination behavior since some might consider the information propositions alone to be the conventional wisdom as to how states make war-termination decisions. In service of this latter goal, many of these key decisions constitute "easy" tests for the information proposition alone. They are episodes in which incoming information was clearly encouraging or discouraging for at least one belligerent, meaning that

TABLE 4.1
Historical Cases

War	Chapter	Belligerent	Time Period
Korean War	5	U.S.	August–September 1950
Korean War	5	U.S.	Early 1951
Korean War	5	U.S.	1951–53
World War II	6	Britain	May 1940
World War II	6	U.S.	Early 1942
World War II	6	Soviet Union	Late 1941
Winter War	7	Soviet Union	December 1939–January 1940
Winter War	7	Soviet Union	February 1940–March 1940
Winter War	7	Finland	February–March 1940
Continuation War	7	Soviet Union	Late 1941
Continuation War	7	Finland	Late 1941
Continuation War	7	Finland	1943–44
Continuation War	7	Soviet Union	1943–44
U.S. Civil War	8	Union	Summer 1862
U.S. Civil War	8	Union	Fall 1862
U.S. Civil War	8	Confederacy	Late 1863
U.S. Civil War	8	Union	Summer 1864
U.S. Civil War	8	Union	February 1865
U.S. Civil War	8	Confederacy	February 1865
World War I	9	Germany	Winter 1917–18
World War II	10	Japan	Mid-1942–July 1945
World War II	10	Japan	August 1945

independent variables of combat outcomes and expectations about the war's future course are easily coded, and the information propositions can make clear predictions. If information (such as combat outcomes) is highly favorable, then an approach focusing just on information would strongly predict that the belligerent should demand more concessions. If information is highly unfavorable, then the information-only approach would strongly predict that the belligerent should offer more concessions.

Table 4.1 lists the twenty-two cases of belligerent war-termination decision-making analyzed across chapters 6–10.

The case studies explore decision-makers' perceptions across a number of variables, including commitment fears, perceptions about the current and future course of the war, the likelihood of third-party intervention, and so on. The cases rely on a variety of types of evidence of decision-makers' perceptions and beliefs, such as public and private statements by the principals themselves. The evidence will be assessed critically since such evidence suffers from at least three potential flaws. First, individuals sometimes misstate their intentions, either strategically or because of simple error. Franklin Roosevelt falsely declared that the idea of unconditional surrender "popped into his mind" at the January 1943 Casablanca conference. We now know that by January 1943 he had been committed to this idea for at least several months.[4] Winston Churchill falsely declared in his history of World War II that no one in May 1940 considered negotiating with Adolf Hitler. U.S. government official John Allison mischaracterized the events of the first weeks of the Korean War in his autobiography.

Some might say that diary entries are the best available source of evidence of intentions. Because they are reflections offered immediately, they are, making them also the freshest recollections, undecayed by the passage of time. They are less likely to be aimed at a particular audience, too (in contrast to, for example, a public speech). However, even diary entries have limitations. Sometimes diary entries are more reflective of emotional tides than a considered opinion that actually motivates decisions and policy-making. For example, in two separate diary entries in 1952, Truman fumed that the only way to break the deadlock in the Korean War negotiations with the Communists would be to threaten them with nuclear destruction. He wrote in his diary that the U.S. should demand that the Communists accept peace terms within ten days, and if they did not, "This means all out war. It means that Moscow, St. Petersburg, Mukden, Vladivostok, Peking, Shanghai, Port Arthur, Darien, Odessa, Stalingrad and every manufacturing plant in China and the Soviet Union will be eliminated. This is the final chance for the Soviet Government to decide whether it desires to survive or not."[5] Of course, the U.S. never adopted such a policy, nor did Truman ever introduce it for discussion among his advisers.

Second, the documentary record is incomplete, and it is sometimes systematically incomplete. For example, an important question regarding the German decision not to negotiate in 1917–18 concerns whether or not German economic special interests influenced German political and military decision-making. One historian claims that the personal records of a key military staff member who may have had industrial ties were systematically purged of any documents that might have indicated a link.[6] The official minutes of the 1942 United States committee that first drew up the unconditional surrender demand were merely summary, generally truncating or omitting the arguments made by the committee members in those sessions.[7] The official minutes of the National Security Council are also quite brief, merely summarizing themes discussed rather than elaborating specific arguments.

Third, scholars themselves sometimes differ in evaluating the same materials. Sometimes differences occur in the translation of foreign language documents into English.[8] Differences also crop up in how to treat different documentary materials. In examination of Japanese war termination at the end of World War II, Tsuyoshi Hasegawa and Robert Frank differ over how to treat documentary records regarding Hirohito's statements at the crucial August 15, 1945 conference in which statements were made describing the motivations behind the Japanese decision to surrender.[9]

The empirical tests also consider competing explanations for the observed war-termination decisions. Perhaps the most prominent alternative set of war-termination explanations concerns domestic politics. Chapter 1 presented two different domestic politics explanations: the first that because democratic leaders are especially casualty-sensitive they are more likely to make concessions as the costs of war mount; and the second being that mixed regimes are more likely to increase their war aims when they face moderate defeat in order to increase the likelihood of achieving a victory that will provide sufficient goods to distribute to the leader's governing coalition, thereby keeping the leader in power. Each chapter will assess one or both of the domestic politics explanations as appropriate, as well as other possibly relevant explanations.

The empirical analysis serves two further functions beyond testing hypotheses. One function is to present and solve specific empirical puzzles. Although external validity and generalizability are leading goals of empirical research, the satisfactory explanation of individual, historically significant episodes is also an important goal. The cases in this book answer some important historical questions, such as: why the United States escalated the Korean War to pursue the conquest of North Korea, a decision that directly led to Chinese involvement and a three-year war costing hundreds of thousands of lives; why the American Civil War dragged on for so long, costing hundreds of thousands of lives and gouging scars in the American social, political, and geographic landscape felt to this day; why Germany in 1917–18 declined the opportunity to end the war and digest its vast gains in the East, choosing instead to fight on, eventually incurring its own decisive defeat; why during World War II even in the darkest moments the Allies refused to concede, and instead pressed on for total victory and the annihilation of humanity's most dangerous creation, militaristic fascism.

A second function is theory building. Political science has greatly benefited from the spare and fruitful bargaining metaphor as a way of enriching our theoretical speculation about the nature of war. However, these very clean ideas have almost never been applied to the very messy reality of actual war. Empirical tests of these ideas will provide greater insight as to which components of the theory are worth keeping, which appear worth limiting or outright rejecting, and where there is unexplained variance demanding greater theoretical elaboration and development. These issues are given special treatment in the conclusion.

THE DIFFICULTIES OF CONDUCTING QUANTITATIVE TESTS

Although quantitative methods would provide advantages of rigor and external validity, severe internal validity problems prevent their application here. Consider first that there are two possible approaches to building a quantitative dataset appropriate for testing the hypotheses of chapters 2 and 3, assuming one has a predefined dataset on all (interstate) wars such as that produced by the Correlates of War project. The first approach would be to break up each war into separate combat events, like battles. Each case would be a single battle, and testing the central information perspective hypothesis would require, in particular, coding the outcome of each battle, which would then have predicted impacts on war-termination behavior. However, some wars, such as insurgencies, do not lend themselves to being accurately characterized as a string of discrete battles. The appropriate size of a battle would also differ across wars, making it difficult to establish a universal definition of battle size.

An alternative to using battle-level data would be to use time units during war as cases, such as the war-month. In this approach, for each war-month (for example) the independent variables are coded (such as which side achieved greater success in battle) and the dependent variables are coded (how did war-termination offers change, if at all). In a particular war-month, there may be no battles, one battle, or several battles, and a single aggregate coding for each war-month would be produced.

Difficulties arise in choosing exactly what time period to choose—for example, war-year, war-month, or war-week. The disadvantage of choosing larger time periods (such as a month or year) is that some wars may last less than a single time period, making it impossible to assess whether the flow of battle information changed war-termination behavior. However, using smaller time periods such as days or weeks introduces problems, as daily and weekly combat performance data is generally unavailable in even the best documented war. Further, reducing the time slice may make it too easy to falsify the information proposition that combat results cause changes in war-termination offers. Leaders rarely have the organizational capacity to make daily adjustments in their war-termination offers, so the record would reveal lots of variance on the independent variable of combat outcomes, and little variance on the dependent variable of war-termination behavior.

The issue of choosing the unit of analysis aside, testing the information proposition requires coding data on intrawar combat performance. To code outcomes quantitatively, there are three general approaches: coding casualties, coding the gain or loss of territory, and a more subjective coding of who wins each battle. A general problem with the first two approaches is the heterogeneity of wars since sometimes leaders focus more on territorial gains and losses than on casualties (such as Germany and the Soviet Union in World War II), and sometimes they focus more on casualties (such as the U.S. in the Vietnam War). It gets more complex. Among belligerents focusing on casualties, sometimes leaders focus on relative casualty rates (such as the U.S. in the Vietnam War), and sometimes they focus on the absolute casualty rates of their adversary (such as Japan in the Pacific War and North Vietnam). This can mean a battle can be both a tactical defeat and a strategic victory. In the December 1862 Battle of Fredericksburg during the U.S. Civil War, even though the Confederates repelled the assault and suffered half as many casualties as Union forces, Lincoln speculated "that if the same battle were to be fought over again, every day, through a week of days, with the same relative results, the army under [Confederate General Robert E.] Lee would be wiped out to its last man, the Army of the Potomac would still be a mighty host, the war would be over, the Confederacy gone."[10] The Confederate leadership saw it the same way. Confederate Vice President Alexander Stephens wrote in his memoirs that the Union "could afford to lose any number of battles, with great losses of men, if they could thereby materially thin our ranks. In this way by attrition alone, they would ultimately wear us out."[11]

Indeed, leaders often talk about accepting tradeoffs between measurable indices of progress, such as territory, lives, and time, and the key point is that what leaders value (and hence what they consider to be an indicator of success) varies widely across wars. Sometimes a military sacrifices lives for time, as when the British government in May 1940 ordered a force contingent at Calais to fight to the death in order to increase the amount of time that the rest of the British Expeditionary Force would have to evacuate from the beaches of Dunkirk.[12] During the October 1941 battles of Bryansk and Vyazma between the German and Soviet armies, the Germans killed, wounded, or captured nearly a million Soviet soldiers at the cost of far fewer German losses. However, this was in some sense a strategic victory for the Soviet Union, as these human losses bought the Red Army critically needed time to ready the defenses of Moscow.[13] Sometimes, giving up territory is part of a military's defensive scheme, such as employing a defense-in-depth strategy to meet a blitzkrieg attack.[14] In 1812, the Russian military welcomed the long French advance towards Moscow, knowing it would be Napoleon's undoing. General Mikhail Kutisov remarked that, "Napoleon is a torrent which we are as yet unable to stem. Moscow will be the sponge that will suck him dry."[15] On an operational level, sometimes an adversary will give up territory temporarily as a feint. Hitler lured France into moving its forces forward into Belgium, making Allied forces vulnerable to encirclement following the German breakthrough in the Ardennes.[16] Making matters even worse, the relative importance of a particular indicator of success may vary not only across wars, but may also vary within wars. In the Korean War, the U.S. (and probably the Communist side as well) shifted in 1951 from a focus on territory to a focus on casualties.[17] Fortunately, these heterogeneity/contextuality problems can be solved with a qualitative approach, appreciation of the specifics of the war and the belligerent's strategy for victory can indicate what constitutes favorable combat outcomes and what constitutes unfavorable combat outcomes.

These conceptual issues aside, there are severe data availability problems. More objective data on combat outcomes is scarce. Data on territorial control during war is even harder to find, and essentially impossible to collect given the generally thin description in the historical record of the exact location of front lines. Casualty data are very difficult to come by. For example, there are not even official aggregate casualty estimates (never mind casualties on a monthly basis) on the Communist side of the Korean War. Estimates vary widely across Chinese and non-Chinese sources, from 152,000 dead to 3 million dead.[18] In the American Civil War, official battle casualty estimates are about 75 percent missing on the Confederate side.[19]

In sum, single indicators of combat success like casualty ratios or territory captured are unlikely to capture the variety of meaning of combat outcomes within and across wars. Another approach might be to code battle outcomes subjectively, classifying them on the basis of a comprehensive view of the historical record as being a win for one side or the other, or a draw. HERO, the only available dataset that provides comprehensive battle-level codings, suffers severe limitations.[20] More generally, a substantial amount of judgment is required for the coding of each case, because it is based on the context of belligerent political–military strategy, and the available evidence on leader perceptions. The better strategy is to make these coding decisions transparent in the context of case studies, rather than obscure the thinking behind each individual coding by merely assigning a numerical value to each coding.

In sum, there are simply too many serious problems to permit the widespread application of quantitative analysis techniques for testing the hypotheses in chapters 2 and 3. The main empirical strategy of this book is the use of case studies. The next six chapters apply case study methods to an array of conflicts, fought over more than a century, to help understand how belligerents try to end their wars.

CHAPTER FIVE

The Korean War

> War's very object is victory—not prolonged indecision. In
> war, indeed, there can be no substitute for victory.
> —General Douglas MacArthur's
> farewell address to Congress, April 1951

THE KOREAN WAR IS A MONUMENT to the inefficiency of war. The war dragged on for three years after North Korea's June 1950 invasion of South Korea, killing millions of people and ending essentially with the reestablishment of the status quo ante, a roughly even split of the Korean peninsula between a Communist North and a non-Communist South. Why did the war drag on for so long? How did the belligerents try to end it, and on what terms?

The war aims and war-termination behavior of the belligerents in the Korean War were fundamentally shaped by both commitment and information dynamics. Neither commitment nor information dynamics in isolation can account for the evolution of war-termination behavior across the war, but together they provide a powerful and comprehensive account. In the first phase of the war from the June 1950 North Korean invasion to the eve of the September 1950 U.S. amphibious landing at Inchon, United States and UN forces suffered a series of combat setbacks that left them on the brink of being swept off the peninsula. Yet before the tide turned the U.S. established very high war aims of seeking the destruction of the Communist regime in North Korea. This decision cannot be accounted for by the hypothesis that belligerents should reduce war aims in reaction to combat setbacks. Rather, the U.S. established high war aims because it feared that any limited settlement leaving North Korea intact would be unstable, tempting a future North Korean attack on South Korea. The U.S. government perceived that only the unification of the Korean peninsula under a single non-Communist government would solve this Communist commitment credibility problem.

In the second phase of the war from mid-September 1950 until spring 1951, American forces experienced initial success following the amphibious landing at Inchon but then catastrophe when in late October China intervened to aid North Korea. Although American fears of Communist postwar noncompliance were not assuaged during this time period, the UN nevertheless reduced its war aims to restoration of the status quo ante. This change reflected shifts in the information environment, namely the U.S. updating its assessments of the likelihood of victory given Chinese intervention, and also its assessment of the costs of victory, as the conquest of North Korea would now likely involve escalation to direct attacks on China and in turn the very costly consequence of involving the Soviet Union in the war directly. As the theory predicts, the key factor that causes the U.S. to abandon its pursuit of absolute victory in the second phase is a rise in the expected cost of pursuing a solution to the commitment problem. In the first phase, the cost of achieving absolute victory to solve the commitment problem, winning a conventional war against North Korea alone, was seen as a price worth paying to achieve the goal of long-term South Korean security. In the second phase, the cost of achieving absolute victory to solve the commitment problem, fighting a nuclear World War III against China and the Soviet Union, was seen as a price not worth paying to achieve the goal of long-term South Korean security.

In the third and final phase from spring 1951 to the end of the war in summer 1953, general stasis existed both on the battlefield, as neither side scored a major victory, and at the diplomatic table, as concessions were scant and relatively minor when they did come. The length of this phase demonstrates the inefficiency of combat as a source of information, since a steady flow of information from combat about capabilities did not create bargaining space for two years. During this third phase, enduring commitment concerns did help shape in particular UN war-termination negotiations, causing the UN to resist a one-for-one POW swap and to resist reestablishing the 38th parallel as the border between North and South Korea.

JUNE 1950–SEPTEMBER 1950

The Korean peninsula was under Japanese control during World War II, and at war's end it was divided into two states, Communist-controlled North Korea (Democratic People's Republic of Korea) and non-Communist South Korea (Republic of Korea), divided by the 38th parallel (latitude) (see figure 5.1).

With the blessings of Moscow and Beijing, North Korea invaded South Korea on June 25, 1950, with the goal of unifying the entire Korean peninsula under a single Communist government.[1] After the North Korean invasion, the initial United Nations demands were for the restoration of the prewar border at the 38th parallel, as expressed in UN Security Coun-

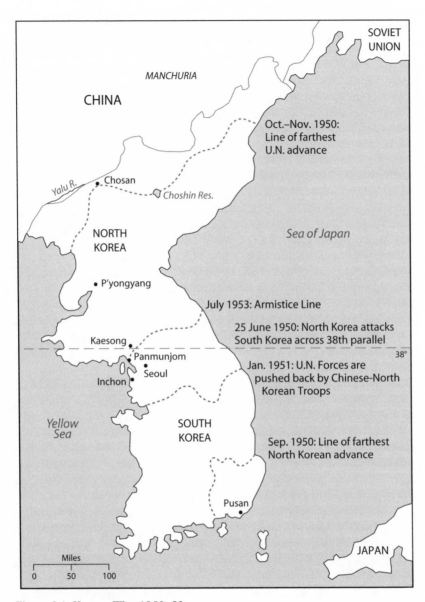

Figure 5.1 Korean War, 1950–53.

cil Resolution 82 of June 25, 1950, supported in public statements by President Harry Truman on June 27 and Secretary of State Dean Acheson on June 29, and discussed by Truman and Acheson during a June 29 National Security Council (NSC) meeting.[2] In a June 28 meeting of the NSC, Truman specifically ruled out military action north of the 38th parallel.[3] However, South Korean President Syngman Rhee had been discussing the possibility of overthrowing the North Korean government even before the June 25 invasion.[4]

Establishing High U.S. War Aims

There was gradual movement among American policymakers from July to September 1950 towards establishing the American war aim of crossing the 38th parallel and eliminating the North Korean government in Pyongyang, and establishing a single Korean state under non-Communist rule. The foundations for such a move were perhaps ironically laid by a 1947 United Nations General Assembly Resolution calling for the peaceful reestablishment of national independence in Korea. A December 1948 UN General Assembly resolution also called for the unification of Korea.[5] Although Truman's initial stated political aims were for the restoration of the status quo ante, the Joint Client of Staff (JCS) did formally approve the use of force north of the 38th parallel as early as June 29, although their message implied that such actions would be taken for purposes of force protection and undermining North Korean logistics, and no mention is made of authorizing the capture of territory above the 38th parallel.[6] The Air Force took a similar position around the same time.[7] Other voices in the U.S. government were calling for broader war aims, however. Director of the Office of Northeast Asian Affairs John M. Allison called for the armed unification of Korea on July 1, and continued to advocate such a goal within government circles for the next several weeks.[8] Perhaps the first public call for crossing the 38th parallel made after the June 25 invasion was Senator Robert Taft's July 6 declaration that United Nations forces should cross the parallel and seize at least a portion of North Korea.[9] Within the U.S. government, debate began to stir between those advocating crossing the 38th parallel (principally at the Defense Department and eventually the State Department Policy Planning Staff), and those opposed to such a move (some at the State Department, such as George Kennan, and the CIA).[10] General Douglas MacArthur, who on July 8 was officially named commander of UN forces in Korea, by mid-July was considering the possible necessity of crossing the 38th parallel to occupy and unite all of Korea.[11]

Truman's thinking was running roughly parallel to MacArthur's in terms of timing and direction. On July 13, Truman declared in a press conference that the question of whether to cross the parallel was on the table, although that same day when South Korean President Syngman Rhee declared that his forces would cross the 38th parallel, a U.S. Army spokesman declared that the U.S. would "use force if necessary" to prevent South Korean forces from crossing the parallel.[12] Six days later, Truman perhaps edged a bit further towards supporting unification by force, declaring in a statement to Congress that his administration supported the UN resolutions, which called for providing "the people of Korea an opportunity to choose their own form of government free from coercion." In a separate speech to the public the same day, though, his language shaded more towards accepting the existence of North Korea, as he declared the U.S. goal to be to "help the Koreans *preserve* their independence."[13] In mid-July, Acheson was beginning to think about the longer-term problems of maintaining South Korean security after the status quo ante had been restored, but he stopped short of recommending reuniting Korea by force.[14] He, Charles Bohlen, and Paul Nitze concurred in a Cabinet meeting at this time that U.S. war aims, especially regarding the question of moving north of the 38th parallel, could not yet be publicly clarified.[15]

By August, the Truman administration began to move closer to calling for the unification of the Korean peninsula under a single, non-Communist regime. On August 1, Secretary of State Dean Acheson sent U.S. ambassador to the United Nations Warren Austin a draft statement which declared the importance of liberating all of Korea.[16] Nine days later, Austin gave a speech to the Security Council reflecting the main themes of Acheson's note. Austin declared, "Shall only a part of the country be assured this freedom? I think not. This question has already been decided by the General Assembly resolutions of 1947, 1948, and 1949 . . . Korea's prospects would be dark if any action of the United Nations were to condemn it to exist indefinitely as 'half slave and half free,' or even one-third slave and two-thirds free. . . . The General Assembly has decided that fair and free elections should be held throughout the whole of the Korean peninsula."[17] The speech was at this point just a political feeler. A week earlier, Truman declared in an NSC meeting that U.S. forces were not yet authorized to launch attacks above the 38th parallel.[18]

U.S. war aims became more ambitious by the end of August. U.S. officials met with British and French representatives, expressing the belief that "the unification and independence of Korea" would be desirable, so long as it avoided general war with the Soviet Union or China.[19] On September 1, the Truman administration agreed to authorize the use of force above the 38th parallel, as long as such actions could be carried out without Chinese or Soviet intervention.[20] In a public speech on that day, Truman declared that U.S. war aims included helping the Koreans become "free, independent, and united."[21] The following day, in off-the-record remarks to the press, Acheson noted that the UN was on record support-ing a united Korea.[22] This decision was codified further in NSC 81/1 is-sued on September 9 (Truman signed the document on September 11), which formally supported using force to cross the 38th parallel and unify North Korea, with the principal caveat that such actions should not incur Soviet or Chinese intervention.[23] This marked an official and important increase in American war aims from the beginning of the war.

Some scholars have viewed U.S. war aims in this period differently. They see NSC 81/1 as a compromise rather than a genuine expansion in war aims, because of the stated condition that unification of the Korean peninsula would be pursued under the assumption that neither China nor the Soviet Union will intervene. The real expansion of U.S. war aims, the argument goes, came in late September, after the success of the Inchon landing, as U.S. fears of Chinese and Soviet intervention eased.[24] However, the decision-makers themselves viewed NSC 81/1 as having marked the real change in U.S. war aims.[25] Chief of Staff Omar Bradley sent a memo to the Secretary of Defense on September 7 stating that the Joint Chiefs of Staff and MacArthur understood U.S. strategy now to be to destroy North Korean military strength above and below the 38th parallel, as a precursor to the establishment of a single non-Communist government for all of Korea.[26] Decades later, Bradley remarked in his memoirs, "NSC 81/1 reflected a drastic change in our concept of the Korean War. Our initial intervention had been launched as an effort to 'save' South Korea. Now we had broadened our war aims to include complete destruction of the North Korean Army and political unification of the country."[27] Tru-man himself made a similar point in his memoirs, as did Secretary of State Dean Acheson. JCS member General J. Lawton Collins also emphasized in his memoirs that the JCS views that MacArthur's mission required destroying the North Korean military and the ability to move north of the 38th parallel were reflected in NSC 81/1.[28]

Combat Outcomes and the Increase in American War Aims

The information proposition in chapter 2 predicts that combat successes encourage war aims to be raised, and combat defeats encourage war aims to be lowered. This proposition would suggest that the increase in Ameri-can war aims in NSC 81/1 followed improving UN fortunes on the battle-field. Combat successes would encourage the political leadership to im-prove its assessment of the relative balance of capabilities, thereby seeking greater gains from the other side as a condition for ending the war.

However, the historical record reveals the opposite pattern: the increase in war aims followed battlefield setbacks. At the outset of the conflict, American decision-makers believed that South Korea had at least a fighting chance to repel a North Korean attack. North Korea enjoyed modest but not overwhelming advantages over the defending forces, as Pyong-yang's forces outnumbered South Korean forces 85,000 to 69,000 (there were about 500 American troops in South Korea at the time of the invasion), and enjoyed some other advantages, such as possessing about 150 tanks to none for South Korea and more combat experience among its troops. South Korea also did not have planes, mines, large mortars, recoilless rifles, or extensive ammunition stocks.[29] However, many were confident that South Korea could defend itself. General William L. Roberts, commander of the American Korean Military Advisory Group (KMAG), told the U.S. ambassador to Japan before the invasion that the South Korean forces could "hold the Commies" in the event of war.[30] Elsewhere, he bragged that the South Korean military was "the best doggoned shooting army outside the United States."[31] Although the U.S. Ambassador to Korea had been requesting an increase in military aid, he did not indicate that South Korea faced military inferiority, and in fact claimed that the South Korean military enjoyed better training, small arms, morale, and leadership. U.S. intelligence agreed.[32] Not all were so bullish, though. A lower-ranking KMAG officer was more pessimistic, reporting before the war to the U.S. ambassador to South Korea that the South Korean military faced serious deficiencies vis-à-vis the North in terms of quality and quantity of military equipment, in areas such as artillery.[33]

The battlefield disasters in the first weeks of the war provided new information that belied peacetime confidence in South Korean fighting power, and caused UN decision-makers to lower their estimates of the likelihood and ease of eventual victory. North Korean forces achieved great combat successes initially and pushed South Korean and American troops steadily southward. American intelligence reports on July 6 and 7 reported North Korean forces as enjoying "extremely high" morale, effective logistics, and tactical competence, while making progress against U.S. forces throughout the Korean peninsula.[34] MacArthur's July 9 message to the Joint Chiefs of Staff begging for an additional four divisions is blunt: "The situation in Korea is critical. . . . to date our efforts against his armor and mechanized forces have been ineffective. His armored equipment is of the best and the service thereof, as reported by qualified veteran observers, as good as any seen at any time in the last year. They further state that the enemy's infantry is of thoroughly first class quality."[35] MacArthur repeated these concerns at a July 13 meeting with Generals Collins and Hoyt Vandenberg.[36] His July 19 communication to Truman was a bit more upbeat, extolling the successes of the Eighth Army at stemming the Communist advance, although stopping short of making definite predictions or discussing imminent victory.[37] At his August 6 meeting with Averell Harriman, MacArthur stressed the continuing need for more troops, even those just armed with small arms, or who were World War II veterans.[38]

MacArthur's reportage aside, the reality on the ground was undeniably grim. By mid-August, South Korean and United Nations forces had been driven into a small perimeter in the southeastern corner of South Korea, around the port city of Pusan (see figure 5.1). North Korean forces had performed better than the UN had anticipated, and it was not clear that the UN forces would be able to maintain even this perimeter. In mid-August, British military leaders estimated that UN forces had only an even chance of maintaining their toehold in Korea, and guessed that pushing back to the 38th parallel would take at least three to four months.[39] The Defense Department in Washington agreed. A Defense memo sent to Truman on August 30 claimed that a military stalemate was likely to develop around the Pusan Perimeter, and that such a stalemate "could last several months."[40] Matters did not improve in early September, when North Korea launched a highly threatening offensive against the Pusan Perimeter, inflicting the highest casualties yet experienced in the war.[41] The most dangerous breakthrough was parried only when a Marine unit, which had been assigned for the planned amphibious landing at Inchon, was redeployed to the front line. The attack was sufficiently threatening that the ground forces commander, General Walton Walker, at one point considered withdrawing from the Pusan Perimeter back to the last ditch "Davidson Line."[42] Walker did order on September 4 that UN military headquarters be moved from Taegu, located on the edge of the Pusan Perimeter and in danger of being overrun, to the town of Pusan itself, located deep inside the perimeter, away from the front lines.[43]

In short, North Korea enjoyed combat successes from late June to early September, and the UN was forced to lower its assessments of the relative balance of power. America's surprising decision to increase its demands of North Korea in the face of combat setbacks is in direct contrast to the predictions of the information proposition of chapter 2. The information proposition should instead predict that the UN ought to lower its aims, perhaps to requesting a ceasefire at the Pusan Perimeter line, or at the minimum to maintain its demand for the restoration of the status quo ante at the 38th parallel.

"I Wish I Had That Man's Optimism"

Perhaps the UN did suffer these short-term defeats in summer 1950, but was confident that soon the tide would turn, so the increase in war aims was consistent with the UN expectations for the likely eventual outcome, if not recent combat outcomes. One might argue that MacArthur's planned amphibious landing behind enemy lines, at the South Korean port of Inchon, created enough hope to inspire the increase in war aims. The September 15 landing was spearheaded by the First Marine Division, and did drastically turn the course of the UN war effort from teetering on the brink of suffering Communist conquest to a rout of North Korean forces. However, the landing occurred *after* the U.S. had officially raised its war aims by formally enacting NSC 81/1. The key question is, before the landing occurred, were American decision-makers highly confident that it would work, enough that they were willing to raise their war aims in the hope of future victory even in the face of recent battlefield failure?

Despite its ultimate success, many military and political decision-makers had grave doubts about the landing's chances. A number of objective factors indicated that the Inchon landing would be extremely risky. The tides at Inchon are the worst in East Asia and among the severest in the world, greatly limiting the amount of time a landing party would have to come ashore. There are no beaches; only piers, seawalls, and mudflats. The approach channel to Inchon is very difficult to navigate, and any invasion fleet would face mines and enemy gunfire in the channel. The channel is also narrow, meaning that if one vessel ran aground or was damaged by enemy fire, ships behind it would be unable to move. The tides also meant that there were only three possible days of landing in the fall of 1950 (and on each of these days the window for landing was narrow), worrisome because it would be easy for the North Koreans to also calculate when these windows of vulnerability were open, and to beef up defenses on those days and times. Securing two islands before the city, a necessity, would sacrifice the element of surprise. There was limited room for landing craft to come ashore to bring troops and supplies, and even once seized the port of Inchon had limited capacity for serving as a beachhead to supply a major UN offensive. The harbor itself enjoyed seawalls 12–14 feet high, requiring ladders to surmount, and while doing so assault forces would come under fire from well-concealed defenders. Further, the landing force would have to be assembled in Japan, an area crawling with Communist spies. Indeed, a North Korean spy was captured in Japan a week before the Inchon landing with the invasion plans in his possession. If North Korea had discovered the UN plans, then MacArthur's crucial advantage of surprise would have been lost. One naval officer declared that, "We drew up a list of every conceivable and natural handicap, and Inchon had 'em all." Another declared, "Make up a list of amphibious 'don'ts,' and you have an exact description of the Inchon operation."[44]

Interestingly, MacArthur chose Inchon as a landing site *because* so many objective factors seemed to line up against the success of an assault. In his thinking, these difficulties made it the last place the North Koreans would expect a landing. The total surprise of such an attack would guarantee its success. MacArthur noted that such an approach of attacking a spot that seemed invulnerable was exactly what allowed forces under the British General James Wolfe to capture Quebec in 1759, climbing lightly guarded cliffs to surprise the French defenders.[45] Indeed, there are other historical examples of military strategies working *because* they are risky, causing target areas to be left undermanned by unsuspecting defenders. Roman forces conquered New Carthage in the Second Punic War when Hannibal's brother Mago left a city wall unprotected because it adjoined a lagoon thought to be impassable. In December 1941, outnumbered Japanese forces entered and eventually conquered Singapore through mangrove swamps thought to be impassable, unmolested by British heavy artillery pointing seaward. German tanks conquered France in weeks in 1940 because French forces left the heavily forested Ardennes region undermanned. German forces made the same move in December 1944 during the Ardennes offensive when American forces repeated the French mistake and left only a small force to guard the region.[46]

Most high-level decision-makers were not nearly as confident as MacArthur. Naval officers, generals, admirals, marines, fliers, and even MacArthur's own staff expressed their opposition to the Inchon plan in August.[47] In late August, Joint Chiefs of Staff (JCS) members General J. Lawton Collins and Admiral Forrest Sherman traveled from Washington to Korea to express their concerns about the plan, and perhaps to talk MacArthur out of it. MacArthur gave a briefing to Collins, Sherman, and other high-level officers, and all recognized MacArthur's presentation to be highly persuasive, although MacArthur conceded (perhaps out of showmanship) that the odds for success were 5,000 to 1.[48] Doubts remained even after the briefing, however. Sherman, Admiral C. Turner Joy, Admiral Arthur Radford, and two Marine Corps generals agreed that Posung-Myon would be a better landing site, and tried to convince MacArthur to change the location of the landing. MacArthur refused.[49] Rear Admiral James Doyle would only allow that the operation was "not impossible."[50] Only after a follow-up one-on-one meeting with MacArthur was Sherman eventually won over, although his lingering concerns are reflected in his remark after this last meeting, "I wish I had that man's optimism."[51] After the August 1950 briefing, Collins and Sherman traveled back to Washington to brief Truman and the Joint Chiefs. The Chairman of the Joint Chiefs, General Omar Bradley, records that Collins was quite pessimistic, "expressing grave doubt that it would work." Bradley himself was unpersuaded, declaring even in hindsight, after the landing had succeeded terrifically, that the proposed Inchon landing "was the riskiest military proposal I had ever heard of. At that time we were not certain MacArthur could even hold the Pusan perimeter. It seemed imprudent that a large portion of his staff be preoccupied with a blue sky scheme like Inchon rather than the immediate and grave threat to Pusan."[52]

Regardless, the JCS officially approved the Inchon operation on August 28, although with some reservation, indicating their desire to continue to receive information about planning and preparation. Secretary of State Dean Acheson records in his memoirs that both the JCS and Truman approved the Inchon plan only "reluctantly." In Truman's handwritten notes of his briefing with Sherman and Collins after their return to Washington, he does not mention the Inchon operation, but does note that "MacArthur is acting up." Years later, after the landing had of course succeeded, Truman wrote in his memoirs that he had had confidence in the plan.[53] Secretary of Defense Louis Johnson supported the plan.[54] On September 7, the JCS sent a second message to MacArthur more firmly expressing their reservations.[55] MacArthur felt the doubts creeping into the second message, later recounting that the message "chilled me to the marrow of my bones. The message expressed doubt of success and implied the whole movement should be abandoned."[56]

In short, the claim that war aims were raised in anticipation of great success at Inchon is unsustainable. The decision to increase American war aims was already well on its way towards adoption in late August, before Truman and the JCS had been persuaded to cross their fingers and approve the landing. Further, there were widespread doubts about the feasibility of the operation at the highest political and military levels, doubts that were based on operational realities. At most, one might expect that confidence in the Inchon landing might have inspired the U.S. to demand the restoration of the status quo ante, but it is unreasonable to propose that the *increase* in American war aims was driven by confidence in the Inchon landing.

Although most American decision-makers did not have great faith in the Inchon plan, perhaps they were spurred to increase American war aims by faith that a wave of American reinforcements would soon tip the balance decisively against North Korea and allow a successful ground offensive. The decision to conquer North Korea, the argument would run, was driven by confidence that such reinforcements were coming. The problem with this claim is that such a wave of reinforcements was at least several months off as of August 1950, and during August–September the ability of UN forces to maintain the Pusan Perimeter for such a period was in doubt. The shortage of manpower in the near and medium term was evident to all. In August, one congressman suggested to Secretary of Defense Johnson that American forces in Korea be equipped with bullet-proof vests because of the limited pool of reinforcements.[57] As a matter of record, no American reinforcements arrived in Korea in 1950 after mid-September. By September, essentially *all* trained units in the American Army other than the 82nd Airborne Division had been sent to Korea.[58] These deployments to Korea strained American global conventional strength. Secretary of Defense George C. Marshall noted in an internal memo on September 26, 1950 that airlift capacity had been redeployed from Europe to Asia, threatening NATO's ability to renew an airlift should the Soviet Union again blockade West Berlin.[59] The National Guard had been called into military service, but would not be ready for combat until March 1951.[60] The risk, therefore, was that by refusing to seek a limited war outcome of either the status quo ante or perhaps an armistice around the Pusan Perimeter, the U.S. and UN were running the risk that the Inchon landing would fail, and U.S./UN forces would be completely swept off the Korean peninsula before reinforcements could arrive in 1951. At that point, the U.S. would either have to concede the annexation of South Korea, or continue the war without a foothold on the Korean peninsula, the latter requiring a risky and costly amphibious landing somewhere in South Korea, launched from Japan.

Additionally, some thought that time was not on the side of UN forces, that the UN could not afford to wait until 1951 for reinforcements. Mac-Arthur argued on August 8 that "a. Time works against us in the Korean situation. b. Early military victory is essential. c. Delay in achieving it increases the chance of direct military participation [by] Chinese Communist or Soviet forces, or both."[61] An August 24, 1950 Defense memo expressed the concern that should a military stalemate develop around the Pusan Perimeter, even if UN forces could eventually build up enough strength to launch a successful offensive, the combination of a Soviet peace offensive, pressure from non-aligned and other UN members, and growing public discontent over casualties might force the UN to accept a settlement rather than press for military victory.[62]

In short, the expansion of American war aims to seek the liquidation of the North Korean government can not be attributed to (increased) American confidence in the balance of capabilities. North Korean forces had fought surprisingly well, up through early September. UN forces were pinned down in the Pusan Perimeter. Substantial reinforcements would not arrive for several months, and the ability of U.S. forces to maintain the Pusan Perimeter for that long was in doubt. The Inchon operation did break open the war, but American war aims expanded or had started to expand before it had been launched and indeed before concerns about the operation had been fully allayed. Many in the military and foreign policy establishment had grave doubts about the likely success of the operation before it was launched.

Reassurance about Soviet/Chinese Intentions?

Another possibility is that Truman became emboldened to conquer North Korea because he became reassured in the first few weeks following the

June 25 invasion that doing so would not risk Soviet or Chinese involve-ment. That is, new information about possible third-party involvement encouraged the U.S. to establish high war aims. One historian argued that in the first few weeks of the war American decision-makers received a number of signals that the USSR and China would not become involved in the fighting (which at that point was all taking place south of the 38th parallel), and these signals helped the Americans consider "further bold steps."[63]

This interpretation has three problems, however. First, the American leadership was fairly confident that the Soviets and Chinese wished to stay out of the Korean conflict even from the very outset of the crisis, when Truman ruled out striking north of the 38th parallel. Several politi-cal and military leaders, including Acheson, Kennan, Admiral Roscoe Hil-lenkoetter, General James Burns, Admiral Sherman, and Ambassador-at-Large Philip Jessup all concluded in the four or five days after the June 25 invasion that the Soviets did not look at the Korean conflict as an opportunity for initiating a general war.[64] Second, even by early Septem-ber, the American leadership was not completely reassured of Soviet/Chinese noninvolvement, as NSC 81/1 allowed for military action north of the 38th parallel only under the condition of Soviet/Chinese noninvolve-ment. Third, the Soviets/Chinese started sending tougher, not weaker, sig-nals as time passed. The Chinese foreign minister made a speech linking North Korean and Chinese security on August 20.[65] More ominously, an article published in China on August 26 proclaimed that "North Korea's defense is our defense. North Korea's victory is our victory."[66]

The Credibility of Communist Commitments

The expansion of American war aims in August–September 1950 is best explained by a focus on American concerns about the credibility of Com-munist commitments to abide by a peace settlement. Recall that the com-mitment proposition in chapter 3 forecasts that a belligerent may pursue the absolute defeat of the opponent, even in the face of combat setbacks, if it fears the adversary might renege on a war-ending settlement. It is especially likely to do so if the cost of solving the commitment problem is acceptable in relation to the severity of the threat posed if the war-ending commitment were to be broken.

In the summer of 1950, this was the principle argument decision-makers made in favor of the expansion of war aims, that North Korea would likely defect on any war-ending agreement, and the only true path to stability on the Korean peninsula was to eliminate the Communist gov-ernment. The general context was a fear in the relative growth of Commu-nist economic and nuclear power. In particular, it was feared that closing the nuclear gap might encourage Communist conventional aggression.[67] American decision-makers were not confident that North Korea would accept a peace settlement restoring the 38th parallel as the Korean–Korean border. The 38th parallel itself was an arbitrary political boundary, not possessing any unique geographic qualities that made the defense of South Korea easier. Any peace restored on the basis of the 38th parallel was likely to be unstable, inviting future Communist attack at a time of their choosing. As General Collins summarized, the JCS felt that "if you stopped at the 38th Parallel, then the North Koreans, supported by the Chinese and the Russians, could once again attack when they were ready to."[68] This was also MacArthur's understanding of the logic behind destroying the North Korean army and unifying the peninsula, and the reasoning behind MacArthur's famous April 5, 1951 statement to Congress which serves as the epigraph for this chapter, that decisive victory should be sought to establish lasting peace: "War's very object is victory—not prolonged indecision. In war, indeed, there can be no substitute for victory."[69] Future Secretary of State John Foster Dulles, then a State Department consultant to Secretary of State Acheson, argued as early as July 14, 1950 that "it would be folly to go back to the division of Korea at the 38th parallel," as doing so would be giving "asylum to the aggressor" which would "allow the North Korean army to retire in good order with its armor and equipment and re-form behind the 38th Parallel from whence it could attack."[70] Allison made similar points in the weeks preceding NSC 81/1.[71] The Department of Defense concurred. A July 31 Defense memorandum stated that if UN forces stopped at the 38th parallel, "the former military instability would again obtain. The USSR could rearm a new striking force for a second attempt. Thus, a return to the *status quo ante bellum* would not promise security."[72]

Acheson was also thinking about the long-term postwar security of South Korea in the first half of July.[73] He understood that the South Korea question would not go away once this North Korean attack had been repelled, and that, "It seems too abstruse to ask the country to sacrifice men and money to retake Korea to support the UN, and then let it slip away by default. . . . I cannot see the end of it. In other words, as the Virginians say, we have bought a colt." He also worried (again, in July 1950) about whether an indefinite American commitment to South Korean security would be a feasible solution to the long-term problem of the North Korean threat: "In the longer run, if we should succeed in reoccupying the South, the question of garrisoning it and supporting it would arise. This would be a hard task for us to take on, and yet it seems hardly sensible to repel the attack and then abandon the country."[74] Indeed, as early as the first week of October 1950, the JCS began making plans for the redeployment of U.S. troops out of Korea.[75]

Even those opposing striking north of the 38th parallel recognized that Communist commitments to peace might not be credible. Kennan, who opposed crossing the 38th parallel, observed that the U.S. rejected the Indian peace proposal (accepted by China on July 10, 1950) of restoring the status quo ante in Korea in exchange for Chinese entry into the United Nations because the U.S. feared doing so would leave South Korea vulnerable to future North Korean attack.[76] He advocated a grander (and probably politically infeasible) approach, in which the U.S. and USSR would agree on several actions, including the restoration of the 38th parallel as the border as well as the American demilitarization of Japan. He speculated that such a multifaceted deal would be self-enforcing, for if one side defected on one part of the deal (for example, a new invasion of South Korea), the other could retaliate by reneging on another part of the deal (for example, the U.S. could remilitarize Japan). In an August 23 memo to Acheson, Kennan wrote that his proposed deal "does not imply any written agreement with the Russians. In fact, to try to negotiate anything of that sort would probably be disastrous. It implies only a general meeting of the minds, the sanction for which would lie in the readiness of either side to proceed with its part of the arrangement. Thus channels should be left open so that further Russian tactlessness in Korea could be followed by an immediate reintroduction of U.S. forces into Japan. If, on the other hand, we were to re-occupy Japan without provocation, the Russians could consider all bets off with respect to Korea."[77]

Why did Truman and other members of the American government doubt the credibility of a Communist commitment to end the war on terms that would respect South Korea's existence? American trust of the Soviet Union had been spiraling downwards since the end of World War II due to a series of events including perceived Soviet reneging on elections in Poland, the blockade of West Berlin, and the Soviet-supported 1949 coup in Czechoslovakia. As one historian pithily put it, "Truman believed the worst about the Soviets by 1950."[78] The invasion of South Korea solidified American mistrust of the Soviet Union and Communism more generally, entrenching the belief that Communism was fundamentally aggressive and opportunistic.[79] As Secretary of Defense Johnson stated in Senate testimony in summer 1950, "The very fact of this aggression . . . constitute[s] undeniable proof that the forces of international communism possess not only the willingness, but also the intention, of attacking and invading any free nation within their reach at any time that they think they can get away with it. The real significance of the North Korean aggression lies in this evidence that, even at the resultant risk of starting a third world war, communism is willing to resort to armed aggression, whenever it believes it can win."[80] Acheson agreed: "The international Communist movement has shown that it does not hesitate to use force to conquer a sovereign and independent nation, where it can hope to do so successfully."[81] The invasion of South Korea was seen by Truman and others as part of an enduring and global Communist strategy, similar to Hitler's strategy in the 1930s, to probe Western weakness at every opportunity.[82] Any regime so deeply embracing opportunistic aggression would be likely to break any commitment to peace, attacking at its first chance, perhaps when the balance of forces had swung fortuitously, even if temporarily, in its direction.

The American decision to establish high war aims in September 1950 demonstrates the importance of expected costs as a crucial intervening factor determining whether commitment or information dynamics will predominate. When the information and commitment proposition make diverging predictions, as when a belligerent fears the adversary will violate a war-ending commitment but it is losing battles, then a relatively low cost of continued fighting in relation to the danger of a broken war-ending commitment can encourage the belligerent to eschew negotiations and press on for absolute victory. In this case, American expectations of the costs of continued fighting, even in pursuit of the conquest of North Korea, were low *as long as* China and the Soviet Union stayed out of the conflict. The U.S. was confident the Chinese and Soviets would not intervene to save North Korea not because the Yalu river (which forms the China–North Korea border) forms an impenetrable military barrier, but rather because the American assumption in August–September 1950 was that China and the Soviet Union wanted to avoid direct clashes with the forces of the U.S. or its allies, and instead use catspaws like North Korea to test Western resolve.[83]

Some might question whether U.S. aims actually increased from late June to early September, or whether U.S. aims are better viewed as emerging over this time period, with initial statements about merely restoring the 38th parallel (in late June) reflecting immediate reactions, with later aims of overthrowing the North Korean government (by early September) evolving from more careful consideration. The evidence seems to be more consistent with the latter view. The initial decision not to strike north of the 38th parallel was secondary to the more important decision to send American and UN forces to South Korea's defense. Debate unfolded in a relatively conventional manner across the summer, as the principal actors from different branches of government weighed in with their views, in meetings, public speeches, and memoranda. Notably, many key advocates within the administration maintained relatively stable views about striking north of the 38th parallel throughout the summer. MacArthur, Allison, Dean Rusk, and other hawks advocated striking above the 38th parallel from as early as mid-July, while Kennan, Chip Bohlen, Paul Nitze, and other doves advocated against striking above the 38th parallel from back around the same period. Ultimately, the debate coalesced with NSC-81/1, a document that in some sense was a compromise between the two views, since it favored attacking north of the 38th parallel and overthrowing the North Korean government, although only under the conditions of Soviet/Chinese noninvolvement. It reflected not so much a change in the terms of debate since late June, but rather the outcome of the policymaking process, of the American desire to solve the Communist commitment problem, but only if the costs of such an accomplishment could be kept reasonable through the localization of the conflict.

SEPTEMBER 1950–SPRING 1951

A very important caveat to the desire to push beyond the 38th parallel was concern about the possibility of Chinese or Soviet intervention into the Korean War. American consideration of this risk is very much in line with the theoretical structure of this book, as a fearful belligerent will seek to solve a credible commitment problem only when doing so is seen as bearing acceptable costs. This condition cropped up repeatedly in discussions of crossing the parallel, was expressed explicitly in NSC-81/1, and was the main criticism of crossing the parallel from people like Kennan. Allison was perhaps the only individual who supported crossing the parallel even if it meant World War III, writing on July 24, "That this may mean war on a global scale is true—the American people should be told and told why and what it will mean to them. When all legal and moral right is on our side why should we hesitate?"[84]

Unfortunately, the presumption that Chinese intervention could be avoided proved to be incorrect, as Chinese military forces began entering North Korea in October, and within a few weeks the wave of American successes since Inchon had been completely reversed. Since the war, scholars have debated as to whether the Chinese might have intervened anyway if the 38th parallel had not been crossed or if UN forces had crossed the parallel but stayed away from the Sino–North Korean border.[85] Regardless, the combat situation in Korea took a disastrous turn in November 1950 with the commencement of the first major Chinese offensive. The true extent of Chinese involvement emerged slowly, although by the end of November it was evident that Chinese intervention was significant and threatening to UN forces. MacArthur reported on November 28 that "we face an entirely new war," and that the possibility of quickly ending the war and unifying Korea was now gone. He later said UN forces would have to be evacuated absent a ceasefire or some radical change in UN military strategy, such as air attacks on—and a blockade of—China, the use of nuclear weapons, and/or the procurement of Nationalist

Chinese reinforcements from Taiwan.[86] That same day, Truman met with the NSC. Talk had already begun about finding some way to end the war soon, perhaps with a ceasefire, as a means of avoiding further escalation and long-term commitment.[87] The military situation was bad enough in early December that Washington considered the possibility that UN forces might have to retreat to beachheads around Inchon, Wonsan, and Pusan, and even these beachheads might not be tenable in the face of Chinese and Russian bombing.[88] There was opposition at this point to offering a ceasefire, because it was seen that doing so after defeat would communicate weakness to the Communists.[89] This view persisted until April, when it was thought that no new peace proposals could be offered until after the spring offensive, for fear of showing weakness.[90] Note that this unwillingness to offer concessions in the face of battlefield setbacks is inconsistent with the chapter 2 information proposition that combat defeats make concessions more likely. It is arguably consistent with a broader information outlook, as American decision-makers feared that the very act of making a concession itself would send a credible signal of weakness.

Even past January 1951 when the military environment began to stabilize, Chinese intervention completely changed the UN decision calculus. The UN had at this point three choices: keep the fighting within Korea, escalate the fighting to include (possibly nuclear) attacks on China, or escalate the fighting to include (most likely nuclear) attacks against China and the Soviet Union. These three options are progressively more costly and risky, but also progressively offered more decisive solutions to the fear of an adversary reneging on a war-ending agreement. Specifically, if conquest, destruction, or foreign-imposed regime change could be visited on North Korea, China, and the USSR, then this of course would offer the most complete solution to the possible Communist non-compliance problem.

The third of these options was dismissed quickly, if for no other reason than American military weakness in relation to the Soviet Union at the time.[91] Indeed, the government exiled the occasional official who called for preventive war against the USSR, such as Secretary of the Navy Francis Matthews, who was made ambassador to Ireland, and General Orville Anderson, who "decided" to retire.[92] When members of Congress in a private August 14, 1950 meeting informed Acheson that public interest in preventive war was growing, Acheson quickly dismissed it as out of the question.[93] The second of these options, attacking China, attracted closer consideration. It, however, was ultimately dismissed. There was fear that attacking China directly might incur Soviet intervention, in part because of the Sino–Soviet alliance. Also, American allies, and Britain in particular, were deeply opposed to risking a general war, and American decision-makers did not want to risk alienating allies, especially because UN forces were highly dependent on the contributions of British forces.[94] As JCS Chairman Bradley memorably put it in 1951, war with China would involve America "in the wrong war, at the wrong place, at the wrong time, and with the wrong enemy."[95]

This left the first option, keeping the fighting contained within the Korean peninsula. Given its unwillingness to expand the war to the Chinese mainland or to the Soviet Union itself, the administration had at least informally abandoned thoughts of reunifying Korea by force and instead was committed to seeking a ceasefire soon after the front stabilized in January 1951.[96] Indeed, in a frank February 2 conversation between then Assistant Secretary of State Dean Rusk and representatives of nations contributing to the UN military coalition in Korea, Rusk indicated that military action beyond the 38th parallel was now essentially off the table, and that the current goal was to achieve a stable ceasefire.[97] On February 7, Acheson said in a confidential memo that unification of Korea by force was "no longer feasible," given Chinese intervention.[98] These views received more formal description in mid-February memos from the State Department.[99]

This reduction in war aims was formally expressed in NSC 48/5, approved by Truman on May 17. While this document retained as a theoretical goal the political (but not military) unification of Korea, it set out as minimum U.S. goals the restoration of the status quo ante—that is, recognition of the authority of the Republic of Korea over all territory south of the 38th parallel.[100] Retired General George Marshall (soon to be Secretary of Defense) expressed these views in a secret meeting with a Chinese contact in Kowloon on the same day, that the U.S. was now interested not in conquering North Korea but rather in restoring as much of the status quo ante as possible.[101] These changes in U.S. war aims were made public by Acheson during public hearings in early June 1951. He stated that the U.S. stood for the political unification of Korea, but that the U.S. would be willing to accept a ceasefire that recognized a political division at the 38th parallel.[102]

American goals were reduced despite enduring American fears that North Korea might violate any war-ending agreement. The credible commitment fears of 1950 certainly did not disappear by 1951. Why, then, did the U.S. reduce its war-termination demands? U.S. concerns about Communist commitment credibility had not diminished. As discussed in chapter 3, information dynamics are more likely to override commitment dynamics, as they did here, when the expected costs of continued war go up and the threat posed by post-agreement defection is less than catastrophic. In this case, the Chinese intervention substantially increased American assessments of pursuing increments of the good beyond the

38th parallel. Further, the defense of South Korea was important but not critical to American national security interests, in relation to goals like defending Western Europe or America itself. If South Korea were completely overrun after peace was struck, this would damage but not severely threaten American national security. This combination of escalating estimates of the costs of continued war, coupled with the lack of a direct and dire threat to national security made the solution of the credible commitment problem prohibitively expensive for the United States.

There was also the first recognition of an alternative approach to alleviating the Communist commitment problem, now that eliminating the Communist government in Pyongyang was off the table. The fear in 1950 had been that after war's end, eventual U.S. force withdrawal from South Korea would shift the balance of power towards the Communist side, creating an opportunity for a second try to conquer South Korea. South Korea might be overrun before U.S. forces could be reintroduced. American decision-makers began to recognize as early as summer 1951 that absent regime change, a long-term solution to South Korean security would be an enduring deployment of U.S. and UN forces there to deter a North Korean attack. In the summer 1951 MacArthur hearings, Republican Senator Alexander Wiley of Wisconsin posed this leading question to Acheson: "And isn't it true, too, that if we were to have some kind of a peace or some kind of armistice with the Reds in Korea, that it would necessitate, in view of our knowledge of Red tactics and the way that they have acted in the past, it would necessitate a large standing force of the United Nations to remain in Southern Korea in order to stabilize it, would it not?" After some hemming and hawing, Acheson conceded that troops would have to remain for "some time" after an armistice.[103]

On the Communist side, there was a significant shift in war-termination goals by around June 1951, away from a demand for unifying the Korean peninsula under Communist leadership and towards some sort of restoration of the status quo ante. Publicly, the Chinese in late June gave indications of their willingness to accept a ceasefire, and North Korea around the same time changed its propaganda demands from driving "the enemy into the sea" to driving "the enemy to the 38th parallel."[104] In internal Chinese deliberations, Peng Dehuai, commander of Chinese forces in Korea, advised Mao on July 1 that "it should be acceptable to both sides to restore the demarcation at the 38th parallel."[105] This reduction in demands probably reflected Chinese recognition of the failure of the Communist offensives of the first half of 1951, meaning that this change is also evidence in support of the information proposition of chapter 2.[106]

SPRING 1951–JULY 1953

The remainder of the war, from mid-1951 to mid-1953, can be character-ized straightforwardly. On the military front, a general stalemate held at a front line that ran across the middle of the peninsula, near the 38th parallel. On the diplomatic front, a slow dribble of concessions emanated from both sides, eventually culminating in an armistice in July 1953. In June 1951, the Communists agreed to delink a Korean ceasefire from other issues, including Taiwan, a withdrawal of foreign forces from Korea, and China's representation at the UN. China also proposed a ceasefire and a return to the 38th parallel as border.[107] Formal negotiations began on July 27. In August, the Communists conceded that the armistice line would be the line of contact between the two forces rather than the 38th parallel itself, the latter of which was viewed by the UN as militarily indefensible. In October, the Communists made small concessions regard-ing the location of the talks. Later that month, the Communists dropped their demand for inspection beyond the to-be-established demilitarized zone. In December and January, the Communists made two further con-cessions, on Soviet representation on the neutral supervisory organ (in exchange for UN concessions on airfields), and on replenishment—in other words, the right of outside actors to replenish the war equipment of foreign forces remaining in Korea after the war.[108]

The lingering unresolved issue in the negotiations was the postwar repa-triation of prisoners of war (POWs). China favored an all-for-all exchange of POWs, although the UN was opposed to forced repatriation of POWs who did want to return to North Korea or China. Since the UN held more Communist POWs than vice versa, it was feared that an all-for-all exchange would provide a substantial manpower boost to the Communist side, potentially shifting the balance of power.[109] Notable POW conces-sions weren't made until April 1953, when the Communists conceded that all POWs who did not desire repatriation be sent to a neutral state. The specifics were hammered out over the following several weeks.[110] The final armistice line is shown in figure 5.1.

In this last long phase, the UN had already abandoned an absolute war outcome as a solution to the commitment problem. However, commit-ment concerns persisted, namely that the Communists might reattack after a war-ending deal had been struck. In the summer 1951 MacArthur hearings, one of the central conclusions of a group of influential senators was that North Korea would reattack "on any flimsy pretext at any conve-nient opportunity."[111] Truman worried in December 1951 that "the Com-munists would build up after an armistice and then come right down the peninsula to Pusan."[112] The following month, he complained bitterly in his diary that Moscow had violated commitments made at Tehran, Yalta, and Potsdam, and that, "Dealing with Communist Governments is like an honest man trying to deal with a numbers racket ring or the head of a dope ring. The Communist Government, the heads of numbers and dope rackets have no sense of honor and no moral code."[113] Four months later, he again vented in his diary that any agreement signed with the Communists "would not be worth the paper it is written on. You've broken every agreement you made at Yalta and Potsdam. You have no morals [and] no honor."[114] These commitment concerns were not empty paranoia. A few weeks *after* the 1953 armistice was signed, Mao remarked to an official in the Soviet embassy in Beijing that "from a purely military point of view it would not be bad to continue to strike the Americans for approximately another year in order to occupy more favorable borders along the Changan River."[115]

These commitment concerns shaped the negotiating positions of the UN during this period in at least two ways. First, as noted, the UN was concerned that an open POW exchange might exacerbate the commitment problem by shifting the balance of power in favor of the Communists. Some in the U.S. government, such as Bradley and Secretary of Defense Robert Lovett, went farther. They feared that if the U.S. forcibly repatriated unwilling POWs now, this would make Communist soldiers less likely to defect in inevitable future conflicts with Communist states.[116] Conversely, refusal to repatriate POWs in the future would increase U.S. power in the future because, as Dulles argued in 1953, "soldiers in these armies who want freedom will be more apt to desert and surrender . . . the Red Armies [will] become less dependable and there is far less risk that the Communists will be tempted to use these armies for aggression."[117] Therefore, it is conceivable (although we do not have evidence from the Chinese side) that the POW issue created a commitment problem for the Chinese, in that if repatriation were made voluntary this would have the effect of increasing U.S. power after an armistice, thereby diminishing (from the Chinese perspective) the credibility of the American commitment to adhere to the terms of the agreement.

Second, commitment concerns affected UN demands for the location of the border at the end of war. The U.S. resisted the Chinese recommendation to return to the 38th parallel as the North–South border, because it was deemed to be militarily indefensible.[118] After the war, Acheson related that he felt no need to respect a "surveyor's line" that might interfere with military prerogatives.[119] Relatedly, U.S. budgetary constraints would have made it difficult to keep a sufficiently large American force deployed in South Korea over the long term to protect as indefensible a border as the 38th parallel.[120] In terms of the theoretical framework of this book, the U.S. was concerned that a Chinese commitment to a war-ending settlement at the 38th parallel would be less credible than a war-ending settlement at the existing battle line, viewed to be more defensible. Therefore, not all increments of the disputed good were equally valuable, as gaining territory up to the 38th parallel was not as valuable as gaining territory that would create a militarily defensible frontier. The U.S. was strongly motivated to hold out for a more defensible border that would make future Communist attacks less likely, and less motivated to gain territory beyond a defensible border.

Information had a sophisticated connection to American war-termination behavior during this period. The negotiators on both sides understood that negotiations were closely connected to battlefield events. The Chinese delegation was directly instructed that "the truce talks could not be separated for even one second from the situation on the battlefield," whereas one member of the UN negotiating team expressed the opinion that battlefield events "had much more results at the conference table than anything said at the conference."[121] However, what is striking is the inability of the accumulation of combat experience to make much impact on war-termination diplomacy. The 1951–53 period saw continuous combat between the two sides as tens of thousands of casualties accumulated. Yet this steady flow of information about relative capabilities was unaccompanied by significant changes in war-termination offers. In other words, combat during this period appeared to be an inefficient means of creating bargaining space. Strangely, battlefield defeats sometimes made the belligerents *less* likely to make concessions, as it was feared that offering concessions after defeat would send a signal of weakness. For example, when the Communists walked out of peace talks on August 23, 1951, it may have been in reaction to a string of real and perceived weaknesses, including the commencement of UN offensives on the central and eastern fronts, logistical failures in a Communist offensive, and reports in the Western media of Communist military failures.[122] Observers also speculated that a Communist POW proposal put forth in June 1952 was withdrawn after UN forces bombed Yalu power stations, as the Communists feared appearing weak.[123] One scholar noted that the Chinese leadership in 1952 allowed that "Chinese policy could change after that time [Spring 1953] because the military situation in Korea would by then certainly have turned in their favor."[124]

COMPETING EXPLANATIONS

Information and commitment factors played a large role in determining war-termination behavior during the Korean War. Were other forces also relevant? A number of arguments linking domestic politics to war-termination behavior in the Korean War have been made. One explanation for the expansion of U.S. war aims to cross the 38th parallel was that Truman saw it as a means to justify to domestic audiences a massive increase in the U.S. defense budget.[125] The evidence that Truman expanded the war in order to achieve an expanded defense budget is weak, however. The only direct piece of evidence is the notation from a November 24, 1950 NSC meeting that "if the Chinese threat evaporates, the President doubts that you could go ahead with a $45 billion program.[126] However, this comment does not speak to Truman's original motivation for expanding the war, and was made after Chinese intervention had occurred. Further, the argument implies that Truman *wanted* Chinese intervention in order to justify the expansion of the defense budget, a view at odds with all his other statements and actions which indicated a strong desire to keep China out of the war, including allowing for crossing the 38th parallel only if it would not bring China into the war. There is no evidence either that Truman crossed the 38th parallel in order to increase defense spending, or that he hoped China would enter the war.

There are other possible domestic politics connections. Some argue that domestic political pressures in 1950 pushed Truman to approve conquering North Korea.[127] Late July State Department reports indicated the popularity of crossing the 38th parallel and unifying Korea.[128] Truman did see the initial U.S. intervention on South Korea's behalf as a means of boosting his anti-Communist credentials and refuting accusations from Senator Joseph McCarthy and others that his administration was soft on Communism.[129] However, Truman was no slave to the shifting winds of public opinion, and was willing to take unpopular stances in the Korean War. Many congressional Republicans attacked the Truman administration and Secretary of State Acheson in particular for having directly caused the North Korean invasion of Korea. Republicans from both houses demanded Acheson's dismissal, some calling him a traitor.[130] More significantly, Truman knew he was making a deeply unpopular move when he fired MacArthur in 1951 for the latter's public deviation from White House policy.[131] Seven million people lined the streets of New York City to welcome MacArthur back when he returned from Asia. A joint session of Congress gave MacArthur a standing ovation. Many were outraged at MacArthur's dismissal and declared it to be a great victory for Communism. Some, including the *Chicago Tribune*, openly called for Truman's impeachment. The then-popular McCarthy declared of Truman to reporters, "The son of a bitch should be impeached."[132] For both men, Truman defied public outrage and stuck to his guns, keeping Acheson and dumping MacArthur.

More generally, the Korean War does not demonstrate well the hypothesis that escalating casualties in a democracy erode support for a war, and push the leadership to offer concessions to end the war.[133] The pattern of opinion on the war was fairly straightforward, with very high support for the war at the outset, including high public and media support for crossing the 38th parallel in September–October 1950,[134] followed by a steep drop in support after Chinese intervention, and from then on support that maintained roughly the same moderate level until the end of the war, even in the face of escalating casualties.[135] Public support across the breadth of the Korean War is described in figure 5.2. John Mueller, the original proponent of the thesis that rising casualties erode public support for war, noted the unexpected lack of a falloff in public support for the war as casualties mounted: *"More striking than the drop in support caused by the Chinese entry is the near-absence of further decline for the remaining 2 years of war.* From early 1951 until the end of the war in the summer of 1953, basic support for the war … remained largely constant—this despite the continually mounting casualties and despite a number of important events."[136]

Neither changes in public opinion nor the occurrence of the 1952 presidential election seems to have had much real effect on American decisions to make war-termination concessions. One might expect that by 1952, escalating domestic concerns about casualties—there were more than 22,000 American dead by the end of 1951[137]—coupled with a Chinese willingness to restore essentially the status quo ante and an impending presidential election (in which admittedly Truman was not a candidate) might have been enough to push Truman to make concessions on POWs and on other issues (notably, even under the Chinese POWs offer all UN POWs would be returned). Perhaps Truman might have launched an October surprise, making a couple of key concessions in autumn 1952 to achieve peace by the November election and aid Adlai Stevenson's Democratic presidential campaign and the campaigns of congressional Democratic candidates. However, Truman did not make concessions, and perhaps not surprisingly the Democrats suffered losses in the 1952 elections, losing control of the White House and both houses of Congress.[138] This outcome is at variance with the view that the escalation of casualties steadily erodes public support for a war and forces an elected leader to make greater concessions in order to stop the fighting.

The end of the war is also not easily explained by U.S. domestic politics—that is, the election was not a vehicle for a new party taking control of the White House in January 1953 to make swift concessions to end an unpopular and bloody war. As a candidate, Dwight Eisenhower's campaign emphasized the need to end the war in Korea, but he proposed no

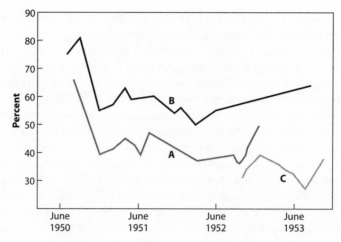

Figure 5.2 American Public Support for the Korean War

A: "Do you think the United States made a mistake in going into the war in Korea, or not?" (AIPO)

B: "Do you think the United States was right or wrong in sending American troops to stop the Communist invasion of South Korea?" (NORC)

C: "As things stand now, do you feel that the war in Korea has been (was) worth fighting, or not?" (NORC)

Source: Mueller (1985)

specific exit plan, and certainly made no promises to make concessions at the negotiating table to bring American troops home.[139] After taking office, President Eisenhower became more inclined to escalate the war as a means to end it.[140] American public opinion was sufficiently mixed to offer Eisenhower freedom of action. Although most supported an end to the war, opinion was mixed over how to accomplish that goal. One December 1952 survey revealed that 39 percent supported escalating the war to attack China directly, 27 percent favored staying the course, and 23 percent favored an American withdrawal.[141] However, Eisenhower opposed both a major new conventional offensive and the use of atomic weapons, the former because it wouldn't work and the latter because of its international political costs. He did, however, favor the use of atomic threats, although again Eisenhower probably did not seriously consider or make plans for the use of atomic weapons by the time the war ended.[142] American nuclear threats probably did not play a major role in ending the Korean War, as the Chinese leadership did not view the American threat to use nuclear weapons, especially the strategic use of such weapons, as credible.[143] Ultimately, Eisenhower was attacked by some from within his own party for a war outcome that essentially restored the status quo ante.[144]

Scholars differ over the role of domestic politics in Communist war-termination behavior. Some have argued that the key event permitting the end of the war was probably the death of Joseph Stalin on March 5, 1953. Stalin had supported continuing the war and taking a hard line at the negotiating table at least in part because the Soviet Union directly benefited from the continuation of the war. The war tied down American forces, drained the American economy, battered the Truman administration domestically, and provided unique opportunities for the USSR to collect intelligence on American military capabilities. Soon after Stalin's death, most importantly in a March 19 resolution passed by the Council of Ministers, Stalin's successors informed North Korea and China that the time had come to end the war. Kim Il-Sung and Mao accepted the new approach.[145] The Communists made a number of moves starting in late March designed to hasten the war's end. On March 28, they agreed to a UN proposal to exchange sick and wounded prisoners even while the war endured. The Chinese proposed renewing negotiations at Panmunjom for an armistice, and offered to handle the repatriation of prisoners through a neutral country. The UN exhibited persistent intransigence over the next few weeks, but eventually an armistice was signed on July 27.[146]

Notably, some have argued that the available evidence does not prove that Stalin's death was necessary to end the Korean War. One scholar noted that Stalin himself decided to make concessions to end the war before his crippling stroke of March 1, 1953, meaning that even if he had avoided the stroke and lived, the war might have ended in 1953.[147] Others propose that Communist concessions in the spring and summer of 1953 were part of a long-term negotiating strategy rather than an abrupt shift.[148]

Domestic politics aside, another factor possibly affecting American war-termination behavior in the Korean War was concern for maintaining and bolstering America's international reputation. American decision-makers recognized the relatively low impact Korea had on the global material balance of power. Indeed, this was the main reason why the American Secretary of the Navy explicitly omitted South Korea from the American defense perimeter in a public speech he made in January 1950. However, after the invasion Truman immediately framed the attack in reputation terms, equating the invasion of South Korea with the fascist probes of the 1930s.[149] A strong American response to defend South Korea would have positive reputation effects worldwide. Truman told one of his aides that Korea is the "Greece of the Far East. If we are tough enough now, if we stand up to them like we did in Greece three years ago, they won't take any steps."[150] Acheson made a similar point in a July 14 Cabinet meeting.[151]

Over the course of that summer, those arguing for expanding war aims sometimes also argued that conquering North Korea would offer broader reputation benefits. MacArthur considered the possibility of unifying Korea in a July 13 conference where he stated that, "We win here or lose everywhere; if we win here, we improve the chances of winning everywhere."[152] Allison told an agreeable Rusk on July 1 that unifying the peninsula would have a "*salutary effect* upon other areas of the world."[153] The July 31, 1950 Defense memo, for example, postulated that the benefits of Korean unification would be "incalculable. The Japanese would see demonstrated a check on Soviet expansion. Elements in the Chinese Communist regime, and particularly important segments of the Chinese population, might be inclined to question their exclusive dependence on the Kremlin. Skillfully manipulated, the Chinese Communists might prefer different arrangements and a new orientation. Throughout Asia, those who foresee only inevitable Soviet conquest would take hope."[154] Other world leaders agreed. Ernest Bevin of Britain wrote to Clement Atlee that the Korea operation would give the West the chance to make the Soviets "realise that they are up against it."[155]

However, not all agreed with the reputation arguments. Writing several years after the war, Acheson was skeptical of the sweeping claims in the July 31 Defense memo, although just after the Inchon operation he did make a reputation-based argument, telling the cabinet that Korea could serve as proof of "what Western Democracy can do to help the underprivileged countries of the world."[156] Under the Eisenhower administration, Secretary of State Dulles' motivation to continue fighting in order to build American reputation met clear disagreement from the President.[157]

COMMITMENT, INFORMATION, AND THE KOREAN WAR

The Korean War well illustrates the interplay between commitment and information dynamics. In the first phase of the war, credible commitment dynamics and specifically American concerns about North Korea possibly reattacking the South following a peace agreement pushed the U.S. to ignore battlefield setbacks and establish the high war aim of seeking the conquest of North Korea. At this stage, the costs of overthrowing the Pyongyang regime—a conventional war with the North Korean army—were acceptable in relation to the benefits of solving the commitment problem. However, after Chinese intervention in autumn 1950, the rising expected costs of continuing to pursue the capture of North Korea, namely the risk of a wider and perhaps nuclear war with China and the Soviet Union, made such a pursuit prohibitively expensive, especially because the stakes were less than the absolute highest for the U.S. In the last long phase of the war, the steady accumulation of information from battlefield activity was generally insufficient to create bargaining space between the two sides. The end of the war may have been delayed by commitment concerns, as the U.S. opposed the restoration of the indefensible 38th parallel, and the deadlock over the exchange of POWs was strengthened by concern that a POW exchange and the forcible repatriation of Communist POWs might shift the balance of power and make any war-ending deal less stable. Worries about unstable war-ending settlements were not unique to the Korean War, though, as shown in the next chapter, which explores the role of such concerns when stakes are even higher.

CHAPTER SIX

The Allies, 1940–42

> If this long island story of ours is to end at last, let it end only when each one of us lies choking in his own blood upon the ground.
> —Winston Churchill, May 28, 1940

> We are fighting this war because we did not have an unconditional surrender at the end of the last one.
> —U.S. Assistant Secretary of State Breckenridge Long, May 1942

NAZI GERMANY POSED the most serious threat of world conquest since ancient Rome. It conquered more territory in shorter order than any country in world history, sweeping aside any lingering thoughts that entrenchments would slow down the advance of armies in the Second World War as they did in the First. What made this threat even more frightening was Germany's alliance with Japan, who in the blink of an eye asserted control of half the Pacific Ocean.

How did the Allied powers, especially Britain in 1940, the United States in 1942, and the Soviet Union in 1941, react to the initial parade of Axis victories? Did they update their senses of the balance of power and seek terms with the attackers, hoping at least to save their own countries from conquest? Or did they instead ignore the bad news, choosing to fight on rather than strike a deal feared to be ultimately doomed to Axis treachery?

Like nearly all of the case studies in this book, the early years of World War II indicate that a complete understanding of war-termination behavior must account for both information and commitment dynamics. Both Britain in May 1940 and the U.S. in the first half of 1942 faced very dire and worsening short-term military environments—Britain because of the fall of France and the threat of an imminent German invasion, and the U.S. because of a six-month string of combat setbacks. A war-termination approach emphasizing information only would forecast that the U.S. and Britain should have used these battlefield outcomes to update their understandings of the balance of power in a pessimistic direction. The U.S. and Britain then should have made concessions to the Axis in the hopes of avoiding absolute defeat. Neither the U.S. nor Britain did so. Britain rejected any move to negotiations, pushing forward in pursuit of eventual victory. The United States went further, not only putting aside any talk of negotiations, but even establishing in the months after Pearl Harbor the aim of pursuing the unconditional surrender of the Axis powers.

The U.S. and Britain rejected negotiations and pushed on for victory for three reasons, all of which fall within the theoretical model laid out in chapters 2 and 3. First and most importantly, both countries thought that the Axis powers would not abide by the terms of any limited peace deal. They feared that any deal reached leaving the Axis powers intact would provide only passing peace before breaking into a new war, just as the ephemeral stability of Versailles was shattered by World War II. Only absolute victory and the attendant opportunity to remake the political, economic, and social landscapes of the Axis nations would provide lasting peace. Second, both countries understood the grave dangers posed by the Axis, and the severe costs that would be posed if they broke their commitments to a peace settlement. The Axis powers were seen as terrible regimes with real and enduring designs on world conquest, and the awful costs of World War I made "never again" a genuine imperative. By contrast, a Communist North Korea left standing in 1950 would pose a serious but not mortal threat to American security, as North Korea could reattack South Korea but not the United States itself. A Nazi Germany or Imperial Japan left standing in the early 1940s would pose an unacceptably high danger to the American and British homelands.

Third, even when times were darkest, both Britain and the U.S. retained hopes for eventual victory, somehow. As described in chapter 2, even when the credibility of the adversary's commitment is very low, a fearful belligerent will only fight on if it thinks there is some chance of eventual victory. If the belligerent sees essentially no chance of winning the war, it will likely accept an unstable peace rather than absorb the costs of fighting on in pursuit of the impossible goal of victory. As France and the Low Countries fell, Britain faced severe military disadvantages and many feared that a German invasion was imminent. However, the British government realized that the strength of the Royal Navy gave it hope to fend off the short-term German invasion threat, especially if the Royal Air Force could win the Battle of Britain in summer 1940. In the longer term, there was hope that eventual American intervention in the war might turn the tide toward victory. That is, the severe commitment problem pushed Britain to reject negotiations, and the faint hope of eventual victory enabled it to imagine someday turning the tide. Conversely, one can imagine a set of conditions (such as Roosevelt losing to an isolationist in the November 1940 presidential campaign, the Luftwaffe defeating the Royal

Air Force [RAF] in the Battle of Britain, and a successful German landing on the beaches of southern England) that would be so discouraging that the British government might be willing to accept peace terms with Hitler rather than continue to fight on. For the United States, its long-term hope was that eventually the full mobilization of its economy would enable it to defeat Nazi Germany and Imperial Japan. If conditions were much darker in 1942, perhaps with the Japanese conquests of Midway, Hawaii, and Australia, the destruction of the American fleet in the Pacific, carrier-launched air raids on West Coast cities, the fall of the Soviet Union, and the neutralization of Britain, perhaps this information environment would have been so awful that it might have encouraged America to settle on limited terms rather than fight on.

It appears that the Soviet Union in October 1941 may have come closer than Britain or the U.S. to the point of no hope, as there is some evidence Stalin considered trying to reach an agreement with Hitler. Stalin had great reason to doubt Hitler would abide by any peace deal, because of Hitler's unhidden, deep hatred of Bolshevism and desire to conquer the USSR, because of Hitler's history of breaking agreements such as the 1939 Molotov–Ribbentrop Pact, and because of Stalin's realist doubt of the significance of any international agreement. And yet it appears that in the darkest moment of the war, in October 1941 when the Wehrmacht appeared to be rolling unstoppably to Moscow, Stalin briefly considered offering terms to Hitler in an attempt to salvage some part of Soviet sovereignty, even if temporarily. Notably, Soviet fortunes in 1941 were much more frightening than were British fortunes in 1940 or American fortunes in 1942, perhaps encouraging Stalin to fear that the German army would overrun the Soviet Union before the Red Army could turn the tide.

These three cases demonstrate the joint importance of both information and commitment. A focus on information alone gets the U.S. and Britain cases wrong. If belligerents' war-termination decisions are driven purely by changes in the information environment as determined by combat outcomes, both should have considered negotiations in their darkest moments. However, credible commitment fears will push a discouraged belligerent to eschew negotiations and fight on. A focus on commitment alone (perhaps) gets the Soviet case wrong. If belligerents' war-termination decisions are driven only by credible commitment fears, then Stalin should never have even considered negotiating with Hitler. If things look sufficiently bleak, even the most fearful belligerent may be willing to accept even an unstable peace rather than fight on with no hope of turning the tide. A complete account of war termination must consider both information and commitment dynamics.

BRITAIN, MAY 1940

The last vestiges of Versailles were shattered when Britain and France declared war on Germany on September 3, 1939, in reaction to Germany's September 1 invasion of Poland. Although Britain and France were formally committed to the defense of Poland, they sent no troops to Poland, nor did they open a second front elsewhere. After Poland fell in late September, there were some superficial exchanges between Britain and Germany about peace talks, although no serious moves were made. Germany sent a delegate to London on September 28, essentially calling for armistice on the basis of British acceptance of the (new) territorial status quo. Hitler publicly laid out the possibility of peace with the Western powers in a speech to the Reichstag on October 9.[1] British Prime Minister Neville Chamberlain rejected Germany's peace "offer," viewing as unacceptable a settlement that would allow Germany to keep its new territorial gains.[2] This rejection should be considered at most very limited evidence against the information proposition of chapter 2 despite the German conquest of Poland. Although Germany quickly and easily defeated Poland's armed forces, Anglo-French forces were as yet untested, probably discouraging Britain from downgrading its estimate of its own balance of capabilities with Germany. Certainly, up until the actual invasion of France in May 1940, the British and French political and military leaderships were extremely confident of the Allied ability to parry a German invasion of the Low Countries and France.[3] More broadly, Chamberlain became increasingly sure through the fall and winter that Hitler could not and would not attack in the West. On September 17, after Poland fell, he doubted that Germany would attack in the West, and instead might next pounce on Romania.[4] He even ventured privately in October and December 1939 that the war might be over by spring, sputtering to a halt because of German war fatigue.[5]

Part of the motivation for Chamberlain's 1939 rejection of Hitler's overture was Chamberlain's concern with the credibility of Hitler's commitment not to reattack after peace would have been struck. The faith of Chamberlain and many other Britons in Hitler was shattered after the March 1939 German invasion of Czechoslovakia. This attack violated the 1938 Munich agreement that gave Germany the Sudetenland in exchange for a promise of peace. The March 1939 action was critical in affecting Chamberlain's perceptions of Hitler's trustworthiness because this directly contravened a bilateral agreement between himself and Hitler.[6] Indeed, at some points Chamberlain viewed regime change in Germany as the only means to provide lasting peace. He wrote to his wife on September 10, 1939 that, "Of course the difficulty is with Hitler himself.

Until he disappears and his system collapses there can be no peace."[7] And, a month later: "The difficulty is that you cant [sic] believe anything Hitler says. . . . the only chance of peace is the disappearance of Hitler."[8] Others, such as permanent under-secretary of the Foreign Office Sir Alexander Cadogan agreed that Hitler must go.[9] On this point, Chamberlain was right, Hitler's peace offers were only a ruse. As early as September 1939, Hitler spoke to his staff about the importance of attacking France in the near future.[10] Around this time he declared that he wanted a German attack "at the earliest possible moment and in the greatest possible strength" through the Low Countries and France "to serve as a base for the successful prosecution of the air and sea war against England."[11]

In the several months following the fall of Poland at the end of September, very little combat occurred. This period was famously known as the Bore War, Phony War, or *Sitzkrieg* (Sitting War). In April 1940, this phase ended when Germany invaded Denmark and Norway. On May 10, Germany launched its invasion in the West against the Low Countries and France. The German offensive went fantastically well, due largely to German strategic exploitation of French intelligence failure.[12] The swift fall of France was a great shock. Lord Halifax wrote in his diary on May 25 that the one constant in the previous two years of defense planning was the solidity of the French Army, and now that had crumbled.[13] By May 23, planning for maritime evacuation of British and other Allied forces from the Belgian coastal town of Dunkirk was underway (the evacuation decision was made on May 25), and the British chiefs of staff formally declared that France was essentially lost.

The Nadir of World War II

The last week of May 1940 was a critical turning point in the war, the real "hinge of fate" according to one historian.[14] It was the lowest point of Allied military fortunes of the war and the closest Hitler came to victory over Britain. If war-termination decisions were exclusively or primarily about information revealed by combat outcomes, then Britain should have offered concessions to Germany to end the war. In fall 1939, Anglo-French forces had not yet been tested against German forces, so despite Germany's walkover against Poland there were not yet sufficient grounds for real pessimism (note Chamberlain's vain hopes in fall 1939 of German collapse). By late May 1940, however, the official British military assessment was quite gloomy, notwithstanding one intelligence report declaring that Germany was being stretched on the home front because of mounting casualties and rising economic shortages.[15] The fall of France was a great shock to Britain. What Wilhelmine Germany failed to do in four years in World War I, Nazi Germany had accomplished in essentially three weeks.

Chamberlain had bluntly stated in December 1939 that if France dropped out of the war, Britain would not be able to carry on alone.[16] On May 19, with the fate of France already clear, Chief of the Imperial General Staff General Sir Edmund Ironside soberly told Secretary of State for War Anthony Eden, "This is the end of the British Empire." Eden grimly agreed with this assessment.[17] As early as May 25, the War Office was considering evacuation of Channel and East Coast towns in England in preparation for a German invasion.[18] On May 26, the Chiefs of Staff delivered their official assessment of Britain's chances in the event that France fell, an eventuality that appeared more likely by the day. The report stressed that the Royal Navy and RAF would be sufficient to block an amphibious invasion of Britain. With decisive damage to the RAF, however, the Navy could not block an invasion indefinitely. The report grimly conceded that British ground forces would be inadequate to stop a German invasion.[19] In a battle for aerial supremacy, Germany would enjoy certain advantages, namely a four-to-one numerical superiority of aircraft (although Winston Churchill, who had succeeded Chamberlain as prime minister earlier that month, claimed the advantage was more like five to two, and the advantage was shrinking given that German planes were getting shot down three times faster than British planes), as well as the asymmetry that the British aircraft industry was vulnerable to aerial bombardment but the German aircraft industry was not.[20] Concerns also existed that bombing against British civilian targets would erode popular will. Lastly, the report declared that without the full economic and financial support of the United States, continuing the war would be hopeless.[21] The report's conclusion rested on a thin reed of hope: "To sum up, our conclusion is that *prima facie* Germany has most of the cards; but the real test is whether the morale of our fighting personnel and civil population will counterbalance the numerical and material advantages which Germany enjoys. We believe it will."[22] Interestingly, this hope that morale and fighting spirit would defeat material superiority was the basis of Japan's ultimately incorrect theory as to how it might beat the materially preponderant U.S. in the Pacific.[23] Churchill on May 28 told his Cabinet Ministers that an invasion was coming, and British intelligence feared that Germany might suspend its military operations in France to launch an immediate invasion of Britain.[24]

Like Churchill, Ironside was deeply concerned about the German invasion threat. He wrote in his diary on May 28, "Up to London to a meeting of the [Home] Defense Executive at the Horse Guards. Not too bad. The state of the armament is catastrophic. I hope that it will get better in a week or two. Hope we get the week or two. . . . Local Defence Volunteers going well. I must get them armed with Molotoff [sic] cocktails in all the villages of England. The only way to deal with a tank."[25] It is difficult to decide what is more ominous: that Ironside feared a German invasion as early as the coming weeks, that the home defense of the most established industrial power in the world would depend on Molotov cocktails (indeed, Ironside also bemoaned the "lack of any kind of tank" available for British home defense against German tanks[26]), or that Ironside felt the need to arm *all* the villages of England, not just those near likely German landing sites on the English Channel coast.

The bleak prospects in late May for the evacuation of the British Army from the collapsing Belgian and French fronts were also grave reasons for concern. During these last days of May, the now famous Dunkirk operation was not yet a success, and estimates projected the evacuation of only 30,000 to 50,000 troops (eventually more than 300,000 Allied troops were evacuated), leaving their equipment behind. In his late afternoon meeting with his entire cabinet on May 28, Churchill estimated that only 50,000 would be evacuated from Dunkirk.[27] Ironside wrote on May 29 that there seemed, "Very little chance of the real B.E.F. coming off. They have now sunk three ships in Dunkirk harbour and so there is very little more chance of getting any units off."[28] Few suffered delusions of imminent victory. One member of Churchill's government, Harold Nicolson, made preparations to commit suicide in the event of a German landing, so as to avoid torture.[29]

British Assessments and Negotiations with Hitler

Facing such danger, did Britain try to stop the war? The logic of the information proposition of chapter 2, that poor military fortunes should inspire concessions to avoid absolute defeat, was clearly expressed in the thinking of Foreign Secretary Lord Halifax, the most pro-negotiations member of the British cabinet. He argued that British war aims should no longer be the decisive defeat of Germany, but rather the maintenance of British independence. He proposed using Benito Mussolini of then-neutral Italy as a mediator.[30] In line with the information proposition, he proposed that Britain would be more likely to get better terms before its military situation really fell off the cliff. He remarked on May 28, "we must not ignore the fact that we might get better terms before France went out of the war and our aircraft factories were bombed, than we might get in three months' time."[31]

Although Germany at this point presented no specific war-termination terms to Britain, there were German diplomatic feelers. On May 18, a Vatican official approached the British ambassador to Rome about possible peace talks.[32] On May 20, Hitler privately declared that Britain could have peace at any time in exchange for restitution of the colonies.[33]

Around the same time, one of Hitler's generals noted privately that Hitler was trying to make contact with Britain to reach a settlement.[34] A week later, Germany sent an oblique inquiry about negotiations to Britain through the Japanese ambassador to Britain.[35] Germany's efforts aside, there were those around Churchill who directly suggested negotiation and concession to end the war. Beyond Halifax there was also the Australian High Commissioner in London and U.S. Ambassador Joseph Kennedy.[36]

These flecks of encouragement to negotiate notwithstanding, at the end of May the British leadership decided not to make concessions or even enter into negotiations. The decision not to negotiate was the conclusion of a critical set of War Cabinet meetings taking place from May 26–28, at the end of which Churchill rallied sufficient opposition to negotiations both within and outside the cabinet. The exclamation point came on the evening of May 28 when Churchill declared to a group of high government officials, "If this long island story of ours is to end at last, let it end only when each one of us lies choking in his own blood upon the ground."[37] Two days later, Churchill refused to even consider a written proposal, authored by the Australian High Commissioner in London, for an international conference with the aim of reaching a peace settlement.[38] Churchill made this position public on June 4, in perhaps his most famous speech of the war when he proclaimed, "We shall go on to the end. We shall fight in France, we shall fight on the seas and oceans . . . we shall defend our island, whatever the cost may be. We shall fight on the beaches, we shall fight on the landing grounds, we shall fight in the fields and in the streets, we shall fight in the hills; we shall never surrender."[39] This decision at the end of May not to negotiate marked a key turning point in British war strategy, as no further official moves to negotiate were made for the rest of the war.[40]

The perspective that war termination is driven completely or even principally by information fails to explain the British decision not to negotiate in late May 1940. This should be an easy case for an information-alone view: the poor performance of the British army and rapid fall of France caused Britain to severely downgrade its estimate of the balance of power, and should have caused Britain to make concessions to Germany. But Britain did not.

Churchill the Appeaser?

The popular image of Churchill is an indomitable bulldog, constitutionally incapable of even considering making concessions to Hitler. Perhaps surprisingly, the historical record indicates a small handful of instances in which Churchill seemed to hint at the possibility of negotiations and concessions. In the May 27 War Cabinet meeting, he said that, "If Herr

Hitler was prepared to make peace on the terms of the restoration of the German colonies and the overlordship of Central Europe, that was one thing. But it was quite unlikely that he would make any such offer." The Foreign Secretary presented the hypothetical of France collapsing and Germany offering terms. Churchill replied that "he would not join France in asking for terms; but if he were told what the terms offered were, he would be prepared to consider them."[41] Churchill also wrote in a letter to the Dominions on May 27 that the decision to continue fighting "is of course without prejudice to consideration of any proposals that might hereafter be put forward for a cessation of hostilities and subject to developments in the military situation."[42] Sometimes Churchill held out for the possibility of negotiating with Hitler after Britain had strengthened its bargaining position by achieving some military successes. Churchill argued in an internal meeting that "if we could get out of this jam by giving up Malta and Gibraltar and some African colonies [I] would jump at it. But the only safe way was to convince Hitler he couldn't beat us."[43] And on May 28, in fending off one of Halifax's last attempts to accept the French proposal to introduce Mussolini as a mediator in peace negotiations, Churchill replied that "the French were trying to get us on to the slippery slope. The position would be entirely different when Germany had made an unsuccessful attempt to invade [Britain]."[44]

It is difficult to know exactly what to make of these comments made in internal debates given Churchill's many other private and public statements about the unacceptability of negotiations, and of course his actions. One possibility is that Churchill's stated position varied depending on to whom he was speaking. In the May 26–28 War Cabinet meetings where Churchill made his most pro-negotiations comments, he may have been trying to appear as moderate as possible to avoid alienating on-the-fence Cabinet members like Chamberlain, and avoid pushing them to the more openly pro-negotiation stance of Halifax. To other audiences, like the British public, he of course showed no sign of openness to negotiation, as the mere act of going to the table would mean that "all the forces of resolution which were now at our disposal would have vanished," even if Hitler's inevitably unacceptable terms were to be rejected.[45] He needed to stiffen the spine of his French allies, so when speaking with French Prime Minister Paul Reynaud in May 26 he declared that even if France fell, "we were not prepared to give in. We should rather go down fighting than be enslaved to Germany."[46] A few days later, as he was preparing to withdraw British military assets from France to fight another day, he told the French leadership, "Better far that the last of the English should fall fighting and *finis* to be written to our history than to linger on as vassals and slaves."[47]

In these crucial debates, Churchill sometimes made a more sophisticated point about the need for Britain to fight and lose rather than surrender. He proposed that Britain must fight, even if to defeat, in order to maintain its international reputation. He declared on May 27 that, "At the moment our prestige in Europe was very low. The only way we could get it back was by showing the world that Germany had not beaten us. If, after two or three months, we could show that we were still unbeaten, our prestige would return. Even if we were beaten, we should be no worse off than we should be if we were now to abandon the struggle."[48] He also argued that "nations which went down fighting rise again, but those which surrendered tamely were finished."[49] Another cabinet member agreed, fretting of the reputation consequences if Britain offered to give up territory in return for peace.[50] Churchill's reputation concerns were sufficiently broad that he rejected Halifax's suggestion of asking Roosevelt to mediate, noting that fighting would earn America's respect, and seeking terms would have the opposite effect.[51] Indeed, later in the war the British Foreign Office tried to squelch reports of an unauthorized June 1940 peace feeler, because, in the words of one government official, "Our stoutheartedness when we stood alone is such a tremendous asset to our prestige in the world—and is likely to remain so."[52]

Also possible is that although Churchill was intellectually willing to entertain the theoretical possibility of a bargain, which he would accept to stop the war, he also recognized that what may have been theoretically possible was practically speaking out of the question, both because of the heavy reputation costs of even opening negotiations, and because Churchill knew that Hitler would never agree to terms that Britain might find acceptable. At one point, Churchill remarked that the odds that Hitler would offer acceptable terms were "a thousand to one against."[53] In a May 26 meeting with some of his War Cabinet Ministers, Churchill remarked that France "would be likely to be offered decent terms by Germany, which we should not. . . . There was no limit to the terms which Germany would impose upon us if she had her way."[54]

Conversely, some might speculate that Churchill's opposition to negotiations was idiosyncratic, and that if it had been Halifax instead of Churchill succeeding Chamberlain as prime minister on May 10, 1940, then British policy would have swung the other way. However, Churchill did not impose autocratically his "no negotiations" policy in late May. Indeed, the central aim of the May 26–28 War Cabinet meetings was to sway the Cabinet in his favor through argument and persuasion. Churchill could not rule by unilateral declaration because his political position at this point was rather weak. He had been appointed prime minister by the king, but did not lead any political party, and he felt the need to include leading national figures (including his political rivals) such

CARL A. RUDISILL LIBRARY
LENOIR-RHYNE UNIVERSITY

as Chamberlain and Halifax in his cabinet because their support was necessary both to make his policies legitimate and to ensure his political survival.[55] The key turning point in the meetings was when Chamberlain, the architect of appeasement, went along with Churchill's decision to eschew negotiations and fight on, remarking on the afternoon of the 28th that "the alternative to fighting on nevertheless involved a considerable gamble."[56] Further, Churchill's decision to fight on was politically popular. When Churchill declared to all his ministers on the evening of the 28th his decision to abandon negotiations, none present expressed dissent, and many verbally offered support.[57] By Churchill's recollection, the reaction was even more positive, and representatives of both parties exuberantly supported Churchill's decision to fight on.[58]

Distrusting "That Man"

Churchill in late May faced the very real possibility of the first conquest of Britain in nine centuries. Why did he risk German invasion by rejecting even the possibility of negotiating with Hitler? Most importantly, like Chamberlain, Churchill did not trust Hitler to adhere to any war-ending commitment. Churchill had had a long-standing wariness of the enduring threat posed by Germany, of the new threat posed by Hitler and Nazism, and of the risk that Germany would violate any war-ending agreement. In the 1920s, Churchill concluded his multivolume history of World War I by wondering whether the Versailles treaty had provided for long-standing peace or whether war with Germany might reerupt. As early as 1930, Churchill told German diplomats that he was concerned that Adolf Hitler, then a somewhat peripheral figure in German politics, might seek to launch a new world war. In the 1930s, Churchill churned out a stream of warnings in his speeches and writings about the serious danger Hitler posed to Britain and European order.[59]

Churchill had great respect for German national power, clearly understood Hitler's revisionist intentions, and distrusted Hitler's willingness to adhere to his international commitments. In the 1930s, appeasers like Chamberlain put faith in the hope that a true settlement granting sufficient concessions to dissuade Hitler from going to war might be possible. Churchill vehemently disagreed. After Germany remilitarized the Rhineland in March 1936, in violation of the Versailles Treaty, Churchill remarked that "Herr Hitler has torn up all the Treaties." Any German commitment to go no further could not be trusted. He argued against the false hope that Germany would stop at the Rhineland. Refortifying the Rhineland would permit Germany to attack France through the Low Countries. Hitler might also be able to challenge Poland, Czechoslovakia, Yugoslavia, Romania, Austria, and the Baltic states.[60] As Germany

CARL A. RUDISILL LIBRARY
LENOIR-RHYNE UNIVERSITY

moved to annex Austria in February 1938, Churchill warned that Hitler could not be counted on to halt there, remarking that a British confrontation with Germany was inevitable. Months later, he made a similar point during the Sudetenland crisis.[61] Churchill told an American journalist in June 1939—before war broke out—that Britain should never surrender, and that he (Churchill) would personally die in battle before accepting surrender.[62]

In late May 1940, Churchill's longstanding beliefs in Germany's long-term threat and inability to commit credibly led him to reject the idea of negotiations. Chamberlain dismissed Hitler's October 1939 peace overture for similar reasons, when Chamberlain viewed Hitler's verbal assurances as worthless.[63] Churchill told members of the House of Commons on May 28 that any German peace terms must be rejected. Hugh Dalton, Minister of Economic Warfare, recalled Churchill's remarks as follows: "And then he said, 'I have thought carefully in these last days whether it was part of my duty to consider entering into negotiations with That Man.' But it was idle to think that, if we tried to make peace now, we should get better terms than if we fought it out. The Germans would demand our fleet—that would be called 'disarmament'—our naval bases, and much else. We should become a slave state, though a British Government which would be Hitler's puppet would be set up—under Mosley or some such person.' And where should we be at the end of all that?"[64]

Churchill feared that peace terms would restrict British military power, allow the relative growth in German power, and thereby give Hitler even greater incentive to renege on any peace deal. As Churchill put it, "It was impossible to imagine that Herr Hitler would be so foolish as to let us continue our re-armament. In effect, his terms would put us completely at his mercy. We should get no worse terms if we went on fighting, even if we were beaten, than were open to us now."[65] In a May 26 meeting, Churchill envisioned that any likely offered terms to Britain from Hitler would "place her entirely at the mercy of Germany through disarmament, cession of naval bases in the Orkneys, etc."[66] That same day, he remarked that Britain could never accept German dominance of Europe, and that "We must ensure our complete liberty and independence." He proclaimed his opposition "to any negotiations which might lead to a derogation of our rights and power."[67] This argument underlay Churchill's public speeches on the war. During his May 13, 1940 speech to the Commons, he stressed the importance of defeating Germany rather than trying to coexist with it, declaring that the British aim is "victory, victory at all costs, victory in spite of all terror, victory, however long and hard the road may be; for without victory there is no survival. Let that be realised; no survival for the British Empire, no survival for all that the British Empire has stood for."[68]

Others saw things in similar terms. Ironside held no hopes that the Germans would honor any peace agreement.[69] Even Halifax, the highest placed proponent of negotiations, saw the danger of an incredible Nazi commitment to end the war. He feared that a German peace offer would strip Britain of her military power, tempting Hitler to violate his war-ending commitment. On May 25, Halifax laid out his thinking in a never-sent telegram to Roosevelt: "It would be natural for Hitler to say that he would include Great Britain in his peace offer but only on terms that would ensure our not taking revenge, which would leave this country entirely at his mercy and which we of course could not accept."[70]

Thin British Hopes for Ultimate Victory

The central reason Britain fought on was distrust of Hitler. A second reason was that British prospects were bleak but not utterly hopeless. If there was absolutely no reasonable case to be made of eventually prevailing, as was the case for France around this time, then as noted at the beginning of the chapter there would be no reason to fight on. Better to at least curtail the bloodshed. At this time, Britain did have some reasons to hope that somehow, perhaps, the war might eventually turn around. However, as will be evident, these hopes rested on shaky ground, and did not steer British leaders away from a fundamental pessimism. With greater faith in the credibility of a German commitment to peace terms, British leadership might have been willing to negotiate for limited terms, as it did with Wilhelmine Germany during the First World War[71]—that is, absent the severe commitment problem Britain might have sought to negotiate in 1940. However, very low German credibility combined with even slim reeds of hope pushed Britain to fight on under very discouraging conditions.

British hopes for survival and victory had short-term and long-term aspects. In the short term, Churchill hoped that a successful evacuation at Dunkirk would boost Britain's ability to parry a German amphibious invasion. He wanted at the least to put off negotiation until seeing how Dunkirk turned out. In a May 26 War Cabinet meeting, Churchill remarked that "it was best to decide nothing until we saw how much of the Army we could re-embark from France. . . . we might save a considerable portion of the Force."[72] He also allowed that the evacuation effort "would afford a real test of air superiority, since the Germans would attempt to bomb the ships and boats."[73]

Churchill's late May wait-and-see approach had its risks, however. The hope was that if things went well in the coming days or weeks, then this would serve as encouragement to fight on. However, if Dunkirk had gone *worse* than predicted, for example if less than 10,000 troops were evacuated and German aircraft proved superior to British aircraft, then this might undermine the British negotiating position even further. Halifax expressed this very point, that Britain would be in a worse position if Britain delayed negotiations a few months and military setbacks continued. He stated in a war cabinet meeting on May 27, "The Prime Minister [has] said that two or three months would show whether we were able to stand up against the air risk. This meant that the future of the country turned on whether the enemy's bombs happened to hit our aircraft factories. [I am] prepared to take that risk if our independence was at stake; but if it was not at stake [I] would think it right to accept an offer which would save the country from unavoidable disaster."[74]

Churchill was willing to take the risk of rejecting negotiation until after Dunkirk had played out, because he viewed any deal struck with Hitler to be essentially worthless. However, waiting was a great risk, as success at Dunkirk was by no means assured. After Dunkirk's great success, some (including British General H. R. Pownall) referred to the outcome as the "miracle" at Dunkirk. Indeed, the great success was in large part due to sheer luck, poor German decisions, and extraordinary British bravery. As for luck, the famously turbulent English Channel exhibited an almost never-seen nine days of smooth waters during the evacuation, an essential precondition for a maritime operation involving such a vast and diverse array of vessels including so many small boats. As for the Germans, on three occasions between May 20 and May 30 Hitler and the German high command strangely ordered their tanks to halt their advance, including on May 24 when General Heinz Guderian's tanks were just ten miles short of Dunkirk, with nothing standing in their way. These pauses in the German advance gave the Allied force just the slight margin it needed to accomplish the evacuation. The Luftwaffe, consistent with its doctrine, did not launch significant attacks against troops on the Dunkirk beaches or the British coastal targets where they landed. As for British bravery, the miracle was made possible by the willingness of a handful of British battalions to stay behind and fight without hope of escape. Of those ordered to stay and fight, almost none escaped.[75]

Importantly, even the miracle at Dunkirk did not end the period of high danger. Persisting British fears about the future belie the image that Churchill breezily passed up on negotiations after the Dunkirk rescue, or even after the Battle of Britain, assuming that better fortunes were just ahead. That is, Britain continued to reject negotiations not because it became confident in ultimate victory, but rather because its doubts in the credibility of any German commitment to end the war persisted. Regarding Dunkirk, even after the successful evacuation of troops, one government official estimated that the loss of the continental English Channel ports undercut British military power by 30 percent. Chief of the Imperial General Staff Sir John Dill thought throughout summer 1940 that a German attack on Ireland, Scotland, England, Iceland, and/or the Orkney Islands was likely, and by late June still worried about the training and discipline of the British defense forces, fretting that they were not up to the task of parrying an invasion. Ironside feared in mid-June a German attack to be likely before October, and arranged for all sixty volumes of his diaries to be shipped off to Canada for safekeeping. He prayed for God to help him "piece together an Army in the most terrible crisis that has ever faced the British Empire." General Alan Brooke, in charge of homeland defense, worried about British invasion defenses, observing a force undertrained, underequipped, and perhaps outnumbered. Even by mid-September, Brooke thought invasion defenses were woefully lacking. By that point, Britain had for invasion defense about twenty-two divisions, only half of which were capable of any kind of mobile operations, whereas in contrast the French frontier had been half the length of the British coastline, and despite some eighty divisions and the Maginot Line, Allied forces failed to deflect the German attack.[76] Desperate measures to defend Britain might be needed. In the event of an actual landing, Churchill advocated the use of chemical weapons against German troops on British beaches, an opinion shared by Dill.[77] On June 4, he wrote in a note to another British political figure that "We are going through v[er]y hard times & I expect worse to come: but I feel quite sure that better days will come! Though whether we shall live to see them is more doubtful." And on June 12 he told his military secretary bluntly, "You and I will be dead in three months time."[78] In late June, the forecast was for German invasion by mid-July, and military and political leaders were doubtful about Britain's ability to foil a German invasion. Cadogan colorfully noted in his June 29 diary entry that a recent report on invasion preparations "makes it seem that the Germans can take a penny steamer to the coast and stroll up to London! . . . As far as I can see we are, after years of leisurely preparation, completely unprepared. We have simply got to die at our posts."[79] In late July, Churchill remarked that Britain faced a threat worse than any since the Spanish Armada of 1588.[80]

Beyond Dunkirk, the September 1940 victory in the Battle of Britain establishing British air superiority over the British Isles did not dismiss British invasion fears. The leadership still feared that Hitler would strike at the first opportunity.[81] As late as April 1941, British generals feared that a German invasion was both possible and likely. The June 1941 German invasion of the Soviet Union did not dispel these fears, given British assumptions about Soviet military weakness. Dill warned against sending additional troops to the Middle East, so as not to strip further the invasion defenses of Britain. That summer, Churchill called for invasion defense preparations to be "at concert pitch" by September 1, 1941.[82] Further, the Battle of Britain did not affect the critical Battle of the Atlantic.

Churchill often remarked, both during the war and after, that the greatest threat to the British war effort was the German U-boat campaign against the maritime supply line linking North America to the British Isles. The U-boat threat did not abate until spring 1943.[83]

Dunkirk and the Battle of Britain provided Britain some reassurance that it might be able to fend off a German invasion in the short term. The longer term hope for victory was in American entry into the war. As Churchill put it, Britain need only hold out until "in God's good time the new world with all its power and might, steps forth to the rescue and liberation of the old."[84]

The key question was how soon American help might arrive. Certainly, Churchill occasionally indulged in wishful thinking that Britain's decision to fight might inspire American intervention.[85] However, it was clear to all in spring and summer 1940 and beyond in 1941 that any substantial American aid was not coming in the near or medium term. In mid-May 1940, Kennedy conveyed America's unwillingness to intercede, telling Churchill that President Roosevelt "would not leave the United States holding the bag for a war in *which the Allies expected to lose*."[86] Kennedy's Anglophobic isolationism notwithstanding, the fall of France did move Roosevelt to fear that the German defeat of Britain was likely in the coming weeks.[87] The British ambassador to the U.S., Phillip Kerr, reported on May 27 that Roosevelt had told him that under the most dire circumstances the U.S. would intervene. However, Roosevelt's comments seemed more geared to carrying on the fight from the Western Hemisphere after the British Isles had fallen, as he spoke of, for example, relocating the British government in Bermuda.[88] At the same time, Kerr suggested to Churchill that Britain might lease to America British airfields in the Western Hemisphere as a means of reducing British war debt. Churchill bitterly refused to consider it, as the "United States had given us practically no help in the war, and now that they saw how great was the danger, their attitude was that they wanted to keep everything which would help us for their own defence."[89]

Skepticism about the imminent appearance of meaningful American aid proved accurate. It was more than a year (September 1941) before Britain and the U.S. struck a deal for the fifty World War I vintage American destroyers that Britain so badly wanted. The Lend Lease program of American assistance to the British war effort remained limited. In the following year, 1941, it only accounted for 2.4 percent of all British munitions.[90] And, of course, the U.S. did not enter the war because of a desire to aid Britain. Rather, it entered the war in the Pacific after the Japanese attack on Pearl Harbor, and it entered the war in Europe after Germany and Italy declared war on the U.S.

Fighting on with Much Fear and a Little Hope

Britain's decision to fight on in May 1940 and after was driven by great fear and a few scraps of hope.[91] Britain (and Churchill in particular) had so little faith that Hitler would adhere to the terms of a war-ending deal that it shunned the possibility of a peace deal with Germany even as its greatest military planning nightmare, the swift fall of France, came to pass. That is, in contrast to the predictions of a purely information-oriented view of war-termination behavior, the revelation of severely discouraging information was insufficient to move Britain to offer concessions. Importantly, Britain fought on both because of its grave doubt that Germany would adhere to the terms of a peace settlement and because Britain's situation, although frightening to be sure, was not completely without hope. As long as Britain could maintain a vision for eventual victory, resting on luck and courage at Dunkirk and in the skies above Britain in the short term and on American intervention in the long term, then Britain would fight on. Conversely, one can imagine a set of circumstances so discouraging, including a disaster at Dunkirk, the destruction of the Royal Air Force, a successful German amphibious landing in England, and the election of an isolationist to the White House in November 1940, that perhaps even Churchill might have swallowed his fears and reached a deal with the Nazi monster.

UNITED STATES, 1942

The summer of 1940 may have been the single darkest moment of the war for the Allies, but it was thereafter certainly not a steady climb to victory. American entry into the war, the event on which Britain had desperately pinned its hopes, did not occur until Japanese forces attacked Pearl Harbor on December 7, 1941. However, even at that point the tide did not immediately turn. From December 1941 to early summer 1942, the Allies suffered their worst combined string of setbacks in the entire war. In the Pacific, there was a rush of Japanese successes, including the Pearl Harbor raid itself which destroyed the bulk of the American Pacific fleet, as well as the Japanese capture of Guam, Wake Island, Singapore, Mandalay, Corregidor, Burma, Hong Kong, Malaya, and the Philippines, among other areas. The only bright spots were perhaps the minor Doolittle air raid on Japanese cities in April and the indecisive Battle of the Coral Sea in May. Generally, by mid-1942 Japan was poised to invade Australia in the south, to seize India in the west, and to strike at Midway Island and then Hawaii in the east, while maintaining a secure northern perimeter through its peace with the Soviet Union and its June seizure of two Aleutian islands.

Roosevelt and Churchill recognized the scope of the Japanese threat. At the Arcadia Conference of December 1941–January 1942, they understood that the West Coast of North America itself could be threatened by naval bombardment, minelaying in ports, suicide attacks on vessels by human torpedoes, aerial bombardment from aircraft carriers, or at the limit perhaps even amphibious invasion. Indeed, these kinds of events did occur during World War II, such as in February 1942 when a Japanese submarine surfaced off the coast of California and shelled a Santa Barbara ranch. Roosevelt and Churchill also recognized that in Asia Japanese troops could threaten India and march to the Middle East, perhaps linking up with German troops moving eastward in their attack on the Soviet Union.[92] Churchill at one point voiced the concern that continued Japanese successes might fuel a "Pan-Asiatic movement" of all "the brown and yellow race" in Asia supporting the Japanese bid for empire.[93] In March 1942 correspondence with Churchill, Roosevelt conceded that the Japanese "deployment has been skilfully [sic] executed and continues to be effective. The energy of the Japanese attack is still very powerful. . . . The U.S. agrees that the Pacific situation is now very grave."[94] Indeed, the bad news in the first two months of the war eventually began to dent American public confidence and optimism. One reporter at a February 10, 1942 presidential news conference made reference to the "matter of 'complacency' in this country, in the face of bad news in the Pacific."[95]

The course of the war did not look brighter outside of Asia. No major Allied offensives had yet commenced. The American bombing campaign of Germany would not start until August, and the Allied landings in North Africa, Operation Torch, would not begin until November. German U-boats continued to sink Allied shipping throughout the Atlantic and even off the American east coast, as close as a few hundred yards from the shoreline.[96] May and June 1942 marked the greatest monthly losses of Allied shipping to U-boat attacks of the entire war.[97] In North Africa, the German Afrika Korps under General Erwin Rommel recaptured Benghazi in January 1942 and drove on Egypt, not to be turned back until the August Battle of Alam el Halfa and in particular the October Battle of El Alamein. In the campaign between the Soviet Union and Germany, the first few months of 1942 were quiet as both sides waited for better weather, although May would see the initiation of a major German advance in the south, moving towards the Caucasus and the city of Stalingrad. Some in the United States fretted about a possible separate peace between the Soviet Union and Germany.[98] South America slowly began to edge towards aligning with the Axis powers.[99] Churchill summed up the grim reality to the Conservative Party leadership in March 1942 in these blunt terms: "[In the last twelve months] we have had an almost unbroken series of military misfortunes. We were driven out of Cyrenaica, and have now only partly re-established ourselves there. We were driven out of Greece and Crete. . . . Hong Kong has fallen; the Malay Peninsula and the possessions of the brave Dutch in the East Indies have been overrun. Singapore has been the scene of the greatest disaster to British arms which our history records. The Allied squadrons in the Netherlands East Indies have been virtually destroyed in the action off Java. Burma is invaded; Rangoon has fallen; very hard fighting is proceeding in Upper Burma. Australia is threatened: India is threatened."[100] U.S. Assistant Secretary of State Breckenridge Long wrote in his diary in early February 1942, "The whole picture is pretty dark—an aggressive foe, well prepared, with a superiority of men, planes and naval support—a scattered front with a very long line of communications—and probable defeat in the western Pacific with a 'long, long pull' to push the enemy out of situations it was much easier to defend than to retake. . . . The truth is we are spreading our butter very thin over the world—even in the United States."[101] In April, Long was even gloomier: "Four months since Pearl Harbor—and the situation has deteriorated every minute since."[102]

If war-termination decisions were driven exclusively by information dynamics, then in the face of six months of steady military setbacks the United States (and Britain, for that matter) should have downgraded its assessments for the prospects for eventual victory and made concessions to the Axis with the aim of ending the war on limited terms. This was certainly an integral part of the Japanese war plan, as the Japanese leadership hoped that running up an impressive string of victories would cause the U.S. to perceive that war with Japan would inevitably be long and bloody, moving the U.S. to offer concessions and seek settlement.[103] However, like Britain, the United States did not consider negotiations. Rather, the United States and its Allies during this period laid out the framework for a policy of unconditional surrender, offering zero concessions.[104] Roosevelt was opposed to negotiation even before Pearl Harbor, as in November 1941 Roosevelt rejected out of a hand a Vichy France request for the United States to either mediate a negotiated settlement between Britain and the Axis or solicit Vatican mediation.[105] His January 6 annual message to Congress was typically emphatic and blunt: "No compromise can end that conflict. There never has been—there never can be—successful compromise between good and evil. Only total victory can reward the champions of tolerance, and decency, and faith."[106] On March 27, he told a British envoy that he favored the postwar dismemberment of Germany.[107]

That spring, the American Subcommittee on Security Problems, composed of an array of civilian and military leaders, convened to consider a number of issues, including what the eventual terms of Axis surrender should be. In May 1942, they advised the president of their conclusions that the Allies should demand the unconditional surrender of Germany and Japan.[108] Roosevelt was sympathetic to their findings, telling Soviet Foreign Minister Vyacheslav Molotov the following month that "he had already developed his ideas about disarming Germany and Japan."[109] Roosevelt restated his firm commitment to unconditional surrender to a British envoy in August 1942.[110] There is also some evidence that the Joint Chiefs of Staff recommended unconditional surrender in December 1942, and forwarded these recommendations to Roosevelt.[111] A committee similar to the Security Problems Committee met in May 1943 to discuss the postwar treatment of Japan. It reached similar conclusions, that Japan posed a long-term threat, and that the absolute defeat of Japan would be necessary to sustain peace in Asia and the Pacific.

Roosevelt's support of the absolute defeat of Japan was not isolated. Many in American society and government supported crushing Japan utterly, some advocating literally the extermination of the Japanese society and/or people. In September 1942, Admiral William Leahy, Roosevelt's chief of staff, equated Japan to Carthage, proposing that the U.S. as Rome "should go ahead and crush her utterly." This was not enough for two members of the State Department's Security Technical Committee, U.S. Navy Captain H. L. Pence and Assistant Chief of the State Department's Division of Southern European Affairs Cavendish Cannon. In May 1943 meetings, they advocated genocide, the virtual elimination of the Japanese race. Their view was not isolated. A December 1944 poll of the American public revealed that 13 percent supported genocide in Japan, and an additional 33 percent supported destroying the Japanese polity. In December 1945, three months *after* the Japanese surrender, nearly one quarter of those polled in one survey mused that they regretted that the U.S. did not have the opportunity to use *more* atomic bombs before the Japanese surrender.[112]

Unconditional Surrender, Commitment Credibility,
and the Shadow of Versailles

Why did the United States decide on a zero concessions, unconditional surrender policy during this early phase of the war when the news from the front was uniformly discouraging? The information proposition of chapter 2 would make the opposite prediction, that the U.S. should make concessions or at least open negotiations under such conditions. However, the U.S. pursued total victory, even at this early stage, for two reasons. More importantly, the U.S. wanted to achieve a lasting peace, and was concerned about the possibility of Axis defection on a peace settlement providing a limited outcome. U.S. concern over Axis noncompliance with a limited outcome peace deal encouraged the pursuit of total victory. Further, although the string of Axis victories was certainly discouraging, the core of American military power—American economic strength—remained unthreatened. Victory would be long in coming and costly, but even in early 1942 American decision-makers saw it could be had once the American economy had been mobilized.

American concern with Axis noncompliance was strongly driven by a motivation to avoid repeating what were perceived as mistakes committed in the World War I–ending peace settlement of Versailles, mistakes that left open the door to renewed German aggression.[113] The Subcommittee on Security Problems chair, Norman Davis, supported studying the 1918 Armistice in thinking about how to end World War II. A general serving on the committee concurred, commenting that the core flaw in the 1918 terms were that they were watered down in their adoption and implementation. Committee members studied the memos drawn up by U.S. General John Pershing in October 1918, in which Pershing declared that "there should be no tendency toward leniency."[114] One general later remarked that he thought the terms of the 1940 French surrender to Germany, which included German occupation of France save for the puppet Vichy government, were a preferable model to the 1918 armistice.[115] Eventually, the committee unanimously supported the pursuit of unconditional surrender, largely because of the shadow of 1918.[116] Long put it succinctly at a May 6, 1942 meeting: "We are fighting this war because we did not have an unconditional surrender at the end of the last one."[117]

The Subcommittee's conclusions were passed on to Roosevelt, who was sympathetic.[118] Indeed, Roosevelt's thinking about foreign policy and the problems of world order were strongly shaped by the lessons and mistakes of World War I.[119] One historian put it this way:

> As Roosevelt sat at the end of the long table in the Cabinet Room working on that speech and other speeches during the war years, he would look up at the portrait of Woodrow Wilson, over the mantelpiece. The tragedy of Wilson was always somewhere within the rim of his consciousness. Roosevelt could never forget Wilson's mistakes . . . Wilson had advocated "peace without victory," he had produced the Fourteen Points as a basis on which Germany could surrender honorably. The violation of these principles had plagued the postwar world, had led to the rise of Hitler and a Second World War, and there was no motivating force in all of Roosevelt's wartime political policy stronger than the determination to prevent repetition of the same mistakes.[120]

Roosevelt made a similar point later in the war, declaring that the lessons of World War I were that the Allies "must not allow the seeds of the evils we shall have crushed to germinate and reproduce themselves in the future."[121] He told the public in an October 1942 radio address: "We have learned that if we do not pull the fangs of the predatory animals of the world, they will multiply and grow in strength—and they will be at our throats once more in a short generation. . . . It is clear to us that if Germany and Italy and Japan—or any one of them—remain armed at the end of this war, or are permitted to rearm, they will again, and inevitably, embark upon an ambitious career of world conquest. They must be disarmed and kept disarmed, and they must abandon the philosophy which has brought so much suffering to the world."[122] In internal discussions in 1944, Roosevelt dismissed the suggestion of a limited outcome with Germany leaving a military-controlled government there, insisting that "A somewhat long study and personal experience in and out of Germany leads me to believe that" the best solution to the German threat would be "total defeat," and that, "To assume otherwise is to assume, of necessity, a period of quiet followed by a third world war."[123] There was great concern that the taproot cause of the war was militarism in Germany and Japan, and only total war followed by fundamental social, political, and economic changes in these countries could provide for peace. The repetition of these themes in a variety of fora increases our confidence that they genuinely reflect Roosevelt's thinking.[124]

Others shared Roosevelt's obsession to avoid repeating the mistakes of Versailles. Some advocated extreme measures against both Germany and Japan. In July 1944, Generals Dwight Eisenhower and Walter Bedell Smith discussed the problem of the enduring threat posed by the German General staff, the core of German militarism. Smith commented that imprisonment of these individuals, some 3,500 officers, would be insufficient, as they would in six or eight years be released from prison. Eisenhower suggested executing the group of them, and he included for good measure all members of the Nazi Party from mayors up as well as all members of the Gestapo. They reassured themselves that if these individuals fell into Russian hands, nature would take care of the problem.[125] Secretary of the Treasury Henry Morgenthau proposed a plan for the postwar treatment of Germany that would include destroying all German heavy industry, internationalizing the Ruhr, Rhineland, and areas north of Kiel, encouraging Germans with industrial skills and training to emigrate from Germany, transferring German industrial plants and equipment to its victim nations, dividing Germany into constituent states and giving some territories to France, closing down all German schools and media outlets until they could be restructured by the Allies, banning all German aircraft, military uniforms, military bands, and military parades, and executing all war criminals.[126]

Similar ideas were expressed about Japan. As noted earlier, some in government and in society more broadly advocated the extermination of the Japanese polity and people. Generally, many saw that the total defeat of Japan was necessary to establish lasting peace in Asia and the Pacific. One U.S. senator warned that the Japanese "don't seek real peace—only an armistice to give some years for preparing another attempt to dominate the entire Far East, and then the remainder of the world." Admiral William "Bull" Halsey agreed, claiming that with limited terms Japan would "use this peace as Germany did before them, to build up for another war."[127]

Preparing for a Long Road to Victory

What was the long-term Allied outlook for victory from late 1941 to mid-1942? Certainly, for Churchill and Britain the attack on Pearl Harbor was perhaps the best possible news, because with America (and the Soviet Union) on Britain's side, the defeat of the Axis was now seen as inevitable.[128] On the American side, the string of defeats were certainly disturbing, but importantly none of them touched America's long-term military–industrial power, its factories, cities, population, shipyards, mines, oil wells, and farms. Certainly, the American government understood from the outset that, at best, victory would take years to achieve. For example, the "Victory Program" drawn up in autumn 1941 did not imagine that the American armed forces would be ready for substantial offensive action until summer 1943, even under conditions of wartime mobilization.[129] This view that large-scale offensive operations would not be possible until 1943 was repeated at the post–Pearl Harbor Arcadia conference between Churchill and Roosevelt.[130] A few months later, in April 1942, Roosevelt wrote to Queen Wilhelmina of the Netherlands that the Dutch Indies and Philippines might not be liberated until 1944 or 1945.[131]

In short, American commitment to unconditional surrender in early 1942, like the British desire to fight on in 1940, was driven by two factors. First, obsession with repeating the mistakes of Versailles made Americans deeply worried about Axis powers reneging on any war-ending commitment. Only complete victory, permitting the rooting out of militarism in Japan, Italy, and Germany would provide a stable peace. Second, the long string of combat setbacks was serious, but did not undermine the foundation of Allied confidence in eventual victory: American economic might. If either condition had not been present, America might have been more open to a limited settlement. If America had been less fearful of Axis treachery, it might have been willing to consider war termination short of total victory. Indeed, this view roughly represents American decision-making in World War I. Through many phases of that war, including up to early 1918, the Allies considered and indeed offered to the Central Powers peace terms that were short of their unconditional surrender (see chapter 9). If American and Allied faith in long-term victory was some-how dented in 1942, with perhaps a combination of Soviet defeat, British exit from the war, Japanese conquest of Midway, Hawaii, and Australia, Japanese bombardment of California, and a total disaster at the first American amphibious landing in the Pacific at Guadalcanal, perhaps ne-gotiations might have looked more attractive.

Are there other explanations of American war-termination behavior during this period? The domestic politics hypothesis would not predict much change over this period since American casualties had not yet esca-lated substantially—though, as noted, the initial setbacks may have slightly reduced public confidence in the war effort in early 1942. Another possible explanation concerns the interactions between Churchill and Roosevelt with Stalin. The proposition would be that Churchill and Roo-sevelt embraced unconditional surrender, especially at their January 1943 Casablanca meeting, in large part to reassure Stalin. Stalin demanded the U.S. and Britain open a second front in the West to alleviate the pressure the Red Army felt from German forces, and Churchill received one report that Stalin was threatening to break with the U.S. and Britain if a second front was not opened soon. Some Soviet officials speculated that the Anglo-American plot was to have the Soviet Union exhaust itself in its war with Germany, after which the U.S. and Britain would cut a deal with Hitler.[132] However, as described, Roosevelt's support for unconditional surrender had emerged long before the Casablanca meeting. Regardless, at Casablanca Stalin was miffed that he had not been consulted about the formal announcement of unconditional surrender, and did not view the announcement as an acceptable substitute for a second front.[133]

USSR, Autumn 1941

Both Britain and the United States refused to panic when their fortunes looked bleakest. Importantly, though, neither country was invaded, and each had bodies of water and powerful navies to thwart invasion. The Soviet Union faced a similar test in 1941, and did not have such reassur-ances. Germany invaded the Soviet Union on June 22, 1941, breaking the August 1939 non-aggression agreement between the Soviet Union and Germany. The conquest of the Soviet Union was at the center of Hitler's plans for world empire, to eradicate the threat posed by Communism, to subdue the inferior Slav people, to provide "living space" for the German people, and to harness the resources of the region for the coming titanic confrontation with the United States. Hitler sought the absolute defeat of the Soviet Union, including at the minimum overthrowing the Communist government of the Soviet Union.[134]

The war initially went well for Germany and poorly for the Soviet Union. German armies advanced deeply into Soviet territory, killing or capturing hundreds of thousands of Soviet soldiers. By early November, nearly three million Soviet prisoners of war were in German captivity, decimating Soviet reserves. Only fifteen tanks were available for the defense of Moscow.[135]

In late September, concern over German advances escalated. During these weeks, German attacks created massive battles at Vyazma and Bryansk, where some 700,000 Soviet soldiers were captured, and another quarter million were dead or wounded. More importantly, the attacks created a three-hundred-mile-wide hole in the Soviet line, leaving Moscow open for conquest. Stalin received the bad news on October 5, at first disbelieving the reports (and, perhaps typically, threatening the court martial of the air force colonel who initially reported the catastrophe, before later promoting him when the reports proved accurate). Once he became persuaded of the veracity of the reports, Stalin reacted by deploying troops to slow the German advance, ordering the retreat and consolidation of the Soviet defensive line, and arranging General Georgi Zhukov's return from Leningrad to assist in the impending defense of Moscow.[136] The German threat at this point was close; the Luftwaffe had already commenced air raids in Moscow. The autumn rains had descended, somewhat slowing the rapid German advance, but the fear was that when the ground froze in winter, German forces might continue their offensive and perhaps capture Leningrad, Moscow, Stalingrad, and Rostov.[137] By October, Stalin himself was sufficiently concerned about German advances that in anticipation of the German attack he ordered the evacuation of Moscow to the city of Kuibyshev, farther to the east, and the destruction of the thousand or so factories located in and around Moscow. When the order to evacuate was announced, panic descended on ordinary Muscovites, as office workers began burning papers and families began preparing for evacuation.[138]

These discouraging events should have pushed the Soviet Union to lower its war-termination demands, and start offering concessions to Germany as a means of stopping the war and hopefully staving off absolute defeat. The record of Soviet decision-making during the war is spotty, but there is some evidence that in October Stalin did decide to offer concessions to Hitler in an attempt to end the war. It appears that on October 7, 1941, Stalin met with Zhukov and NKVD chief Lavrenti Beria, ordering Beria to work through diplomatic channels to explore negotiations with Germany. Stalin was pessimistic about the future course of the war, and wanted to explore the possibility of a second Brest-Litovsk agreement. This March 1918 deal between Russia and Germany established peace between those two countries, at the price of substantial Russian territorial concessions. Stalin authorized the cession of several Soviet territories, including Lithuania, Latvia, Estonia, Moldova, Belorussia, and portions of Ukraine. Soon after the October 7 meeting, Stalin and Beria met with a senior Bulgarian official in Moscow to convey the terms to Berlin. By some accounts, the Bulgarian refused to act as intermediary, telling Stalin that the USSR could still defeat Germany, even if a retreat to the Ural Mountains was necessary. By other accounts, there are some indications that the deal was transmitted to Hitler, who rejected it out of hand because of his confidence in German military prospects.[139]

Some historians have voiced doubt about the occurrence of this episode, so the available evidence should be examined closely.[140] A few sources corroborate the basic facts of the story.[141] A Soviet general recounted the outlines of the story in a 1957 Soviet defense ministry meeting, which had in turn been provided to him by Beria when the latter was being interrogated in 1953, after Beria's arrest and prior to his execution.[142] Some historians doubt the veracity of this source because there is no available written record of the interrogation, and because the information may have been produced under torture.[143] Some sources of corroboration exist, however. In 1989, Dimitar Peyev, a junior Bulgarian diplomat in Moscow in 1941, gave a television interview in which he confirmed the details of the story.[144] Around the same time, Nikolai Pavlenko, a Soviet general, recalled a conversation he had had with Zhukov in the 1960s in which Zhukov described the episode.[145] The senior Bulgarian diplomat serving in Moscow in 1941, Ivan Stamenov, outlined the details of the meeting some years later in a conversation with a Soviet investigator.[146] Conversely, there have been some denials. Vyacheslav Molotov in an official 1971 interview not unexpectedly denied that there were any contacts between Stalin and Germany during the war.[147] A former NKVD officer claimed in a 1994 memoir that the entire affair never occurred, that instead there was a disinformation campaign at the time to spread rumors about Soviet interest in peace terms. Its object was "to weaken German resolve," a speculation at odds with the information proposition, which would predict that offering concessions would strengthen German resolve.[148]

On balance, the evidence indicates that such a contact probably did take place since some evidence came from several principles with direct knowledge of the endeavor: Beria, Stamenov, and Zhukov. Molotov's 1971 offhand denial in an official Soviet government publication carries little weight. The NKVD officer's denial is also insufficiently documented to persuade.

Stalin's negotiations proposal is surprising, given his deep distrust of Hitler. He knew that Nazi ideology called for expansion in the east[149] and had long suspected that war with Germany would come eventually.

Further, Stalin likely doubted that agreements with Hitler would offer much protection. Hitler had a long record of breaking international commitments, including the Versailles Treaty in the 1930s and the October 1938 Munich agreement on the Sudetenland. The June 1941 invasion was itself a violation of the August 1939 neutrality agreement between the Soviet Union and Germany. Stalin also might have had reason to doubt the German inclination to cooperate after Germany treated captured Soviet soldiers brutally, in violation of the terms of the Geneva Convention to which Germany was a signatory. Although the Soviet Union was not a signatory, Moscow had declared in July and August 1941 that it would be willing to abide by the terms of the Geneva Convention and respect POW rights, although the Germans, through diplomatic channels, rejected the Soviet offer, and declared themselves unbound by the Geneva Convention in their treatment of captured Soviet soldiers, because the Soviet Union was not an official signatory of the treaty.[150] More generally, Stalin himself was a hardboiled realist with no idealistic hopes about the protections international agreements might offer. He once declared that "a diplomat's words must have no relation to actions—otherwise what kind of diplomacy is it? . . . Good words are a concealment of bad deeds. Sincere diplomacy is no more possible than dry water or iron wood."[151] Stalin was surprised by the June 1941 attack not because he assumed that Hitler would adhere to the 1939 neutrality pact, but rather because he thought Hitler was not willing to fight a two-front war, and Stalin thought in 1941 that Britain would not be eliminated or neutralized until 1942 at the earliest.[152] Later in the war, Stalin suggested to Harry Hopkins that if for some reason the Allies did settle on more moderate terms with Japan, once Allied occupation forces arrived in Japan the Allies should renege on the limited terms agreement and essentially impose an absolute outcome by effecting widespread regime change.[153]

Why, then, was Stalin willing to strike a deal so unlikely to be honored? One might be tempted to write off Stalin's decision as reflecting stress and panic, as individuals under extreme stress can exhibit symptoms of depression, and experience a collapse in self-confidence and severe resignation.[154] However, Stalin had already experienced such an emotional collapse in the first days following the June invasion, and since then had seemed to recover.[155] The historical record is too thin to provide definitive explanations for Stalin's actions, but certainly a primary reason must have been his panic about Soviet military prospects. Unlike Britain in 1940 and the U.S. in 1942, the Soviet Union had been invaded; there was no body of water coupled with a strong navy to shield the Bolshevik state from the Wehrmacht. Worse, the German invaders had in the first months of the war captured a very hefty chunk of the Soviet economy. By late November 1941, the territory abandoned by the Soviets to the Germans contained

63 percent of all Soviet coal production, 68 percent of pig iron, 58 percent of steel, 60 percent of aluminum, 41 percent of railway lines, 84 percent of sugar, 38 percent of grain, and 60 percent of pigs.[156] Economic factors aside, the Red Army had been easily and substantially dismembered by German forces. Several times as many Soviet soldiers had been killed or captured by October 1941 in four months of war as British soldiers had been rescued at the miracle at Dunkirk. The road to Moscow was open. The forces defending Moscow and indeed the rest of the country were meager. Stalin certainly had no illusions about Hitler's aims, but things looked so bad that perhaps he was willing to take his chances on a limited peace rather than face the costs of what looked like near certain absolute defeat anyway. In comparison, Churchill might have reached a similar conclusion had German forces successfully landed on the beaches of England, annihilated substantial portions of the British Army, and stood poised to march on London.

Notably, both Stalin and Molotov framed the October 1941 approach to Hitler as an opportunity for a second Brest-Litovsk agreement.[157] The March 1918 Brest-Litovsk agreement established peace between Germany and Russia in exchange for widespread Russian territorial concessions. Imperial Germany did honor the terms of the agreement in that it did not reattack Russia before the Brest-Litovsk agreement was invalidated by the cluster of treaties that ended World War I and rearranged the territorial borders in Eastern Europe. Stalin may have thought that Imperial Germany in World War I complied with the Brest-Litovsk agreement if for no other reason than Germany used the opportunity of peace with Russia to focus its energies on the Western front. Perhaps Hitler might do the same, accept a limited aims agreement with Stalin to neutralize Britain. Although not establishing long-term peace, such an agreement would at least buy the Soviet Union time to reconstitute its military. But this is all speculative, given the thinness of the historical record.

Confronting the Great Evil of the Millennium

From 1940 to 1942, each of the major Allies faced a critical choice: fight on to victory, or try to negotiate an end to the war with the Axis powers. All three, the U.S., Britain, and the Soviet Union, confronted discouraging battle outcomes, and all three doubted the likelihood that the Axis powers would honor the terms of any war-ending agreement. Of these three, the U.S. and Britain rejected the option of negotiations with the Axis, instead deciding to fight on to victory. In contrast, there is at least some evidence that the Soviet Union flinched at the moment of greatest peril, reaching out to Hitler in October 1941 in pursuit of a peace deal. The U.S. and

British cases demonstrate that a purely information-oriented approach to understanding war-termination behavior is incomplete. The Soviet case, assuming that Stalin did authorize negotiations, demonstrates that a purely commitment-oriented approach is incomplete.

What explains the variance in behavior among these three states? Probably the key is the degree of faith each belligerent had in its ultimate ability to prevail. The U.S. probably had the greatest faith, relatively speaking. It was confident its economic power would overwhelm its adversaries, and would be untouched by enemy attacks. It established the highest war aims, unconditional surrender. Britain had the next most faith. Things looked very black in 1940. However, in the short term, Britain could hope that the Dunkirk evacuation would rescue the bulk of the British Expeditionary Force, that the Royal Navy could parry a German invasion of England itself, and that the qualitative (if not quantitative) superiority of the RAF over the Luftwaffe could maintain British air superiority over Britain itself. In the longer term, there was the hope that eventually American entry into the war would help turn the tide. Britain also had high war aims, rejecting negotiations and generally calling for war until victory, although without laying out in 1940 what war's end would look like. The American and British cases demonstrate that when belligerents have severe commitment concerns and have at least some distant hope of eventual victory, they will be willing to ignore battle outcomes, reject negotiations, and fight on.

The Soviet Union had the least faith in its prospects. Germany had invaded, there was no uncrossed moat guarded by a large navy to protect Soviet territory. The Red Army had been decimated, perhaps half of the Soviet economy had been seized or destroyed, and the German Army stood poised to march on Moscow. The Soviet Union had the lowest war aims, apparently being willing to make territorial concessions to accomplish a limited outcome to the war. The Soviet case demonstrates that even a belligerent with severe commitment credibility concerns may be forced to consider terms, if it faces an apparently imminent defeat promising to impose extremely high costs.

Like the Korean War, the early World War II cases demonstrate the importance of both information and commitment dynamics in explaining war-termination behavior. The next chapter explores another pair of cases, the Winter War and Continuation War, which also illustrate how information and commitment factors work both in contrast and complement.

CHAPTER SEVEN

The Logic of War: Finland and the USSR, 1939–44

> First, when you speak of Hanko, you proceed from the conversation with Stalin in the autumn of 1939. But we have warned you that we are laying down new conditions since there have been combat operations and blood has been spilled. . . . If these negotiations drag on, I cannot be sure at all, let me say it again, that the demands we have now presented will not be increased.
> —Soviet Foreign Minister Vyacheslav Molotov to Finnish ambassador to Sweden Juho Paasikivi, March 19, 1940

PRIOR TO WORLD WAR I, Finland was one of many ethnic regions that fell under the rule of the Russian tsars. After war broke out between Russia and Germany in 1914, many Finns saw that a German victory might provide political independence from Russia. About two thousand Finns traveled to Germany in 1915 and 1916 for military training and to serve in the Imperial German army to fight Russia. Following its exit from the war, Russia disgorged several new states, including Poland, Estonia, Latvia, Lithuania, and Finland. Finland emerged as independent and non-Communist in May 1918, and with assistance from Imperial Germany proceeded to crush Bolshevik-supported Communist resistance to the new Finnish government. The new government in Helsinki signed a treaty of peace and recognition, the Treaty of Tartu, with the new Soviet government in 1920. This was followed by a treaty of non-aggression in 1932.[1] The 1932 agreement did not prove enduring, however, as Finland and the Soviet Union fought two wars over the next twelve years, the 1939–40 Winter War, and the so-called Continuation War, in which alongside Nazi Germany Finland fought the Soviet Union from 1941–44.

This chapter explores war termination during these two wars, examining both Soviet and Finnish war-termination decisions. How did the Helsinki and Moscow governments think about ending these wars? More pointedly, why did the Soviet Union not pursue an absolute victory in either war, despite in both wars enjoying (eventual) military successes and a large power advantage over Finland?

Information factors were perhaps as dominant here as for any other cases examined in this book, as war aims tended to move in concert with battlefield outcomes. In the Winter War, the initial wave of Finnish military successes caused Stalin to decrease Soviet war aims, and then new Soviet military successes in the latter portion of the war caused Soviet war aims to creep up. Increases in Soviet demands were curtailed by new information about impending Anglo-French intervention on behalf of the Finns, pushing the Soviets to accept limited gains rather than the absolute defeat of the Finns. Similarly, in the Continuation War the Finns kept high war aims at the outset while the Soviets made concessions during the initial period of Finnish/German military success. As the tide of the war turned against Finland and Nazi Germany, Soviet war aims increased and Finnish aims decreased. The Soviets accepted limited victory over Finland short of absolute conquest in 1944 because of pressing military needs elsewhere.

Although each side doubted the trustworthiness of its adversary, high costs often prevented either side from pursuing absolute victory, as predicted by chapter 3. For the Soviets, pursuing absolute victory in the Winter War risked Anglo-French intervention, an unacceptable danger. In the Continuation War, absolute victory over Finland was not worth the cost of distraction from the defeat of Nazi Germany. For the Finns, the costs emerging from the military impossibility of conquering the Soviet Union alone in the Winter War, and with a weakened Germany ally in the latter phase of the Continuation War, precluded the pursuit of absolute victory. Costs aside, Moscow was more willing to accept limited war outcomes despite commitment fears because in each war it was able to acquire strategic pieces of territory thought to improve Soviet border security and reduced the likelihood of Finland breaking its war-ending commitments and reattacking.

CAUSES OF THE WINTER WAR: THE SOVIET SEARCH FOR SECURITY

The first steps to the 1939–40 Winter War were taken in the infamous August 1939 Molotov–Ribbentrop Pact between Germany and the Soviet Union. This nonaggression agreement and its secret protocol secured Germany's eastern front in the short term from Soviet attack, giving Germany time to make conquests in the near east (Poland), the north (Denmark and Norway), and the West (France, Belgium, the Netherlands, and Luxembourg). In exchange for Soviet neutrality, the agreement recognized an expansion of the Soviet sphere of influence into the Baltic region, specifically including Finland within its sphere. It also bought the Soviet Union time, in the sense that it opened the door to a possible long war between Germany, Britain, and France. Stalin hoped such a war might leave all three states exhausted, thereby enhancing Soviet security and creating political and other opportunities.[2]

After the German–Soviet dismemberment of Poland in October 1939, Moscow replaced the soft tone of its diplomacy towards Finland with a harder, more demanding edge.[3] The Molotov–Ribbentrop Pact boosted Stalin's confidence that he could consolidate the Soviet position in the region without German interference.[4] Specifically, the Soviets were able to focus on improving their military posture in the Baltic Sea. The disappearance of the Baltic States, as essentially provided for in the Molotov–Ribbentrop Pact, opened the door for the reemergence of the Soviet Baltic fleet, based in Leningrad. The Baltic States occupied the southern shore of the Gulf of Finland, a waterway through which the Soviet Baltic fleet would have to pass after exiting its homeport of Leningrad. If the Soviet Union could also secure the northern shore of the Gulf of Finland, territory that in fall 1939 was part of sovereign Finland, it would give the Baltic Fleet the opportunity to navigate the entire Baltic Sea with impunity, enhancing Soviet influence in the region. Further, more complete control of the Gulf of Finland would improve the security of Leningrad, located at the eastern edge of the Gulf of Finland.[5]

Around this time, a Soviet Naval War Commission studied the security environment in the region. The concern was that if Finland were to join the Anglo-French or German belligerent blocs, then an invasion could be launched from Finnish territory. Absent an outright invasion, Soviet naval passage through the Gulf of Finland could come under serious threat from mines or coastal artillery. The Soviets also worried that Finnish airfields might be used by a foreign power to launch airstrikes against the Soviet Baltic and Northern Fleets. The Commission recommended that the USSR acquire bases and coastal artillery batteries on the Hanko and Porkkala-Udd peninsulas and control the Suursaari and Suur-Tiutärsaari islands.[6]

In negotiations beginning on October 12, 1939, the Soviet delegation made a series of demands of Finland reflecting these security concerns. The delegation demanded that the USSR and Finland sign a mutual assistance pact, a Red Army base be established on the Hanko peninsula, all islands in the Gulf of Finland be ceded to the USSR, Finland hand over anchorage facilities at the port of Lappohja, and Finland make territorial concessions in the areas around Leningrad and Murmansk to improve the security of those two cities. In justifying these demands, Stalin bluntly told the Finns that these concessions were necessary to protect Leningrad in the event of war with either Britain or Germany (as discussed in the previous chapter, Stalin placed little faith in agreements with Hitler). In the course of the negotiations, the Finns made some concessions to Soviet demands, but they were not sufficient to satisfy Stalin. The Soviet Union renounced the 1932 nonaggression pact on November 28.[7] On November 30, 1939, the Soviet Union attacked Finland, initiating the Winter War (see figure 7.1).

THE COURSE OF THE WINTER WAR

At the outset of the Winter War, the Soviets sought to impose regime change on Finland as a means of achieving absolute victory. The Soviets set up the "Democratic Government of Finland" under Finnish Communist O. W. Kuusinen. This was known as the Terijoki government, as it was set up in the Finnish border village of Terijoki. A treaty of recognition was signed between the Terijoki government and Moscow.[8] Soviet desires for regime change in Finland were strongly driven by concerns about Finland's trustworthiness, and the credibility of its commitments. Soviet Foreign Affairs Minister Vyacheslav Molotov informed the Soviet ambassador to Berlin on November 30 that

> ... we have not found it possible to come to terms with the present Government of Finland and we see that we won't get anywhere. Whatever promises it has given [have] been broken right away. The Government of Finland has all along been seeking to cheat us. You cannot rule out the possibility of Finland having a different government, one friendly towards the Soviet Union as well as towards Germany. That government will not be Soviet, but one of a democratic republic. Nobody is going to set up Soviets over there, but we hope it will be a government we can come to terms with so as to ensure the security of Leningrad.[9]

At the outset of the war, Moscow expected a rapid victory. The leadership planned for twelve days of combat, but thought that fighting might be unnecessary, as the Finns might simply surrender at the outset of hostilities.[10] Such expectations were not completely outlandish, as the USSR began the war with substantial material advantages, including ratios of three to one in manpower, 80 to 1 in tanks, five to one in artillery, and more than five to one in aircraft, seemingly more than enough to ensure swift victory, especially if one follows the standard military rule of thumb that an attacker needs a three to one advantage to prevail.[11]

The course of the war can be broken into two phases, the first half of the war during which the Finns successfully parried the Soviet advance, and the second half of the war when the Red Army (finally) enjoyed battlefield success. In the first phase, the Red Army suffered a string of embarrassing defeats, failing to achieve decisive victory within the twelve days

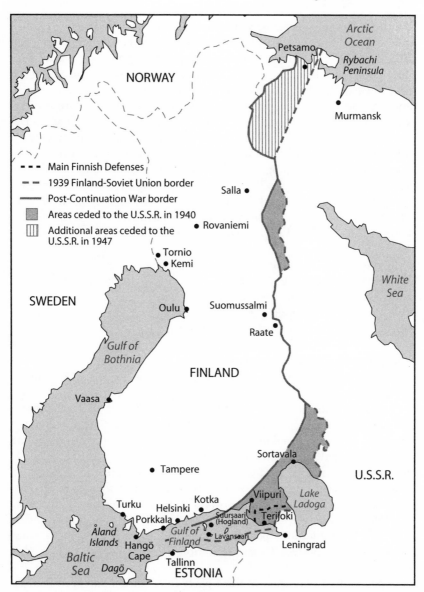

Figure 7.1 Winter War and Continuation War, 1939–44

allotted by its prewar plans.[12] The Soviet advance was slowed by Finnish mines, poor Soviet command and control, insufficient Soviet preparation to conduct river crossings, lack of training or equipment for winter warfare, poor Finnish roads, and Finnish guerrilla tactics. At the end of the first week of combat, the bulk of the Finnish army was able to escape annihilation or capture, retreating behind the system of fortifications known as the Mannerheim Line. A new Soviet offensive launched on December 15 fell short, as Soviet forces suffered heavy casualties (three fifths of Soviet tanks thrown in to the massive attack were destroyed). As the Soviets were planning a new offensive against the city of Viipuri[13] around December 23, the Finns launched a preemptive counteroffensive, disrupting Soviet plans and destroying two Soviet divisions. The Soviets officially declared their operation Ladoga to have failed on December 28. Finnish forces enjoyed impressive successes elsewhere in late December, as well.[14]

By the end of December, Moscow decided on a change in course. The Soviets concluded that concessions were necessary to end the war quickly. Most straightforwardly, the Soviets were confronted with the unavoidable reality of the poor performance of their troops against Finnish forces, a performance much worse than they had hoped for before the war broke out. Stalin's decision to lower Soviet war aims in the wake of unexpectedly poor Soviet battlefield performance is consistent with the information proposition that discouraging combat outcomes encourage concessions.

Stalin was also concerned about the effects of the war on Soviet reputation. A conventional reputation hypothesis might be that a belligerent ought to be wary of making concessions, as doing so might undermine its international reputation for toughness. However, Soviet behavior reflected an opposite dynamic, as reputation concerns contributed to Stalin's decision to *offer* concessions. In a meeting at the end of December, Stalin worried that world powers were watching the Winter War carefully, and that the show of weakness against the Finns might undermine Soviet reputation, perhaps emboldening other powers to enter the conflict. To protect Soviet reputation, the war needed to be ended quickly.[15]

Importantly, Soviet fears of third-party intervention had been increasing since the USSR was ejected from the League of Nations on December 14.[16] In the weeks to follow, Moscow received a steady stream of signals indicating a growing likelihood of British and French intervention in favor of Finland. Indeed, by January 29, Britain and France had approved sending a brigade group to Finland. They were to sail on March 12, arriving on March 20, although the dispatch of these forces was contingent on Norway and Sweden granting transit rights.[17] Indeed, the Allies were considering even broader military action against the Soviet Union as a means of aiding Finland. One French general stationed in the Middle East suggested France strike Soviet oil fields in the Caucuses, a proposal consonant with the thinking of at least some Paris politicians.[18]

As the information proposition predicts, Soviet war-termination behavior shifted in response to battlefield and diplomatic developments. On the military side, Moscow revamped its strategy towards more limited territorial ambitions within Finland, and appointed a new commander of Soviet forces.[19] On the diplomatic front, the Soviets reestablished contact with Helsinki by the end of January, and the Soviets dropped their demand for foreign-imposed regime change by recognizing the Helsinki government and cutting ties with the Terijoki government.[20]

The second phase of the Winter War began when the Red Army broke through the Finnish Mannerheim Line on February 13, opening the door for the advance of Red Army forces and the encirclement of the Finnish army. One historian proposed that this development "utterly transformed" the negotiations.[21] In reality, the political effects were not immediate. The Soviets did slightly increase their terms on about February 21, adding two small towns to their demands, although they did not mention demands for territorial gains in the Petsamo area or the Åland Islands.[22] At this stage, the Finns made no concessions past their earlier negotiations stance.

Matters changed towards the end of February. When a new round of bad news from the defenders of Viipuri reached the Finnish leadership on February 29, the Finnish leadership finally decided to make concessions. But, on March 1, after the official Finnish reply to Soviet demands had been drafted but not yet sent, France and Britain substantially increased their offer of assistance, raising it from 20,000 troops to 50,000 troops and 150 bombers, and promising the arrival of these forces by late March. This decision was enough to encourage the Finns to hold off on agreeing to Soviet terms, and the official Finnish reply was not (yet) sent to Moscow.[23]

Further important military and diplomatic changes occurred in early March. On March 3, the Finnish foreign minister informed the Soviets that peace could be had if Finland could keep the towns of Viipuri and Sortavala.[24] On March 5, and before replying, the Soviets enjoyed an important battlefield success, when they crossed the frozen Gulf of Viipuri and established a foothold on the shore, close to the town of Viipuri. This advance threatened the entire front, and Finnish resources were being stretched. All the Finnish reserves had been committed to battle, and the Finns were now starting to rely on the very young and very old to fill the ranks. At this time, the military command bluntly informed the political leadership that the situation was dire, and the front faced complete collapse absent imminent British or French military assistance or a ceasefire.[25]

On March 5, the Soviets rejected the Finnish request to keep Viipuri and Sortavala. They also threatened to reintroduce the possibility of recognizing the Terijoki government and the pursuit of regime change in Finland, if the Finns did not accept the Soviet terms soon. The following day, they invited a Finnish delegation to Moscow to negotiate, but the Soviets rejected the idea of permitting a cease fire during the talks.[26] When negotiations in Moscow began on March 8, the Soviets increased their demands, requiring Finnish concessions on Hanko, the so-called Fisherman's Peninsula, all of Karelia including Viipuri and Sortavala to the frontier established by Peter the Great, parts of Kuusamo and Salla, the Finnish construction of a railroad across Finland to improve Soviet communications with Sweden, and a Finnish commitment not to join an anti-Soviet alliance. Highly consistent with the information proposition of chapter 2, Molotov directly connected the increase in Soviet demands with Soviet battlefield successes, calling such a dynamic the "logic of war."[27] Molotov told Finnish ambassador to Sweden Juho Paasikivi on March 19, 1940, "First, when you speak of Hanko, you proceed from the conversation with Stalin in the autumn of 1939. But we have warned you that we are laying down new conditions since there have been combat operations and blood has been spilled."[28] A key Soviet emissary in the talks, Soviet ambassador to Sweden Alexandra Kollontai took a similar line when she told Finnish Foreign Minister Väinö Tanner on February 27: "Moscow's first proposal to the Finnish government was more advantageous to you but you didn't accept anything and missed your chance. If you turn down this proposal as well, my government may advance still tougher conditions."[29] In reaction to demands placed by the Finns on March 10, Molotov stonewalled and replied, "If these negotiations drag on, I cannot be sure at all, let me say it again, that the demands we have now presented will not be increased."[30] The Finns recognized their deteriorating situation, and that they now faced the choice of giving in to Soviet demands or, in the words of Finnish foreign minister Elias Erkko, being "wiped off the map."[31] A March 9 Finnish military report stated that "the present state of the army is such that further military operations would lead to nothing but the continuing weakening of the situation and fresh losses of territory."[32] The Finns signed the treaty on March 12, making substantial territorial concessions (for territory exchanges, see figure 7.1).[33] The war killed about 25,000 Finns, and perhaps ten times the number of Soviets. Actual casualty numbers are imprecise, in part because many bodies were lost in the snow, left uncounted. In his memoirs, Nikita Khrushchev estimated as many as a million Soviet dead.[34]

The information proposition accurately describes much of the war-termination behavior in the Winter War case. As predicted, when the Soviets suffered surprising setbacks on the battlefield during the first phase of the war, they lowered their war-termination offers from seeking regime change to seeking territorial gains. Notable, however, is the Soviet willingness to accept a limited war outcome as the Finnish military was collapsing in early March. This decision is inconsistent with the form of the information proposition which focuses on combat outcomes, as information from the battlefield indicated that the Soviets could have inflicted an absolute defeat upon Finland within a few weeks. However, it is consistent with the form of the information proposition that focuses on third-party intervention, as Soviet acceptance of a limited victory is probably best explained by increasingly strong signals of imminent Anglo-French intervention. Certainly, the Soviet Union feared that the balance of power would shift against them if British and French forces arrived, and for geopolitical reasons they very much wanted to avoid conflict with the Western powers. Absent that threat, the Soviet Union might have fought on longer to achieve a decisive and complete victory over Finnish forces, allowing it to impose a friendly government in Helsinki. The prospect of Anglo-French intervention was ultimately not enough to encourage the Finns to continue fighting on, given their deteriorating battle prospects. Finnish leaders feared that Helsinki might fall before Western help could arrive.[35]

The role played by credible commitment fears in determining war-termination decision-making is mixed. The Soviets initially feared Finnish noncompliance with a war-ending commitment, in that their general fear was that Finland might in the future pose a threat if it aligned or allied with a great power. Stalin viewed written promises as inadequate. Despite the existence of the 1932 nonaggression pact, in prewar negotiations he still demanded territorial concessions to bolster the defenses of the Soviet border and Leningrad in particular, as a solution to the commitment problem. When Finland rejected these territorial demands, Stalin sought regime change in Helsinki as a more complete solution to the commitment problem.

For their part, the Finns had good reason to doubt Soviet credibility. The Finns knew that the Soviets had recognized Finland's history of anti-Communism. The 1939 Soviet attack was itself a violation of the 1932 Soviet–Finnish nonaggression pact.[36] There was concern that low Soviet commitment credibility would mean that any deal ending the Winter War might not last long. Tanner made this argument to the Swedish government on February 26, 1940 when he argued for a Scandinavian defense pact: "In Finland it is believed that if peace is made now, it will not turn out to be a lasting one. The Soviet party may later present new demands, and the consequence may be a new war."[37] Finnish willingness to accept a limited outcome reflected their understanding that a Finnish absolute defeat of the Red Army followed by a march on Moscow was practically speaking out of the question (or at least prohibitively costly). It might have been conceivable with major power support, but Germany sent no signals about sending military aid to Finland, and certainly British and French intervention would have been only for the defense of Finnish borders, not the overthrow of the Soviet government. As predicted by chapter 3, high costs served to force a fearful Finland to forgo the luxury of achieving a more enduring solution to a credible commitment problem.

The calculus for Finland shifted as its military fortunes declined in February and March. Despite facing an untrustworthy adversary, Finland saw that a limited outcome with substantial territorial losses and the possibility of Soviet defection was preferable to the looming alternative, Finland's absolute defeat. On March 12, after reading a dire military report declaring that "the present state of the army is such that continued military operations can lead to nothing but further debilitation and fresh losses of territory," Tanner told the cabinet that, "Our situation is such that we are faced by a forced peace. We must make haste before the collapse occurs. After that our views would not be asked."[38] The Finns apparently took little comfort in Germany's February 1940 suggestion that any concessions Finland might offer now as part of a war-ending deal would be regained once the general war amongst the major power wars ended.[39]

A domestic politics proposition for Finnish war-termination behavior might argue that the Finnish government began to make concessions because of mounting public concern over casualties. However, the dynamic was more the opposite, as Finnish leaders feared that the public would not accept peace at the price of concessions, eager instead to fight on in the hopes of external military assistance. Even as the Red Army turned the military tide in February and March and Finnish casualties mounted, there was grave concern among the Helsinki leadership that the public would reject peace as a means of stopping the bloodshed.[40]

The Continuation War, 1941–44

In 1939, the Soviet Union was concerned about the possibility of Finland joining or being used by a great power adversary to attack the Soviet Union. The optimal solution was foreign-imposed regime change, and the lesser solution, ultimately adopted, was the acquisition of key strategic territories as a means of improving the defense of the Soviet homeland. In an April 1940 high-level Soviet government conference on the lessons of the Winter War, Stalin declared the war to have been inevitable and necessary as a means of, in particular, shoring up the defense of Leningrad.[41] In one sense, the Soviets hoped the territorial exchange brought by the end of the war would solve the credible commitment problem of the Finns allying with a major power and posing a grave threat to Soviet territory.

As it turned out, the Winter War failed to provide such security. Part of the problem was Finnish recognition that the Soviet Union was unlikely to be satisfied with territorial concessions as a means to increase its security. Indeed, the Soviets viewed the control of small buffer states as critical to their security vis-à-vis Germany.[42] They viewed France as having made a great mistake in not occupying Belgium prior to the German attack, and did not want to make the same mistake themselves. This was the motivation behind the de facto 1940 Soviet annexation of the Baltic States, and Moscow saw the control of Finland also as ultimately being necessary. Molotov bluntly told the Lithuanian foreign minister that, "You must be realistic enough to understand that in the future small states will disappear. Your Lithuania together with the other Baltic states, including Finland, will be included within the honourable family of Soviet peoples."[43] Finland recognized this mounting threat. For example, there was a war scare in summer 1940 when the USSR annexed the Baltic States and mobilized thirty divisions on the Finnish and Estonian borders, leading Finland to mobilize its military forces in anticipation of an imminent Soviet invasion. Rumors were circulating in Moscow that the Soviets would strike Finland after Germany invaded Britain. German intelligence predicted a Soviet attack on Finland in mid-August. Rumors circulated Helsinki in November 1940 that Moscow was seeking German acquiescence to a Soviet move to annex Finland.[44]

During this period, the Soviet Union began to present Finland with new demands, many of which exceeded the terms of the treaty ending the Winter War. Moscow demanded mining rights to nickel deposits in the Pechenga area of Finland, the destruction of fortifications built on the Åland Islands during and after the Winter War, and the use of Finnish railroads for transporting Soviet troops between the USSR and the newly Soviet-controlled area of Hanko. The Finns conceded on the fortifications and rail demands, but not on mining rights.[45] When discussion about a possible union between Finland and Sweden emerged, Moscow's threatening rhetoric in opposition killed the idea.[46]

These moves greatly increased Finnish anxiety about Moscow's willingness to adhere to the treaty ending the Winter War. All saw the end which befell the Baltic States, and there was concern that such a fate might await Finland. Sweden's unwillingness to risk Soviet enmity by backing Finland, Finnish fears of the looming Soviet threat, and Finnish hopes of recovering its Winter War territorial losses all pushed Finland towards expanding its ties with Germany in 1940.[47]

Germany, in turn, saw Finland as likely to be useful in the coming war with the Soviet Union, and sought to strengthen its military and economic ties with Finland. In August 1940, Germany started selling munitions to Finland, secretly, in exchange for a Finnish agreement to allow the transit of German troops en route to German-occupied northern Norway. After the Winter War, Germany directly warned the Soviets not to invade Finland, notably during a visit Molotov made to Berlin in November 1940. These warnings probably helped squelch Soviet plans for a new attack on Finland aimed at seizing the entire country. On the economic side, Germany coveted access to Finnish nickel deposits, and encouraged Finland to reject new Soviet demands regarding the nickel mines in Pechenga in January 1941. Germany's interest in the region was driven in part by its control of the Baltic Sea, since such control provided an area for undisturbed U-boat crews to train to attack Anglo-American shipping in the critical Battle of the Atlantic. A hostile Red Navy able to break out of the Gulf of Finland would make the Baltic unusable for German U-boat training. By early June 1941, there were formal military agreements for Finnish–German cooperation in a war against the Soviet Union. By this time, there were 30,000 German troops in Finland, and some 100,000 square kilometers of Finnish territory were under German military control.[48]

When Germany attacked the Soviet Union on June 22, 1941, Finland initially did not officially join the German attack. However, Finland took a number of actions around the time of the attack that pushed the boundaries of its official neutrality. Specifically, German mining vessels hid in Finnish waters the week before the attack, Finland allowed German troop transports through Lapland, Finnish submarines mined Estonian harbors the night before the attack, German bombers flew from Finnish bases to attack Soviet targets, and Finnish aircraft flew over the Soviet border, albeit on nonlethal missions. Finnish neutrality was more decisively breached when Soviet aircraft bombed Finnish bases being used by the German air force on June 25. These attacks inflicted considerable collateral damage on Finnish towns, and gave the Finnish government the cover it needed to declare war in the context of Soviet aggression against Finland. The Finnish attack on Soviet forces began around July 10, beginning the "Continuation War."[49]

Finland's war aims in 1941 went beyond the restoration of the territory lost in the 1939–40 Winter War. Even before the June 22 attack on the Soviet Union, Finland declared (privately) its agreement with the German war aim of absolute victory over the Soviet Union, and most importantly the overthrow of the Bolshevik government in Moscow.[50] Now that it was partnered with a revisionist major power, Germany, Finland saw that it was militarily feasible to overthrow the Soviet government. Finnish leaders declared their interest in such an outcome. General Carl Mannerheim often framed the war as an anti-Communist crusade, hoping that this war would destroy "Bolshevism once and for all." For him, the eradication of Bolshevism was necessary to prevent Finland itself from being destroyed, noting in July 1941 that the war would "save us from 'being wiped from the face of the earth' which otherwise, knowing the Bolsheviks' methods, would quite certainly have taken place in the near future."[51] Finnish President Risto Ryti described the war as the "final struggle against Bolshevism." To a parliamentary delegation on July 21, Ryti remarked that war between Germany and the Soviet Union "is Finland's only salvation. The Soviet Union will never give up its attempt to conquer Finland . . . if Germany now crushes the Soviet army, we may perhaps enjoy a century of peace." The chairman of the Finnish Social Democratic Party and Finnish General Erik Heinrichs also supported overthrowing the Bolshevik government, the latter remarking that Soviet regime change could safeguard Finnish security for the first time in a millennium.[52] Finnish leaders made similar points in (private) diplomatic conversations, arguing that the Soviet regime was likely to collapse following Germany's defeat of the Red Army, and conversely that a Nazi defeat would open the floodgates to the spread of Communism in Europe.[53] Certainly, there was general confidence in Finland that Germany would win a war against the Soviet Union, borne from German victories in 1940. Before the German invasion, both Paasikivi and Mannerheim were confident that Germany was likely to win.[54] In September 1941, then Minister of Commerce Tanner told the American ambassador to Finland that there was, "No doubt [the] U. S. S. R. will lose [the] war against Germany."[55] The following month, the American ambassador to Finland reported that Finnish president Ryti had told him that "with expected fall of Leningrad situation on Finnish front would largely clear and he hoped this would be the matter of few weeks only. He [Ryti] likewise expected fall of Moscow in relatively short time and German success further south was completing defeat of Bolshevik regime."[56]

The Continuation War initially went quite well for Finland, as did the larger German campaign against the Soviet Union. By December 1941, Finnish and German forces had advanced dozens of kilometers forward along a broad front past the 1941 Finnish–Soviet border. As noted in chapter 6, Stalin probably attempted to make territorial concessions to Hitler in October 1941 to end the war short of absolute defeat. Stalin also attempted in August to make a separate peace with Finland, offering territorial concessions in exchange for Finnish disengagement from Germany. The Finns ignored the offer, at least in part because they doubted the Soviets would observe the terms of any peace treaty.[57]

In the first several months of the war, the role of third parties in Finnish war aims was complex. Britain and the United States certainly opposed Finnish collaboration with Nazi Germany, and tried to pressure Finland to exit the war, or at least not move beyond its pre–Winter War borders. Although Finland desired to maintain good relations with the Western powers, it also recognized its commitment to Germany, and hence did not comply with British and American requests. Under pressure from Moscow and despite lingering sympathy for Finland, Britain formally declared war on Finland on December 6, 1941.[58]

By early 1943, the exhaustion of troops and material resources brought the Finnish offensive to a halt. The Finns remained confident in eventual German victory through early fall 1942, but by early 1943 their optimism had waned, largely in reaction to Allied successes at Stalingrad, North Africa, and elsewhere. Belief in German victory for members of Finland's Coalition Party declined from 95 percent in September 1942 to 50 percent in February 1943, for members of the Agrarian Party from 95 percent to 46 percent, and for members of the Social Democratic Party from 65 percent to 19 percent.[59]

On February 3, 1943, the Finnish leadership decided to seek a separate peace, albeit one that would not endanger its critical economic (and other) ties with Germany. Members of the Finnish government discussed reestablishing the 1939 border, although no official approach to the Soviets was made.[60] The top leadership agreed that it would be willing to sacrifice Eastern Karelia to achieve peace, if need be, although this decision was not communicated to the Soviets, nor was it debated in the Finnish parliament.[61] A major reason for the shift was growing Finnish concern about the course of the German–Soviet war, highlighted by the Soviet victory at Stalingrad in late January and early February 1943.[62]

The Soviet Union had, since the dark days of August 1941, grown its war aims vis-à-vis Finland. In December 1941, Stalin told visiting British Foreign Secretary Anthony Eden that the Soviet Union demanded the restoration of the 1940 border, acquisition of the nickel-rich Pechenga area, rights to military bases in Finland, a defense pact with Finland, and reparations. Rumors also arose, spreading from Stockholm to Helsinki, that Stalin sought regime change in Finland, although elsewhere it appeared that Stalin was more interested in subjugating the Baltic States than Finland. The December 1941 terms were more or less restated in March 1943 to American representatives, with the addition that the Finnish army be reduced to peacetime strength. The same position was reiterated at the December 1943 Teheran conference.[63]

The Finns continued to observe with concern the slide in Axis military fortunes throughout 1943, including the Soviet victory at the titanic battle of Kursk in July, the Western landing at Sicily, and Mussolini's fall from power. Contact was made between Helsinki and Moscow in July, and the Finns suggested peace essentially on the basis of the 1939 borders. The Soviets rejected this offer out of hand.[64] At this stage of the war, some elements of Finnish society opposed the idea of a separate peace, doubting that any peace would endure.[65]

Matters worsened for the Finns in January 1944. The Soviets broke through the blockade around Leningrad, pushing the Germans back some 200 kilometers, threatening Germany's connection to Finland. The President and Prime Minister themselves agreed to settle on the 1940 border, although they had their doubts about public support for such a settlement. The Soviet negotiating position was at this point quite fluid. Stalin seemed to indicate at the Teheran conference with Churchill and Roosevelt in December 1943 that he was willing to accept a limited outcome with Finland, but a secret Soviet document drawn up around the same time called for the brutal military occupation of Finland at war's end. On February 21, the Soviets established preconditions for negotiations, including severing relations with Germany, interning German forces, restoring the 1940 border, and returning all Soviet POWs. The Finnish government, with the support of the parliament, rejected the preconditions but supported continuing dialogue. In talks in late March, Molotov refused to reduce the preconditions, making the information proposition argument that, "I don't understand why we should make concessions to you. Germany has already lost this war, and you are allies of Germany, so you can just accept a position that befits a defeated country." The only concession Molotov offered was that German forces could be expelled rather than interned, although he further demanded the demobilization of the Finnish military. The Finns rejected the Soviet terms, in part because they provided no assurance that the Soviets would not eventually annihilate Finland. The Finnish president fretted that, "These conditions will destroy our independence."[66]

Domestic politics played a role in the Finnish rejection of Soviet terms. Väinö Tanner, a leading Social Democrat and member of the ruling government, believed that any exit strategy from the war must be broadly popular. At this juncture, however, there was broad dissatisfaction with the Soviet terms both because they were seen as too harsh, and because some did not want to make a separate peace and abandon Finland's ally, Germany.[67] Interestingly, this effect of domestic forces prolonging war is opposite to the domestic politics proposition that, especially in democratic settings, war fatigue will hasten war termination. Popular opposition to swift war termination is especially surprising considering that the Finnish population was suffering economically, with escalating food shortages in particular.[68]

Finnish military fortunes continued to deteriorate in the months to follow. The Soviets launched a major offensive in June 1944, advancing quickly in the face of Finnish military inferiority and, in some cases, panic. Having learned from their tactical mistakes in the Winter War, the Red Army was this time able to capture Viipuri, suffering far fewer losses than it had in 1939–40. The Finns soon evacuated Eastern Karelia. Finnish lines stabilized in mid-June, and Germany sent additional troops in support. However, in exchange for this support, Germany in June extracted from the Finnish president a written commitment that Finland would not make a separate peace with the Soviet Union.[69]

The Soviet offensive came to a halt by the end of June in an area north of Viipuri, due to the strengthening of Finnish defenses and the need for Soviet resources to be devoted to the offensive against German forces in Byelorussia. The last major battle of the war took place at Ilomantsi from July 30–August 9. The Finnish victory there ended the Soviet offensive into Finland and persuaded the Soviets to give up their demand for Finland's unconditional surrender. The door to a settlement at last opened.[70] Around this time, in late July, Ryti stepped down as president and was replaced by Mannerheim. This move was seen within Finland as necessary to make peace with the Soviet Union since the Finnish commitment to Germany was in the form of a letter from Ryti to the Berlin government, and therefore binding on Ryti but not on any successor. Mannerheim was also widely respected as the former Commander in Chief, and he could make peace moves without suffering domestic political attacks.[71]

Peace talks began again in late August. On August 29, the Soviet Union communicated new, more lenient terms, agreeing to receive a Finnish delegation only under the conditions that Finland cut its ties with Germany and evict German troops. This constituted a reduction in demands since the Soviets no longer demanded surrender. The Finnish parliament agreed to Soviet terms for negotiations, and the two sides agreed on a ceasefire, starting on September 5.[72]

Negotiations began on September 14. Soviet demands were more extensive than they had been earlier in the year. They now demanded not only the restoration of the 1940 border, the exit of German forces from Finland, the annexation of Pechenga, war reparations, and the demobilization of the Finnish army, but now also the lease of the Porkkala promontory in southern Finland, the acceptance of Soviet intervention in Finnish domestic affairs, and Finnish assistance in the punishment of war criminals. The Porkkala demand was especially troubling to the Finns, as that area was less than twenty kilometers from Helsinki. The Soviets wanted it because coastal gun emplacements there helped them secure the Gulf of Finland from naval threats. Eventually, the size of the war reparation demand was reduced and the two sides agreed to terms on September 19 (figure 7.1 describes territorial exchanges of the peace settlement).[73]

War-termination behavior in the Continuation War demonstrates the importance of information. When the war was going badly in the initial months, Stalin offered concessions, which Finland in turn rejected because of its confidence in eventual Soviet defeat.[74] As the tide of war turned, the Finns shifted towards making concessions while the Soviets raised their demands. Peace became more likely as the summer 1944 Soviet offensive bogged down a bit, and more pressing Soviet needs elsewhere pushed them to start making concessions.

There were elements demonstrating the importance of commitment credibility, as well. Finland saw the war as offering the opportunity to solve the problem of an enduring Soviet threat by effecting regime change in Moscow. The Finns also explored other solutions to the commitment problem. When the United States urged Finland to accept Stalin's August 1941 peace offer, the Finns inquired whether the U.S. or Britain might be able to offer some guarantees against the possible Soviet violation of a peace agreement.[75] Notably, the very territorial concessions that the Soviets demanded were intended to help alleviate the credible commitment problem by improving Soviet border security. From the Soviet perspective, Finland had reneged on the agreement ending the Winter War by allying with Germany and preparing for war. The Soviets demanded Finnish demobilization to neuter the Finnish offensive threat, as their concern was that Finland might rejoin Germany before the latter had been completely defeated. This was made apparent in an exchange between Molotov and Paasikivi during peace talks on March 27, 1944:

Mr. Molotov: As long as the World War lasts, the Finnish Army must [demobilize and] have its peacetime strength.

Mr. Paasikivi: Why so? Once the peace treaty has been signed, we will not fight with anybody.

Mr. Molotov: But the Soviet Union continues its war against Germany, whereas Finland is no longer at war.

. . .

Mr. Paasikivi: Do you really believe that we will attack you immediately after the peace treaty has been signed?

Mr. Molotov: Our security policy demands the demobilization of the Finnish armed forces.[76]

The territorial demands were intended to reduce the chances of Finnish violation of any war-ending agreement. Acquiring the Porkkala promontory both gave the Soviets greater control over the Gulf of Finland, directly improving the naval posture of the Soviet navy in the Baltic Sea and improving the defenses of Leningrad, and put the Soviets in close striking range to Helsinki, posing a direct threat to the Finnish capital in the event of another war.[77] The fear of Finnish commitments being incredible was an important part of the Soviet desire for other territorial acquisitions as well. When Paasikivi offered the economically important Petsamo area for the strategically important Hanko and Northern Karelia areas in the 1944 negotiations, Molotov replied, "We do not agree to that. Three wars in twenty-five years is really too much. . . . We cannot tolerate that Finland every seven or eight years attacks us."[78]

As forecast by the theory, the fear of rising costs of fighting pushed Stalin to accept a limited war outcome with Finland, rather than pursue absolute victory. It is possible that the successful D-Day landings of June 1944 encouraged Stalin to settle with Finland quickly so as to permit a rapid march on Berlin.[79] Further, part of the limited war arrangement was the commitment by Finland to use its own military forces to expel the hundreds of thousands of German troops stationed in Finnish territory. This the Finns did, at the expense of some 1,000 Finnish dead and 3,000 wounded, thereby further freeing up Soviet resources for the drive to Berlin, as well as eliminating any possibility of renewed Finnish–German cooperation.[80] Moscow also saw that imposing foreign-imposed regime change on Finland might be prohibitively costly, because the Finnish Communists were small in number and weak by 1944.[81]

The theory explains the interplay of information and commitment dynamics during the Continuation War. The preferences of the two sides for various war settlements is well-explained by commitment concerns. Finland initially sought foreign-imposed regime change to eliminate permanently their untrustworthy Bolshevik neighbor. The Soviets desired a permanent solution to Finnish treachery. The flow of information from combat eventually convinced both sides that solving their commitment problems would be prohibitively costly, for the Finns because the tide of the larger German–Soviet war (and the Finnish role in it) eventually turned, and for the Soviets because of other pressing demands in the larger war, especially Stalin's desire to crush Hitler quickly and decisively without distraction by the Finnish sideshow. Moscow's willingness to accept the 1944 limited outcome was boosted by its recognition that the territorial exchanges in this settlement would provide a partial solution to the commitment problem.

FINLAND, THE SOVIET UNION, AND THE EBB AND FLOW OF WAR

Finnish–Soviet relations from 1939–44 were defined by the surge and recession of the tides of war. Each side unsuccessfully sought to destroy the other. Both eventually accepted coexistence. These appetites for destruction were tamed by the flow of information from combat and international diplomacy, and on Moscow's side they were sated by the acquisition of strategic territory guarding the approaches to the Soviet northwest. Information does not always play this prominent a role, however. The next chapter examines a war in which a steady flow of information failed to prevent a fight to the bloody finish.

CHAPTER EIGHT

The American Civil War

> We must free the slaves or be ourselves subdued.
> —Abraham Lincoln, July 1862

> The war came and now it must go on till the last man of this
> generation falls in his tracks, and his children seize his
> musket and fight our battle.
> —Jefferson Davis, July 1864

> Will we ever awake from this hideous nightmare?
> —Mary Lincoln, December 1863

THE CIVIL WAR IS THE SINGLE MOST IMPORTANT event in American history since the Revolutionary War. In December 1860, several Southern states seceded from the United States of America (the Union), aiming to avoid federal intrusion into state-recognized rights of whites to own individuals of African descent as slaves. These seceding states formed the Confederate States of America (CSA) in early 1861. Abraham Lincoln was elected president of the Union in November 1860, taking office the following March. During his presidential campaign he had reaffirmed the rights of southern states to allow their citizens to own slaves, although he vehemently denied the existence of any right to secede. The secession dispute escalated to violence in April 1861 when Southern forces attacked the Union's Fort Sumter located in South Carolina, a slave state. Full-scale war soon broke out. The conflict raged for four years across much of the pre-secession United States, with major battles occurring as far north as Pennsylvania, as far south as Georgia, and as far west as Louisiana. More than 620,000 soldiers on both sides died (2 percent of the 1860 U.S. population) before the secession was ultimately crushed, the Union restored, and slavery banned under the thirteenth amendment to the U.S. constitution.

Although carefully pored over by historians, the Civil War has oddly been understudied by conflict scholars, perhaps because students of interstate war view it as a civil conflict, and students of civil conflict tend to focus on the post-1945 period. I examine it here to demonstrate that the theory developed in chapters 2 and 3 can apply to civil as well as international conflicts.[1] What were the determinants of war-termination dynamics during the conflict? Did information dynamics affect intrawar negotiations or the war's outcome? Did commitment concerns have significant effects? Why did the war drag on for so long?

The Civil War is perhaps the strongest evidence in this book that information factors alone comprise an incomplete explanation of war-termination behavior. Despite the steady flow of information provided by four years of battlefield carnage, the two sides almost never budged from their war-termination offers. This intransigence was driven by commitment fears. The Union feared that southern states could not credibly commit to avoid making greater demands following a limited settlement, especially if such a settlement undermined Northern military power by requiring the revocation of the Emancipation Proclamation. Somewhat relatedly, the Union government in Washington was also concerned about the commitment credibility of Northern states within the Union, as permitting secession of the Southern states might encourage Northern states to secede, causing the entire Union to unravel.

Credible commitment fears played a more nuanced role in the South. The CSA strategy was to prevent Union absolute victory, namely the destruction of the Confederate Army and/or the Union occupation of the South, and impose high enough costs on the Union to force Lincoln to accept secession as the only way to stop the bloodshed. So, an important part of the CSA strategy involved information, namely the CSA ability to send credible signals about its military strength and its ability to inflict costs on the Union without itself suffering military exhaustion.

If information alone could explain CSA behavior, then we would observe the CSA making a range of war-termination offers throughout the war as the fortunes of war ebbed and flowed. These offers might range from CSA independence to the southern States returning to the Union but with constitutional guarantees of state slavery rights to a return to the Union and the abolition of slavery, and everything in between. However, commitment fears truncated the CSA bargaining space. The CSA was unwilling to accept any war-termination arrangement short of CSA independence because it feared that Northern politicians, especially radical Republicans, would renege on any moderate deal once the CSA government dissolved. Northern acceptance of CSA independence, after the CSA had demonstrated on the battlefield that Northern conquest of the CSA would be impossible or at least prohibitively costly, would be the only reasonable means of assuring that the Union would accept the sovereignty of southern states over matters such as slavery. The inability of the North to commit credibly to a moderate deal short of CSA sovereignty made that whole range of moderate options unacceptable to the CSA. CSA credible commitment fears forced the CSA to fight as long as the Union refused to accept CSA independence. Union credible commitment fears forced them to fight as long as the CSA insisted on independence. The resulting collision produced one of the world's bloodiest wars in the century framed by Napoleon's final defeat in 1815 and the outbreak of World War I in 1914.

BATTLES, INFORMATION, AND THE AMERICAN CIVIL WAR

When the American Civil War broke out, there were significant differences in the two sides' estimations of the relative balance of power. Each side entered the war expecting swift victory. In one sense, then, the war began under conditions consistent with an information-oriented view on the causes of conflict. Southerners forecast that the merchants of the north had no stomach for war. Former governor of Virginia Henry Wise boasted, "Let brave men advance with flint locks and old-fashioned bayonets, on the popinjays of Northern cities . . . and he would answer for it with his life, that [sic] the Yankees would break and run." A North Carolinian put it more colorfully, "Just throw three or four shells among those blue-bellied Yankees and they'll scatter like sheep."[2] The North was similarly confident. Secretary of State William Seward thought war would be over in two short months, writing on war's eve that "there would be no serious fighting after all; the South would collapse and everything be serenely adjusted."[3] Hundreds of (Union) Washingtonians eagerly brought picnic baskets and opera glasses to Manassas, Virginia to watch the Battle of Bull Run in July 1861, hoping to catch a glimpse of the excitement before it all ended.[4]

Some at the time saw the war from an information-oriented perspective. The two sides did not agree on who would win, and only fighting could resolve the disagreement. The future Postmaster General Montgomery Blair remarked in January 1861, "The real cause of our trouble arises from the notion generally entertained at the South that the men of the North are inferiors. . . . They will not submit, they say, to mere numbers made up of *Mudsills*, the factory people and shop keepers of North. . . . And it is my deliberate opinion that nothing will do so much to secure real and permanent fraternity between the Sections as a decisive defeat on this field. It will show the Southern people that they wholly mistake the quality of the men they are taught by demagogues to despise."[5] The two sides' initial war aims were straightforward. The CSA demanded Union recognition of its independence, and the Union demanded the return of the CSA member states to the Union. Importantly, President Lincoln did not (initially) demand that Southern states abolish slavery as a condition of reentering the Union.

War initiation aside, was war-termination behavior during the Civil War strictly determined by information flows? Did the belligerents use combat outcomes to update their beliefs about the balance of power, and in turn change their war-termination offers accordingly? More specifically, did concessions generally follow combat defeats, and did raises in war-termination demands generally follow combat victories?

I present two separate empirical analyses of an information-only explanation of war termination in the Civil War, that combat outcomes affected war-termination offers. The first analysis uses more systematic data, combat outcomes for sixty-three battles across the war.[6] Though, as discussed in chapter 4, there are real dangers in using battles in a more quantitative way, these dangers are reduced if the analysis is confined to a single war, and if the combat dynamic in that war can be captured by a focus on conventional battles (as opposed to a war dominated by guerrilla operations). Data on intrawar negotiations come from primary and secondary sources.[7] The unit of analysis was a single month during the war. For each month, the independent variable, combat outcomes, was the total number of battle victories experienced by the Union minus its total number of battle defeats. Using casualty ratios is unfortunately impractical, as there are missing data on casualties on at least one side for many of the battles.[8] The dependent variable is categorical. If there was no change in war-termination offers in a particular month, the variable was coded 0. If the Union demanded more as a condition of terminating the war, the variable was coded 1. If the Union demanded less as a condition of terminating the war, the variable was coded −1. An information approach, namely the information proposition from chapter 2, predicts that these two variables should be positively correlated, that as the Union does better in battle it should demand more, and as it does worse it should demand less.

Figure 8.1 presents these data graphically. The x axis is time (war-months). The combat outcomes are shown on one line, and negotiating behavior on the other. Again, the information perspective would predict that these lines should move together, as combat success should cause the Union to demand more, and combat defeat should cause the Union to demand less. Instead, figure 8.1 shows that these lines do not move in tandem. Although there is substantial movement in combat outcomes, reflecting the many ebbs and flows of the war, there is almost no movement in negotiation behavior. Confederate diplomacy is not shown, but it would indicate an even flatter line, as the CSA made no concessions until it surrendered at war's end.

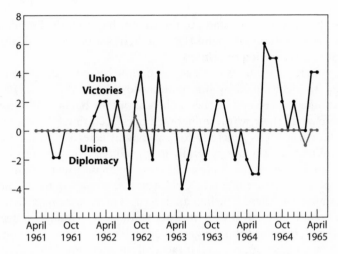

Figure 8.1 Battle Outcomes and Diplomacy—American Civil War

FIVE TURNING POINTS IN THE WAR

The preceding test has some limitations. The cited measures are crude proxies of combat outcomes.[9] It may also be that the quantitative test is too demanding of the information proposition, essentially requiring one side or the other to change its war-termination offer after even minor battles. An easier test for the information proposition would be to focus on the critical turning points in the war. If the information proposition is correct, each side should be most likely to update its estimate of capabilities and change its war-termination offer after combat events recognized as more salient, when fortunes appeared to be at especially low or high tides.

The eminent Civil War historian James McPherson outlined four turning points in the war, to which one might add a fifth turning point of the war's endgame. The five turning points include summer 1862, when CSA counteroffensives in Virginia and the West stopped what appeared to be a forthcoming Union victory; autumn 1862, when Union victories at Antietam and Perryville stopped a CSA invasion of the North and headed off possible European intervention for the CSA; summer/autumn 1863 when Union victories at Gettysburg, Vicksburg, and Chattanooga again seemed to mark a march to ultimate Union victory; summer 1864 when the Confederate victories increased war fatigue in the Union; and fall 1864–spring 1865 when the Union capture of Atlanta and the destruction of CSA General Jubal Early's army in Virginia seemed finally to spell the doom of the CSA.[10] Of these five turning points, there was a change in war-termination offers after only two, in autumn 1862 and in February 1865. Closer examination reveals that neither change in war-termination offers is consistent with the expectations of the information proposition, and that more generally war-termination behavior in the Civil War is not consistent with an information-only perspective on war termination.

Summer 1862: The Confederacy Persists and Attacks

The summer of 1862 saw many engagements between Union and CSA forces in Virginia in particular. The general pattern in June and July was not a long string of tactical victories for the CSA (although some did occur, such as at Malvern Hill). However, Union sentiment became increasingly gloomy, especially after the unsuccessful Peninsula campaign of May and June.[11] In August and early September, things grew worse with the CSA victory at the Second Battle of Bull Run. After hearing the bad news, Lincoln was so despondent he thought to himself that "we may as well stop fighting."[12]

This string of military developments had three important strategic consequences. First, the Union failed to destroy the CSA army. This was critical, because the CSA could win its war aims of sovereignty merely by continuing to exist and maintain its ability to inflict costs on the Union army, whereas the Union needed to crush the CSA in order to accomplish its key war aim of restoring the Union.[13] Second, and relatedly, it was becoming increasingly apparent that the war would not end quickly, and that the Union would require a new round of mobilization and recruitment for the longer haul. Third, Union forces retreated from Virginia back into Maryland, opening the door for a possible strategic CSA offensive. Indeed, the CSA crossed the Potomac River and invaded Maryland on September 4.[14]

The information proposition of chapter 2 might predict that the Union at this point would consider reducing its war aims, both because of a lowered estimate of its relative capability, and because of a raised estimate of the likely costs and duration of the war. However, although morale in the North was low, Lincoln never considered compromise or lowering Union war aims. Indeed, it was during this period that Lincoln first began to consider *raising* Union war aims, as he told his cabinet on July 22 of his general intention to announce the emancipation of the slaves.[15] More generally, rather than cut back on Union war aims, Lincoln focused on trying to right the ship of the Army of the Potomac, dismissing the ineffectual General John Pope and giving sole command to General George McClellan, the Union's great hope for victory and peace.[16] As described in the following section, Lincoln's commitment and other fears blocked him from considering any deal that would allow for secession, the core CSA demand.

Autumn 1862: Antietam

A second turning point in the war occurred later that year in September, when Union forces turned back the CSA invasion of Maryland at the battle of Antietam. The day of the battle, September 17, was the bloodiest single day of combat in American history, worse than D-Day or Pearl Harbor, killing some 6,000. It was soon followed by Lincoln's announcement of the Emancipation Proclamation, decided on September 22, which would liberate slaves in all states in rebellion on January 1, 1863. The Proclamation was immediately recognized as an abrupt and important change in course. Lincoln had had his doubts about emancipation, both regarding whether emancipation was constitutional, and whether it would have political and military costs, perhaps sparking a backlash within the Union army and border states.[17] Indeed, as recently as May 1862, Lincoln had revoked the order of a Union general freeing the slaves within Union control on a handful of islands off the coast of South Carolina.[18] Although the Proclamation itself only applied to slave states and was strictly speaking an emergency war measure rather than something more enduring like a Congressional law or constitutional amendment, it was seen at the time (and later) as a fundamental change in the Union's war aims and the war itself. Soon after the Proclamation was made public, high-level Union officials scoffed at the error the rebels had made, as if to say that had the Southern states remained in the Union peacefully they could have kept slaves for decades, but now the Proclamation made slavery a doomed institution.[19]

At first glance, this episode would seem to be evidence in favor of the information proposition. The Union enjoyed battlefield success at Antietam, and an increase in Union war aims, a change from the initial demand of allowing slavery to persist in the South to the new demand that Southern slaves be emancipated, soon followed. Indeed, Lincoln told his cabinet that he had made a vow to God that if the Union won at Antietam, he would free the slaves.[20]

There are some problems with interpreting this episode as evidence favoring the proposition that new and favorable combat information provided by the Antietam outcome caused a reassessment of the balance of power and in turn an increase in war aims. Even though the outcome of Antietam was a strategic Union victory in that it turned back the CSA invasion of Maryland, Antietam was not a decisive tactical Union victory and did not reveal a substantial Union military advantage. Union victory came in the context of a nearly two-to-one numerical Union advantage over CSA forces, and the outcome was not a rout of the Confederate army.[21] Casualties were even, with the Union suffering 11,657 killed or wounded and the CSA suffering 11,724 killed or wounded.[22] Lincoln at the time was not terribly bullish about the future, nor was he terribly impressed with the performance of the Union Army. After Antietam, he told the cabinet of his desire to free the slaves, but cautioned, "I wish it were a better time. I wish that we were in a better condition. The action of the army against the rebels has not been quite what I should have best liked."[23] Secretary of the Navy Gideon Welles was also pessimistic about the course of the war, writing in his diary just after Antietam that, "A favorable termination of this terrible conflict seems more remote with every moment."[24]

In fact, the motivation of the Emancipation Proclamation was not a reflection of Lincoln's new post-Antietam confidence in Union fighting abilities, but rather the opposite, his concerns about the future course of the war. Lincoln recognized that the war was far from won and that the Union suffered important military deficiencies. He hoped the Emancipation Proclamation would boost Union fighting power. Specifically, he hoped that the Proclamation would increase Union capabilities by encouraging Southern blacks to join the Union army and fight for their freedom. Liberal Republicans such as Senator Charles Sumner, Secretary of War Simon Cameron, and Secretary of the Treasury Salmon Chase had made this argument in a number of forms as early as July 1861, that the slaves should somehow be directly incorporated into the Union war effort.[25] The black abolitionist Frederick Douglass had long argued for the inclusion of blacks into the Union war effort, both as necessary for Union victory and as a critical step towards legitimizing black citizenship.[26]

Although Lincoln rejected the idea in 1861, by the following year events had forced him to reconsider. In early spring 1862, he was encouraging slave states to embrace voluntary emancipation, recommending to Congress that the federal government offer financial aid to any state taking such an action.[27] As noted, in the summer of 1862, the Union suffered a string of battlefield disappointments, and in vain battlefield commanders (McClellan in particular) demanded more troops to defeat the enemy.[28] Sumner saw emancipation as being a solution, telling Lincoln on July 4, 1862 that, "You need more men, not only at the North, but at the South, in the rear of the rebels: you need the slaves."[29]

By late summer 1862, Lincoln was coming around to Sumner's point of view. Lincoln began to see more clearly the shortcomings of the Union army when he reviewed Union troops at Harrison's Landing in early July. He also saw that emancipation of the slaves would be one way to shift the balance of power, both because it might attract blacks to support the Union cause, and because it might make slaves less willing to support the Confederate war effort. Although slaves were not (yet) serving in the Confederate Army, Lincoln saw that their labor was put to great use by the CSA, as field laborers, domestic servants, attendants for Confederate armies, waiters, and as construction laborers building Confederate fortifications and entrenchments.[30] In addressing border state representatives on July 12, he urged them to support (gradual) emancipation not on the grounds that battlefield successes now allowed the Union to raise its war aims, but rather because emancipation would bring victory quicker. He told them that "if you all had voted for the resolution of gradual emancipation last March, the war would now be substantially ended. . . . How much better for you, and for your people, to take the step which, at once, shortens the war."[31] Later, in reflection, Lincoln explained that it was the general worsening of the Union's military fortunes that summer that spurred him to embrace emancipation: "It had got to be midsummer 1862. Things had gone on from bad to worse, until I felt that we had reached the end of our rope on the plan of operations we had been pursuing; that we had about played our last card, and must change our tactics, or lose the game. I now determined upon the adoption of the emancipation policy."[32] Indeed, this was just the argument he made in a private informal conversation with two cabinet members on July 13, arguing, as Secretary Welles later recalled, that emancipation "was a military necessity, absolutely essential to the preservation of the Union. We must free the slaves or be ourselves subdued."[33] He made the same argument to the entire cabinet on July 22.[34]

Interestingly, the Emancipation Proclamation may have had a separate effect on the balance of military power during the American Civil War, aside from encouraging Southern blacks to fight for the Union. The CSA placed great faith on the possibility of European (especially British or French) intervention on their side, whether in the form of formal recognition, direct military assistance, or anything in between. By mid-1862, Britain in particular was en route to recognizing the CSA formally. However, the Proclamation served to stave off European aid to the CSA because of European queasiness about slavery. In particular, emancipation encouraged the British cabinet in October to reject a French proposal to intercede in favor of an armistice recognizing Southern independence.[35]

Some, such as Blair and McClellan, feared that the Proclamation might undermine Union capability. They thought that emancipation might encourage border states to abandon the Union's war effort. It might also undermine Union army morale, as perhaps some Union soldiers would not be motivated to fight and die to free the slaves. It might also thwart Union recruitment efforts.[36] Lincoln finessed the first problem by exempting border states and other areas from the Proclamation. The second and third problems turned out not to be significant, as soldiers enlisted and fought on regardless. Even McClellan, who deeply opposed the Proclamation, eventually fell into line.[37]

His comment about his "vow to God" notwithstanding, Lincoln likely did not see the Proclamation as a declaration or reflection of Union military power. Although the Proclamation was an increase in war aims and came after a Union victory, Lincoln was to the contrary concerned that this action would be seen as a sign of weakness rather than strength. As Seward argued (to Lincoln's agreement), "The depression of the public mind, consequent upon our repeated reverses, is so great that I fear the effect of so important a step [as Emancipation]. It may be viewed as the last measure of an exhausted government, a cry for help; the government stretching forth its hands to Ethiopia, instead of Ethiopia stretching forth her hands to the government." Seward suggested that instead Lincoln should wait "until the eagle of victory takes his flight . . . [in order to] hang your proclamation about his neck." Lincoln saw Seward's point as that emancipation would be considered "our last *shriek*, on the retreat," undertaken by a frantic government in its last throes. He feared that Emancipation would be seen by the Northern public as accepting an otherwise undesirable policy as a necessary evil to increase the Union's military power.[38]

Importantly, Lincoln's gambit worked. Emancipation strengthened the ranks of the Union army, as both ex-slaves and Northern blacks became more eager to serve. In total, between 9 and 10 percent of all Union troops during the war were black.[39] In many engagements, African-American troops fought at least as well as if not better than white troops.[40] It also allowed the Union access to the (civilian) labor of some hundreds of thousands of fugitive slaves residing in the North.

Some might reply that the Emancipation Proclamation was driven more by Lincoln's normative beliefs than by strategic considerations, as Lincoln freed the slaves not because of strategic advantages but simply because he thought it was the right thing to do. Although Lincoln certainly thought about the ethical dimensions of slavery, such factors were most likely not predominant in his emancipation decision-making. Indeed, he had been willing to accept slavery in the South from the time of his 1860 presidential campaign up through summer 1862. As discussed in the following, he also seemed to offer in February 1865 a retreat from emancipation if it might end the war. Perhaps most importantly, Lincoln himself around the time he decided for emancipation quite clearly framed it as a strategic decision to save the Union, and that he was motivated first and foremost by the imperative of saving the Union. He wrote on August 22, 1862 in an open letter to newspaperman Horace Greeley, "My paramount object in the struggle *is* to save the Union, and is *not* either to save or destroy slavery. If I could save the Union without freeing *any* slave I would do it, and if I could save it by freeing *all* the slaves I would do it; and if I could save it by freeing some and leaving others alone, I would also do that."[41]

The boost in Union war aims via the Emancipation Proclamation was not caused by Lincoln's newfound confidence in Union fighting capabilities following Antietam. To the contrary, Lincoln undertook this bold step because of his concerns about enduring Union military *weakness*. As for the CSA, it did not see the defeat at Antietam as a signal to lower its war-termination demands. At most, the leadership in Richmond was hopeful that CSA success would have encouraged Union concessions, whereas defeat meant the continuation of fighting.[42]

Summer–Autumn 1863: Great Northern Victories

The Union enjoyed two great victories on July 4, 1863. In the west, General Ulysses S. Grant executed a brilliant campaign in Mississippi, culminating with the capture of the city of Vicksburg. Among other things, this success provided the Union control of the Mississippi river, cleaving the Confederacy in two. Grant perhaps immodestly claimed after the war that "the fate of the Confederacy was sealed when Vicksburg fell." Others have agreed with this assessment. One historian declared that, "The capture of Vicksburg was the most important northern strategic victory of the war." Lincoln recognized that the campaign proved Grant's extraordinary abilities as a commander, a critical revelation given that perhaps the Union's greatest weakness in the early years of war was the incompetent military leadership of generals such as Pope and McClellan.[43] Perhaps the more famous Union success on July 4 was at Gettysburg, Pennsylvania, at which Union forces turned back the sole major Confederate incursion above the Mason–Dixon Line.[44]

The Confederates in mid-July recognized the dark turn of their fortunes provided at Vicksburg and Gettysburg. Lee offered his resignation (it was refused). Southerners saw this as the (to that point) darkest day of the war. The Chief of Confederate Ordinance Josiah Gorgas wrote in his diary at the end of July that, "The Confederacy totters to its destruction."[45]

CSA fortunes improved marginally over the next several weeks. The Union failed to press the advantage sufficiently in Pennsylvania, and the remainder of Lee's army escaped across the Potomac River to safety. However, in early September Union forces under General William Rosecrans captured Knoxville, the heart of union sentiment in east Tennessee, and Chattanooga, a critical Confederate rail center. Hope again dwindled in the Confederacy. CSA President Jefferson Davis wrote in his diary that he was "in the depths of gloom. . . . We are now in the darkest hour of our political existence."[46] The CSA mounted a counterattack, enjoying a battle success near Chattanooga at Chickamauga. However, they failed to dislodge Union forces from Chattanooga itself, and eventually Confederate forces in the area retreated in a rout. By November, a dread for the future had returned to the CSA.[47]

Both a domestic politics and information proposition would predict that at this stage the CSA should start making concessions in hopes of ending the war sooner rather than later, short of absolute defeat. As a domestic politics proposition might claim, the accumulation of casualties and a downturn in military fortunes helped advance pro-peace sentiments in the Confederacy in late 1863, culminating with some pro-peace candidates winning office in the CSA congressional elections of 1863. The CSA's setbacks on the battlefield were coupled with the absence of any indication that assistance from Britain and France was imminent or likely.[48]

But despite these political, military, and international events, Davis did not offer concessions to Lincoln to end the war, in contrast to the forecasts of the information and domestic politics propositions. Davis would not accept any terms requiring the dissolution of the CSA, and for him the CSA must convince the Union that it would continue to fight on and shed Northern blood until CSA independence was accepted. Only after Union military confidence had been dented could the CSA consider entering into talks; accepting negotiations before that point risked signaling CSA weakness to the Union. Davis' thinking is revealed perhaps most clearly in a January 8, 1864 letter to North Carolina Governor Zebulon Vance, pursuant to the latter's suggestion that the Confederacy negotiate. Davis remarked, "the purpose of the enemy [is] to refuse all terms to the South except absolute, unconditional subjugation or extermination. . . . To obtain the sole terms to which you or I could listen, this struggle must continue until the enemy is beaten out of his vain confidence in our subjugation. Then and not till then will it be possible to treat of peace. Till then all tender of terms to the enemy will be received as proof that we are ready for submission, and will encourage him in the atrocious warfare he is waging."[49]

Summer 1864: The Union Nears Exhaustion

Summer 1864 saw a new turn in the war, and the growth of pessimism in the Union. Grant launched a major offensive in Virginia on May 3, entering an area called the Wilderness. The fighting was extremely heavy. By mid-June, the Wilderness campaign left 65,000 Union troops killed, wounded, or missing, some 60 percent of the total casualties inflicted on the Army of the Potomac in the first three years of war.[50] The CSA suffered heavy casualties as well, but the critical problem, again, was that the CSA army was not destroyed, since Lee at Cold Harbor and elsewhere stayed behind his defenses rather than engage openly. Grant failed to capture Petersburg. Sherman's progress towards Atlanta was (at this point) slow. In July, to the surprise of the Union, CSA forces crossed the Potomac, entered Maryland, and marched on Washington, getting as far as the outer defenses at Fort Stevens. When Lincoln himself traveled to the fort to observe the action, he exposed himself to direct fire from CSA riflemen. The rebels were close enough that bullets flew past the President, striking a soldier nearby. Lincoln finally ducked when (future Supreme Court Justice) Captain Oliver Wendell Holmes yelled, "get down, you damn fool, before you get shot!"[51]

The relatively poor Union fortunes in 1864 became a serious domestic political problem for Lincoln. His concern was not so much that CSA forces would likely soon inflict decisive defeat on Union forces, but rather that defeatism amongst the Union public would spread, a growing concern given the impending November presidential elections. Lincoln knew his chances of losing the election were quite real. He told one officer that summer that, "I am going to be beaten, and unless some great change takes place *badly* beaten."[52] Although he won his party's nomination, he faced the possibility of being defeated by the pro-negotiations Democratic nominee, Lincoln's own former commander General McClellan. Henry Raymond, editor of *The New York Times* and chairman of the Republican National Committee, wrote Lincoln on August 22 of the rising tide of political opposition to Lincoln in the Union. "Two special causes are assigned to this great reaction in public sentiment, —the want of military successes, and the impression in some minds, the fear and suspicion in others, that we are not to have peace *in any event* under this administration until Slavery is abandoned. In some way or other the suspicion is widely diffused that we *can* have peace with Union if we would."[53] By August, all, including Lincoln's own political allies, were convinced that he would lose in November.[54] The venerable political kingmaker Thurlow Weed told Lincoln in early August "that his re-election was an impossibility."[55]

Lincoln did hold one card that might save his political career: reducing Union war aims to allow for the continuation of slavery in the South as a means to end the war. Some advocated this avenue as Lincoln's only chance. Taking such an approach would have eliminated the principal political difference between himself and McClellan, as the latter advocated supporting negotiations although specifically rejecting the idea of peace at any price, that is, recognizing the sovereignty of the CSA.[56] This approach should have been attractive to Lincoln, as he had originally embraced emancipation purely strategically, and lowering his war aims in this manner would of course have allowed him to maintain his core value of saving the Union (assuming the CSA accepted his terms). Such a move would be consistent with the information proposition, as it would have been a reduction of war aims after battlefield setbacks. It would also be consistent with the domestic politics hypothesis, that the escalation of casualties in a democracy increases the likelihood the elected leader will offer concessions.

However, Lincoln rejected abandoning emancipation as a way to stop the war and save his presidency. Even facing declining military fortunes and growing domestic political threats, Lincoln refused to revoke the Emancipation Proclamation, because he believed it to be critical to Union military power. He feared that reversing the Proclamation would end the recruitment of blacks to the Union Army, and cause blacks currently serving the Union Army to desert.[57] A critic might speculate that even if revoking Emancipation undermined military power, this concern is irrelevant if such a move also ended the war, removing the (immediate) need for Union military power. However, Lincoln worried that such a concession would shift the balance of power and cause CSA states to insist on independence. In an August 19, 1864 meeting, Lincoln stated that, "There are now between 1 & 200 thousand black men now in the service of the Union. These men will be disbanded [if emancipation were repealed], returned to slavery & we will have to fight two nations instead of one. I have tried it. You cannot concilliate [sic] the South, when the mastery & control of millions of blacks makes them sure of ultimate success. You cannot concilliate [sic] the South, when you place yourself in such a position, that they see they can achieve their independence." Such a strategy would "result in the dismemberment of the Union."[58] In an August 17 letter to a Wisconsin War Democrat, he rejected the possibility of revoking Emancipation before the war had ended, that is, revoking Emancipation while fighting capability was still needed.[59]

Lincoln held fast all summer. He reiterated his war-termination offer demanding both restoration of the Union and the end of slavery in a letter to CSA representatives on July 18, and in private discussion with cabinet members on August 24.[60] The closest he came to wavering on the slavery issue was when he penned an unsent letter on August 17 concluding, "If Jefferson Davis . . . wishes to know what I would do if he were to offer peace and re-union, saying nothing about slavery, let him try me."[61] Lincoln at this time rejected the idea of initiating peace talks with the CSA, even under the condition that the peace talks would require recognition of the supremacy of the U.S. Constitution. Lincoln saw such a tentative move, suggested by the Republican National Committee, as "worse than losing the [November 1864] Presidential contest—it would be ignominiously surrendering it in advance."[62] Indeed, Lincoln's commitment to emancipation seemed if anything to be strengthening. At the Republication convention in Baltimore that summer, Lincoln insisted that the party's 1864 presidential election platform include a plank calling for a constitutional amendment abolishing slavery, ensuring that emancipation would outlast the war and his presidency.[63] In contrast to the information proposition and a domestic politics approach, Lincoln refused to make concessions, even as the fortunes of both his political career and his nation's military were sinking. Lincoln could not bear the loss of the black contribution to Union military power.

Winter 1864–65: The Confederacy Collapses

The war took a decisive and final turn in favor of the Union in the latter half of 1864. The CSA suffered a string of defeats, including the Union's capture of Atlanta, General William Sherman's devastating march across Georgia, and the fall of Fort Fisher in North Carolina, the last CSA seaport. The capture of Fort Fisher was especially crushing to CSA logistics and hopes, termed in hindsight by one former Confederate leader as "one of the greatest disasters which had befallen our Cause from the beginning of the war—not excepting the loss of Vicksburg or Atlanta."[64] The reelection of Lincoln in November was also a heavy blow, as a McClellan victory would have given the CSA hope of a settlement conceding its independence. The information proposition would predict that at this point the CSA would start to consider reducing its war-termination offer, to extract concessions short of the absolute Union victory that appeared to impend.

And yet, the CSA made no concessions on its key issue, independence, even in the hopes of soliciting Union concessions on slavery. Davis had made this quite clear during some preliminary peace talks in July 1864, framing the key issue as "independence or subjugation," and that "I shall at any time be pleased to receive proposals for peace on the basis of our independence. It will be useless to approach me with any other."[65] Interestingly, the CSA might have been willing to entertain terms that included CSA independence *and* emancipation. Like Lincoln, Davis saw emancipation as linked to military power, as in late 1864 when Davis unsuccessfully offered to European governments emancipation of the slaves in the hopes of drawing European intervention into the war.[66] Davis also seemed to allow for the possibility of CSA independence with emancipation in the July 1864 talks, when he remarked that, "We are not fighting for slavery. We are fighting for independence, and that, or extermination, we *will* have."[67]

The window to war termination opened slightly with the break of the new year of 1865. In January, the Northern politician Francis Blair, Sr. traveled in a generally unofficial capacity—although with Lincoln's consent—to Virginia with an unusual peace proposal for Davis. Blair proposed that the CSA and Union unite military forces for the purpose of invading Mexico, in reaction to French interference in Mexican politics, an ostensible violation of the Monroe Doctrine. Davis wrote a letter to Lincoln in response to Blair's proposal that offered nothing but closed no doors. Importantly, he expressed an interest in convening a "conference *with a view to secure peace to the two countries*," that is, a peace that would recognize Confederate independence.[68]

Although Blair's bizarre Mexico suggestion did not bear fruit, it lay the groundwork for further efforts. Soon after his visit, the Union and CSA agreed that CSA representatives would travel to the Union and have a peace parley with Lincoln himself in February at Hampton Roads. This was the only official peace negotiation of the war, and the willingness of Lincoln himself to meet with the CSA representatives offered a very real chance for the CSA to have a new war-termination offer taken seriously. During the negotiations, Lincoln quite surprisingly offered some concessions to the Confederates in return for the restoration of the Union, including reparations in the neighborhood of $400 million. Lincoln also may have opened the door to concession on the slavery issue. According to one participant in the meeting, Lincoln noted that the January 1863 Emancipation Proclamation was a "war measure," and that in his opinion it would cease to be operative once the war ended, although he allowed that the courts might differ on this interpretation. During the meeting, Seward noted that the Thirteenth Amendment, which would abolish slavery, had received the necessary two-thirds vote in the House some days before (the Senate had given two-thirds approval in 1863). He gave the impression that if the CSA laid down its arms, then those former CSA states could return as recognized states in the Union, and as such could block the amendment, as the U.S. Constitution provides that any amendment receiving two-thirds approval by the Senate and House must then receive approval from at least three quarters of state legislatures. Any ten of the thirty-six states in the Union would be able to block the amendment, and the CSA included more than ten states. Lincoln also talked about the possibility of prospective ratification of the Amendment, perhaps taking effect in five years rather than immediately.[69]

However, CSA President Davis refused to discuss any terms that included the restoration of the Union and the demise of the CSA. His instructions to his representatives at Hampton Roads indicated that they were authorized to speak with Lincoln with "the purpose of securing peace to the two countries." Davis may have consented to doomed peace talks as a means of publicly highlighting the Northern demand for unconditional surrender, and demonstrating that the CSA's back was against the wall, thereby inspiring the Southern public to fight on.[70] In other words, both Lincoln and Davis used war-termination diplomacy to increase military power, with Lincoln using emancipation to inspire blacks to fight for the Union, and Davis using failed peace talks to boost Southern morale.[71]

The information environment at the time makes Davis' obstinacy puzzling. The CSA had endured a string of combat defeats, and its resources were low and dwindling. Union forces were advancing under the superior generalship of officers like Grant, Sheridan, and Sherman, having abandoned the chronically timid McClellan. Indeed, the war did end with the virtually unconditional surrender of the CSA some two months later at Appomattox, bringing with it the national abolition of slavery under the (ratified) Thirteenth Amendment. The information proposition would predict that Davis should have at least considered negotiating with Lincoln at Hampton Roads, perhaps at least attempting to extract more concessions, such as stronger guarantees of states' rights over slavery or other issues, a commitment not to imprison CSA political or military leaders, or greater financial compensation. Instead, Davis rejected the peace opening, and attempted to reinvigorate the Southern war effort. One historian expressed the Hampton Roads puzzle as such: "Faced with almost certain defeat, anyhow, Confederates might come out of defeat with much better terms by negotiating now than if they continued on and forced the North to beat them into definitive subjugation when they no longer had anything, even surrender, with which to bargain."[72]

CREDIBLE COMMITMENTS

The Civil War presents a puzzle for an information-only perspective on war termination. Both more quantitative examination of the evidence and closer analysis of key turning points in the war reveal essentially no connection between combat outcomes and war-termination diplomacy, as defeats did not cause concessions, and victories generally did not encourage greater demands. Instead, each side clung to its core demands, the Union calling for restoration and the CSA calling for independence. Changes in the tides of war were not matched by changes in war-termination behavior. The sole exception might be the Emancipation Proclamation following the Union's victory at Antietam which increased Union demands. However, closer examination of this episode reveals that the battle was not interpreted by Lincoln as evidence of Union military superiority, and the Proclamation was driven by concerns about Union military weakness rather than confidence in Union military strength.

The commitment proposition can help explain this lack of connection between combat outcomes and war-termination offers. On the Union side, Lincoln maintained great concern over what the future would hold if concessions were made to the CSA. That is, he doubted the credibility of a CSA commitment to adhere to a deal that included Union concessions. Before the war, commitment concerns colored Lincoln's thinking. Specifically, in late 1860 several Congressmen floated the so-called Crittenden Compromise as a last ditch effort to avoid secession and war. It called for a series of constitutional amendments that would guarantee slavery in southern states. However, Lincoln was concerned that making this concession in response to a threat of secession would set a dangerous precedent, encouraging Southerners to wield the threat of secession again to renege on the terms of the Crittenden Compromise and extract more concessions. Certainly, the threat of secession was a familiar tool to Southerners. They had wielded it as a domestic political tool through the 1850s.[73] In December 1860, to a compromise-oriented Missouri newspaper editor, Lincoln described his take on the Crittenden Compromise: "I am not at liberty to shift my ground—that is out of the question. . . . The secessionists, *per se* believing they had alarmed me, would clamor all the louder."[74] In a reply the following month to Congressman James Hale, one of the supporters of the Compromise, Lincoln noted that if this concession was made, "They will repeat the experiment upon us *ad libitum*. A year will not pass, till we shall have to take Cuba as a condition upon which they will stay in the Union."[75] Many Southerners indeed looked to grow the slave empire. On the eve of the attack on Fort Sumter, a former governor of South Carolina declared, "Mexico and Cuba are ready, now, to fall into our hands, and before two years have passed, with or without the Border States, we shall count twenty millions. . . . Our territory will extend from the Atlantic to the Pacific, and as far south as the Isthmus. We are founding, sir, an empire that will be able to defy all Europe—one grander than the world has seen since the age of Pericles!"[76]

Later, an additional commitment concern emerged. During the dark summer of 1864, some suggested to Lincoln that he consider conceding on slavery (although not CSA independence) in the hopes that this might make peace possible. For Lincoln, the problem was that making this concession would create a commitment problem, as it would cause blacks to abandon the Union cause, decisively swinging the military balance against the Union, and thereby allow the CSA to harden its bargaining position and pursue independence) through war. Lincoln wrote in an August 17, 1864 letter that if emancipation were repealed,

All recruiting of colored men would instantly cease, and all colored men now in our service, would instantly desert us. And rightfully too. Why should they give their lives for us, with full notice of our purpose to betray them? Drive back to the support of the rebellion the physical force which the colored people now give, and promise us, and neither the present, nor any coming administration, *can* save the Union. Take from us, and give to the enemy, the hundred and thirty, forty, or fifty thousand colored persons now serving us as soldiers, seamen, and laborers, and we can not longer maintain the contest.[77]

That is, Lincoln was especially strongly motivated to stand by emancipation because this was a good the two sides were bargaining over that directly affected the military balance, as was the case for POWs in the Korean War and strategic territory in the wars between Finland and the Soviet Union.

There were also commitment concerns on the CSA side. At least part of Davis' motivation not to concede on CSA independence, even in the dark days of early 1865, was worry over whether the North would adhere to a war-ending agreement. The war itself was caused in part by commitment concerns, as Southerners greatly feared and opposed the election of the Republican Lincoln, despite his many statements that he was not an abolitionist. Prior to the late 1850s, southern states had felt more assured that their slavery rights would not be threatened because of a balance in the Union between free and slave states, affording each side a veto in the Senate over highly contentious issues such as anti-slavery amendments to the constitution. The balance in the Senate gave the South a tool to enforce the verbal Northern commitment not to pursue abolition. This balance, and thereby the credibility of the North's commitment, was perceived to be deeply threatened in 1858, when the Congress refused to admit Kansas as a slave state to balance the 1850 admission of California as a free state.[78]

This fear became entrenched after the Emancipation Proclamation, seen by Southerners as a reversal of Lincoln's prewar and wartime declarations that he would not free the slaves, and as vindication of Southern suspicions that earlier statements of moderation issued by Lincoln and the Union government could not be trusted. In his January 12, 1863 speech to the Confederate Congress, Davis declared that the Emancipation Proclamation "affords to our whole people the complete and crowning proof of the true nature of the designs of the party which elevated to power the present occupant of the Presidential chair at Washington and which sought to conceal its purpose by every variety of artful device and by the perfidious use of the most solemn and repeated pledges on every possible occasion."[79]

CSA commitment concerns were driven by observations about Union domestic politics, as well as doubts about Lincoln's word. Union violations of civil liberties during the war moved Davis to doubt that the North could be trusted to respect individual freedoms in the South if the war

ended with the abandonment of CSA sovereignty.[80] Even if Lincoln ultimately promised and genuinely intended moderate terms of peace settlement, Davis and the CSA feared that Northern Radicals might take over
any reconstruction process and impose a very harsh set of peace terms on
the South, pushing aside Lincoln's past promises of moderation.[81] Blair,
on an unofficial mission from the Union, told Davis in January 1865 that
"Mr. Lincoln did not sympathize with the radical men who desired the
devastation and subjugation of the Southern States; but that he was unable to control the extreme party which now had great power in the Congress and would at the next session have still more."[82] James Gilmore,
another peace emissary, had made a similar point to Lincoln some six
months earlier.[83]

Certainly, splits in Northern opinion about postwar reconstruction of
the South emerged in the months following the Emancipation Proclamation. Lincoln's relatively moderate Proclamation of Amnesty and Reconstruction issued on December 8, 1863 demonstrated the growing cleav-
ages in the North. This policy allowed that a seceding state could
reacquire its representation in Washington if 10 percent of its voting population made an oath of loyalty to the Union and agreed to accept emancipation, and if the state's constitution was amended to abolish slavery.
However, the new state constitution could enact temporary measures in
the transition to abolition, and no requirements were declared that post-
slavery states make provisions for black suffrage or equality before the
law.[84] Northern Radical Republicans soon criticized what became known
as the Ten Percent Plan, in part because they feared its demands were
too lenient, and would allow Southerners to renege on their war-ending
commitments.

Other lightning rods for Union disagreement arose beyond the Ten Percent Plan. Northern radicals and others voiced growing concern about
the emerging post-secession government in Louisiana. The new system
seemed to be a disturbing example of a post-secession state offering insufficient protection of, and assistance to, blacks.[85] As Senator Jacob Howard
declared in the Senate:

> . . . we shall be acting a very childish and very foolish part to demand
> no other security from the leaders of the rebellion than a promise, on
> their already violated oath, that hereafter they will support the Consti-
> tution of the United States. Sir, I will never be wheedled and cheated in
> this way. . . . the people of the North are not such fools as to fight
> through such a war as this . . . and then turn around and say to the
> traitors, 'All you have to do is to come back into the councils of the
> nation and take an oath that henceforth you will be true to the Govern-
> ment.' Sir, it would be simple imbecility, folly; and for one I will

never, whatever may be the cost or the consequences of this war, or however long it may continue, be consciously guilty of such weakness and such folly.[86]

The Radicals offered an alternative in July 1864, the Wade–Davis Plan, which declared that Reconstruction in a state could not begin until a majority of white males pledged loyalty to the Union, required that only those who took the loyalty oath could vote on a post-slavery state constitution, and allowed for some guarantees of equality before the law for blacks. Lincoln vetoed the bill, although it enjoyed almost complete support from Republicans in Congress. Indeed, the extremely inflammatory Wade–Davis manifesto, published in August, sharply opposed Lincoln's veto in the most extravagant terms, claiming among other things that Lincoln's veto was motivated by a desire to hold the "electoral votes of the rebel States at the dictation of his personal ambition." It included a thinly veiled threat: "If he wishes our support he must confine himself to his executive duties—to obey and to execute, not make the laws—to suppress by arms armed Rebellion, and leave political reörganization to Congress."[87] That fall, after Lincoln's presidential prospects improved dramatically following the capture of Atlanta, the radicals fell in line to support Lincoln's reelection, with the ultimate aim to guide Lincoln's war policies from within towards seeking abolition and more extreme war aims, rather than attack Lincoln's perceived moderation from without.[88]

More and more Radicals began to clamor for an even more ambitious Reconstruction, calling for black education, black suffrage, and land reform to give land to ex-slaves. An example of such actions included General William Sherman's Special Field Order Number 15, which established the Georgia and southern South Carolina coastal areas as zones for black settlement, allowing that each black family in the region be granted forty acres of land and a mule.[89] The inability of Lincoln to commit to a moderate reconstruction in the context of these domestic political problems contributed to the failure of the February 1865 Hampton Roads Conference. One CSA attendee at the conference observed later that Lincoln and Seward seemed "terribly afraid of their constituents."[90] Davis was so unconvinced of Lincoln's abilities to implement moderate promises that he doubted the $400 million compensation pledge had ever been made at Hampton Roads (Davis did not personally attend the conference), griping that "nothing could be more absurd" than the compensation story since "it would have been idle if he had made it because he had no power to fulfil [sic] it."[91]

Northerners recognized that CSA fear of Union commitment credibility was the key barrier to Confederate willingness to accept an end to their sovereignty as part of a war-ending deal. In summer 1864, Former Secretary of State Jeremiah Black mused on possible solutions that might both preserve the Union and alleviate CSA commitment fears: "[Self-government for the CSA] does not mean the separate nationality of the South. They are not opposed to the federal *Government* (using the word government in the sense of the Constitution and laws). . . . They struck for independence because it was the simplest and readiest means of saving the rights of the States from violation. . . . If they could now have some absolutely certain guarantee that the same end might be accomplished in the federal Union they are not so perverse as to fight an army of half a million and expose their country to desolation for a punctilio."[92] When Blair proposed his Mexico gambit to Davis in January 1865, he held out that driving France from Mexico might enable the annexation of Mexican territory, which would in turn restore the "Equipoise" of North and South.[93] Such a restoration of balance between slave and free states within the Union towards a pre–Civil War (or pre-1850) environment might satisfy the CSA states that its prerogatives would remain respected.

The Confederate fear of the Union expanding its war aims after war's end proved to be Lincoln's personal undoing. John Wilkes Booth interpreted a Lincoln speech on reconstruction given on April 11, 1865 as a move towards radical changes in the South. Booth told an associate after hearing the speech, "That means nigger citizenship. Now, by God, I'll put him through. That is the last speech he will ever make."[94] Booth made good on his oath, fatally shooting Lincoln at Ford's Theater in Washington three days later, a week after Lee had surrendered his armies to Grant in the Virginia village of Appomattox Courthouse.

ALTERNATE EXPLANATIONS

Are there other possible explanations of war-termination behavior during the Civil War? Some have argued that reputation concerns can affect war-termination behavior during civil wars. Specifically, in civil wars, the national government may be concerned that making concessions to secessionists will give it a reputation for weakness among other substate groups, encouraging them to attempt secession, as well.[95] This is to some degree also a credible commitment problem, but the difference is that here the question is whether the commitment of the subnational units to stay in the country is credible, whereas the argument laid out in chapter 3 is about whether the commitment of the belligerent to adhere to the terms of the agreement is credible.

For the Union during the American Civil War, the problem was not exactly that each state or concentrated ethnic group would demand more autonomy, but rather that secession would undermine the core legal foundation of the Union, unraveling its entire political structure. The American constitution of 1787 allowed for a relatively weak federal government and comparatively powerful states, but importantly it made no provisions for secession. Taking the next step and permitting secession would undermine the viability of the Constitution, and perhaps cause more individual states to secede and abandon the Union. President James Buchanan, who left office just before the war began, expressed his concerns in December 1860 that if secession was deemed legitimate, the Union would become "a rope of sand," and "our thirty-three States may resolve themselves into as many petty, jarring, and hostile republics. . . . By such a dread catastrophe the hopes of the friends of freedom throughout the world would be destroyed."[96]

This concern was an important part of Lincoln's opposition to secession, the belief that acceptance of secession would destroy the Union. For him, secession was the "essence of anarchy." Majoritarian rule must reject secession. The heart of the Union cause "is the necessity of proving that popular government is not an absurdity. We must settle this question now, whether in a free government the minority have the right to break up the government whenever they choose."[97] Lincoln was also concerned about encouraging future secession attempts. In his message to Congress on July 4, 1861, he declared, "Again, if one State may secede, so may another. . . . If we now recognize this doctrine, by allowing the seceders to go in peace, it is difficult to see what we can do, if others choose to go, or to extort terms upon which they will promise to remain."[98]

A second alternative explanation for war-termination behavior concerns domestic politics. Of course, in some sense all aspects of the American Civil War are about domestic politics. A narrower cut is to examine how domestic political factors affected the war-termination offers of the two sides. There is the specific hypothesis that escalating casualties will erode popular support for a war, and, especially in belligerents with elected governments, push leaders to make concessions in the hope of ending the war.

Although casualties accumulated steadily and the tides of fortune shifted back and forth throughout the war, domestic politics were never a strong enough factor to affect war-termination demands. Lincoln supported the Emancipation Proclamation, despite his concerns about its lack of popularity in the North. Indeed, its announcement in the North encouraged the Democratic opposition, and may have led to some Republican losses in the 1862 midterm elections.[99]

Probably the most critical phase was the summer of 1864. As noted, the Union's war effort had stalled, and there was growing discontent in the north, culminating with the Democratic nomination of McClellan. During that summer, Lincoln expected to lose to McClellan in the coming election. All expected Lincoln's defeat. Domestic politics would predict that Lincoln might have sought accommodation with the CSA as a means of undercutting the Democratic threat and improve his chances of remaining in office. The information proposition might make a similar prediction in particular given a string of recent Union military failures, including the CSA parrying the Union advance on Atlanta through June and July, an advance of CSA forces on Washington to within five miles of the White House in early July, a separate advance across the Mason–Dixon Line into Pennsylvania, and failure in the Union siege of Petersburg (including the infamous Battle of the Crater). The information proposition and a domestic politics interpretation intertwine, as illustrated by the statement of an editorial in one Democratic newspaper at the time: "If nothing else would impress upon the people the absolute necessity of stopping this war, its utter failure to accomplish any results would be sufficient."[100]

Yet, Lincoln would not budge. He refused to back down from his core demand of restoring the Union, even though doing so threatened to oust him from office. The President called in mid-July for an additional half million recruits, knowing that doing so would hurt his electoral chances.[101] By his thinking, dominated by a view of the legal indivisibility of the Union, an armistice leading to likely acceptance of secession would doom the Union, so given his likely defeat and ouster from office in early 1865, his only course of action was to try to win a decisive victory and save the Union before McClellan took office and destroyed it. On August 23, he wrote a private letter conceding that "it seems exceedingly probable that this Administration will not be re-elected. Then it will be my duty to so co-operate with the President elect, as to save the Union between the election and the inauguration; as he will have secured his election on such ground that he can not possibly save it afterwards." He planned to tell McClellan upon the latter's victory: "Now let us together, you with your influence and I with all the executive power of the Government, try to save the country. You raise as many troops as you possibly can for this final trial, and I will devote all my energies to assisting and finishing the war."[102]

ENDING THE LONG NATIONAL NIGHTMARE

The bloody inferno of the American Civil War was fated to drag on until the Confederate Army was completely crushed or the Union cracked under the strain and flew apart. Neither side was willing to concede on the central issue of CSA independence. Lincoln feared that the South could not credibly commit not to make greater demands if the North caved to secession threats or granted secession. He also worried that secession could possibly lead to the very unraveling of the American political fabric. The CSA worried that the Union could not credibly commit to even a theoretically acceptable settlement that removed Southern sovereignty, both because of doubts that Lincoln would keep his word, and concerns that Northern Republicans would force Lincoln to renege on a moderate settlement and reconstruction plan. Each side went so far as to consider making concessions on the critical issue of slavery, although Lincoln's concerns about the contribution that emancipation made to Northern military power made him generally hesitant to do so. In this conflict, the steady accumulation of casualties did not perform the informative function of teaching the two sides about the balance of power, pushing them, towards eventually reaching a war-ending settlement. Bloodshed had no silver lining of information in this war. It was simply a grotesque horror, fated to continue until one side collapsed.

CHAPTER NINE

Germany, 1917–18

> Our future military needs would not be satisfied if Belgium
> should remain a free state in any form. . . . It is absolutely
> necessary that we force through the military requirement that
> we be able to use Belgium as a concentration area.
> —German Major Georg Wetzell, September 1917

> The central issue of the whole world war is our relationship
> to England and to Anglo-Americanism. . . . Germany and not
> England must hold sway over Belgium.
> —German Admiral Alfred von Tirpitz, November 1917

BY EARLY 1918, after three and a half years of the worst war in world history, the stage seemed to have been set for Germany to declare victory and go home. Germany had acquired a titanic slab of Russia—including a full third of Russia's population, some 55 million people—through the one-sided March 1918 Treaty of Brest-Litovsk.[1] Fresh American military forces had not yet arrived in the West to bolster the battered French and British armies.[2] And yet Germany's thirst for war was not yet quenched. It launched a major new offensive on the Western Front in spring 1918, unsatisfied with the millions of square kilometers acquired in the East, and still hungry for gains in the West as well.

Germany's decision to fight on in early 1918 caused the Central Powers to lose World War I. This had sweeping implications for the entire global order. Consider the consequences if an early 1918 peace deal recognizing German gains in the East and the status quo ante in the West. Germany would have retained possession of wide swaths of Eastern Europe, including Finland, Poland, Belarus, the Baltic States, and Ukraine. The Bolshevik government in Moscow would have been severely hobbled by the loss of such a substantial fraction of its population and industry. An end to the war in early 1918 might have prevented the Austro-Hungarian and Ottoman Empires from disintegrating. America's participation in the war would never have exceeded the token forces dispatched in 1917. Perhaps most importantly, the German monarchy would have survived the end of the war, and Germany would have emerged as the world's most powerful nation. Absent the humiliation of Versailles, Adolf Hitler would probably never have taken power.

A critical factor driving the German decision to continue fighting was concern about credible commitments. Germany doubted the willingness of France or Britain to accept a peace deal into the future. The Germans believed it critical that they shore up their Western borders to neutralize the long-term Anglo-French threat. Accomplishing this task required a peace settlement permitting German control of Belgium, an outcome that was not in the offing in early 1918, but which the Germans felt could be achieved with a new offensive. That is, Germany perceived there to be a credible commitment problem (from Britain and France), they felt that the good under dispute (the post-war political status of Belgium, among other things) affected the severity of the credible commitment problem, and they felt that continuing the war into 1918 would offer them the opportunity to acquire more of the disputed good, enough to reduce substantially the commitment problem. There were other commitment problems at this stage, as well. The pending arrival of large numbers of American troops threatened to shift the balance of power in favor of the Allies, and as a result Germany put little faith that negotiations alone would produce a satisfactory and stable outcome. Additionally, the possibility that Germany could digest its Russian gains and become much more powerful in the years following a limited war outcome pushed Britain to seek a decisive victory to prevent this eventuality. These three commitment factors blocked a limited war settlement in the winter of 1917–18, and made a more decisive fight to the finish inevitable.

Information and the State of the War in Winter 1917–18

The War to End All Wars broke out in summer 1914. It commenced under conditions consistent with an information account, as all sides predicted swift victory for themselves.[3] German forces came within artillery range of Paris in the opening weeks of fighting, but no closer. In the West, the war soon stabilized into an abattoir for soldiers of both sides, millions dying in battles fought between trenches running through France and Belgium. The other principal campaign, in Russia, was more dynamic, with the Russian war effort collapsing by the end of 1917, due both to external pressure from the German and Austro-Hungarian armies and to internal pressure from the Bolshevik Revolution.

As noted, the negotiations with Russia in the winter of 1917–18, culminating with the March 1918 Treaty of Brest-Litovsk, yielded tremendous territorial gains for Germany. The remaining question for Germany was what to do in the West. Should Germany fight on in pursuit of territorial gains in the West, or should it propose a peace settlement of some form of territorial status quo ante in the West, allowing it to digest the extraordinary gains in the East?

The predictions of the information proposition as to what Germany should have done at this stage are mixed.[4] On one hand, if the war was being driven fundamentally by information asymmetries, then the heavy continual fighting with the highest casualties of any armed conflict in world history should have generated the convergence of expectations about the true balance of power. That is, if war is fundamentally about information, if war begins because of incomplete information and disagreement about the balance of power and/or resolve, and if the function of fighting is to reveal information towards eventually opening bargaining space and permitting war termination, then the huge quantity of information revealed by the battles taking place between 1914 and 1917 should have been sufficient to open bargaining space and permit a deal to be struck between Germany, France, and Britain. But it was not.

On the other hand, factors existed that might have served to encourage the two sides to think that past combat outcomes might not serve as strong predictors of the likely future outcome of war. If this is the case, then the lack of war termination by the end of 1917 is not so terribly surprising, because each side had some reason to hope the future might be better. On the Allied side, the great hope lay in the impending arrival of substantial detachments of American troops. Although the American Congress had formally declared war in April 1917, large amounts of American troops were not due to arrive in Europe until 1918. With these fresh forces, the Allies might have been able to tip the balance of power in their favor in the West.

On the German side, there were two sources of encouragement. Perhaps counteracting the American contribution, the Russian exit from the war would allow the redeployment of German troops from the East to the West. These redeployed forces might have given Germany hope for victory in the West, perhaps because they were combat veterans, and perhaps because they might arrive before the Americans.[5] Troop assignments aside, the Germans were developing new infantry tactics that presented the possibility of breaking through enemy entrenchments in the West, even without massive quantitative superiority or new superweapons.[6]

CREDIBLE COMMITMENTS FEARS: BELGIUM, AMERICA, AND RUSSIA

Germany's war policy was largely about ensuring German security after the war.[7] To that end, a central motivation behind German war aims in the West was acquiring Belgium and perhaps territory in northern France to address a credible commitment problem posed by Britain and France. The German leadership believed that control of Belgium would make an attack on German territory less likely, and more generally would undercut British power. Throughout the war, establishing control over Belgium remained Germany's principal war aim in the West.[8]

Public and private arguments for the importance of acquiring Belgium for German security were made from the very beginning to the very end of the war. During the first weeks of the summer 1914 crisis, German foreign policy relied on the assumption that Britain would stand aside in any escalating conflict between Germany and Russia or Germany and France. The German leadership even hoped that Britain might remain neutral in the event of the planned German invasion of Belgium, British treaty commitments to Belgian borders notwithstanding. By the end of July, it became increasingly clear that Britain would not stay out of the war, and indeed Britain entered the war on August 4. British entry caused a wild upsurge of Anglophobia in Germany, as many within both government and society saw Britain as now the great enemy, bent on emasculating if not destroying Germany, for the sake of maximizing British profits and strengthening the British empire. Some saw the central goal of the war to be the creation of a lasting solution to the threat of British perfidy. One nationalist newspaper in Germany declared on September 29, 1914 that peace would not be made until "we can re-sheathe the sword, which we have been forced to unsheathe, in full confidence that the world will be safe from English aggression for decades to come."[9]

Germany saw Belgium as a key bulwark against the Anglo-French threat. Indeed, some have argued that in August 1914 the initial operational goal of German forces in the West was not the conquest of France but rather the occupation of Belgium.[10] German naval officers such as Deputy Chief of the Admiralty Staff Rear Admiral Paul Behncke stressed the strategic importance of Belgium in September 1914, arguing specifically that German control of Belgium would undermine British and French power.[11] In his September 9, 1914 memo, Chancellor Theobald von Bethmann Hollweg laid out German plans for Belgium, which included military control of its coast and the reduction of Belgium to vassal status if not outright annexation. More generally, this memo noted that "the general aim of the war" was "security for the German Reich in west and east for all imaginable time."[12]

German focus on the postwar security benefits of controlling Belgium persisted. Following the September memo, in October and December 1914, separate memos addressing the Belgian question were drawn up by high-ranking officials of the German government. Both memos advocated bringing Belgium under permanent German control, to prevent its future use as a base of military operations against Germany.[13] German politicians agreed. The leading Conservative in the Reichstag supported these aims, writing the Chancellor, "If a lasting peace is to be won, Belgium must be rendered harmless. We must gain military, political and economic guarantees that England or France will not be able to use Belgium against us in future political controversies. Such guarantees require at least the military and economic dependence of that country upon Germany."[14] In late 1915, Berlin informed the Belgian king that negotiated peace would require eliminating Belgium's army, granting occupation and transit rights to Germany, and German control of the port of Antwerp and Belgian railways.[15]

The military strongly supported the control, if not annexation, of Belgium as a critical war aim. Admiral Alfred von Tirpitz wrote to Bethmann Hollweg in January 1915 that the maintenance of German power required a secure position on the Channel coast across from England, including the German use of the Belgian port of Antwerp. He was blunt: "If we fail to keep secure the possibilities of development offered in Belgium, I should regard the war, considered in relation to Germany's world power status, as lost; with Belgium, as won."[16] In April 1916, Tirpitz declared German control of Belgium to be "the cornerstone on which one can build a German world power equal to that of the Anglo-Saxons and the Russians." Other admirals agreed with Tirpitz.[17] The German navy officially recommended German control of the Belgian coast in December 1916, arguing that controlling Belgium would be a critical step towards breaking British national power and maritime supremacy.[18] The May 1917 naval war aims program restated the importance of controlling Belgium to Kaiser Wilhelm.[19]

Even the so-called moderates in German society and government who diverged from the more extreme view of the annexationists argued for the importance of controlling Belgium for German security. They sometimes differed over how much control was needed, sometimes proposing that solutions short of the annexation of the entire country might suffice. However, they generally agreed with the core point that any war-ending settlement must include a settlement of the Belgium issue satisfactory for German security. One industrialist moderate argued in 1915, "I take the standpoint, as you know, that we must gain access to the sea if we do not want to live through a repeat version of this terrible war in the near future."[20]

The significance of Belgium in German war aims persisted throughout 1917. Notably, the German government did not express infinite demands in the West, and even occasionally seemed to indicate willingness to make concessions in the West. For example, in June 1917 Bethmann indicated to a Papal peace mediator that although Germany would not concede on German control of Belgium, it might be willing to make concessions on

Alsace and Lorraine, two French territories that Germany had acquired in the 1870–71 Franco-Prussian War.[21] There remained a very strong sentiment among military and other government officials during autumn 1917 that the control of Belgium was critical for Germany's postwar security. By early September, foreign minister Richard von Kühlmann had concluded that conceding Belgium might produce a separate peace with Britain, but this suggestion went nowhere within the German government since Chancellor Georg Michaelis, Bethmann Hollweg's successor, told Kühlmann quite clearly that such concessions were out of the question.[22] In a September 15 letter, Chief of the General Staff Paul von Hindenburg stressed to Michaelis the importance of maintaining control of Belgium for security reasons.[23] The importance of Belgium for German war aims was also emphasized in a September 30 memo by Major Georg Wetzell. This memo was well-received by General Erich von Ludendorff, who by this point—along with Hindenburg—ruled Germany essentially as military dictators. Wetzell framed German war aims in terms of preparation for future war, noting that "from a military viewpoint, we cannot come out of this peace strong enough by any means." For Wetzell, German military control of Belgium was essential: "Our future military needs would not be satisfied if Belgium should remain a free state in any form. . . . It is absolutely necessary that we force through the military requirement that we be able to use Belgium as a concentration area."[24] Hindenburg reemphasized the importance of Belgium for German security around November 1917, writing that "Every one must admit that our Rhenish-Westphalian industry would be greatly endangered through a Belgian state leaning towards England and France."[25] Hindenburg reinforced these points in a December 11 memo to Chancellor Georg von Hertling, recalling an April memo, approved by the Kaiser, which demanded the control of Belgium for reasons of German security.[26]

The German leadership decided formally on December 18, 1917— again, as Russia was collapsing—that controlling Belgium remained a critical war aim, especially maintaining German-built fortifications on the Belgian coast and resisting British influence in Belgium.[27] The dominant strand of thinking was that control of Belgium was necessary to safeguard Germany against future attacks. On January 23, 1918, Hertling wrote to the Emperor that, "It need not be especially stressed that questions of military security will not be overlooked. In what way they will be achieved, depends upon the political and military situation at the time peace is concluded. We shall have to take into consideration how far our future economic and political relations to this neighbor [i.e. Belgium] and especially the development of our Flemish policy will diminish the probability of a future war with her and thus decrease the necessity for military safeguards."[28] In a speech to the Reichstag on February 25, even while trying to make Germany look as pacific as possible to Allied publics, Hertling could not evade the central point that German postwar security required German control of Belgium: "Over and over again it has been said in this place that we do not think of retaining Belgium, of making the Belgian State a component part of the German Empire, but that we, as was pointed out in the Papal Note of 1st August last year, must be preserved from the danger that a country that which we wish after the war once more to live in peace with and friendship should become the object or the base of enemy machinations."[29]

Ludendorff emphasized the importance of German postwar control of Belgium during a high-level meeting of government ministers on February 4, and refused to budge on Belgium during peace negotiations with the Allies during March and April.[30] As late as May 1918, Hindenburg hoped the capture of the Belgian coast would allow the direct artillery bombardment of the English coast itself and perhaps eventually even of London. He saw this as having implications for postwar security as well as the termination of the present war since such a threat "would be a serious prospect for Great Britain, not only for the moment but for her whole future!" Such an accomplishment might be "regarded as a guarantee of peace."[31]

In short, acquiring the control or outright ownership of Belgium to improve German security had become the central German war aim in the West.[32] One historian summarized Ludendorff's thoughts around February 1918 bluntly: "Belgium must remain in German hands at all costs."[33] Ludendorff himself declared, "A peace which only guarantees the territorial *status quo* would mean that we lost the war. . . . Matters are still uncertain as far as the west is concerned. But if we keep our old frontiers, we shall be in a less favorable position after the war than before. . . . We must improve the protection of our western coal regions through rectification of the frontier."[34]

Germany's recognition of Belgium as important to international security and power was probably reasonable. A sovereign and independent Belgium certainly was central to British strategy and national power, and it was the challenge to Belgian independence that brought Britain into war in 1914. Indeed, keeping the Low Countries region independent of the influence of a continental great power had been a cornerstone of British foreign policy for centuries.[35] Further, after Germany's defeat in 1918, Belgium was included in Anglo-French military planning since Belgium and France signed a defense agreement in 1920. French war plans also called for the early movement of French troops into Belgium in 1940.[36]

This obsession with the security provided by the control of Belgium provides one answer as to why Germany decided to fight on in early 1918, rather than stop the war to digest its eastern gains. Germany did not trust Britain and France to adhere to a war-ending peace settlement, and wanted to achieve a settlement that would substantially decrease the odds of new British and French attacks in the future. Germany saw the control of Belgium as a supervaluable increment of the disputed good, in that controlling Belgium would make it much more costly for Britain or France to attack Germany in the future. They did not see the absolute defeat of Britain and France as necessary to satisfy German security needs, or at least the incremental improvement in German security provided by absolute victory was not worth the cost. Because Germany placed such high value on controlling Belgium, and because Germany thought that a peace settlement that restored the status quo ante might be unstable and tempt future attacks, Germany continued the war in early 1918, looking to make territorial gains in the West.

German obsession with Belgium as a solution to the credible commitment problem presented a major impediment to war termination in 1918. Beyond Belgium, there were two other credible commitment factors at this stage that also blocked war termination. A short-term credible commitment problem was the impending arrival of greater numbers of American troops. Germany feared that the arrival of more American troops on the Western Front throughout 1918 would shift the balance of power. Unrestricted submarine warfare could at this point not be relied upon to win the war for Germany, as its payoffs were by the end of 1917 seen as disappointing.[37] The changing balance of power caused by the arrival of substantial American forces might make any early 1918 Allied commitment to a peace deal incredible. Germany sought to solve this credible commitment problem by launching an offensive in early 1918 to win the war before the Americans arrived in force. Hopefully, with the British forces swept from the continent and the French will to fight completely broken, peace talks would hand Germany the Western gains it so desperately wanted before American forces could make a difference. A defensive posture in the West, conversely, could not guarantee victory before the arrival of the Americans.[38] The head of operations for the German general staff, Major Wetzell, wrote a position paper in October 1917 laying out this concern. He added that the Allies would make it through the 1917–18 winter, and by spring the United States would add ten to fifteen divisions to the Western Front. Wetzell argued that the only hope was "to deliver an annihilating blow to the British before American aid can become effective."[39] Ludendorff agreed with Wetzell's outlook.[40] Both sides knew that the arrival of American troops would shift the balance of forces significantly in the Allies' favor, and Germany's fear was that Britain and France would bide their time until the arrival of American troops.

Germany assessed Allied war planning accurately. On the British side, the hope of American assistance encouraged Prime Minister David Lloyd George in September 1917 to continue fighting rather than sue for peace. On the French side, French Premier and Foreign Affairs Minister Alexandre Ribot that same month informed the French ambassador to the United States that, "until the United States has made the decisive effort it is preparing, we shall not be in a favourable position to negotiate."[41] In December 1917, the Commander in Chief of the French Army, Henri Pétain, issued a directive on Allied strategy that stated: "The Entente Powers will reach numerical superiority only when sufficient American troops can enter the line. Until that time, it will be necessary for us, unless we wish to use up our forces irretrievably, to assume a waiting attitude, with the express purpose of taking up the offensive as soon as we are able to do so; for only the offensive will bring us final victory."[42]

A last credible commitment problem, on the Allied side, concerned Allied fears about the likelihood that Germany would comply with a limited war outcome. A growing British concern in late 1917 was that a settlement at that point would grant Germany large territorial gains in the East, given Russia's ongoing collapse. These gains would encourage a medium- and long-term shift in the balance of power in Germany's favor, making a limited war outcome unstable. The only real solution for Britain would be to reject any limited outcome, and fight on to the complete defeat of Germany. These views were expressed in a pair of critical meetings of the British leadership in late September 1917. A member of the British cabinet argued that a limited outcome with Germany at this point would mean Germany "coming out of the war more powerful than she entered it and another war in ten years time." Sir Douglas Haig, Field Marshal for the British Army, agreed, worrying that a limited war outcome "would mean . . . the almost certain renewal of the War hereafter at a time of Germany's choosing." Chief of the Imperial General Staff William Robertson opposed a limited outcome, as it would allow Germany to "organize a fresh attempt for securing that world dominion which she had failed to obtain in the present war." Later that year, Lloyd George put it this way, "If they [the Germans] make a separate peace with Russia, there's no compensation you can give them. It is war to the end." The French shared these concerns.[43] Shifts in the balance of power aside, the severe concessions imposed by Germany on defeated Russia raised grave doubts about German ambitions more broadly, diminishing Allied (and American in particular) hopes that a stable limited war outcome was possible.[44]

Notably, British concerns with the postwar balance of power interacted with impending American intervention. Lloyd George in late 1917 wanted to put off a major Allied offensive until after a substantial American force arrived. If Britain launched an offensive before the American contingent arrived, then an Allied victory would be Pyrrhic, as the British army would be shattered by the effort, and likely overshadowed by the postwar military power of the U.S. and Russia. If it waited until the Americans arrived, then American blood could take the place of British blood, helping ensure postwar British military dominance.[45] In short, commitment fears contributed to an unwillingness to negotiate a limited outcome on both the German and Allied sides in winter 1917–18.

DOMESTIC POLITICS AND WAR-TERMINATION BEHAVIOR

Hein Goemans has produced a novel explanation of war-termination behavior based on domestic politics, testing it on war-termination behavior during World War I.[46] To recap the summary of the argument from chapter 2 of this book, the central proposition is that leaders of semirepressive, moderately exclusionary political systems worry about facing severe personal punishments (such as exile, imprisonment, or death) in the event of moderate or severe military defeat, because unlike democratic leaders they cannot expect to be left alone in peace after falling from power, and unlike dictators they cannot use the tools of repression to stave off all but the gravest of internal threats to their rule. To avoid such severe punishments, leaders of these systems may raise their war aims when their nations are losing wars, attempting to gather enough gains in a peace settlement to pay off their supporters to remain in power. Relatedly, leaders may engage in risky military strategies, so-called "gambles for resurrection," which may increase their states' chances of military victory, at the expense of also increasing the chances of decisive military defeat. Goemans noted that such behavior is in contrast to the information proposition, which predicts that a belligerent would lower its war aims when information indicates that the war is going badly.

Germany during World War I is the leading example of a moderately exclusionary, semirepressive state engaging in this kind of war-termination behavior.[47] Perhaps the strongest case supporting Goemans' argument is the cluster of German decisions to increase war aims in late 1916 and launch unrestricted submarine warfare in January 1917, the latter being a gamble for resurrection intended to support the former. The specific hope was that unrestricted submarine warfare would tighten the blockade around Britain, and force Britain to exit the war rather than face civilian starvation. Germany made these decisions despite receiving in the latter half of 1916 an array of discouraging information from the war: the failure of the German Verdun offensive; the demonstration of British resolve indicated by the Somme offensive and the adoption of conscription; the Brusilov offensive, which demonstrated Russian military power and Austro-Hungarian weakness; the Romanian declaration of war against the Central Powers, and growing food shortages and unrest in Germany itself.[48] Despite these developments, Germany increased its war aims in late 1916, specifically demanding more Polish concessions, the annexation of Courland and Lithuania as well as other Russian territories, and more territorial concessions from France.[49] These 1916–17 war-termination decisions, Goemans argues, were motivated by a desire to increase the profits Germany would gather from victory in war, profits that could be distributed to the population to counteract the rising costs of war and quell a possible postwar political threat to the regime. Distributing the spoils of war was seen by the regime as a revolution-avoiding strategy preferable to adopting political reforms.

Three mild caveats to Goemans' interpretation of the events of 1916–17 are worth noting, the first two of which point to the information proposition as playing perhaps a larger role for the expansion of German war aims than Goemans allows. First, although the entry of Romania into the war in August 1916 was discouraging, Romania's defeat and exit from the war in early December 1916 had the opposite effect, in particular because Germany perceived that Romania's fall would keep Denmark, the Netherlands, and other neutrals out of the war.[50] Evaluating the timing of the Romanian decision in relation to the increase in war demands is difficult; specifically, if Romania's December exit was on balance encouraging, this might have been one force pushing Germany to raise its war aims. There was approval within the German government to increase war aims in early November 1916. However, the Germans delayed the release of their Peace Note that invited negotiations (without specifics) until after the fall of Romania in early December 1916, perhaps because they did not want the Note to appear as a sign of weakness.[51]

Second, although the decision to launch unrestricted submarine warfare in early 1917 can be portrayed as a gigantic risk because it would likely bring the United States into the war, there is some evidence that at the time key German decision-makers did not see the move as so risky. In the planning stages, the high military command estimated that unrestricted submarine warfare would force Britain out of the war within months. Tirpitz guessed Britain would fold within two months.[52] The German ambassador to the United States, Arthur Zimmerman, sent dispatches that the American public wanted to avoid war. Ludendorff was confident that America did not have the shipping to bring substantial numbers of troops and supplies across the Atlantic, that the British did not have the ships to spare for the conveyance and protection of American forces, and that any U.S. forces that were sent would be sunk by German submarines.[53] At the critical January 8, 1917 meeting at which the final decision to launch unrestricted submarine warfare was made, the Kaiser stated that he "fully expected America's entry into war," but dismissed such an eventuality as "irrelevant." Ludendorff declared, "I don't give a damn about America," and Hindenburg dismissed any American contribution to be "minimal, in any case not decisive."[54] Admiral Henning von Holtzendorff had also dismissed the factor of American entry, claiming the war would end before American forces or money could make a difference.[55] Some, such as the German admiralty staff chief, even made the contrary argument that expanding the U-boat campaign would show German strength and resolve, and might help keep neutrals out of the war.[56] Further, even if unrestricted submarine warfare had brought the United States into the war, it more importantly might have forced Britain from the war, likely before American forces could make a decisive contribution in the West. An early January 1917 memo to the Chancellor claimed that unrestricted submarine warfare could starve Britain out of the war in five months.[57] As late as May 1917, Ludendorff was arguing internally that unrestricted submarine warfare would force Britain from the war in two or three months.[58]

German optimism about British vulnerability to unrestricted submarine warfare was not deluded speculation.[59] In October 1916, before Germany imposed unrestricted submarine warfare, British Admiral John Jellicoe forecast that merchant losses from the submarine threat might force British acceptance of unfavorable peace terms by early summer 1917. Other members of the British political and military leadership in late 1916 and early 1917 worried that the submarine threat was dire. After the war, former Prime Minister David Lloyd George bluntly stated that "the submarine was the crucial problem upon which the issue of the War would depend. If we failed to counter its ravages, the Allies were irretrievably beaten."[60] In his multivolume history of World War I, Winston Churchill (himself Minister of Munitions during World War I) offered a similar view, as did Henry Newbolt in the official history, the latter commenting that, "Everything, indeed, combined to show that the Allies were really within sight of disaster."[61] These grim assessments were based on equally grim statistics. At the worst of it in April 1917, if a ship left Britain for a destination beyond Gibraltar, its chances of safely returning were only one in four.[62] Importantly, British maritime collapse was avoided not because of American entry into the war, but because the British navy switched to a convoy strategy in April 1917, which improved its ability to protect commercial vessels and sink German U-boats.[63]

Third, Bethmann, the nominal civilian leader, opposed pursuing unrestricted submarine warfare for fear of bringing the U.S. into the war, although the military leaders supported it. Therefore, the decision to pursue unrestricted submarine warfare might be best understood as a function of poor civilian control of the military in Germany rather than the civilian leadership seeking to achieve decisive victory to acquire more war aims for distribution to political supporters. Indeed, an early 1916 push to implement unrestricted submarine warfare failed, perhaps in part because the Duo of Ludendorff and Hindenburg had not yet taken power from the civilian leaders. They both supported unrestricted submarine warfare, and once they installed a de facto military dictatorship in summer 1916, unrestricted submarine warfare became politically possible as a German military strategy.[64] Assuming that unrestricted submarine warfare was a poor strategic choice, this view is consistent with broader theorizing that states make bad strategic and doctrinal choices when there is weak civilian control of the military.[65]

Putting 1916–17 decision-making aside, Goemans also proposes that German war-termination decisions in 1917–18 can be explained by domestic political factors. Not only did Germany elect not to pursue peace in the West that winter, but Germany went further, launching a massive spring 1918 offensive to make further territorial gains. Goemans proposes that the primary motive for the new offensive was that the regime needed to hold together its supportive political coalition. Maintaining the coalition in turn required making territorial gains in the West to provide profits to the industrialists, which were necessary to balance off the gains in the East and their associated profits to the Prussian Junkers.[66]

However, certain shortcomings of this interpretation undermine support for the domestic politics hypothesis. The decision to continue the war in the West was not an unpopular one driven solely by an insecure autocrat struggling to hold together a wobbly and narrow coalition. German politics during this period are often characterized as being dominated by an iron and rye coalition, an alliance of industrialists and shipbuilders seeking gains in the West and the agriculturally based Prussian Junkers seeking gains in the East. However, expansion in the West and the reduction of British power was a leading war aim of the Conservative Party, the leading political party (along with the associated Agrarian League) of the Prussian Junkers. That is, territorial gains in the West were a widely popular war aim, not a pet project of one narrow segment of German politics. The historian Hans Gatzke wrote:

> Despite their divergent interests, however, the aristocracy of blood and the aristocracy of coal and iron (ranged respectively behind the Conservative and National Liberal Parties) had much in common. . . . In the foreign field they shared (although for different reasons) a common hatred of Great Britain. Germany's industrial and commercial interests saw England as their most dangerous competitor; while Germany's agricultural interests looked upon England as the birthplace and embodiment of that liberal and democratic tradition which threatened the

maintenance of their privileges. . . . The hatred of the Conservatives for Great Britain [was] based not merely on ideological grounds, but on an equally important element of patriotism (Anglo-German naval rivalry, after all, was not merely a matter of commercial competition but equally one of national prestige) . . . [67]

Indeed, the Conservatives placed a higher priority on the defeat of England than on annexation in Russia. At some points in the war (especially before the 1917–18 Russian military collapse), the Conservatives expressed willingness to support a separate peace with Russia in order to better prosecute the war in the West.[68] The Conservative leader Count Kuno von Westarp discussed political strategy in a November 9, 1915 letter to fellow Conservative leader Ernst von Heydebrand, posing the following: "We could present the problem this way: do you want half-efforts on both fronts or wouldn't you agree that it would be wiser to drop the eastern aims as much as is necessary and achieve a full victory in the west?"[69] As debate stirred in late 1916 about the expansion of German war aims, both Conservative and industrial newspapers stressed western and colonial gains over eastern gains.[70] Indeed, in his postwar memoirs, Westarp stated unequivocally, "The demand for the most vigorous war effort against England was, in essence, the basis of Conservative policy in the war."[71] More generally, throughout Germany fear and hatred of Britain spiraled upward into blind fury as the war continued, the Satan of Britain and its materialistic values representing the sworn enemy of Germany and its Teutonic values of honor and virtue.[72]

The industrial interests and the Conservative Party were not alone in pursuing the continuation of war in the West in 1918. Many within German society had advocated nationalist annexation in the West from the outset of the war. The annexationist Army League argued in March 1915 that "Germany's permanent possession of Belgium is an absolute necessity for military, *völkisch*, and economic reasons," and that "Belgium is ours. Our self-preservation demands that she remain in German hands."[73] After the war, Bethmann Hollweg dismissed the possibility of a 1915 peace based on restored Belgian independence and neutrality, commenting that such a concession would have aroused "the most bitter feeling among the German people."[74] In September 1917, Tirpitz and a Prussian bureaucrat founded the German Fatherland Party, which favored expansionist war aims, arguing that the failure to put Belgium in German hands would mean "Germany's demise and the victory of Anglo-American capitalism."[75] Tirpitz and other members of the Fatherland Party argued that establishing control of Belgium must be a central German war aim. For example, one history professor declared in October 1917 that "the only guarantee which we could have of England's future good behaviour is military possession of the Flanders coast." The following month, Tirpitz made a similar point in a public speech, arguing that "the central issue of the whole world war is our relationship to England and to Anglo-Americanism," meaning that "Germany and not England must hold sway over Belgium."[76] This party was not a hollow front used to advance the interests of narrow industrial interests. By early 1918, it had 1.25 million members, making it larger than the Social Democratic Party, and indeed the largest political organization in Germany.[77] In consonance with the information proposition, the tremendous successes in the East helped raise the prestige of the German army in the eyes of the public, and the public became less willing to oppose the army's plans for continued expansion in the West.[78]

Popularity of the issue aside, the German political system at this point might be more accurately characterized as a dictatorship rather than a moderately exclusionary, semirepressive regime. That is to say, German war-termination decisions were determined more by what the Duo, Hindenburg and Ludendorff, saw as the national interest, and not so much by their domestic political fears. Hindenburg and Ludendorff had ascended to supreme command of the German military (technically, First and Second Chiefs of Staff) in August 1916, succeeding General Erich von Falkenhayn. This was a critical step towards the establishment essentially of a military dictatorship, called by some the silent dictatorship.[79] Notably, the ascent was itself not the maneuver of a narrow industrial clique, and many segments of German society—beyond annexationists—supported Hindenburg in particular.[80] But, once given formal command of the military, their grip on political power tightened. Ludendorff helped engineer the dismissal of the more moderate Bethmann Hollweg as Chancellor in July 1917, replacing him with the General Staff puppet Michaelis.[81] This maneuver established the Duo as de facto dictators.[82] True, Michaelis surprised the Duo by advocating concessions in the West, and the Duo responded not only by snuffing out the suggestion but also maneuvering by early November to have Michaelis replaced with the even more compliant Hertling.[83]

The Kaiser was too weak to control the Duo. He at some points expressed sympathy with the gambit of offering concessions on Belgium in an attempt to split the Allies. However, he knew such a position would be very unpopular with the Navy in particular, and he feared their power. In a September 10, 1917 letter to Michaelis, the Kaiser worried that Belgian concessions, especially regarding the Belgian coast, would cause "strong dissension" in the "officer circles ... of the fleet." He further fretted that, "For me *personally*, in my relations with my navy, the question is so *serious*, that *without compensations* for the loss of the Flanders coast I could no longer show myself among the executive officer corps."

The political storm that would emerge from such a move "compared to which the July days and Bethmann's dismissal were child's play." In closing, the Kaiser practically begged Michaelis: "I urgently ask you once again not to underestimate the mood of my executive officer corps, where many hidden supporters of Tirpitz remain, and to pay heed to my very difficult situation vis-à-vis this group."[84] The civilian leadership grew even weaker as time passed. In January 1918, Hindenburg and Ludendorff rebuffed the (civilian) Chancellor's assertion that peace negotiations were the province of the civilian leadership, Hindenburg declaring that "we feel ourselves justly responsible to the German nation, history and our own conscience for the form which peace takes. No formal declaration can relieve us of that sense of responsibility."[85] Around the same time, in the midst of peace negotiations with Russia, the Kaiser brightly suggested to the Duo that Germany required the annexation of relatively little territory from Poland for German security needs. The Duo collectively turned purple in rage, openly insulting the Kaiser. Ludendorff slammed the door as he stormed out of the room. Needless to say, the Kaiser's suggestion was quickly forgotten.[86] By June 1918, Ludendorff was openly placing the interests of the German nation ahead of those of the Kaiser.[87]

The previous section argued that German pursuit of Belgium was strongly driven by security needs. Some might propose that (even private) arguments made by German politicians and military leaders about the importance of Belgium to German security masked what were fundamentally economic motivations of the Western industrialists, specifically the protection of the mines and factories in the region.[88] It is impossible to disprove completely an ulterior motives claim such as this, as one can always speculate that statements are strategic facades for an actor's true motives, which go undocumented. Further, an individual's motives are often a swirl of factors, so the presence of one motive (concerns for postwar German security) does not necessarily exclude the presence of another motive (advancing German industrial interests).

In the case of World War I Germany, the available evidence does increase our confidence that security concerns were the leading motives of the Duo, and that they were, at the minimum, not puppets controlled by industrial and other interests. It does not quite fit to see the Duo as fronts for other interests since the Duo were themselves generals and came to power by the pleasure of Chancellor Bethmann Hollweg and Kaiser Wilhelm, not by Reichstag vote or some other means. In other words, they did not come to power by decision of political parties, which in turn represented special interests. It is also inaccurate to see the Duo as actors without agency, doing the bidding of others. Indeed, in 1917 it was the army that requested heavy industry increase its pro-annexation/imperial propaganda, rather than the reverse.[89] A safer statement would be that the Duo supported politics that were consonant with many preferences of the industrialists, including annexation in the West. Ludendorff had advocated even before the war positions similar to those of the industrialists, such as the importance of coordination between army and industry, the need for a drastic increase in the size of the army, and the importance of total war and total mobilization.[90]

If Ludendorff was long known to have preferences in line with German industry, this then begs the question of whether the industrialists were behind the Duo's succession of Falkenhayn in August 1916. Such an interpretation is probably too simple. Falkenhayn fell from power in August 1916 principally because of dissatisfaction with his military leadership. Indeed, some annexationists wanted to promote Falkenhayn to Chancellor, hoping he would be the strong presence needed at the negotiating table, replacing Bethmann, who they saw as weak.[91] Resentment about Falkenhayn's military leadership capabilities had been growing. They accelerated in summer 1916 in the face of several setbacks, including the Brusilov offensive in June, the emerging pointlessness of the Verdun meat grinder, and the British assault on the Somme in July. The key event that caused his ouster was probably Romania's August 1916 entry into the war on the side of the Allies.[92] One historian claimed that Colonel Max Bauer of the German General Staff played a key role in overthrowing Falkenhayn and supporting Ludendorff, speculating that Bauer had close ties to the industrialists.[93] Others portray a different process, noting that many supported Falkenhayn's ouster, and in particular that Bethmann Hollweg engineered Falkenhayn's exit ironically as a means of opening the door for a negotiated annexationist peace, using the appointment of Hindenburg as political cover, by garnering support for Falkenhayn's support along the way from important allies such as the Kaiser's military adjutant, the Crown Prince, and the War Minister.[94]

Even if one concludes that the industrialists were somehow critical in bringing Hindenburg and Ludendorff to power, the completion of Goemans' argument requires understanding the domestic political consequences if the Duo abandoned annexation in the West in favor of the status quo ante. The domestic politics theory predicts that the Duo and elements of the German leadership refused to abandon Western aims because of the fear that doing so would lead to their loss of political power, and eventually they would individually suffer the severe punishments of exile, death, or prison. There are two problems with this conjecture. First, it is not clear that the Duo relied on a supporting coalition to stay in power, they were rather appointed generals who had steadily expanded their political power such that by late 1917 they were de facto dictators. Second, even if the Duo had lost power as a result of seeking peace in the West, they likely would not have suffered severe punishment, such as exile, death, or prison. As military officers, in any political transition short of violent revolution they likely would have been reassigned to other military duties, as Falkenhayn was when he was ousted in 1916, or perhaps forced to retire. It is quite difficult to imagine severe personal punishment for the Duo in the early 1918 context of a peace deal ensuring substantial gains in the East and perhaps the status quo ante in the West. Some fears arose in January 1918 of the possibility of a violent revolution echoing the Bolshevik's, but the fears were of revolutionaries from the left demanding peace and democracy, not of upheaval from the right by annexationists demanding war and empire.[95] Notably, when Germany faced the much worse outcome of decisive defeat in November 1918 (in comparison to a late 1917 negotiated peace leaving Germany with its Eastern gains), Hindenburg did not suffer severe punishment, and indeed he did not even leave his post until 1919, after which he resumed a public life in Germany, some years later even running successfully for political office. Ludendorff resigned in October 1918 and did soon flee to Sweden out of fear for his personal safety from revolutionaries, although he returned to Germany and to German politics in 1920.[96]

One twist on the argument might be that Ludendorff and the ruling class greatly feared political reforms, including broader suffrage, and saw the continuation/expansion of war aims as one means of forestalling this threat. There was growing pressure for domestic political reforms in Germany, and great victories might have relieved the pressure for political reforms, especially if such victories enlarged the spoils of war, which could be distributed to the workers demanding political change. Certainly, Ludendorff himself greatly feared and opposed expanding the franchise. Some argue that he saw continued war as a means of avoiding having to face the disaster of suffrage.[97] Ludendorff's concerns about pressures for democratization were real, as in early 1918 Germany faced a wave of internal unrest and strikes. The protesters demanded suffrage, the end of the war, and other concessions. In late January, 500,000 workers in Berlin alone went on strike.[98]

However, it is odd to speculate that by not giving in on one of the demands, peace negotiations, it would make the strikers more willing to concede on another demand, internal political reform. Some within the German government recognized that the goals of annexation and blocking domestic reforms were in competition with each other. Bethmann fretted in a June 1917 memo that if it got out that the pursuit of Courland and Lithuania had prevented a peace settlement, Germany would face domestic "collapse."[99] The Prussian minister of the interior Bill Drews also drew the connection, suggesting that the leadership could ameliorate the internal pressure by conceding on some although not all issues, specifically, making political reforms to allow a freer hand in foreign policy.[100] Ludendorff and the leadership rejected this approach, instead foregoing concessions and cracking down on striking workers. The leadership eventually arrested some 150 leaders of the strikes, sent 50,000 striking workers to the front, and closed down labor newspapers. These actions strengthened the Duo's political power.[101]

Perhaps a more general problem with the domestic politics argument that the captured booty from annexations was intended to stem demands for political reforms is that the political context in Germany had changed from the early years of the war to its later years. In the earlier years of the war, a number of political and industrial leaders argued that the spoils of war could be used to buy off the public and forestall demands for political reform. However, by 1917 the political and economic climate had changed, and this claim was no longer made. The demands of the politically threatening segment of German society were by 1917–18 straightforward: political reforms, food, and peace, and these demands could no longer be satisfied with the promises of gains in war.[102] One historian put it this way: "But war aims were no longer the placebo they had been in 1914–1916. Few worker-soldiers in 1917 had the slightest interest in, or willingness, to continue to fight for Courland or Wallachia or Liège. Few women who daily lined up for 150 g of flour or an egg were willing to suffer hardships for a slice of Montenegro, Luxembourg, or Lithuania."[103]

Another proposition related to the domestic politics interpretation of this time period is that the demand for gains in the West in 1917–18 pushed Germany to embrace a gamble for resurrection, the spring 1918 Western offensives. This point is partly correct. The offensive was a gamble in comparison with negotiations, in that the offensive increased the chances both of decisive victory (annexation in East and West) and decisive defeat (loss of the war) in comparison with negotiations, which increased the chance of moderate victory (annexations only in the East). However, the offensive is probably not genuinely a gamble in comparison to other military options, such as maintaining the defensive in the West. Ludendorff, Hindenburg and others became convinced in late 1917 that the offensive was the only option. The Central Powers could not play a waiting game because their military fortunes would only decline over time, given the eventual arrival of American troops and the fears that Austria–Hungary might soon no longer make much of a contribution to the war effort.[104]

Further, the spring offensive was not complete madness from a military perspective. The balance of forces by early March in the West had swung in Germany's favor. German troops had been steadily flowing from East to West, and by March German troop strength had increased some 30 percent over what it had been in November 1917, whereas British troop strength was down 25 percent over its levels in summer 1917. At this moment, German troops for the first time in the war outnumbered Allied troops in the West.[105] The spring offensives did have some successes, in part because of the implementation of new force employment tactics. These tactics, termed at the time "stormtrooper" tactics and later the "modern system" of force employment, emphasized the dispersal of formations, stressed the use of cover and concealment offered by terrain, changed preparatory artillery barrage procedures to maximize surprise, used combined arms techniques, and permitted more independence to smaller units to maximize rates of advance. This new approach was revolutionary. The Germans achieved tactical success in four of the five battles from March to July 1918, and made greater advances on the Western Front during this period than any army had to that point achieved. Germany wrecked the British Fifth Army and defeated the French at Chemin des Dames. The English Channel ports and even Paris itself were threatened. Britain thought France was close to seeking terms, and France thought Britain was close to abandoning the war. Had the Germans developed better operational plans for this campaign they might have been able to split the Allies and push the British Expeditionary Force off the continent, perhaps causing the French government to fall and putting Germany at the least in a better negotiating position with the Allies to extract concessions on matters such as Belgium.[106]

A Doomed Search for Security

In August 1914, Kaiser Wilhelm told German troops, "You will be home before the leaves have fallen from the trees."[107] This, like so many other forecasts about the First World War, proved tragically wrong, as the casualty lists grew from the hundreds to the thousands to the millions. The brief decisive war expected by all in summer 1914 disappeared, swallowed by the mud of the trench system of the Western front, the latter being so infused with death that one British poet described it as "the long grave already dug."[108]

Germany's decision not to end the war in late 1917 and early 1918 is part of the puzzle of why World War I lasted so long. It is difficult to assess the role of information factors, because the changing military environment gave each side hope notwithstanding all the information provided by three years of intensive combat. Credible commitment concerns played an important role in Germany's decision to fight on, certainly more than domestic politics.[109] The looming arrival of hundreds of thousands of fresh American troops promised to shift the balance of power decisively against Germany, which both precluded the possibility of getting Belgium in a winter 1918 peace deal, and made the strategic option of shifting to a defensive posture in the West unattractive. Britain's fear of the postwar growth in German power because of gains in the East pushed the British to pursue a decisive victory. But most importantly, the German leadership refused to accept the half a loaf of western Russia, its enduring paranoia of Britain and France pushing it to grab Belgium to provide long-term security. For Germany, only the acquisition of Belgium would prevent future Anglo-French aggression.

CHAPTER TEN

Japan, 1944–45

> I agreed to the showdown battle of Leyte thinking that if we
> attacked at Leyte and America flinched, then we would
> probably be able to find room to negotiate.
> —Emperor Hirohito, 1946

JAPAN'S PLAN for victory against the United States in World War II was straightforward. Run up a string of decisive victories in the first several months of war, smash American military and naval power in the Pacific, establish a stout defensive perimeter, and then present America with the prospect of a long and bloody war. Japan hoped that America would become discouraged and sue for peace, accepting a Japanese empire covering most of the Pacific and East Asia. Japan understood America's tremendous industrial advantages, and recognized that in a long war, America would eventually be able to wield considerable material superiority.

The plan did not work. America withstood the first six months of Japanese advances, after which Japan achieved no major victories for the remaining three years of the war. Oddly, Japan did not react to its steady downward slide during these three years by seeking to end the war. It did not even open war-termination negotiations until the very last days of war in August 1945.

This is a puzzle. According to the information proposition of chapter 2, the combination of American military victories and the absence of American concessions should have as early as 1942 begun to convince Japan that its initial plan for victory was not going to work. Japan should have improved its assessment of American power and resolve. Further, Japan should have opened negotiations with the United States and offered concessions with the aim of seeking a limited end to the war. However, Japan remained silent until the very end.

In some regards, Japan in World War II is similar to the Confederacy in the American Civil War. Neither Japan nor the CSA sought the absolute defeat of its adversary, and each wanted to achieve its aims by inflicting costs sufficient to coerce its adversary into making critical concessions:

accepting the Japanese empire and accepting CSA independence, respectively. As described in chapter 8, commitment credibility fears discouraged the CSA from considering concessions because the CSA feared the Union would renege on any moderate terms. Japan faced a different problem, since the United States demanded unconditional surrender essentially from the outset (see chapter 5), meaning there was not even an American suggestion of moderate terms for them to consider. So, why did the Japanese fight to the very end without offering concessions or even opening negotiations with the United States?

The central answer to this puzzle is that after the June 1942 Battle of Midway, Japanese leaders became convinced that Japan could not enter into negotiations, much less offer concessions, until it had scored an additional major battle victory. The U.S. demanded unconditional surrender, and because Japan had no hope of inflicting absolute defeat on the U.S., Japan's only hope of pushing the U.S. to abandon unconditional surrender was to raise American estimates of the costs of pursuing unconditional surrender. Hence, consistent with the logic laid out in chapter 3, commitment and information dynamics interacted, as credible commitment fears pushed the U.S. to pursue absolute victory (as described in chapter 5), but Japan hoped to make the attainment of absolute victory a prohibitively expensive luxury, similar to how the threat of nuclear escalation after the November 1950 Chinese intervention in the Korean War made the pursuit of absolute victory in that war prohibitively expensive for the United States. Japan believed it could only accomplish this goal of raising U.S. cost estimates of pursuing unconditional surrender by winning at least one decisive battle. Entering negotiations with the U.S. before attaining a decisive victory would doom such an effort to failure, as without itself facing a battlefield setback the U.S. would not deviate from its commitment to unconditional surrender. Worse, offering an olive branch might also stiffen American resolve to continue, as suggesting negotiations might be taken as a sign that Japanese resolve was flagging. Japan waited for a great victory to allow it to negotiate from a position of strength, a victory that never came.

THE JAPANESE STRATEGY FOR VICTORY

Even before Pearl Harbor, many in the Japanese government recognized America's industrial superiority, and conceded that Japan could not win a long war with the United States. Japan's strategy for victory was not to seek the literal conquest of the U.S. but rather to accumulate enough initial combat successes and to promise enough future punishment to persuade the United States to accept a massive Japanese Asian and Pacific empire and seek peace. At a September 6, 1941 Imperial Conference, this strategy was laid out as follows: "Although America's total defeat is judged utterly impossible, it is not inconceivable that a shift in American public opinion due to our victories in Southeast Asia or to England's surrender might bring the war to an end."[1] The leadership developed a strategy of inflicting a string of defeats on American forces, establishing a strong defensive perimeter in the Central Pacific, and then presenting to the United States and the American public in particular the prospect of a long and bloody conflict. The American public could not stomach a long and costly war, Japanese thinking went, and faced with such a war the public would force the American government to seek terms and accept an extensive Japanese empire.[2] Just before the Pearl Harbor attack, the Japanese admiral Isoroku Yamamoto put it colorfully: "One thing we could do now is disperse as many submarines as possible around the South Pacific so as to make the other side feel they've been set upon by a swarm of hornets. If the hornets around it buzz loudly enough, even a hefty animal like a horse or a cow will get worried, at least. American public opinion has always been very changeable, so the only hope is to make them feel as soon as possible that it's no use tackling a swarm of lethal stingers."[3]

Japan began the war with substantial war aims, seeking to expand the Japanese empire as far east as the central Pacific, as far south as Australia, as far west as India, and as far north as the Aleutian Islands. In the six months following Pearl Harbor, Japan rolled up a string of victories that helped advance these goals. In early March 1942, it reaffirmed its prewar strategy, committing to expanding its Pacific offensive to break the American will to fight.[4] The limits of Japan's World War II conquests are illustrated in figure 10.1.

The tide turned against Japan in mid-1942. In May, American forces turned back the planned Japanese landing at Port Moresby in the Battle of the Coral Sea. Soon after, American forces inflicted substantial damage on Japanese naval and air assets and rebuffed an invasion force headed for the island of Midway. In August, American forces invaded Guadalcanal, marking the beginning of America's island-hopping campaign. The decline in Japanese military ventures was slow but steady over the next three years, as in particular the American island-hopping campaign enjoyed success and slowly marched westward. The vulnerability of the Japanese home islands to aerial attacks accelerated in 1944–45, with the capture of the islands of Saipan, Iwo Jima, and Okinawa. August 1945 saw the twin blows of the atomic bombings of Hiroshima and Nagasaki and the Soviet declaration of war on Japan. At last, in mid-August Japan abandoned its dreams of empire and surrendered.

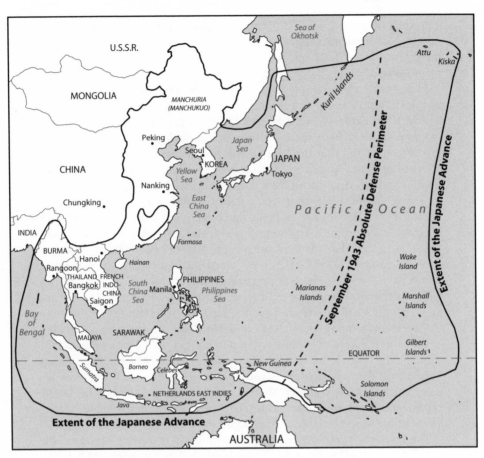

Figure 10.1 Japanese Empire, World War II

The Japanese Quest to Negotiate from Strength

What was the nature of Japanese war-termination behavior? The information proposition from chapter 2 predicts that the string of defeats from summer 1942 forward should have reduced the divergence of the expectations of the two sides about the future course of the war, and in particular should have pushed Japan to make concessions in an attempt to end the war short of absolute defeat. However, Japan made no official concessions and did not even open negotiations with the Allies until August 11, 1945, after the two atomic bombings and the Soviet entry into the war, when Japan offered a conditional acceptance of the Potsdam Proclamation. Notably, the lack of peace negotiations between Japan and the Allies was not a product of the absence of diplomatic contacts, as there were discussions about peace settlement terms between a Japanese naval officer and U.S. intelligence in Switzerland, but as late as May 1945 the Tokyo government refused to use this conduit.[5]

Importantly, the Japanese leadership was not blind to its declining military fortunes. As early as February 1942, Lord Keeper of the Privy Seal Koichi Kido expressed to Emperor Hirohito his concerns that the war would not end in swift success given the inevitable rise in American military strength, and that the Pearl Harbor attack had had the unexpected effect of unifying American opinion in support of the war.[6] In late 1945 interviews with American officials, a number of Japanese naval officers, including Admiral Soema Toyoda, Navy Minister and Admiral Mitsumasa Yonai, Chief of the Imperial Japanese Navy General Staff Osami Nagano, Rear Admiral Toshitane Takata, and Admiral Kichisaburō Nomura, indicated that they considered the June 1942 defeat at Midway and/or the successful 1942 U.S. invasion of Guadalcanal to be the turning points of the war.[7] As the war progressed, the Japanese leadership recognized a variety of danger signs, including growing American material superiority, the steady destruction of the Japanese naval and maritime fleet by American submarines, and the rapid American construction of airfields in the central Pacific. The military leadership saw that Japan was in danger of losing the Solomons and New Guinea area, the Marshall and Caroline Islands, the two Aleutian islands it had seized, and the Burma–Sumatra–Java defensive perimeter. Worrisomely, the loss of these areas could expose the Japanese home islands to American bombing.[8] Even archhawk Prime Minister Hideki Tojo began to temper his public optimism.[9]

The Emperor's confidence in Japanese military prospects began to ebb after Midway. Following a major sea battle in late October 1942, Hirohito issued a message congratulating the navy for sinking the American aircraft carrier *Hornet* and a destroyer, but tempered his message by remarking that "the war situation is critical. Officers and men, exert yourselves to even greater efforts."[10] In the latter half of 1942, Hirohito's recognition that the Japanese-held island of Guadalcanal was doomed to American capture coupled with his concerns about Axis fortunes in Europe encouraged him to cancel Operation Gogō, a major ground offensive in China.[11] Through early 1943, the Emperor remained very concerned about the course of the war, in part because of Germany's worsening fortunes.[12]

The Japanese leadership reacted to these adverse developments from mid-1942 on by adjusting its military strategy and ambitions, rather than by opening negotiations with the Allies and/or offering concessions. In reaction to Allied successes, the Japanese leadership de facto retracted its war ambitions, without formally declaring a reduction of demands as part of negotiations with the Allies. Following the first American victory at Midway in early June 1942, Japan canceled plans to invade the islands of New Caledonia, Fiji, and Samoa, and plans to expand into the Indian Ocean.[13] As noted, they soon after canceled a major offensive in China.

On September 30, 1943, the Japanese leadership approved the establishment and reinforcement of an "absolute defense perimeter." The goal was to strengthen Japan's defenses in preparation for the coming Allied offensive (see figure 10.1). This new perimeter was a reduction of territory in comparison to the high water mark of Japanese expansion in mid-1942, and included only the Japanese home islands, the Kuriles, the Bonin Islands, Iwo Jima, the Marianas, the Philippines, the Dutch East Indies, and the Andaman and Nicobar Islands in the Indian Ocean. It excluded Rabaul, the central Solomons, eastern New Guinea, the Marshalls, Makin, and Tarawa. This move recognized Allied successes, the growing threat of further Allied advances, and finite Japanese resources. Regarding this last point, forces on mainland Asia were transferred to the new absolute defense perimeter in the Pacific.[14] Not all saw this shift as a panacea. At the meeting where the leadership proclaimed this new defensive perimeter, Chief of the Imperial Japanese Naval Staff General Admiral Nagano stated that even with a new perimeter and even if annual aircraft production more than doubled to 40,000 aircraft per year, "I cannot assure the future of the war situation."[15] Two months later, Rear Admiral Sōkichi Takagi assembled and presented to two other high-ranking naval officers a comprehensive report on the war, which concluded that Japan could not win.[16]

Japan's military fortunes did not improve significantly over the next several months. A June 1944 report from the army general staff's Conduct of War Section conceded that there was "now no hope to reverse the unfavourable war situation."[17] The July 1944 fall of Saipan was recognized by all as a major setback, convincing the army leadership that the war was lost. The defeat forced Emperor Hirohito to remove Prime Minister Tojo from power.[18]

In reaction to its decline in military fortunes, Japan also sought to amass more power. To that end, it recognized that it would need greater cooperation from other Asians. Japan decided in 1943 to offer more rights and independence to Japanese-controlled areas in China and Southeast Asia in the hopes that under better political conditions Asians would be more willing to contribute to the war effort against the Allies. Like Lincoln's decision to free the slaves, Japan was manipulating its (colonial) war aims in order to increase its military power.[19]

Why did Japan not offer concessions to the Allies as these battle defeats accumulated? A cluster of factors contributed to Japan's refusal to negotiate as it approached literal immolation. Centrally, the Japanese leadership took American demands of unconditional surrender as genuine rather than as strategic posturing. For some, such as Foreign Minister Mamoru Shigemitsu, the reiteration of the unconditional surrender demand in the Allies' December 1943 Cairo Declaration confirmed Allied aims.[20] The Japanese deeply opposed unconditional surrender, as they at all costs wanted to maintain the institution and personal safety of the Emperor and the integrity of the Japanese polity (*kokutai*) more generally.[21] As late as July 12, 1945 the Emperor ruled out the option of direct negotiations with the United States, knowing that the U.S. demanded unconditional surrender, which would mean the destruction of the *kokutai*.[22] As the U.S. steadily marched across the Pacific from mid-1942 forward without any major setbacks, the U.S. gave no indications that it was ready to back down from its unconditional surrender demand. Hence, Japan had no motivation to offer concessions, as Japan perceived that concessions would not be reciprocated by an Allied abandonment of unconditional surrender. Further, as discussed in chapter 2, the mere act of offering concessions might be taken as a signal of Japanese weakness.

If Japan could not use negotiations to get the U.S. to retreat from its unconditional surrender demand, what options were left for saving the Emperor and the *kokutai*? The outright conquest of the United States was inconceivable even to the most deluded militarist. This left as Japan's only option persuading the U.S. to abandon its demand for unconditional surrender. Japan had to somehow convince the U.S. that pursuing unconditional surrender would be prohibitively costly. If the U.S. reached that conclusion, it might then be ready to make concessions. This was a natural evolution of Japanese strategy from the beginning of the war, when it hoped to threaten a war long and bloody enough to persuade the Americans to accept the new Japanese empire. Now, as that empire was being broken by American industrial might and a string of successful island campaigns, Japan sought to persuade America that the last phase of conquering Japan itself would be extraordinarily costly, enough so that America would have to accept the endurance of the Japanese monarchy, albeit one shorn of much of its Asian and Pacific conquests.

The Japanese believed that winning a decisive battle was the best and perhaps only way to persuade the U.S. that pursuing unconditional surrender would be unacceptably costly. The idea that a decisive battle could turn the course of the war and break the will of the opponent was perhaps driven by the Japanese interpretation of the 1904–05 Russo-Japanese War, during which the Japanese victory at the naval battle of Tsushima was seen as the critical blow forcing Russian capitulation.[23] In the late December 1942 discussion about withdrawing from Guadalcanal, the Emperor urged Japanese military leaders to work towards achieving a victory over American forces that would move the Allies to negotiate.[24]

This approach pushed the Emperor to put heavy emphasis on offensive tactics especially in late 1942 and 1943, looking to capture a decisive victory in the face of setbacks in the South Pacific.[25] Indeed, as conditions continued to worsen in mid-1944, the Emperor's reaction was not to consider concessions to the Allies as the information proposition posits, but rather to seek a decisive victory as at Tsushima. He exhorted Vice Chief of Staff Admiral Shigetarō Shimada on June 17, 1944, "Rise to the challenge; make a tremendous effort; achieve a splendid victory like at the time of the Japan Sea naval battle [of Tsushima]."[26] Talking after the war about the October 1944 decision to fight a major battle at Leyte in the Philippines, Hirohito remarked, "I agreed to the showdown battle of Leyte thinking that if we attacked at Leyte and America flinched, then we would probably be able to find room to negotiate."[27]

Many in the Japanese government opposed negotiation until after a great victory had been won. In early January 1944, Kido developed a proposal for opening negotiations, but opposed presenting the proposal to the Allies if Germany collapsed. That is, negotiations could not be risked in the context of growing Japanese weakness.[28] That fall, Prime Minister Kuniaki Koiso framed Japanese strategy in this manner at a meeting of the Supreme Council for the Direction of the War, that Japan would negotiate an end to the war after achieving one decisive victory. For Koiso, the alternative of negotiating terms right after Saipan would have doomed Japan to "merciless terms," and perhaps a serious domestic political crisis. The Council officially approved Koiso's plan in August 1944.[29] Around this time, the Japanese leadership laid out a specific plan, called Sho-Go, for achieving such a decisive victory, aiming to lure American forces into a decisive battle in one of four areas, the Philippines, Formosa (Taiwan) and the Ryukyu Islands, the Japanese home islands other than Hokkaido, and/or Hokkaido itself.[30]

By early 1945, Japanese strategy began to focus on preparing for a decisive battle on the Japanese home islands. On January 20, the Emperor approved a new strategy that called for the use of the home islands for the final decisive battle of the war, again as part of the larger strategy of creating the proper conditions for inducing American retreat from its unconditional surrender demands.[31] On February 14, 1945, Prince Fumimaro Konoe urged immediate negotiation to end the war, but Hirohito disagreed, noting that ending the war would be "very difficult unless we make one more military gain."[32] Hirohito placed his faith in particular on the ability of Japanese spiritual superiority to trump American military superiority, and on Japanese kamikaze tactics.[33] Around this time, General Yoshijiro Umezu and the navy advocated luring the U.S. into a decisive battle off of Taiwan, as a decisive Japanese victory would then make negotiations possible.[34] At the same time, the Imperial General Headquarters drew up a report emphasizing that Japanese military weakness could be offset by exploiting American casualty sensitivity. This idea was the center of the Ketsu-go defense strategy adopted in March.[35] In June 1945, General Korechika Anami, the Army Minister, demurred on a suggestion from Kido to immediately negotiate an end to the war, commenting that a diplomatic initiative would be more likely to succeed if it was launched "after the United States has sustained heavy losses."[36] Prime Minister Kantarō Suzuki agreed with Anami, at least initially.[37] The army leaders understood the great material disadvantage they faced, but they felt that they could accomplish the political goal of encouraging American concessions only by promising exorbitant costs. The Imperial General Headquarters staff held out hope for this strategy in mid-1945, after Germany had surrendered:

> The enemy is mustering enormous and overwhelming military power for use against us; the issue will be joined between now and next spring. Although Japan is faced with an exceedingly precarious overall situation, certain circumstances are working to her advantage. While the end of the war in Europe has given the USA a comfortable reserve of national war potential, industrial mobilization and reconversion have already begun, due to the desire to grab postwar profits. The fighting morale of the United States is being weakened by fear of large casualty tolls. There has been an increase in labor strife, criticism of the military, and agitation from the ranks to engage in a precipitous demobilization. Should the USA be defeated in the battle for Japan itself, public confidence in the President and military leaders will decline abruptly, fighting spirit will deteriorate in the flurry of recriminations, and Japan will find herself in a much more favorable strategic position.[38]

The chief of the Japanese intelligence section, Lieutenant General Arisue Seizo, told American interrogators after the end of the war: "If we could defeat the enemy in Kyushu or inflict tremendous losses, forcing him to realize the strong fighting spirit of the Japanese Army and people, it would be possible, we hoped, to bring about the termination of hostilities on comparatively favorable terms."[39] Notably, although the army hoped to use the invasion of Japan as its last, best opportunity for inflicting a decisive defeat on the U.S., the navy had abandoned its optimism for such an outcome after the June 1945 loss of Okinawa, at which its surface fleet was destroyed and its air strength decimated.[40]

The obsession with demonstrating strength led to some odd perceptions within the Japanese leadership. Indeed, as late as early August 1945 (although before Hiroshima) some in Japan interpreted the July 26 Allied Potsdam Declaration, which called for unconditional surrender, disarmament, regime change, military occupation, and the prosecution of war criminals, as an indication of *buckling* Allied resolve because it also allowed for the possibility of Japan reentering the world economy. Prime Minister Suzuki remarked on August 3 (three days before the first atomic bombing), "For the enemy to say something like that means circumstances have arisen that force them also to end the war. That is why they are talking about unconditional surrender. Precisely at a time like this, if we hold firm, then they will yield before we do. Just because they broadcast their declaration, it is not necessary to stop fighting. You advisors may ask me to reconsider, but I don't think there is any need to stop [the war]."[41]

The strategy of trying to convince America that pursuing total victory would be too costly had a dark side for Japan. Because Japan could at this stage only inflict costs through ground combat (as opposed to bombing the American mainland), part of the signal about the high costs of continued war would have to be that Japan would be willing to accept high costs in its effort to inflict high costs on the U.S. This point was made rather bluntly by the War Journal of Imperial Headquarters after the failure in the Marianas in July 1944, "We can no longer direct the war with any hope of success. The only course left is for Japan's one hundred million people to sacrifice their lives by charging the enemy to make them lose the will to fight."[42] Similarly, Prince Higashikuni remarked, "If Japan's determination to be annihilated is comprehended abroad, then Britain, America, and Russia might hesitate to wage a battle to the finish with us, and might reconsider matters."[43] As a result, by 1945 high Japanese casualties in campaigns such as Iwo Jima and Okinawa *supported* the Japanese strategy since the Japanese willingness to suffer such casualties without offering concessions offered proof to the U.S. that Japan would be willing to suffer exorbitant casualties in the defense of its homeland, as it sought to slaughter the invading American troops.

In sum, Japan framed its war-termination strategy in informational terms: its central military objective was to win a major battle in order to convince the United States that Japan could inflict high casualties if the war continued, and it wanted to avoid sending a signal of Japanese weakness by making concessions following battle defeat. However, the information proposition in chapter 2 does not describe Japanese war-termination behavior well. Because the Allies enjoyed relatively steady military success from mid-1942 onwards, the Japanese should have made concessions, but they did not. Rather, they refused to take any real diplomatic steps towards ending the war until they achieved a great battle victory. Perhaps ironically, at least some on the American side upheld the same view, that concessions should be considered only after victory. That is why Assistant Secretary of War John McCloy rejected an internal proposal in May 1945 to lower the American war-termination offer below unconditional surrender, because Okinawa had not yet been conquered. McCloy felt that an American concession before victory might send a signal of weakening resolve, especially in the context of the stalwart and bloody resistance then being offered by Japanese forces at Okinawa.[44]

A SOBER RECOGNITION OF IMPENDING DEFEAT

Slowly, the course of combat events became sufficiently clear that the Japanese leadership at last began to see the need for negotiations even without a decisive battlefield victory. A crucial event for many was the American capture of the island of Okinawa in June 1945. Kido saw in June that negotiations could not wait for a decisive victory, but rather that negotiations should begin immediately before things worsened even further and Japan might "not attain even our supreme objective of safeguarding the Imperial Household and preserving the national polity."[45] When Chief of Staff Umezu laid out his thoughts on peace negotiations in June, the Emperor asked him directly if he meant that peace moves should be delayed "until after we strike yet another blow at the enemy." Umezu indicated that that was not what he meant.[46]

Hirohito finally decided formally at a June 22 conference to pursue a negotiated peace using the Soviet Union as an intermediary. The significance of this decision should not be exaggerated, however, since no consensus was reached by the top leadership as to what terms for peace would be offered to the Allies or even what terms would be acceptable for Japan.[47] The decision can be seen as partially supportive of the information proposition from chapter 2, in that battlefield setbacks eventually moved the Japanese to consider concessions, but it is evidence of the inefficiency of battlefield information towards causing diplomatic movement because the decision to negotiate was made after three consecutive years of bad military fortunes. Also, the decision itself was limited, in that no actual concessions were decided upon, and the decision was only to open negotiations to draw the participation of a third-party mediator, as opposed to opening negotiations directly with the adversary.

The decisive change in Japanese war-termination behavior came in the second week of August, after the U.S. dropped atomic bombs on two Japanese cities and the Soviet Union declared war on Japan, attacking Japanese forces in Manchuria. These events all happened within four days, from August 6–9, and on August 10 Japan decided to accept the Potsdam Proclamation, which essentially demanded unconditional surrender, with the proviso that the "prerogatives of His Majesty as a sovereign ruler" not be compromised.[48] The United States in its reply (the so-called "Byrnes Note") finessed the Japanese condition, holding to the letter of the Potsdam Proclamation, but repeating that the Proclamation allowed for the Japanese form of government to be chosen by the Japanese people. This vague assurance of the protection of the Emperor ultimately proved sufficient for Japan, and Hirohito broadcast Japan's surrender on August 15.

Scholars differ on exactly why Japan surrendered, with most arguing that surrender was caused by the atomic bombings, the Soviet entry into the war, the destruction of the Japanese merchant marine, and/or the collapse in Japanese confidence in its homeland defenses.[49] Lack of faith in homeland defenses was especially damaging to the Japanese strategy, which was predicated on the ability to inflict high casualties on American forces invading the home islands. Hirohito and other members of the Japanese government had grown increasingly pessimistic about the ability of Japanese forces to achieve a decisive victory against American invasion forces, and correspondingly became increasingly willing to end the war. On June 12 and 13, 1945, Hirohito received a pair of reports declaring preparations for defense of the home islands to be severely inadequate. One report concluded that the war must be ended immediately.[50] These and other reports were steadily undermining the army's claims of strong invasion preparedness.[51] Two months later, after the decision to surrender had been made, Hirohito told the imperial princes that one reason for the decision was because he had lost faith in the military due to its record since the 1944 Leyte operation.[52]

Importantly, these interpretations, attributing the surrender to the atomic bombings, to Soviet entry into the war, and to lack of Japanese confidence in Japanese defensive capabilities, offer evidence favoring the information proposition.[53] The atomic bombings provided new evidence of American military superiority, and critically the American ability to punish Japan without suffering (American) casualties. The Soviet intervention provided information that Japanese hopes for Soviet mediation were now completely baseless, provided new information about the balance of forces facing Japan, and undermined confidence in the effectiveness of Japanese ground forces, which would be used to parry an American invasion of the home islands.

However, looking at the entire war provides a more nuanced view of the role of information in war termination. The information proposition of chapter 2, that combat outcomes affect war-termination decision-making, was unsupported over much of the war, given the Japanese refusal to negotiate in the face of a steady course of military setbacks. Notably, the American decision to make the slight concession on unconditional surrender is inconsistent with the information proposition of chapter 2, as in the face of good military and diplomatic news (the successful atomic bombings and the Soviet entry into the war), the information proposition would predict that the U.S. would hold fast to its demands, and not make concessions. Secretary of State James Byrnes made this exact point that the concession was being offered as both sides were collecting more information about the decline in relative Japanese military capability, fretting that "at Potsdam [in June 1945] the big-3 said 'unconditional surrender.' Then there was [no] atomic bomb and no Russia in the war. I cannot understand why now we should go further than we were willing to go at Potsdam when we had no atomic bomb, and Russia was not in the war."[54] However, Japanese refusal to negotiate even in the face of military decline can be put in an information framework, albeit one different from that described in the information proposition of chapter 2. The Japanese ignored their setbacks not because they were indifferent about sending signals, but because they knew that to do otherwise might send a signal, specifically a signal of weakness. Simultaneously, the Japanese sought to send a signal of their own, winning a decisive battle to send a credible signal of their military power. As described in chapter 3, Japan thought that if they could convince the Americans that pursuit of unconditional surrender would be prohibitively costly, perhaps the Americans would accept a deal leaving the Japanese imperial leadership in place, their credible commitment fears notwithstanding.

JAPANESE DOMESTIC POLITICS AND THE TERMINATION OF THE PACIFIC WAR

What of the role of domestic politics? Like World War I Germany, World War II Japan was a moderately repressive, semi-exclusionary state, making relevant the Goemans domestic politics proposition that leaders of such states may raise their war aims and/or engage in gambles for resurrection to maintain their holds on power and avoid severe personal punishment.[55] In both World War I Germany and World War II Japan, there was a monarch with limited powers, a formal parliament with limited powers, and jockeying among special interest groups and military branches in particular for control of foreign policy. In both regimes, democracy and freedom deteriorated as war progressed.[56] Although World War II Japan was certainly not a democracy, it also should not be classed as a dictatorship. No single individual (or branch of the military) ruled Japan as Hitler did in Nazi Germany or Stalin did in the Soviet Union, although Prime Minister Tojo began to aggregate political power before he fell from power in 1944. Although the party system had been essentially abolished, there was a quasi-democratic structure called the Imperial Rule Assistance Association established in 1940, which held elections in April 1942. Although officially recommended candidates ran in these elections, nonrecommended candidates did run and sometimes even won. Wartime prime ministers, including Tojo, were neither all-powerful nor puppets. There was political repression of the opposition, although not as severe as in Nazi Germany, as political opponents such as Communists who were imprisoned were released after renouncing their political beliefs. There were no concentration camps, and no extermination of opposition figures. One former parliamentary member actively attempted to overthrow (peacefully) the Tojo government in 1943, and although he was initially imprisoned he was soon released by judicial order. There was also jostling among factions within the government, including between the army and navy, and between the civil bureaucracy and the military.[57]

Domestic political institutions aside, Goemans' theory should apply well to World War II Japan. The war was fought over private goods (economic empire), the war was long, the costs of war escalated as the war progressed, and Japan suffered a steady string of military setbacks from mid-1942 forward. Goemans' theory should predict that as the war continued and the costs of war escalated, the Japanese leadership ought to have increased its war aims in order to increase the payoffs to coalition members to maintain political support. Although Japan's bid for empire was already ambitious, it could have expanded its war aims further by seeking greater territorial conquests in India, the Soviet Union, or North America. Or, the mixed regime hypothesis might predict that Japan could have decided in 1944–45 to abandon its 1943 "absolute defensive perimeter," reestablishing its more extensive imperial goals of 1941–42. Further, Japan might have engaged in a risky military strategy, a gamble for resurrection, in a desperate effort to secure a decisive war victory providing substantial territorial or other gains at the risk of increasing the chances of total defeat.

Contrary to the predictions of the theory, none of these patterns of behavior came to pass. Japan did not increase and if anything decreased its de facto war aims as its military fortunes declined. In other words, as the war progressed the leadership took actions that reduced the amount of private goods it would have at its disposal to distribute to coalition supporters. It trimmed its expansion plans following the defeat at Midway in 1942, and canceled an offensive in China. It decreased its war aims by deciding in September 1943 to fall back to its absolute defense perimeter, and did not reverse this decision in the last years of the war. Further, perhaps in contrast to the Goemans hypothesis, the Japanese leadership was willing to make concessions, including concessions on economically profitable private goods. In 1943, the Emperor instructed Foreign Minister Shigemitsu that retention of the colonies should not stand in the way of a speedy end to the war.[58] In January 1944, Tojo announced an agreement with the pro-Japanese Wang-Ching Wei regime in Nanking,

China in which Japan abandoned its treaty-port settlements and extraterritorial privileges in China. It was hoped that doing so would allow the redirection of troops from China to the Pacific.[59] In September 1944, the Japanese leadership approved a number of concessions to the Soviet Union to improve Soviet–Japanese relations and secure Soviet mediation, including offering maritime and commercial fishing concessions, abandoning the Chinese Eastern Railway, returning southern Sakhalin, surrendering the Northern Kurils, exiting the Anti-Communist Pact and the Tripartite Pact, permitting peaceful Soviet activities in Manchuria, Inner Mongolia, China, and elsewhere in East Asia, and recognizing Soviet spheres of influence in Manchuria and Inner Mongolia.[60] Similar concessions were offered to the Soviet Union in July 1945 talks between Soviet Foreign Minister Vyacheslav Molotov and Japanese ambassador to Moscow Naotoke Sato.[61] Around the same time, Foreign Minister Shigenori Togo declared in secret correspondence that in war-termination negotiations mediated by Moscow Japan would declare that it "has absolutely no idea of annexing or holding the territories which she occupied during the war."[62]

On the military strategy side, Japan did not engage in any gambles for resurrection. Three strategies are worth discussing as possible gambles for the resurrection of Japan during the 1944–45 period. The first is a Japanese diplomatic gambit to secure a favorable Soviet attitude, either a renewed commitment to neutrality, mediation of a negotiated termination, and/or an alliance with Japan. One Japanese military officer who favored the approach to the USSR framed Japanese diplomacy as a gamble. In an April 29, 1945 report circulated at very high levels, Colonel Suketaka Tamemura compared the Japanese position to a sumo wrestler nearly pushed out of the ring. The wrestler's only hope of victory is a desperate backwards move with only a one-in-ten chance of success. For Tamemura, Japan was in such a situation, and needed to pursue the improbable gamble of securing a favorable Soviet attitude in order to win the war.[63] Although Japan did attempt to engage Soviet mediation from at least late 1944 onward, this was not truly a gamble as intended here. Despite it being a strategy with a low probability of success, it was a maneuver without danger, especially since—when the Japanese did approach the Soviets—they did not present an actual set of concessions they wished the Soviets to pass on to the Allies. Further, the Soviet gambit would not have fit well with Goemans' theory, as the Japanese were offering substantial economic concessions to attract Soviet interest, but within Goemans' theory the point of the gamble for resurrection was to secure decisive victory and acquire more economic gains for distribution to coalition members.

The second possible gamble-for-resurrection candidate is the strategy of launching kamikaze missions. Kamikaze missions, suicide attacks by Japanese aircraft and naval vessels against American naval vessels in particular, are in some sense the definition of desperation, foregoing conventional attacks in the hope that suicidally ramming the enemy might more effectively degrade enemy forces. However, Japanese suicide attacks did not constitute a gamble for resurrection, either, for the simple reason that these attacks were a relatively efficient use of Japanese military resources.[64] By 1943 especially, Japanese air forces were suffering from increasing barriers to effective operations, including steep declines in the number and quality of Japanese pilots, improvements in interception by American fighter aircraft, and the development of the proximity fuse for anti-aircraft shells. Kamikaze tactics reduced some of these problems since such attacks could be conducted with more basic flying skills and more obsolete aircraft. Further, a Japanese plane struck by a proximity-fused shell could still ram its target, although it would likely be unable to deliver a bomb or strafe its target.[65] Kamikaze attacks inflicted heavy damage on U.S. forces. Air attacks sank or put permanently out of action 164 Allied vessels. Another eighty-five experienced substantial structural damage, human casualties, or both, and minor damage was inflicted on a further 221. About sixty kamikazes collided with B-29 bombers in mid-air. Suicide boats sank eight small vessels, heavily damaged an additional eight, and caused minor damage to seven. Human torpedoes known as *kaiten* sank two vessels.[66] More casualties were caused by suicide attacks on U.S. vessels off Okinawa than were inflicted on U.S. troops fighting on the ground there.[67] Consider also the results of a conventional air–sea battle fought off Formosa on October 15, 1944. The Japanese Navy heavily damaged two American cruisers at a cost of 126 aircraft, in comparison with a kamikaze attack ten days later that sank one aircraft carrier and damaged six others at a cost of sixteen aircraft.[68] Two historians have asserted that in the face of kamikaze attacks, "No other power [aside from the United States] could have sustained such losses and continued to fight an offensive naval war."[69] One might rebut that it was mere luck that kamikaze attacks just happened to work, and that it was a true gamble to see if they would succeed. However, kamikaze attacks were relatively low in cost, because attacks were launched initially in a very piecemeal fashion, so the utter failure of the attacks would have meant the loss of a very small number of men and aircraft. In contrast, Germany's 1918 Operation Michael and December 1944 Ardennes offensives were more committing, as each required the decisive commitment of final reserves, and the failure of the attack would (and did) mean exhaustion and rapid military collapse. Also, Germany's 1917 unrestricted submarine warfare was politically committing, since the diplomatic risks of incurring American involvement in the war were incurred as soon as the campaign began.

A third possible gamble-for-resurrection tactic would have been the widespread use by Japan of biological weapons against Allied troops or civilians. Japan had a massive biological weapons program, probably the most substantial of any belligerent in history. It could have deployed biological weapons towards the end of the war as a desperate gambit, increasing the chances for victory by inflicting massive casualties, but also increasing the chances of decisive defeat by steeling the resolve of the Americans to fight to the finish and prosecute Japanese political and military leaders for war crimes.[70]

However, Japan did not embrace biological weapons only as their fortunes worsened in 1944 and 1945. The Japanese leadership approved the use of biological weapons against American troops in the first months of war, during the initial period of great Japanese success. Plans were drawn up as early as March 1942 for the deployment of 1,000 kilograms of fleas infected with the plague against Allied troops in the Philippines, although Japanese forces achieved victory there before the fleas were ready for dispersal. Other plans for the use of biological weapons were also considered. Further, when defeat did loom in 1945, Japan ultimately declined to use biological weapons against American civilians. In March 1945, the Japanese Chiefs of Staff approved operation "Cherry Blossoms at Night," a plan to use submarine-launched planes and ship-borne commandos to distribute cholera and bubonic plague among civilian populations in southern California. The head of the chiefs of staff, Umezu, canceled the operation before it could be carried out because he recognized that such a mission would accomplish no military objectives and would only stoke American fury.[71]

A further question is whether internal political dynamics within Japan fit the hypothesized internal processes forecast by the Goemans hypothesis. Did Hirohito and the Japanese leadership fear they would be thrown from power in the event of moderate defeat? Did they fear that such an eventuality would cause them to suffer severe political punishment such as death or imprisonment?

Japanese leaders did not make domestic political calculations in this manner. There was a fear of domestic internal threat, but the leaders believed this threat would be heightened by *continuing* the privations of war, not from *terminating* the war with insufficient private goods to distribute. As early as February 1943 in the aftermath of the defeat at Guadalcanal, Prince Konoe expressed the view, to the agreement of Kido and Marquis Matsudaira, that immediate war termination was imperative to prevent the emergence of a Communist threat within Japan.[72] Konoe returned to this point two years later when the war looked much worse, urging Hirohito to begin war-termination negotiations immediately to avert a Communist revolution, which might overthrow the *kokutai*, because of growing economic strains and popular discontent.[73] Although Hirohito rejected Konoe's suggestion, he did recognize (in February 1945) the dangers in letting the war continue indefinitely, remarking later that day, "If we persist in this war, I'm absolutely convinced of victory, but until then I worry whether or not the people will be able to endure."[74] Domestic political threats were discussed at an April 4 meeting, at which Kido fretted that the recent surge in antimilitarism could lead to public upheaval.[75] An official high-level report issued in May 1945 worried about the possibility of worsening food shortages and even famines that might undermine domestic order.[76] On July 11, internal correspondence from the Foreign Minister declared that the government was moving to terminate the war "because of the pressing situation which confronts Japan both at home and abroad."[77] Indeed, the Emperor's intervention on August 10 to command conditional acceptance of the Potsdam Declaration was motivated by concerns over threats of domestic upheaval from the continued privations of war, as well as fears of the atomic bomb and Soviet intervention.[78] In the high-level deliberations following the Nagasaki bombing and Soviet intervention, Baron Kiichirō Hiranuma expressed grave concern about domestic conditions and food shortages in particular. He predicted that the "continuation of the war will create greater domestic disturbances than would termination of the war." Prime Minister Suzuki concurred, arguing that the people "cannot withstand the air-raids any longer."[79] After the decision to surrender had been made, one Japanese observer saw the atomic bombings and Soviet intervention as fortunate, since these events facilitated surrender before domestic disorder might have erupted: "I think the term is perhaps inappropriate, but the atomic bombs and the Soviet entry into the war are, in a sense, gifts from the gods. This way we don't have to say that we quit the war because of domestic circumstances. I've long been advocating control of our crisis, but neither from fear of an enemy attack nor because of the atomic bombs and the Soviet entry into the war. The main reason is my anxiety over the domestic situation. So, it is rather fortunate that we can now control matters without revealing the domestic situation."[80] One August 1945 police report noted a substantial increase in antiwar sentiment in comparison to 1943 and 1944.[81] The Japanese historian Saburo Ienaga noted that by the summer of 1945, "The ruling classes' judgment that to continue the war endangered the 'national polity' had ample basis in fact."[82] In short, the Japanese leadership saw the solution to domestic political threats to the government as terminating the war rather than expanding it.

Myths of Empire?

The Goemans hypothesis proposes that leaders of mixed regimes like Japan are motivated to increase war aims and gamble for resurrection when they face moderate military defeat. A related proposition is that such mixed regimes embrace ambitious war aims and imperial over-expansion to hold together ruling coalitions. Specifically, such regimes are often led by oligarchic coalitions of military and industrial interests, and such coalitions are prone to logrolled foreign policies aimed to satisfy all of its members. However, such logrolling can cause a state to bite off far more that it can chew, as satisfying all members of the coalition means an aggregate foreign policy that confronts more enemies than the state has the capability to confront. Relatedly, other scholars have claimed that these dynamics coupled with insufficient press and speech freedoms and weak civilian control of the military spawn pro-imperial mythmaking. Branches of the military and militarist economic sectors encourage the spread of ideas that encourage the embrace of imperial adventures, such as exaggerating the state's own national power, emphasizing the impor-tance of attacking first, and so on. These ideas have been applied to ex-plain Japan's pursuit of empire in Asia in the 1930s and its attack on Pearl Harbor.[83]

These theoretical ideas could also be applied to understand Japanese war-termination decisions during the Pacific War. The general prediction might be that the Japanese leadership should be slow to negotiate settle-ment terms because of domestic political forces. The various members of the oligarchic coalition would resist abandoning foreign policy goals that they had championed. Further, pro-imperial myths might blind the government to the discouraging course of the war, pushing the gov-ernment to resist concessions even as losses mounted. Relatedly, informa-tion monopolies of the military branches in particular might slow the process by which the government came to understood that the war was going badly.

Although the Japanese leadership was willing to give up its empire as the war worsened, the other claims deserve close consideration. Notably, as described earlier and contrary to the speculations of the mythmaking theory, many members of the government inside and outside the military recognized the basic course of the war, that it was a steady tide of bad news from Midway forward, although to be sure there were instances in which some members of government were given inaccurate accounts of battle outcomes, such as following the battle of Midway, the March 1944 airstrike against Majuro, during clashes in the Marianas in mid-1944, and in the early stages of the autumn 1944 Leyte campaign.[84]

One piece of evidence favoring the mythmaking theory might be Prime Minister Tojo's famous postwar complaint that he "did not hear of the Midway defeat till more than a month after it occurred. Even now I do not know the details."[85] Tojo's postwar claim made to American interrogators, conveniently diminishing his own guilt in prolonging the war, may have been disingenuous, however. There was in Japan public discussion of the disaster at Midway as early as a few days after the battle. On June 10, 1942, a spokesman for the Japanese navy was quoted in the *Asahi* newspaper that "one cannot always expect victories and we must be able to stand losses." A few days later, Tokyo radio conceded that the losses at Midway were "not inconsiderable" and that they were "the greatest suffered since the beginning of the war."[86] Tojo himself did get a flow of information about the course of the war. His wife recalled that Tojo was informed, and shaken, when American forces recaptured the Aleutian island of Attu in May 1943. His public language slowly turned less confident throughout the war. He even allowed for the possibility of defeat in public remarks in March 1943, and the following January conceded that "there is only a hairbreadth between victory and defeat," and that the Japanese nation would face "more and more severe" difficulties.[87]

That being said, Tojo at times refused to accept gloomy reports about the course of the war, occasionally killing the messenger, literally. When a colonel presented a report in early 1944 recommending an end to the war, Tojo responded by ordering the colonel's transfer to the China front the following day.[88] Major Tsukamoto also voiced his doubts about the course of the war to Tojo in 1944, and found himself transferred to Saipan the following day, where he was killed in action. Ultimately, Tojo transferred at least seventy-two individuals who voiced opposition to his war plans, who presented political threats, or whom he simply did not like.[89]

However, as described, many key members of government beyond Tojo were reasonably well-informed, and few could avoid seeing the handwriting on the wall as the war progressed. Although some members of government did not get a complete briefing on the outcome of the Battle of Midway, the navy leadership understood what happened at Midway, the Emperor himself was fully briefed, and the public was informed at least in general terms of a significant defeat.[90] As noted, many high-ranking leaders recognized that Midway, or perhaps Guadalcanal, was the turning point in the war. In other instances, an initially rose-colored report on a battle outcome was eventually disproved by further battlefield developments. For example, the promising October 1944 reports about the Leyte campaign had to be abandoned when the Imperial Headquarters declared the battle lost in December, and the Emperor himself became worried by American successes there.[91] Tojo's May 1944 claim that Saipan was invulnerable to conquest was, of course, completely discredited when the island fell in early July, and the deflation of Tojo's outlandish boast contributed to his ouster on July 18.[92] The army certainly understood the seriousness of the loss of Saipan.[93] In November 1944, Premier Koiso claimed publicly that Japan could turn the tide of the war in the Philippines, equating the fighting there to a battle fought in Japan in 1582 when General Hideyoshi won a critical battle at Tennōzan mountain in the Kansai district of Japan, which in turn paved the way for his rise to power. Koiso's claim that "If Japan wins on Leyte, she wins the war!" backfired to Koiso's embarrassment when the U.S. announced on Christmas 1944 that Leyte had fallen.[94] The continued attempts of the government to claim that Leyte, then Luzon, then Iwo Jima, then Okinawa would be the new Tennōzan grew increasingly incredible to the Japanese population at large, as some Tokyo residents joked that Koiso apparently had the power to move mountains.[95]

In sum, the evidence indicates that it would be inaccurate to characterize the Japanese leadership as completely deluded in its contemporary assessment of the progress of the war. This contrasts with the rosy and exaggerated hope for Japanese victory before Pearl Harbor. It may be that myths about one's own superiority and the enemy's weakness are much easier to make when combat is not actually taking place. Once real war starts, it is increasingly difficult to maintain such myths when territory is being lost, cities in the homeland are being bombed, and friendly casualties accumulate.

A slightly different domestic politics hypothesis might be that weak civilian control of the military, a frequent aspect of mixed regimes, slowed war termination. The hypothesis would propose that civilian leaders, with more of a concern for the national good and a more clear-eyed view of Japan's military prospects, wanted to end the war sooner. Therefore, the war would have ended sooner had there been firmer civilian control of the military, reducing civilian fears of a military reaction or even a coup d'état to block serious peace moves. Certainly, differences existed between some civilians and some members of the military over exactly when such negotiations should occur, although notably there were civilian hawks and military doves. Some supported peace negotiations in the first flush of victory, as early as December 1941.[96] The more hawkish elements waited in vain for a decisive military victory, opposing negotiations even after the atomic bombings and Soviet intervention in August 1945.

Did a coup d'état threat slow war termination? The Japanese military certainly took an active role in political life, to the point of assassinating disliked civilian politicians. The 1930s were rife with such actions, including most infamously the February 26, 1936 incident, in which rogue military units assassinated the finance minister, the privy seal, and the inspector-general of military training, among others.[97]

The Emperor and other members of the civilian leadership did worry about the possibility of a coup during the war. In 1946, the Emperor recalled that in 1941 there was sufficient confidence in Japanese military strength that if he had stifled advocacy of war after the American oil embargo had been imposed, he would have risked inciting a coup.[98] However, it may have been politically convenient for Hirohito to claim after the fact that he was forced into war by a domestic military threat; notably, many modern scholars proposed that Hirohito supported the decision to attack Pearl Harbor.[99] Prince Takamatsu privately expressed concern in May 1943 that the demands of the military would be a significant barrier to peace negotiations, although he noted that royal intervention for peace could keep the military in line.[100] In July 1944, before Tojo stepped down, Konoe told Kido that the army was planning on removing the Emperor to Manchuria or replacing him with a prince less inclined to pursue peace negotiations.[101] In April 1945, during discussions over the formation of a new cabinet, both Kido and Tojo expressed concern that the emergence of a more pro-negotiations cabinet might incite military resistance, although former Prime Ministers Keisuke Okada and Baron Reijiro Wakatsuki disagreed.[102] The historian Edward Drea proposed that Hirohito's general timidity and conservatism prevented him from pursuing peace with the Allies in June 1945, even following the June 22 decision to formally seek Soviet mediation. Drea noted that part of this timidity was Hirohito's lingering fear of a military coup if he moved to end the conflict too quickly.[103] The Emperor also claimed after the war that he feared that any mention of peace during the war would have incited tremendous internal violence. His chamberlain went farther, proposing that anyone even mentioning the word peace would have been assassinated by the military.[104] Eventually, the Emperor decided on August 10, 1945 to agree to a conditional version of the Potsdam Declaration, accepting the threat of a coup. There was talk of a military coup at the highest levels immediately after the Emperor made his decision, but the leaders of the military met separately and not only agreed to follow the Emperor's decision, but put their decision to follow the Emperor in writing. There was, however, a coup attempt made by lower ranking officers, who unsuccessfully attempted to seize the recording the Emperor had made announcing his surrender decision, scheduled to be played on broadcast radio on August 15.[105]

These coup fears may have made an earlier move to negotiations less likely, but these effects should not be exaggerated. Many civilians, including the Emperor, opposed entering negotiations at least until Japan had scored a major victory. The Emperor clung to this strategy well into 1945. Even after the loss of Okinawa in June 1945, the Emperor hoped that perhaps a victory over American and British forces at Yunnan might provide some hope, although the army and navy leadership recognized that such an attack was logistically infeasible. The army focused on the American invasion of Japan itself as the last best chance to inflict a decisive defeat.[106] Further, both groups advocated a diplomatic approach to the Soviet Union to secure Soviet neutrality and to attract Soviet mediation to end the war. The war faction saw that Soviet neutrality was necessary to permit a successful defense of the home islands, and the peace faction saw Soviet mediation as the best hope for jumpstarting negotiations with the United States and Britain.[107]

As for the Emperor himself, it would be inaccurate to view him as a closet dove, fearful of speaking out until catastrophe loomed for fear of being thrown from power. In truth, the Emperor supported the attack on Pearl Harbor, and an aggressive pursuit of victory. He was not politically isolated from the hawks. For example, the Emperor supported the arch-hawk General Tojo when the latter was prime minister, and looked unfavorably on plots to overthrow Tojo in 1943.[108] Further, the Emperor often intervened in Japanese politics and military planning, forcing an outcome at odds with military preferences. Before the war, he helped bring down the Tanaka cabinet in 1928, he helped stop the rebels during the February 26, 1936 incident, and his objections helped prevent the 1938 Changkufeng Incident with the Soviet Union from escalating. He was occasionally able to guide military decisions directly during the war, as when he forced Army Chief of Staff Sugiyama to renew Japanese attacks on American forces in the Bataan peninsula of the Philippines in January 1942, pushed Sugiyama to redeploy air assets to support the Guadalcanal campaign in autumn 1942, ordered an immediate offensive against New Guinea once the order to withdraw from Guadalcanal had been given, overrode one of his general's requests by ordering an attack on Leyte in October 1944 rather than a defense of Luzon, and ordered a counteroffensive on the island of Okinawa after America's 1945 landing there.[109]

Some might argue that biases made the Japanese military overoptimistic about its ability to inflict such a decisive defeat on the Americans. Severe bias in the Japanese military would be evidence for the importance of domestic politics, as false military confidence in the ability to inflict casualties, coupled with the inability of the Emperor and civilian leaders to override military preferences on peace talks, caused the war to drag on longer than it should have. It is of course difficult to assess the accuracy of judgments about events that did not happen, specifically, whether Japan could have inflicted enough casualties on American forces invading Japan to move Truman to make concessions permitting the continuation of the *kokutai* as part of a peace deal. However, while the faith in the Japanese military to inflict decisive casualties in the event of an American invasion of the home islands may have been inflated, it was not completely detached from reality. Of course, such a battle would have meant utterly titanic Japanese civilians and military casualties, but this was a cost supporters of the "decisive battle in Japan" strategy were willing to accept in order to save the *kokutai*. In August 1945, Admiral Takijiro Onishi, Vice Chief of Naval General Staff, expressed the extreme form of this view, demanding that Japan continue the war: "we are prepared to sacrifice 20,000,000 Japanese lives in a special attack [kamikaze] effort, victory will be ours!"[110]

American casualties following an invasion might have been enough to encourage major American concessions in negotiations, such as leaving the Japanese political system intact. Estimates of U.S. casualties from an invasion made at the time and after the war vary widely, ranging from the tens of thousands to the hundreds of thousands.[111] More importantly, it is at least conceivable that such casualties may have been sufficient to move the American government to make concessions. Some American leaders at the time were concerned about invasion casualties and their political consequences. Chief of Staff General George Marshall was concerned about the political effects of such gigantic casualties from an American landing in Japan, urging General Douglas MacArthur to reject planning estimates of over 100,000 American casualties.[112] In May 1945, Admiral Chester Nimitz argued that because of the likely heavy casualties and insufficient preparation, the Allies might be better off eschewing invasion and instead embracing a strategy of isolation coupled with naval and air attack.[113] Some contemporary historians have argued that absent the atomic bombings or Soviet entry into the war, Ketsu-go might have succeeded in its goals of pushing the Allies to make substantial concessions after having faced massive casualties in an invasion of the Japanese home islands.[114]

Ending the Pacific War

The accumulation of information from the string of combat setbacks from mid-1942 forward should have pushed Japan to negotiate much earlier, according to the information proposition of chapter 2. Japan's decision to fight on without negotiating was the result primarily of a mix of information and commitment dynamics. Negotiations would be useless until the U.S. could be forced to budge from its demand for unconditional surrender. As described in chapter 6, the U.S. advocated unconditional surrender because of credible commitment concerns. The only way to move the U.S. from unconditional surrender would be to convince the U.S. through a great military victory that pursuing unconditional surrender would be prohibitively costly. Until such a victory could be achieved, Japan feared entering negotiations, as doing so might send a dangerous signal of weakness. Fear of a possible military coup in reaction to peace negotiations might also have delayed peace talks, although there is no support for the hypothesis that moderately repressive semi-exclusionary states fighting long losing wars like Japan in World War II raise their war aims in order to have more goods to distribute to their supporters.

CHAPTER ELEVEN

Conclusions

> War, what is it good for? Absolutely nothing.
>
> —Edwin Starr

WHAT IS THE FUNCTION OF WAR? Poets, artists, and ordinary people have long agreed with the words of the popular song that war is good for "absolutely nothing," providing only death and destruction. And yet wars continue to occur by the deliberate choices of national leaders, encouraging the conclusion that wars must have some purpose, must be politics "by other means."

This book has described two functions of war, two purposes that fighting is meant to serve: providing information and solving commitment problems. These answers undergird a single theoretical approach to war termination focusing on how states seek to maximize benefits and minimize costs. These answers also constitute the core of broader international relations theory about the causes of war: wars happen because states are uncertain about each others' intentions and capabilities, and because states cannot sign binding agreements by which they agree not to attack each other. I have extended these insights about the causes of war to understand the prosecution and termination of war, exploring how war is used to solve the problems that lead to its outbreak.

This concluding chapter has two tasks. The first is summary and synthesis. The findings of the twenty-two war-termination decisions examined are summarized, grouped, and analyzed, towards providing more general conclusions as to how wars end, and how information and commitment factors interrelate in explaining war termination and international relations more broadly. The second is the discussion of the empirical finding for contemporary American foreign policy. What recommendations do these findings hold for the conduct of American foreign policy in the twenty-first century?

HOW STATES ENDED WAR

The empirical chapters in this book surveyed twenty-two war-termination decisions across six wars. Although the small and nonrandom nature of the sample precludes quantitative analysis, the data provide strong support for the model presented in chapters 2 and 3, and the general notion that both information and commitment factors are necessary to provide a complete understanding of war-termination decision-making. This section uses sets of the twenty-two cases to demonstrate several patterns predicted by the theoretical model.

Higher War-Termination Demands with Discouraging Information, Commitment Credibility Concerns, and Hope for Ultimate Victory

The conventional information-oriented wisdom (as expressed by the information proposition in chapter 2) is that combat setbacks should encourage negotiation and concessions, and combat successes should encourage increases in war-termination demands. The theoretical model, as fully developed in chapter 3, develops a set of propositions that explain the conditions under which the information proposition ought to predict accurately war-termination behavior, and conditions under which it will not accurately predict war-termination behavior. Specifically, chapter 3 develops propositions that predict the conditions under which a belligerent may maintain high war-termination demands or even raise them, even when the belligerent is experiencing combat setbacks. The theoretical argument is that a belligerent will eschew concessions in the face of bad news when it thinks the adversary will not credibly commit to a war-ending commitment, and if the belligerent has some hope of eventually winning the war at an acceptable cost in relation to the stakes at hand.

Seven cases fit this mold of a belligerent maintaining high war aims (or even increasing its war aims) despite battlefield setbacks, because of severe commitment concerns and a hope of eventually winning the war. They include the absence of Union concessions in summer 1862, the Confederacy's decision not to negotiate in late 1863, the Union's decision not to negotiate in the summer of 1864, the Confederacy's decision not to make concessions in early 1865, Britain's decision not to negotiate with Hitler in May 1940, the American commitment to the unconditional surrender of the Axis in early 1942, and the American decision to press for the conquest of North Korea in August–September 1950.[1]

In each case, the belligerent in question had suffered severe setbacks. A focus on information alone would predict that the losing belligerent should have reacted to its battlefield setbacks by reducing its war-termination demands in the hopes of ending the war sooner and avoiding the risks of fighting on. However, in each case the belligerent elected to fight on because of concerns that making concessions and/or accepting a limited war outcome would jeopardize the belligerent's longer-term security. Jefferson Davis feared that the Radical Republicans would force a harsh reconstruction. Lincoln feared the southern states would soon demand slavery in more than just the existing slave states. Churchill feared that Hitler would demand concessions, leaving Britain at his mercy. Roosevelt feared a repetition of the Versailles debacle. Truman feared that North Korea would take asylum behind any armistice line, lying in wait for a favorable opportunity to strike again. Further, in each case the belligerent was able to maintain some hope that eventually the tide might turn, the recent setbacks notwithstanding. Britain in 1940 hoped for eventual American rescue. The U.S. in 1942 assumed that eventually mobilization of its economy would overwhelm the Axis. The CSA hoped that escalating Northern war fatigue would force the Union to end the war on terms recognizing Confederate independence. Truman hoped that American forces could hold on until reinforcements could arrive, or MacArthur's great gamble at Inchon might turn the tide.

Beyond these seven cases, Japan from mid-1942 to mid-1945 is perhaps an eighth case. Like the other cases, Japan experienced a steady stream of combat setbacks, yet chose not to negotiate or make concessions. Also like the other cases, Japan clung to some hope of extracting a more acceptable war outcome, by persuading the United States that pursuing unconditional surrender would be prohibitively costly. This case is a bit different from others in that Japan did not face quite the same commitment problem. Its adversary, the U.S., kept to its demand for unconditional surrender, meaning the Japanese did not consider the possibility of the U.S. pushing for a limited war settlement that they would then go on to break.

These cases are the strongest evidence that a complete understanding of war termination cannot focus exclusively on information dynamics. These are all easy cases for an information-only approach, in that in each case the independent variable of battle outcomes is very clearly coded as providing discouraging information from combat outcomes, thereby predicting a reduction in war-termination demands. Yet in each case the belligerent raises or maintains high war-termination demands. They all demonstrate that commitment dynamics play an important role in understanding a belligerent's war-termination decisions.

Lower War-Termination Demands with Discouraging Information, Commitment Credibility Concerns, and Almost No Hope for Ultimate Victory

Another group of cases is similar to the preceding group with one difference. Like the preceding group, these belligerents received discouraging information from combat outcomes and sustained credible commitment concerns about their adversaries. However, unlike the previous group the belligerents in this group held almost no hope in eventual victory. For them, the nontrivial costs of continuing to fight were enough to encourage concessions to reach even an unstable peace, rather than fight on in hopes of a victory unlikely to occur.

The first two cases are Finland in 1940 and 1944. In both periods, Finland experienced combat setbacks in its war with the Soviet Union. Finland had reason to distrust Soviet commitment credibility, if for no other reason than both the 1939 and 1941 Soviet attacks broke neutrality agreements. Yet in both cases Finland decided to make concessions and accept a limited end to the war. Both times, Finland recognized that its military prospects were collapsing rapidly, and that absolute defeat loomed as a possibility. Relatedly, Finland understood on both occasions that there was little hope for eventual victory, especially given that third parties would not be able to turn back Soviet might (in 1940, British and French aid would arrive too late, and in 1944, Germany was collapsing under the assault of the Red Army).

A third case, with thin evidence, is the Soviet Union in autumn 1941. The Soviet Union faced a much grimmer outlook in 1941 than did Britain in 1940 or the U.S. in 1942. All three Allied belligerents faced very worrisome combat setbacks at these three points in time, and all three gravely doubted the credibility of any war-ending Axis commitment to peace. However, the Soviet Union faced a much bleaker outlook in 1941 than did Britain in 1940 or the U.S. in 1942. Nazi Germany had invaded and conquered huge chunks of the Soviet Union by autumn 1941, including roughly a third to a half of the Soviet economy, and stood on the brink of seizing Moscow itself. Both Britain and the U.S. could hope that the oceans, naval power, and air power could provide enough defenses to prevent their own homelands from being invaded, although of course the U.S. felt much more secure on this score than did Britain. The theory predicts that the U.S. and Britain would reject negotiations in pursuit of an unstable limited war peace, and instead fight on, whereas the Soviet Union would in desperation offer concessions in an effort to stave off its apparently inevitable defeat. The existing evidence indicates that Stalin did decide to offer Hitler a basket of territorial concessions in October 1941, as a desperate move to end the war and save the Bolshevik state, although it is unclear whether these concessions were ever communicated to Berlin.

A final case in this group is Japan in August 1945. Up to this point in the war, Japan had continued the war despite combat setbacks, in the hopes that eventually it could threaten to impose enough costs on the U.S. to persuade it to abandon unconditional surrender. It finally agreed to make concessions and accept near-unconditional surrender once its faith in its ability to impose high costs on the U.S. collapsed, a development caused principally by Soviet entry into the war and discouraging reports about Japanese homeland defenses.

Lower War-Termination Demands with Discouraging Information, Commitment Credibility Concerns, and Prohibitively High Costs of Continued Warfare

Related to collapsing hopes of victory, another factor that can cause a belligerent facing combat setbacks and retaining credible commitment concerns to lower its war-termination aims is the prospect of prohibitively high costs of continuing to fight. The U.S. in early 1951 represents this dynamic. Its hopes of solving its credible commitment problem by over-throwing the Pyongyang government were dashed once China entered the war in autumn 1950. Chinese entry redefined the credible commitment problem: now, solving the credible commitment problem in Korea would mean escalation to war with China, and perhaps even nuclear war with the Soviet Union. As the theory predicts, the Washington decision-makers concluded that the costs of securing the luxury of solving the credible commitment problem proved too high in relation to the dangers posed by a violation of the commitment (the future conquest of South Korea). Chastened, the U.S. lowered its war-termination demands, no longer seeking the conquest of North Korea.

Japan in August 1945 also represents this dynamic. The previous section noted that Japan accepted defeat in August 1945 in part because it lost faith in its ability to impose costs on the United States. It also recognized that continuing to fight would impose exorbitant and unacceptable costs. The atomic bombings of Hiroshima and Nagasaki demonstrated the American ability to inflict several tens of thousands of casualties with a single bomb, without risking American casualties. The prospect of the literal annihilation of Japanese civilization was too much for the leadership in Tokyo to bear.

Encouraging Information Causing Higher War-Termination Demands

A few cases demonstrate the logic of war contained within the information proposition of chapter 2, when good news from the battlefront encouraged a state to demand more of its adversary. The Soviet Union in 1940 and 1944, after initial setbacks, finally reached a position of military dominance over Finland. In both instances, it took advantage of its military successes to increase its war-termination demands. Notably, its increased demands in each case were finite, as external factors (the impending Anglo-French intervention in 1940 and the remaining need to crush Germany in 1944) provided impetus to end each war quickly.

The Union in autumn 1862 is worth noting as a case that does not fit in this group. On the surface, it might seem to belong, as the Union raised its war-termination demands to seek the emancipation of the slaves after having won at Antietam. Closer examination reveals that the victory at Antietam did little to boost the Union's confidence in its ultimate military prospects. Further, the Union raised its war aims out of concerns with its weakness, not because it was encouraged by demonstration of its strength, since Lincoln thought that emancipating the slaves would encourage Northern and Southern blacks to support the Union cause and increase its strength.

When the Nature of the Good Affects the Commitment Problem

Imposing an absolute war outcome is one solution to the credible commitment problem since it removes the adversary's sovereignty. In some instances, the severity of the commitment problem can be affected by allocations of the good short of an absolute outcome; if the good can substantially reduce the likelihood, the adversary will break the peace agreement. Territory is the best example of this dynamic, since a belligerent's possession of strategic territory like high ground can make defense easier, thereby making it less attractive for a defeated adversary to defect and reattack, meaning the commitment problem is reduced. The Finnish–Soviet conflicts from 1939–44 illustrate this dynamic, because the Soviets sought the acquisition of critical portions of Finnish territory to make the Soviet border more secure, to improve the defenses of Leningrad and especially naval access to the Baltic Sea, and to make Helsinki more vulnerable to attack. Although commitment factors were critical in creating Soviet preferences, in both the Winter War and Continuation War changes in Finnish and Soviet war-termination demands are well explained by a focus on information. Similarly, the cornerstone of World War I Germany's war aims in the West was the postwar control of Belgium, to decrease the likelihood of a future British or French attack.

Other cases also demonstrate how reallocations of the disputed good can affect the commitment problem. In 1940, Churchill rejected negotiations with Hitler in part because he knew Hitler would demand reductions in British military and naval power, which would put Britain even further at Germany's mercy. In the Korean War, negotiations over prisoners of war dragged on in part because (at least) the UN/American side recognized that the settlement of this issue would directly affect the postwar balance of power, since the UN held more Communist prisoners than vice versa, and the Chinese proposal of an all-for-all trade would provide the Communists with a relative gain in postwar manpower levels. Sending the Communist prisoners back might also make Communist soldiers less likely to surrender in future conflicts. In summer 1864 as Union fortunes looked bleak, Lincoln refused to consider retreating on emancipation, because he knew this would undermine the willingness of blacks to support the Union and thereby undercut Union military power. Raising war aims can improve the balance of power in other circumstances as well, since belligerents may broadly hope that transforming a conflict into a war of liberation may cause individuals to flock to their cause. Emancipation was motivated primarily as a tool to recruit blacks to the Union cause. In 1943, Japan hoped that offering more rights and freedoms in conquered areas would attract greater support. More generally, revolutionary regimes are likely to think that launching wars of liberation may attract oppressed peoples to their sides.[2]

These cases illustrate the idiosyncrasy of how divisions of the good affect the commitment problem. The good can affect the commitment problem (and, more broadly, military power) in a number of ways, including possessing important territory, affecting the motivation or ability of individuals to fight for one side or the other, and possessing specific military assets. Further, not all increments of the good may affect the commitment problem equally, as not all increments of land are equally valuable and not all military assets are equally important to the balance of power.

More generally, if the nature of the good affects the commitment problem, this mediates the effects of information and commitment dynamics. When a state captures an element of the good that reduces the commitment problem, it may feel more willing to end the war and accept a limited outcome, even if it has enjoyed a string of military victories, and especially if it fears the escalation of the costs of war. Further, even when a belligerent fears that its adversary may consider violating the terms of a war-ending agreement, the belligerent may be willing to abandon absolute war aims and accept a limited outcome if the limited outcome allows the belligerent to acquire an element of the good that will reduce the commitment problem. This dynamic allowed the Soviets to accept limited victories over Finland in 1940 and 1944.

Domestic Politics

Surprisingly, the role of domestic politics in this book's cases of war-termination decision-making was limited. The possible effects of domestic politics on war termination are several, and this book considered two possible relationships. The first is the mainstream idea that the escalation of casualties increases the likelihood of concessions, especially in democracies. This hypothesis received strikingly little support. Sometimes, democratic publics were *more* opposed to making concessions than were democratic leaders, as was the case perhaps most clearly in Finland during the

Winter War and Continuation War. This is consistent with the pattern observed elsewhere that sometimes fighting wars is more popular with the public than the leadership.[3] Sometimes, the escalation of casualties makes neither the public nor the leadership significantly more interested in negotiating, as was the case for the U.S. during the Korean War from 1951 to 1953. Sometimes, public opinion is sufficiently unformed that an elected leader has the ability to push public opinion away from considering concessions, as Churchill was able to do in 1940 with his public addresses, some of the most famous and effective wartime speeches in history.[4] Sometimes, rising casualties may make democratic publics more highly motivated to grant the adversary concessions in order to end the war, but leaders may be willing to swim against the tide and fight on regardless. Roosevelt shook off a few specks of public doubt in early 1942. More dangerously, in the summer of 1864, continuing the Civil War was so unpopular in the North that Lincoln accepted that it would cost him the November presidential election, but he chose to fight on and probably lose office rather than negotiate in an attempt to save his reelection bid.

Even the Vietnam War, although not examined here, has limitations as an example of a war in which mounting casualties forced a democracy to make concessions. There is strong evidence that mounting casualties did erode American public support for the war, and encouraged President Johnson not to run for reelection in 1968.[5] However, while this mounting opposition eventually affected American military strategy, especially President Nixon's policy of Vietnamization and the gradual withdrawal of American troops, it did not cause the United States to offer a stream of concessions as casualties increased and support decreased. The first major American concession did not come until 1970, some five years after the major American ground troop escalation and some two years after the Tet Offensive.[6] This surprising pattern points to a puzzle: If escalating casualties do not pressure democracies to make concessions, why are wars involving democracies shorter? One answer to this puzzle may be that democracies are especially likely to initiate wars that promise to be short, but once war starts their war-termination behavior will converge with the behavior of autocratic states.[7]

A small set of the cases also explored the domestic politics hypothesis that semirepressive, moderately exclusionary regimes like World War I Germany may raise their demands as the war evolves into a long losing effort. Chapters 9 and 10 examined two semirepressive, moderately exclusionary belligerents fighting long losing wars. Evidence supporting the hypothesized dynamic was quite limited. The first episode that offers at best weak support for the hypothesis was the German decision not to settle in the West in 1917–18 after the defeat of Russia, and instead launch a major offensive in March 1918. The historical particulars of this case are not consistent with the hypothesis, and the evidence that Germany fought on to improve its security by acquiring Belgium is at least as strong as the evidence for the domestic politics claim. The other case, Japan in World War II, provides almost no support. As things went from bad to worse from mid-1942 through summer 1945, Japan did not raise its war aims. It also refused to make diplomatic concessions to the Allies, although not because of a desire to retain the fruits of empire to reward coalition supporters, but rather because the Japanese believed that concessions should not be made after defeat because they would show weakness, and that the Allies were pushing for unconditional surrender anyway. Further, although Japan made no formal concessions until after August 1945, as early as 1943 it did decide to retreat to a smaller defense perimeter, thereby de facto abandoning goods that could be distributed to coalition supporters. Japan also formally offered material concessions to the USSR as incentive for them to mediate. If anything, the Emperor and others in the leadership saw a greater domestic political threat from public war fatigue than from bringing home insufficient gains in the war. Their fear that continuing the war would create grave internal instability was an important factor pushing them to accept a modified form of the Potsdam Declaration in August 1945.

The absence of strong evidence favoring this latter domestic politics claim in this small number of cases is important, given that the mixed regime hypothesis applies to only a small band of cases within the universe of interstate wars. The set of losing, semirepressive, moderately exclusionary regimes that fought long wars (such regimes fighting long losing wars is the category of belligerents the theory applies to) is relatively limited. The average duration of wars from 1816–1991 was about fourteen months, and of the more than 200 belligerents that fought more than ninety wars since 1816, only nine were mixed regimes fighting losing wars that lasted longer than fourteen months.[8] Beyond the cases discussed here of Germany in World War I (Germany 1916–17, as discussed in chapter 9, providing more support for the Goemans hypothesis than Germany 1917–18) and Japan in World War II, it is difficult to find supportive evidence. For example, the evidence on Russia during World War I is both thin and mixed.[9] In the Mexican–American War, the war-termination behavior of Mexico (a semi-exclusionary, moderately repressive regime fighting a long losing war) is inconsistent with the predictions of the theory. Mexican president Antonio López Santa Anna did not increase Mexican war aims in the face of battlefield defeats and escalating losses. Indeed, he sought to make concessions and negotiate even before Mexico City had fallen. Aside from predicting war-termination behavior, the Goemans hypothesis would forecast that, following defeat in the war, Mexico's primary wartime leader, Santa Anna, should have lost power and suffered severe personal punishment, such as exile, death, or imprisonment. On the surface, the case does seem to offer supporting evidence, since after the war Santa Anna did flee to Venezuela in exile. However, the particulars of his fate do not neatly follow the model. Santa Anna resigned the presidency voluntarily, he did so while the war was ongoing (September 1847), and even after he resigned as president he kept his position as leader of Mexico's army. The new president appointed by Santa Anna, Manuel Peña y Peña, did soon remove Santa Anna from his position as commander in chief, in preparation for a court martial. Santa Anna sought (and received) exile in Venezuela, although he may have been more concerned with personal threats from renegade Texas Rangers for revenge than with threats from angry Mexicans. Notably, any Mexican antipathy to Santa Anna was temporary, as Santa Anna became Mexican president again some five years after his flight to Venezuela.[10] Lastly, it was Peña and not Santa Anna who signed the war-ending Treaty of Guadelupe Hidalgo the following year, and Peña himself was not thrown from power after signing the treaty.[11] Peña voluntarily resigned, and resumed his seat on the Mexican Supreme Court. In short, the evidence supporting the mixed regime domestic politics hypothesis is thin.

Some suggestive evidence exists for a variant on this hypothesis, however. Various scholars have proposed that militaries have different preferences for fighting wars than do civilians—for example, that militaries prefer fighting for decisive rather than incomplete, negotiated victories.[12] When there is weak civilian control of the military, then this may delay war termination, as the civilians may fear a military coup d'état if they move too aggressively towards peace. This dynamic was demonstrated most clearly in the Japan case, where the Emperor and other civilians at times expressed fear of a military coup d'état if the civilians moved to a peace deal that would threaten the Japanese polity. It was also seen in the Germany case, when Kaiser Wilhelm may have feared speaking out against the escalation to unrestricted submarine warfare in 1916–17 because of domestic political threats from the navy. In 1917–18 it is a bit more complicated. Since there was a military dictatorship of the Duo, it appears that both civilians and military officers supported continuing the war in the West in order to secure Belgium.

The Inefficiency of Combat

A general point from many of the cases is that combat is a relatively inefficient means of hastening war termination through information transmission. There are many reasons why combat does not efficiently provide information that in turn directly affects war-termination behavior. The fog of war makes combat outcomes often quite ambiguous, impeding the process by which expectations might converge sufficiently to permit war termination.[13] Making matters worse, decision-makers are motivated to obscure true outcomes, as leaders of a state experiencing battle defeat may wish to underplay the magnitude of the loss so as not to encourage the adversary. For example, a week after the Japanese attack on Pearl Harbor, Assistant Secretary of State Breckenridge Long wrote in his diary, "The real damage at Honolulu has not been disclosed. Apparently Japan does not accurately know. To advise her would be foolish—as well as dangerous." Reciprocally, the Japanese kept silent about the damage inflicted by the April 1942 Doolittle raid on Tokyo.[14] Laboratory experiments have revealed that expectations are less likely to converge when subjects are exposed to more ambiguous information than when exposed to information with a more straightforward interpretation.[15]

Even when combat outcomes clearly indicate success for one side and setbacks for the other, such information still does not always encourage shifts in war-termination behavior. Belligerents such as the Confederacy in early 1865, Britain in 1940, the U.S. in 1942, and the U.S. in 1950 all refused to lower their war-termination demands even in the face of serious combat losses. The case study findings are consistent with evidence from quantitative scholarship on war duration, that wars do not become more likely to end the longer they last—that is, the accumulation of information from ongoing combat does not steadily increase the chance of war termination.[16] What accounts for this inefficiency?

The cases here provide three possible explanations. First, as described in chapter 3, fears of adversarial noncompliance with war-ending agreements sometimes moot the connection between information and war-termination behavior. Although fighting on looks decreasingly attractive, the alternative of seeking a limited war outcome deal is even less attractive, as it allows the adversary to reattack in the future.

A second source of the inefficiency of the combat-information/war-termination connection is the fear decision-makers sometimes have that making concessions will send signals of weakness. Decision-makers fear communicating weakness especially during war, and may want to wait until they have demonstrated strength on the battlefield before risking any concessions or even negotiations. This dynamic reverses the prediction forecast by the information proposition, as it posits that setbacks ought to make a decision-maker less likely rather than more likely to make concessions, again disrupting the proposed combat-information/war-termination dynamic of converging expectations and eventual war termination. Among the cases described here, Japan in World War II perhaps best illustrates this negotiation-from-strength dynamic.

Third, leaders can be patient. They are often unwilling to draw conclusive inferences from individual battles about the balance of power. Even when they admit to themselves that things are going poorly they are reluctant to take the next step and offer concessions. This patience likely emerges from a number of interrelated factors. Leaders recognize there is a large variance around their estimates of the balance of power, and they are often unlikely to change their beliefs too drastically after a single battle.[17] Some leaders, such as Roosevelt in 1942, have the luxury of knowing that the war will be a long one, and that the true balance of power will not be revealed until military mobilization has been completed, some months or years in the future. Part of the unwillingness to offer concessions may be confidence, if not overconfidence.[18] Overconfident leaders may view battle outcomes with bias, playing down defeats and placing too much emphasis on victories. In particular, some losing leaders assume that nonmaterial factors will eventually allow their side to surmount overwhelming material odds. Examples of such (over)confidence include Churchill trusting that British moral fortitude will eventually win out, and putting the best possible spin on the aerial balance-of-power numbers; the Japanese leadership trusting that Japanese spiritual superiority will somehow trump American material power; and Davis' belief that the fighting élan of the Southern man will triumph over the factories, mills, and foundries of the Union.

Variation in Commitment Fears

The cases provide somewhat less traction in understanding consequential variance in belligerents' fears about commitment credibility. Regime type provides little purchase. Some belligerents were unwilling to accept a limited war outcome with autocratic adversaries (such as Britain and the U.S. against the Axis powers in World War II and the U.S. in the first portion of the Korean War), and other belligerents were more willing to accept a limited peace with autocratic adversaries (such as the Soviet Union against Germany in 1941, Finland against the Soviet Union, and the U.S. in the latter stages of the Korean War). Some belligerents were more willing to accept a limited war outcome with democratic adversaries (such as North Korea/China in the latter stages of the Korean War, and the Soviet Union in the Winter War and Continuation War), and other belligerents were less trusting of democratic adversaries to adhere to war-ending commitments (such as the CSA during the Civil War and the Soviet Union in the first stage of the Winter War).

Perhaps the single most important factor affecting variation in commitment fears is the past behavior of the adversary. Churchill and Chamberlain recalled Hitler's treachery at Munich. Roosevelt was haunted by the dashed hopes of Versailles. Lincoln knew the Southern penchant for wielding the secession threat. In the later years of the Civil War, Davis looked back to the Emancipation Proclamation as a clear retreat by Lincoln on his most important prewar promise. Truman saw the invasion of South Korea as a repeat of the dark fascist theater of the 1930s. And yet, there are episodes in which the lines from historical experience to war-termination behavior are not as straight. Stalin knew all too well of Finnish efforts to overthrow Soviet Bolshevism in 1918 and 1941, and yet in 1940 and 1944 was willing to accept a limited outcome because of countervailing factors. In 1941, Stalin looked past the obvious lessons provided by Hitler's abrogation of the 1939 nonaggression pact, and instead grasped for the straws of Brest-Litovsk, hoping against hope that major territorial concessions might save Soviet socialism. In 1951, Truman swallowed his fears of walking in Chamberlain's footsteps when fears of escalation pushed him and Dean Acheson to scale back their war aims in Korea.

Commitment Credibility and International Relations

The findings have broad implications for international relations more generally. Both information and commitment dynamics are fundamental and essential dynamics driving war behavior. The conventional wisdom is correct that information does matter, but this book found that wars are not about information all the way down. Fears of commitment noncompliance have long been understood to affect how wars start, and this book has shown that they also affect how wars end.

Other areas of international relations have also emphasized the importance of credible commitments. Scholarship on international institutions has explored factors affecting the likelihood of state compliance with institutional dictates such as institutional design, domestic politics, interdependence, and others. This book has developed a new factor that can reduce the likelihood that an international commitment will be broken: absolute war outcomes. In fighting war, states can brutally solve the noncompliance problem by eliminating the other side, or at least eliminating the other side's ability to make a choice. Note that this is a solution to the commitment noncompliance problem inapplicable to international institutions covering areas such as trade, finance, or the environment, since one state would be unlikely to consider conquering another state to prevent it from erecting illegal trade barriers, for example.

Implications for American Foreign Policy in the Twenty-First Century

Many of the theoretical issues discussed in this book are centrally important to American foreign policy in the twenty-first century. How should the United States think about ending its wars? How can the U.S. achieve its foreign policy aims while paying as few costs in blood and treasure as possible?

One policy conclusion might be that the most effective conflict resolution policy tools are those that can reduce credible commitment fears. However, the empirical evidence on the effectiveness of these foreign policy tools is mixed. One study of all interstate wars from 1914–2001 found that tools that seem to reduce commitment fears, such as peacekeeping forces, arms control, and confidence building measures, did not significantly increase the duration of peace after war—that is, they did not reduce the chances of a belligerent breaking a peace settlement.[19] Conversely, there is evidence that such tools can help resolve intrastate conflicts.[20]

The 9/11 attacks have increased the concerns of many American foreign-policy makers that America's most worrisome foes—rogue states and terrorist groups—cannot be bargained with, coerced, or frightened. These foes are seen as being willing to engage in gigantically costly, even suicidal operations, because authoritarian leaders and terrorists have no concerns about civilian casualties, and they are sufficiently irrational or fundamentalist to be willing to accept even their own deaths. This makes war termination difficult, both because one might never be able to impose enough costs on such actors to persuade them to negotiate, and because one can not rely on such actors to adhere to war-ending agreements.

The George W. Bush administration framed post-9/11 conflicts in this manner, and laid out a foreign policy to address these new threats. The new foreign policy was presented in the September 2002 National Security Strategy (NSS), also known as the Bush Doctrine. It argued that deterrence would not work against leaders of rogue states and terrorist groups, and as a result the United States may need under some circumstances to strike preemptively or preventively to eliminate emerging threats.[21] Iraq under Saddam Hussein served as the leading example for the Bush administration of a state undeterrable because of its leader's callous disregard of civilian casualties, and of a state that would not abide by its international commitments, as evidenced by its apparent disregard in the 1990s of United Nations resolutions calling for dismantling its WMD and missile programs. Iran and North Korea, the other two members of the "axis of evil," were also seen as authoritarian states willing to disregard international commitments such as those required by their signatures to the Nuclear Non-Proliferation Treaty.

The NSS is well explained by the theoretical framework developed here. The underlying assumption of the NSS was that policy toward rogue actors should not be understood as an information problem. Because rogues are willing to accept huge costs and even their own demise, the revelation of information to rogues will not work. That is, even if America could reveal enough information to convince the rogue that America has both the ability and the willingness to destroy the rogue, such revelation would be insufficient to deter the rogue, because the rogue is willing to risk suicide.

The NSS instead framed rogue actors as constituting a commitment problem. At the simplest level, rogue actors cannot be counted on to adhere to international agreements or accepted norms of behavior. War, and especially preventive war, was seen as a potential solution to the commitment problem that rogue actors present. Two categories of preventive attacks have been suggested as possible solutions to the commitment problems of rogue actors: more limited attacks aimed at destroying WMD or the scientific/industrial infrastructure used to produce such weapons, or more comprehensive attacks aimed at overthrowing the rogue leadership and imposing regime change. In the category of limited attacks, the idea is that if such a limited attack can destroy a state's WMD capability, then the commitment problem is solved by preventing the rogue from having the military power to consider violation of any non-proliferation commitments. In some sense, it belongs to the category of wars in which acquiring an increment of the good, in this case physically destroying a state's WMD program, helps reduce the commitment problem. In the category of regime change attacks, the commitment problem is solved more decisively through absolute war outcome.

A central question for American foreign policy is: Should preventive war be used to solve credible commitment problems? If so, under what conditions? Again, answering these questions has critical importance for American foreign policy in the twenty-first century. The U.S. will face dangerous adversaries in the years to come, including North Korea, Syria, Iran, and others, who are feared to likely renege on their international commitments. The use of preventive force is one possible solution.

A first question is whether or not the use of force works as a means of solving commitment problems. The historical record provides tentative support for the idea that at least absolute war can solve credible commitment problems. In interstate wars since 1816, when a defeated state has suffered foreign-imposed regime change or state death, it has almost never reattacked the victor.[22] However, for the U.S. in the twenty-first century, absolute war will mean imposed democratization, which is a difficult strategy to execute successfully. Sometimes, the U.S. has successfully imposed democracy in the wake of absolute military defeat, such as in Japan and Germany after World War II, in Grenada after the 1983 U.S. invasion, and in Panama after the 1989 invasion. Such efforts are not always successful, however, as demonstrated by a number of other American interventions in Latin America in the twentieth century, especially before 1945. More systematic analyses have indicated that the use of force is not a reliable tool to spread democracy.[23] At this writing (September 2008), it is not clear that democracy will flourish and survive in Afghanistan and Iraq following the 2001 and 2003 interventions in each of those nations. However, even if democracy fails to emerge, neither state is likely to pose an interstate threat to the United States in the short or medium term, because each war smashed the power of the Taliban and Saddam Hussein governments, and that power is not quickly or easily rebuilt. Chaos or civil war might ensue, but undesirable as these outcomes might be, they would not permit the reemergence of an interstate threat.[24]

That being said, pursuing absolute war as a foreign policy tool has two major problems. First, such wars can bear very high costs. Most simply, wars inflict human costs, both deaths and nonfatal injuries, on both the attacking power and on the civilians in the target state. The American military death toll from the Iraq War is in the thousands, with nonfatal injuries in the tens of thousands. At least several tens of thousands of Iraqi civilians have been killed in the violence since the outbreak of war in 2003. Sometimes human costs must be accepted in the pursuit of the protection of the nation, but that does not mean that those costs should be forgotten.

Such wars are also financially costly, potentially running tabs into the hundreds of billions or trillions of dollars. Guns versus butter concerns aside, there are many spending priorities into which those funds could be poured to improve American security against threats from WMDs and terrorism in particular, such as more aggressive acquisition of fissile materials from the former Soviet Union, improved port security at American and foreign ports, more widespread radiation detectors (especially at airports and border crossings), missile defense, foreign aid to attract support in the global war on terror and to stabilize friendly regimes, and others.

These wars also damage the military itself. The American military will most likely remain an all-volunteer force in the short and medium term since neither the Pentagon nor the American public desire a return to conscription. Because of this, very real limits exist on the total size of the American military, and fighting wars such as the Iraq War strain American military capacity, both because forces tied down in one operation cannot be used elsewhere, and because fighting such operations makes recruitment more difficult, having the effect of threatening the quality and quantity of available recruits.[25]

Perhaps most worrisomely, wars with the aim of regime change can have severe diplomatic costs for the United States. At the minimum, the exercise of American power to overthrow a foreign leader makes states uncomfortable, as it violates national sovereignty norms. In the application, such wars are invariably messy, drawing American military forces into behaviors that tarnish the American image abroad, including killing civilians and committing war crimes. The hope is that the world community would recognize that such wars have humanitarian ends, the overthrow of a dictator and the installation of democratic regimes, but the reality is that such actions are often seen in the worst light. America's actions are not given fair comparison to actions taken by other regimes, and America does not get credit for its successes. The 2003 Iraq War caused anti-Americanism around the world to soar, cementing America's image as a new imperialist power bent on killing Muslims and savaging the Muslim world. This despite the overthrow of Saddam Hussein who killed more Muslims than any other individual in history, America's use of force in the 1990s to save Muslim Kosovars and Bosnians from marauding Serb forces, the substantial amount of economic aid given by the United States to Muslim regimes such as Turkey, Egypt, and Pakistan, the wave of disaster relief following the 2005 Pakistan earthquake, and so forth. These concerns are not new to twenty-first century American foreign policy. Indeed, one reason Britain elected not to overthrow the Turkish Sultan after World War I was because of its concerns that doing so would spark a worldwide anti-British backlash, especially among Muslims in the British colony of India.[26]

Anti-Americanism is not merely the loss of a popularity contest, it is a direct threat to American national security. The sources of terrorism are poorly understood, and although experts are divided on the effects of factors such as economic conditions, political institutions, and religious ideology, there is broader consensus that anti-Americanism stimulates terrorist recruitment and action. If terrorism, and WMD terrorism in particular, constitutes one of (if not the greatest) threats to American national security, the surge of global anti-Americanism must be viewed with great concern.

If the first major drawback to such wars is high costs, a second major drawback is that the benefits of such wars as compared to doing nothing and leaving the rogue state in place may be overstated. Sometimes, fears of a rogue state's WMD capabilities may be exaggerated. During World War II, Germany was far less advanced in its nuclear weapons program then the United States feared. Iraq's WMD capabilities were substantially less advanced at the time of the 2003 attack than was presumed by the

Bush administration. The 2005 American National Intelligence Estimate (NIE) declared that Iran was pursuing a nuclear arsenal, but the 2007 NIE reversed course, proposing that Iran had abandoned its nuclear weapons program in 2003.[27]

Further, even when a state does possess WMD, there are other means of addressing the WMD threat than attacks intended to impose regime change. Deterrence of WMD attack has been an extremely successful policy tool. The United States has deterred a number of WMD-armed, anti-American dictators, such as Joseph Stalin, Nikita Khrushchev, Leonid Brezhnev, Mao Tse-tung, Saddam Hussein, and Kim Jong Il from launching WMD attacks against the U.S. or its allies. Israel likely deterred Saddam Hussein from launching biological or chemical weapons against Israeli cities during the 1991 Gulf War. Deterrence can likely succeed in the future as a means of preventing the state-to-state use of WMD. Deterrence aside, diplomacy has been able to ameliorate and even eliminate a number of WMD programs and threats. The existence of the NPT helped persuade nations such as Argentina, Brazil, and South Africa to abandon their nuclear programs. A combination of carrots and (economic) sticks pushed Libya to declare and abandon its WMD programs in 2004. Although North Korea likely violated aspects of the 1995 Agreed Framework, the agreement likely did constrain the size of the North Korean arsenal, and in 2007 it signed a follow-up agreement with the Bush Administration. And the arms control process has substantially reduced the Soviet/Russian nuclear threat since the late 1980s.

Beyond wars aimed to change a rogue's leadership, limited wars can be used to solve credible commitment problems. However, the empirical record is less encouraging of the conclusion that limited wars can serve this function, even if one side can change the balance of power or capture an element of the good that can make future defection by the other side more costly or less likely to succeed. Among the cases in this book, the Soviet Union hoped that its territorial acquisitions following the Winter War would improve the security of its northwest region. These hopes were not met, as after the war Finland permitted Germany to base troops on Finnish soil, and Finland joined Germany's June 1941 attack on the Soviet Union. Israel hoped that its acquisition of the West Bank, the Golan Heights, and the Sinai peninsula in the 1967 Six-Day War would dissuade its Arab neighbors from attacking again in the future, although Egypt initiated the War of Attrition in 1969, Egypt and Syria both attacked to initiate the 1973 Yom Kippur War, and in 2006 Hezbollah launched missile attacks on Israeli territory from beyond the Golan, in Lebanon.

Another limited war strategy, more pertinent to twenty-first-century American foreign policy, and which can reduce commitment credibility problems, is to degrade directly the adversary's military capabilities, in particular the adversary's WMD capabilities. This is often seen as an attractive approach to addressing WMD threats, because rather than launching a more general war intended to overthrow a rogue leader and climb the long steep hill to democracy, one can launch air or missile strikes against WMD facilities. Such attacks are especially attractive because they are seen to have very low human costs, either of friendly forces or of collateral damage in the target state, they impose less strain on military resources, and the international backlash would likely be less. The 1981 Israeli attack on the Iraqi reactor at Osiraq is often pointed to as a leading example of how successful such attacks can be, and American decision-makers have often considered such attacks against Iran and North Korea in particular. The Bush Administration even considered the possible use of nuclear weapons in carrying out attacks against WMD targets.[28]

The principle shortcoming of such limited attacks against WMD facilities is that they are unlikely to ameliorate the WMD threat. The historical record is rather discouraging.[29] The Osiraq attack destroyed a reactor unlikely to have made much contribution to a weapons program, because of the design of the reactor, the presence of international inspectors, and the Iraqi dependence on the French supply of reactor fuel. Further, the attack probably accelerated the Iraqi weapons program, by increasing Saddam's material commitment to acquiring nuclear weapons, and by driving it underground.[30]

The record of other attacks is similarly unimpressive. Some limited attacks, such as airstrikes on Iraqi WMD facilities in 1991, inflict relatively little damage, because the bulk of the targets are hidden and therefore untargeted. Dispersal and concealment is a direct reaction to the threat of airstrikes. The 1981 attack caused Iraq to disperse and conceal their WMD production and storage facilities. Other states such as Iran and North Korea have learned the same lesson, and an important reason why the United States elected not to attack North Korean nuclear facilities in the mid-1990s or later was because of the fear that there were likely many secret sites that would be undamaged in any air attack. Some limited attacks were launched against programs that either likely did not exist, such as the Clinton administration's 1998 missile attacks against alleged chemical weapons facilities in Sudan, or were ultimately unlikely to succeed anyway, such as the bombing raids against the German nuclear weapons program in World War II. Perhaps the most successful such limited attack against a WMD program were Iraqi airstrikes against the Iranian Bushehr nuclear reactor in the 1980s, which may have delayed the Iranian nuclear weapons program, although information on this episode is scant. Similarly, little is known about the context or effects of Israel's 2007 attack on a Syrian facility thought to be part of a nuclear program.

Another important critique is that just as the success rate of launching such limited attacks is underwhelming, the success rate of not launching such attacks is quite impressive, in that no state that considered launching such an attack but elected not to ultimately regretted that decision, especially given that some preventive attacks were nuclear in nature and would have incurred massive casualties and perhaps nuclear retaliation. The United States considered launching preventive attacks against the nuclear programs of the Soviet Union in the 1940s and 1950s, against China in the 1960s, and against North Korea in the 1990s. In each case, hindsight has proven that restraint was the wiser option. The Soviet Union never used its nuclear arsenal against the United States, and never used it politically to extract substantial diplomatic gains at American expense. Further, the Soviet Union eventually crumbled, and the Soviet/Russian nuclear arsenal was substantially scaled back. China neither used its nuclear arsenal nor attacked any American ally after it conducted its first nuclear test in 1964, and it is now evolving into a peaceful commerce-oriented competitor rather than a militarized major power rival. North Korea at this writing is still a militarized nuclear state ruled by an anti-American dictator, but it has not launched any interstate aggression since preventive attacks were first considered in the early 1990s. The 2007 nuclear agreement gives hope that diplomacy may yet yield progress.

Other states have benefited from forgoing preventive WMD attacks. Egypt (and, some argue, the Soviet Union) considered launching preventive airstrikes against the Israeli nuclear reactor at Dimona in the 1960s.[31] Although Israel and Egypt fought three wars in the 1967–73 period, all were conventional, and in the late 1970s the Camp David peace process achieved for Egypt tremendous gains, including peace with Israel, the return of the Sinai peninsula, and a lucrative alliance with the United States. These gains were all eventually realized without preventive nuclear attacks, and of course Israel has not launched nuclear attacks against Egypt in the interim. The Soviet Union considered launching preventive attacks against the Chinese nuclear program in the late 1960s, and since then not only have those two countries avoided military conflict, but they also have achieved a substantial and mutually beneficial rapprochement. India and Pakistan have both considered launching preventive attacks against each other's nuclear programs, but neither state has ever used its nuclear arsenal against the other, and the two states have enjoyed a peaceful and slowly warming relationship since 1999.[32]

In short, war to solve commitment problems has not been and would not be a panacea. American foreign-policy makers in the twenty-first century need to recognize the limits and costs of using wars in this manner. Other foreign policy tools such as diplomacy and deterrence may be less costly and more effective.

Notes

CHAPTER ONE
ENDING WARS

1. Paul Kecskemeti (1958) was especially interested in what he called "strategic surrender," the decision to lay down one's arms before one's military had been utterly defeated. Although his book broke new ground in thinking about surrender as an important political phenomenon, his theoretical discussion tended to be more descriptive than predictive, and he focused more narrowly only on why a losing belligerent accepts strategic surrender, excluding questions like why states decide to fight to the absolute end, why states negotiate to terminate wars short of strategic surrender, and why states decide to pursue total victory. Fred Iklé's 1971 (2005) book *Every War Must End*, likely inspired by the mess of the Vietnam War still ongoing when he wrote it, is deeply skeptical of rosy prewar plans for fighting wars to short victorious conclusions. The book is deeply infused with respect for the Clausewitzian fog of war and other factors that make even simple things in war so difficult, and speculates on the importance of domestic politics for war termination. Other major war-termination books include Pillar (1983) and Goemans (2000).

2. Schelling (1960, 5).

3. Clausewitz (1976, 69). Italics in original.

4. Thucydides (1998).

5. Fearon (2004); Walter (2002). This book builds on past theoretical work. For example, Walter (2002, esp. chapter 2) says little about belligerent wartime behavior when noncompliance fears are high (in her application, when third-party security guarantors are absent). For example, her models allow for post-settlement defection outcomes, but do not allow for the possibility of absolute war outcomes, only for the continuation of war. Powell (2006) does not explore exactly how war solves the commitment problem, but rather merely assumes that launching the war solves, or provides the chance to solve, the commitment problem.

CHAPTER TWO
BARGAINING, INFORMATION, AND ENDING WARS

1. Helmuth von Moltke. Quoted in Brodie (1973), 11.

2. On the bargaining model of war, see Powell (2002); Reiter (2003).

3. See Goldstein (2001).

4. Powell (2006).

5. Mansfield and Snyder (2005).

6. Chapman and Reiter (2004); Lai and Reiter (2005); Baum (2002).

7. Goodwin (2005, 342).

232 • Notes to Chapter Two

8. Harcave (2004, 109).

9. Berman (1982, 145–53).

10. Mansfield and Snyder (2005); Gelpi (1997); Fordham (2002); Pickering and Kisangani (2005); Meernik (2001); Oneal and Tir (2006); Lai and Slater (2006)

11. Leeds and Davis (1997). Chiozza and Goemans (2004b) argue that international conflict—even unsuccessful conflict—does not necessarily impose domestic political costs on political leaders. Hence, if one argues that state leaders assess the costs and benefits of war only in terms of domestic politics, one might not agree with the assumption that war is always costly, as war does not always impose domestic political costs.

12. Fearon (1995b).

13. For a formal critique of the point that mutual optimism makes war more likely, see Fey and Ramsay (2007). Their basic point is that in the prewar phase, a belligerent observes the optimism of its adversary, updates its beliefs accordingly, and war-avoiding bargaining space will open. Note that their model does not allow for a belligerent to believe that its opponent has a false faith in its military strength or might be bluffing.

14. See Stam (1996) and Reiter and Stam (2002). Studies have discovered that certain factors are systematically related to war-causing disagreement about the balance of power. Specifically, war-causing disagreement about military–industrial capability is likely to be lower between states that have higher levels of trade with each other (Reed 2003a), between states with international ties such as alliance or joint membership in international governmental organizations (Boehmer et al 2004; Bearce et al 2006), and as the power disparity between two states grows (Reed 2003b).

15. Förster (1988, esp. 94–95).

16. Quoted in Guderian (1952, 190).

17. Myllyniemi (1997, 80).

18. See Reiter and Stam (2002, 16–17).

19. Gordon and Trainor (1995)

20. Byman and Waxman (2000).

21. Pollack (2002a, 104–14).

22. On the importance of military strategy and force employment for determining battle and war outcomes, see Biddle (2004); Stam (1996).

23. May (2000).

24. Oren (2002).

25. Fearon (1994).

26. Quoted in Reiter and Stam (2002, 22).

27. Quoted in Goodman (1978, 96).

28. Pape (1996).

29. Quoted in Mueller (1980, 497).

30. Yuen (2007).

31. Owsley (1931, 24–25)

32. Huth (1988, 129–38); Press (2005, 46–62).

33. Quoted in Stueck (1995, 63).

34. After the Six-Day War, Egypt became more confident in its relative military power by securing Saudi coordination on the use of the oil weapon against the West as well as Soviet logistical and political support, helping encourage it to attack Israel in October 1973. Herzog (1998, esp. 31).

35. Lai (2004).

36. See, e.g., Fearon (1995b).

37. Some scholars have critiqued this information approach. There is a broad body of literature critical of the idea that individuals update their beliefs in accordance with Bayes' Rule, an assumption of the formal information models (Kahneman, Slovic, and Tverseky 1982; Rosen 2005). Dominic Johnson (2004) offered a more innovative critique, using evolutionary biology to predict that individuals are generally predisposed to be overconfident, meaning that political and military leaders might be unlikely to draw the correct inferences from observed battle outcomes. Others have proposed that the assumption that there is a common metric of combat performance used by all belligerents within a war may not be valid, impeding the process by which information revealed by combat facilitates war termination (Garner 1998; Garofano 2002; Kirshner 2000). A further critique is that decision-makers during wartime when faced with bad news from the battlefield may change military strategy rather than offer diplomatic concessions (Gartner 1997).

38. Simmel (1904, 501); Kecskemeti (1958, 9); Coser (1961); Blainey (1988, originally published 1973, 56, 122); Rosen (1972). Paul Pillar's 1983 book was perhaps the first to propose that war termination should be thought of as bargaining, and to draw on the bargaining literature from economics. I build on Pillar's work in important ways. As discussed in this and the following chapter, my theory is framed around two fundamental problems in bargaining—incomplete information and commitment credibility—concepts that develop Pillar's ideas about bargaining. I also provide deeper empirical examinations, exploring how bargaining between belligerents played out during actual wars.

39. Wagner (2000); Filson and Werner (2002); Slantchev (2003b); Smith and Stam (2004); Powell (2004); see also Goemans (2000). It would be fruitless to try to identify one model as clearly superior to the others, since the constraining nature of the technology of formal modeling often means that although a model may be more sophisticated in one area, it may be less sophisticated in another. For example, one model may have the advantage of incorporating domestic politics, but the drawback of having only a finite number of possible battles (Filson and Werner 2004). Another model may relax the assumption of common prior beliefs, but omit the possibility of signaling through diplomacy (Smith and Stam 2004).

40. This assumption that the likelihood of winning any particular battle is strong and perhaps controversial. In chapter 3, I relax this assumption by allowing that the exchange of parts of the disputed good can shift the balance of power. More generally, one might propose that states might try to increase their chances of winning battles during war, perhaps by increasing mobilization or changing military strategy (Gartner 1997). As noted in the conclusion, if this is true, then this may be a reason why combat outcomes do not efficiently translate into

changes in war-termination offers as predicted, since a losing belligerent may still hold on to hope that the tide of war will change.

41. There are some complete information bargaining models of war, including Slantchev (2003b), Tarar and Levontoğlu (2006), Levontoğlu and Slantchev (2007), and Powell (2006). Smith and Stam (2004) is also technically a complete information model, although it takes the unconventional approach of relaxing the assumption that the two belligerents have common prior beliefs.

42. Wagner (2000); Clausewitz (1976).

43. Werner (2000) presents a model in which a belligerent adjusts its war termination offer in order to affect the decision of a third party to intervene.

44. Slantchev (2003b); Filson and Werner (2002); Powell (2004). Of course, this basic insight that one's own diplomatic moves affect the beliefs and diplomatic moves of the other side is not new, nor is it unique to formal analysis. See Iklé (1964, 194).

45. Admati and Perry (1987); Cramton (1992).

46. Goemans (2000).

47. An emerging domestic politics proposition is that war termination becomes more likely after one or more of the belligerents experiences regime change. See Stanley-Mitchell (2002); Croco (2007).

48. Mueller (1985); Gartner and Segura (1998); Gelpi et al (2005); Berinsky (2007).

49. Reiter and Stam (2002, chapter 6)

50. www.military-quotes.com/otto-von-bismarck.htm (accessed November 9, 2007).

CHAPTER THREE
CREDIBLE COMMITMENTS AND WAR TERMINATION

1. Barbara Walter (2002) applied it to the termination of civil wars, arguing that civil wars are more likely to end in a negotiated settlement if third parties are willing to intervene and enforce the settlement terms.

2. Morgenthau (1967); Blainey (1988, originally published 1973); Waltz (1979), Mearsheimer (2001). Wagner (2007) is an extensive discussion of bargaining and war, but focuses primarily on the causes of war. He (chapter 5) notes that not all war-agreements enjoy compliance, although he does not explore absolute war as a solution to the problem of noncompliance.

3. Eric Labs (1997) folded the basic logic of the commitment and information hypotheses into a single offensive realist theory. He proposed that states expand their war aims given opportunity and threat, and opportunity roughly correlates with victory in the battlefield (as envisioned by the information proposition in chapter 2), and threat roughly correlates with fear of the adversary attacking in the future.

4. Muthoo (1999, 339–40). Note that even the economics models on the "ratchet effect" described here assume that contracts are enforced, but examine an environment of short-term contracts that are frequently renegotiated.

5. See, e.g., Wagner (2000), Filson and Werner (2002, 2004), Powell (2004), Slantchev (2003b).

6. Mearsheimer (2001); Downs, Rocke, and Barsoom (1996).

7. Keohane (1984). Gelpi (2003) was perhaps a bit more optimistic, proposing that the mere existence of an agreement creates a norm that makes further conflict less likely.

8. Wendt (1999).

9. Downs, Rocke and Barsoom (1996); Fearon (1998); Koremenos et al (2001); Blaydes (2004).

10. Clausewitz (1976, 80).

11. Fortna (2004b); Werner and Yuen (2005); Werner (1999); Lo, Hashimoto, and Reiter (2008).

12. Lo, Hashimoto, and Reiter (2008). See also Fortna (2004), Werner (1999).

13. Axelrod (1984); Kydd (2005).

14. Blainey (1988, 183).

15. Clausewitz (1976, 77).

16. Thucydides (1998, 301).

17. Clodfelter (2002, 361).

18. Sanford (2005). At the 1943 Teheran conference, Stalin jokingly suggested executing 50,000–100,000 German military officers (Bohlen 1973, 147). Germany applied the annihilationist approach elsewhere, for example making plans in autumn 1941 for the elimination of all two million of Leningrad's civilians to follow the city's capture by German forces (Dunmore (2001, i). During World War II, the American public and leadership also considered genocide as possible solutions to the postwar commitment problem (see chapter 6).

19. Valentino et al (2004).

20. Fazal (2007).

21. On foreign-imposed regime change solving commitment problems, see Bueno de Mesquita et al (2003, 419–21; 2006). See also Werner (1996, esp. 69–70); Lo, Hashimoto, and Reiter (2008).

22. On the post–World War II transformations of Japan and Germany, see Dower (1999) and Berger (1998).

23. http://net.lib.byu.edu/~rdh7/wwi/1917/wilswarm.html (downloaded January 25, 2007).

24. *The New York Times*, 8 October 2002.

25. Beschloss (2002, 115–17).

26. The document declares that German military forces can only be used for national defense, or for purposes explicitly allowed for in the Basic Law. Basic Law is available at www.jurisprudentia.de/jurisprudentia.html (downloaded on October 30, 2006).

27. Available at www.solon.org/Constitutions/Japan/English/english-Constitution.html (downloaded October 30, 2006).

28. Available at www.oefre.unibe.ch/law/icl/it00000_.html (downloaded January 25, 2007).

29. Available at www.oefre.unibe.ch/law/icl/af00000_.html (downloaded November 17, 2006).

30. Available at www.washingtonpost.com/wp-dyn/content/article/2005/10/12/AR2005101201450.html (downloaded November 17, 2006).

31. On the transformation of post–World War II Germany and Japan, see Berger (1998); Dower (1999).

32. Clausewitz (1976, 77, 69, 488).

33. Biddiscombe (1998).

34. Frank (1999, 315–21).

35. Clausewitz (1976, 580–81). Italics in original.

36. McPherson (1988, 849); Goodwin (2005, 713); Sherman (1990, 810–17).

37. Hasegawa (2005, 219).

38. This is from the August 10, 1945 Byrnes Note sent from the U.S. to Japan, which Japan soon accepted. Quoted in Hasegawa (2005, 221).

39. Reiter (2006b).

40. McPherson (1988, 848).

41. On the structural determinants of insurgency, see Fearon and Laitin (2003). On the effectiveness of work or starve threats, see Liberman (1996). On the failures of the post-2003 occupation of Iraq, see Ricks (2006).

42. Reiss (1970, 96).

43. Wolford, Reiter, and Carrubba (2008).

44. Kolb (1989, 154). Thanks to Philipp Fuerst for translation from the original German.

45. Howard (1961, 371).

46. Quoted in Howard (1961, 372–73).

47. Slantchev (2003b, 628); Filson and Werner (2002, 821); Wagner (2000, 472).

48. Pillar (1983, 18–23) codes outcomes of all wars back to about 1800, but his categories are ill-suited for the discussion here since his Capitulation category combines absolute and limited outcomes.

49. Fazal (2007, 1). State death is defined as the "formal loss of control over foreign policy making to another state."

50. Sarkees (1997).

51. Reiter and Stam (2007). See also Stam (1996), Reiter and Stam (2002).

52. Werner (1999); Lo, Hashimoto, and Reiter (2008).

53. Werner (1999).

54. There is also a debate about whether or not regime type affects war aims. See Mearsheimer (1981); Werner (1996, 1998); Bueno de Mesquita et al (2003, 2006).

55. Fearon (1995b); Powell (2006).

56. Werner (1999); Fortna (2004b); Werner and Yuen (2005); Lo, Hashimoto, and Reiter (2008); Mattes (2008). See also Weisiger (2008).

57. Lai (2004).

58. Van Evera (1999); Biddle (2004); Lieber (2000); Reiter (1995).

59. On leadership change and resolve, see Wolford (2007).

60. Walt (1996).

61. Bennett (1998).

62. Constructivism provides an additional answer, as norms or international behavior may prioritize respect for regime sovereignty and push states away from

considering liquidating their neighbors. Under what Alexander Wendt (1999) calls Hobbesian anarchy, absolute war outcomes are more likely, whereas under Lockean anarchy, limited war outcomes are more likely. Page Fortna (2005) found that among interstate wars, draws are more common after 1945 than before, a pattern that is arguably consistent with the observation that there has been a shift since around 1945 away from Hobbesian anarchy towards Lockean anarchy. Wendt does not demark the beginning of Lockean anarchy at a particular point. Fortna's win/lose versus draw distinction does not exactly map onto the limited versus absolute distinction drawn here. Some might also argue that democracies might be more likely to adhere to their international agreements. Notably, the empirical evidence that democracies are less likely to violate their international commitments is mixed. Gaubatz (1996); Leeds (1999); Lipson (2003); Reiter and Stam (2002, chapter 4); Leeds (2003); Gartzke and Gleditsch (2004); Simmons (2000, 2002); Mitchell and Hensel (2007); Lo, Hashimoto, and Reiter (2008).

63. Wolford, Reiter, and Carrubba (2008).

64. Gartner (1997).

65. Pollack (2002b, 71); Hamza (2000, 244).

66. Blainey (1988, 197).

67. Herzog (1998).

68. Weems (1974, 162).

69. Pletcher (1973, 561). See also Fuller (1936).

70. Pletcher (1973, chapter 6).

71. Quoted in Jervis (1989, 4n, 4).

72. Baker (1995, 436–38); Woodward (2006, 11–12); Ricks (2006).

73. Ricks (2006).

74. Fortna (2004b).

75. On what conflicts attract peacekeepers, see Fortna (2004a).

76. Fortna (2004b); Diehl et al (1996); Werner (1999); Werner and Yuen (2005); Lo, Hashimoto, and Reiter (2008); Beardsley and Schmidt (2007); Tanner (1993); Long (2007).

77. Oren (2002).

78. Schelling (1966).

79. Gaddis (1982).

80. Stam (1996); Jervis (1978); Fearon (1995a); Van Evera (1999). Military geography contains many different aspects, and some geographic features may make some kinds of operations more difficult and others easier (Collins 1998). For example, although rough terrain like mountains can make interstate wars less likely, it can make civil wars more likely, as it provides areas for insurgents to hide (Fearon and Laitin 2003).

81. Quoted in Wawro (2003, 227).

82. Quoted in Kolb (1989, 152, 213); quoted in Howard (1961, 231–32).

83. Van Evera (1999).

84. Liberman (1996).

85. Murray (1984, 292).

86. Fearon (1997); Smith and Stam (2001); see also Wagner (2000, 479–80). Bargaining models in economics do not really capture this insight. The closest perhaps may be repeated bargaining models, which allow for the interdependence

of rounds of bargaining, but this framework does not quite capture the dynamic envisioned here, in which bargaining outcomes affect bargaining power. See Muthoo (1999, chapter 10).

87. Fearon (1997); Smith and Stam (2001). This last idea is also generated in the offense-defense literature. See Van Evera (1999).

88. American and Soviet decision-makers in the Cold War saw asymmetries in value across different areas, despite their rhetoric about the world being zero-sum. West Berlin in particular was seen as a "superdomino," and conversely the USSR saw East Germany as a "super-ally" more important than others (Harrison 2003).

89. Oren (2002, 302–4); Segev (2007, esp. 387); Schiff (1974, 181).

90. Mueller (1994, 121–23); Bush and Scowcroft (1998, 488–90); Baker (1995, 436). Others have speculated that the Bush administration thought Saddam's regime might collapse anyway after Kuwait's liberation. Pollack (2002b, 46–47).

91. Woodward (1999, 185).

92. Bush and Scowcroft (1998, 477); Powell (1995, 485–86).

93. Bush and Scowcroft (1998, 473); Schwartzkopf (1992, 516).

94. Pape (1996, 217). Notably, although the war itself was seen as necessary to smash Iraqi conventional military power as well as liberate Kuwait, substantial elements of the Iraqi military, including parts of the Republican Guard, escaped. Pollack (2002b, 45–46); Ricks (2006, 6).

95. Pollack (2002b, 52).

96. Reiter (2006b).

97. Fearon (1995b).

98. Hassner (2003). See also Goddard (2006).

99. Schelling (1966); Selten (1978); Toft (2003); Walter (2006a).

100. Powell (2006); Fearon (2005b).

101. Tarar and Levontoğlu (2006) state that a leader might claim all of a good publicly in order to generate audience costs, which in turn creates issue indivisibility and make war more likely. They discuss three episodes, none of which support the argument. The first is the Cuban Missile Crisis, in which the claim is that Kennedy demanded removal of Soviet missiles but would not have publicly agreed to removal of the Turkish missiles because of audience costs. However, Kennedy was willing to make further concessions if necessary to avoid war, specifically offering a public trade of Turkish missiles if Khrushchev rejected the offer of a secret trade (Bundy 1988, 435). The second is the 1991 Gulf War, and the interpretation is that Bush underestimated Iraq's resolve for war and demanded too much. To the contrary, the Bush administration actually preferred the liberation of Kuwait through war rather than Iraq's peaceful withdrawal from Kuwait, as the former would allow the destruction of Iraq's military power as well as the liberation of Kuwait (Reiter and Stam 2002, 150–51). The third is the Fashoda Crisis in which Britain demanded total withdrawal from the small East African village in question. Here, the avoidance of war shows that Britain correctly estimated that French preferences would guide them to concede entirely rather than risk war.

102. Tarar and Levontoğlu (2006).
103. Quoted in Palm (1971, 71–72).
104. Ritter (1973, vol. 4, 66).

CHAPTER FOUR
CONDUCTING EMPIRICAL TESTS

1. George and Bennett (2005, 179). See also George and McKeown (1985, 35).
2. George and Bennett (2005, 176).
3. On the importance of commitment problems in civil war termination, see Walter (2002).
4. See, e.g., Balfour (1979 281–82), and chapter 6.
5. Longhand personal notes of Truman, January 27, 1952, "Longhand Notes File, 1930–1955," PSF, Box 282, Truman Library. See also the diary entry for May 18.
6. Kitchen (1976, 39). German officials systematically purged the documentary record of World War I to, among other things, reduce evidence of German war guilt. Herwig (1987).
7. Israel (1966, 264).
8. See, e.g., Goemans' (2000, 101n–2n) critique of one of Gatzke's (1950) translations.
9. Hasegawa (2005, 297–98; 2007); Frank (1999).
10. Stoddard (1890, 179).
11. Stephens (1870, vol. 2, 588).
12. Gilbert (1983, vol. 6, 405–6).
13. Braithwaite (2006, 222).
14. Mearsheimer (1983).
15. Quoted in Nicolson (1985, 88).
16. May (2000).
17. Gartner and Myers (1995); Zhang (1995, 154–55).
18. Li, Millett, and Yu (2001, 6, 246n).
19. Livermore (1957).
20. Desch (2002); Brooks (2003). Biddle and Long (2004) slightly revise the HERO dataset, making few corrections. Thanks to Stephen Biddle for providing me with the revised version of the dataset. Those corrections notwithstanding, HERO's treatment of wars remains highly asymmetrical. Some twentieth-century conflicts coded as wars by the Correlates of War project are not included by HERO, such as the Chaco War, the 1929 Japan–Soviet clash, the Russo-Hungarian War, the Sino-Indian War, the War of Attrition between Egypt and Israel, the Italo-Ethiopian War, the 1948 Indo-Pakistani War, the 1965 Indo-Pakistani War, the Soccer War, the 1971 Bangladesh War, the Cyprus War, the Uganda-Tanzania War, the Sino-Vietnamese War, and others. Of those wars which are included, some wars (especially wars involving the United States) get much more extensive inclusion (that is, many more of their battles are included), whereas other wars get more scant coverage. For example, the single World War II cam-

paign to capture the Pacific island of Iwo Jima is treated as twenty-seven separate battles, whereas the entire 1939–40 Winter War between Russia and Finland is treated as a single battle. Purely naval battles, such as the critical Battle of Tsushima in the 1904–05 Russo-Japanese War, are excluded. Besides generating problems of heterogeneity across wars, it also means that for those wars with few battles, there is insufficient information about how the ebb and flow of combat throughout the war informed the political leadership and may have affected war termination decisions.

CHAPTER FIVE
THE KOREAN WAR

1. Kim Il Sung made a speech to the North Korean military on June 5, 1950 declaring that in the event of war, North Korea would attempt to reunify the peninsula (Stueck 1995, 44). The Soviet Union supported the invasion in part because it hoped to secure a psychological advance from a Communist military victory there, and believed that the United States would not offer substantial military assistance. This belief stemmed from the Soviet reading of U.S. internal and public statements defining the American defense perimeter in the Pacific as excluding mainland Asian territories (Stueck 2002, 73). Most famously, perhaps, Secretary of State Dean Acheson in a public speech on January 12, 1950 defined the American defense perimeter in the Asia/Pacific region in such a way that it seemed to exclude Korea from its reach (Acheson 1969, 357). The Chairman of the Senate Foreign Relations Committee in May went further, noting that the Soviet Union could conquer South Korea without U.S. interference because South Korea was not "very greatly important" (quoted in Leckie 1962, 37).

2. www.un.org/documents/sc/res/1950/scres50.htm; Truman (1956, vol. 2, 338–39); Acheson (1969, 450); Schnabel and Watson (1979, vol. 3, pt. 1, 107).

3. "Minutes of the 58th Meeting of the National Security Council," June 28, 1950, 2, National Archives, College Park, Maryland.

4. Leffler (1992, 365).

5. www.un.org/documents/resga.htm (accessed November 24, 2008).

6. Schnabel and Watson (1979, vol. 3, pt. 1, 109); FRUS 1950 (1977, vol. 1, 328).

7. Kennan (1967, 487).

8. FRUS 1950 (1977, vol. 7, 272); Foot (1985, 72–73). Note that Allison's portrayal of his opinions during this period in his memoirs, is, in the words of one historian, "at best, misleading" (Gaddis 1980, 111n). The documentary record provides a clearer view of what he advocated at the time.

9. Foot (1985, 69).

10. Nerhem (2000); Kennan (1967). On the CIA, see FRUS 1950 (1977, vol. 7, 600–602); Stueck (1983).

11. Whitney (1955, 338); Collins (1969, 83); Schnabel and Watson (1979, vol. 3, pt. 1, 222).

12. Foot (1985, 68). Other South Korean calls for crossing the parallel were made before Austin's August 10 speech. In late July, there were unconfirmed re-

ports from the Kuomintang news agency that the chairman of the South Korean National Assembly called for South Korean forces to be allowed to cross the 38th parallel. Daily Korea Summaries, Intelligence File Series, PSF, Truman Papers, Truman Library, July 24, 1950 (hereafter DKS). The DKS were daily summaries of the combat and political developments in the Korean War sent by the Director of Central Intelligence, Rear Admiral R. N. Hillenkoetter, to Truman. In early August, the commander of South Korean forces declared that annihilation of North Korean forces would make it possible to cross the 38th parallel and unify the peninsula (DKS, August 8, 1950).

13. "Special Message to the Congress Reporting on the Situation in Korea," July 19, 1950, www.presidency.ucsb.edu/ws/index.php?pid=13560&st=&st1= (accessed September 7, 2006); "Radio and Television Address to the American People on the Situation in Korea," July 19, 1950, www.presidency.ucsb.edu/ws/ index.php?pid=13561&st=&st1= (accessed September 7, 2006), italics added.

14. Acheson (1969, 451); see also Beisner (2006, 395–98).

15. Minutes of July 14 meeting, "Memoranda of Conversations File, 1949–1953," Box 67, Acheson papers, 3, Truman Library.

16. Stueck (1995, 383n). See also Kennan (1967, 488–89).

17. Austin (1950, 331).

18. Decisions made at the August 3, 1950 NSC meeting, "NSC Meetings File," PSF Box 180, Truman Library.

19. *Foreign Relations of the United States, 1950*, volume 3 (Washington: U.S. Government Printing Office, 1977), 1154.

20. Acheson (1969, 452).

21. Truman (1956, 358–59).

22. Memo of off-the-record comments between Acheson and correspondents, September 2, 1950, in folder Co–Cz of Acheson Personal Correspondence, 1949–1952, Acheson papers, Box 63, Truman Library.

23. "A Report to the President by the National Security Council on United States Courses of Action With Respect to Korea," September 9, 1950, www .trumanlibrary.org/whistlestop/study_collections/korea/large/sec4/nsc81-3.htm (accessed September 7, 2006).

24. Labs (1997, 35–37). Specifically, one might mark the date of expansion as September 29, when Secretary of Defense Marshall formally told MacArthur that he now had the authority to advance north of the 38th parallel. Foot (1985, 74).

25. Note that the core political strategy throughout September did not change: UN forces should conquer North Korea, providing there was no intervention on the part of China and the Soviet Union. This was stated publicly by Truman on September 1, and was codified in NSC 81/1. The September 29 communication to MacArthur formally giving MacArthur authority to move north of the 38th parallel (as well as the September 27 JCS communication to MacArthur) concerned military strategy rather than political aims, and can best be termed a clarification of (rather than a change in) military strategy. Indeed, MacArthur had been informed on September 15, the day the Inchon operation began, that NSC 81/1 gave him legal authority to operate above the 38th parallel (Schnabel and Watson 1979, vol. 3, pt. 1, 228).

26. Memo from Bradley to Secretary of Defense, September 7, 1950, "NSC Meetings File," PSF, Box 180, Truman Library.

27. Bradley and Blair (1983, 561).

28. Truman (1956, vol. 2, 359); Stueck (1995, 89); Acheson (1969, 452); Collins (1969, 146–47).

29. Leckie (1962, 39). MacArthur claimed in his memoirs that the pre-invasion South Korean military was deliberately left as an underequipped essentially constabulary force, so as to prevent it from attacking North Korea. Stueck (2002, 61–62); MacArthur (1964, 328–30); Hickey (1999, 27).

30. Quoted in Wainstock (1999, 7).

31. Quoted in Leckie (1962, 37). See also Bradley and Blair (1983, 530).

32. Leffler (1992, 365); Offner (2002, 358).

33. Ridgway (1988, 16).

34. DKS, July 6 and 7, 1950.

35. Schnabel and Watson (1979, vol. 3, pt. 1, 184).

36. Collins (1969, 81–85)

37. www.presidency.ucsb.edu/ws/index.php?pid=13561&st=&st1= (accessed September 7, 2006).

38. Truman (1956, 351).

39. Stueck (1995, 77).

40. "Peace Offensives Concerning Korea," August 24, 1950, in Merrill (1997, 432).

41. Stueck (2002, 88).

42. Schnabel and Watson (1979, vol. 3, pt. 1, 212–13).

43. DKS September 6, 1950.

44. Cagle and Manson (1957, 78–81).

45. Collins (1969, 125).

46. Collins (1998, 7).

47. Manchester (1978, 574).

48. Cagle and Manson (1957, 76).

49. Schnabel and Watson (1979, vol. 3, 210).

50. Quoted in Ridgway (1988, 39).

51. Quoted in Karig, Cagle, and Manson (1952, 169). In hindsight, Collins gives no hint about whether at the time he thought the plan likely to succeed or fail, either in his memoirs or at a 1976 retrospective conference. Collins (1969, 126–27); Heller (1977, 24–25); Schnabel and Watson (1979, vol. 3, pt. 1, 211n); MacArthur (1964, 347–49).

52. Bradley and Blair (1983, 544).

53. Acheson (1969, 448); Truman memo of briefing by Collins and Sherman, August 27, 1950, "Longhand Notes File, 1930–1955," Box 281, PSF, Truman Library; Truman (1956, 358).

54. Schnabel and Watson (1979, 211).

55. Ibid. (1979, vol. 3, pt. 1, 211–13); Whitney (1955, 350–53).

56. MacArthur (1964, 351).

57. Merrill (1997, 383).

58. Schnabel and Watson (1979, vol. 3, pt. 1, 199–200; 213).

59. "Memorandum for the Executive Secretary, National Security Council," September 26, 1950, folder 63, National Archives, College Park, Maryland.

60. Truman (1956, 386).

61. *FRUS 1950* (1977, vol. 7, 541).

62. "Memorandum for the Secretary of Defense. Subject: Peace Offensives Concerning Korea." From Frank Pace, Dan A. Kimball, and Thomas K. Finletter. August 24, 1950, General Data Folder, PSF, Box 206, Truman Library.

63. Foot (1985, 62).

64. Offner (1992, 367–68); Hamby (2005, 535).

65. Stueck (2002, 104).

66. Quoted in Sartori (2005, 23). The U.S. ignored increasingly strident Chinese warnings through the fall not to approach the Sino–Korean border. Scholars have offered a number of explanations as to why these warnings were ignored, including cognitive psychological accounts for ignoring discrepant information, and reputation-based accounts that propose China's reputation in American eyes had suffered because of hollow threats China had made over Taiwan. Lebow (1981); Sartori (2005).

67. See "NSC-68: United States Objectives and Programs for National Security," April 14, 1950, available at www.fas.org/irp/offdocs/nsc-hst/nsc-68.htm (downloaded August 4, 2008), Tractehberg (1991, chapter 3).

68. Quoted in Heller (1977, 26–27). See also Collins (1969, 144–46).

69. www.claremont.org/publications/precepts/id.163/precept_detail.asp (downloaded November 24, 2008).

70. LaFeber (1974, 83); *FRUS 1950* (1977, vol. 7, 386).

71. See, e.g., *FRUS 1977* (1950, vol. 7, 458–61).

72. *FRUS 1950* (1977, vol. 7, 503).

73. Offner (2002, 380).

74. Note from Acheson to Paul Nitze, July 12, 1950, Acheson papers, "Memoranda of Conversations File, 1949–1953," Box 67, Truman Library; Christiansen (1995, 270).

75. Schnabel and Watson (1979, vol. 3, pt. 1, 270–71).

76. Kennan (1967, 488, 491).

77. Memo from Kennan to Acheson, August 23, 1950, "Memoranda of Conversations File, 1949–1953," Box 67, Acheson papers, Truman Library.

78. Offner (2002, 358).

79. Jervis (1980); Kydd (2005, 113–115).

80. *Supplemental Appropriations for 1951* (1950, 272).

81. Ibid., 268.

82. Truman (1956, vol. 2, 332–33).

83. Leffler (1992, 376–377).

84. *FRUS 1950* (1977, 461).

85. See, for example, Jian (1994); Zhang (1992); Christensen (1996).

86. Acheson (1969, 469, 477).

87. Ibid., 471; Truman (1956, 387–88).

88. Acheson (1969, 472).

89. Ibid., 476, 513.

90. George M. Elsey to Charles Murphy, April 24, 1951, Korea: New Peace Proposal 1951, Subject File, Harry S. Truman Administration, Elsey Papers, Student Research File: "The Korean War: The Prisoner of War Issue and the Search for Peace," Truman Library.

91. Trachtenberg (1991, 122–23). Later in the war, at his most exasperated Truman would vent in his diary that the only way to break the negotiations logjam was to threaten the USSR and China directly and openly with nuclear war if they did not immediately accept peace terms. It does not appear that he ever voiced these frustrations as serious policy proposals, however. Longhand personal notes of Truman, January 27 and May 18, 1952, "Longhand Notes File, 1930–1955," PSF, Box 282, Truman Library.

92. Acheson (1969, 478).

93. Minutes of August 14 meeting, "Memoranda of Conversations File, 1949–1953," Box 67, Acheson papers, Truman Library.

94. Foot (1985, 123–30); Risse-Kappen (1995, 46–51).

95. Quoted in Foot (1985, 23).

96. Schnabel and Watson (1979, vol. 3, pt. 1, 439).

97. *FRUS 1951* (1977, vol. 7, pt. 1, 152–54).

98. Ibid., 159.

99. Ibid., 164–67; 189–94.

100. Schnabel and Watson (1979, vol. 3, pt. 1, 480–81).

101. Stueck (1995, 207).

102. Acheson (1969, 531).

103. U.S. Congress, Senate, *Military Situation in the Far East* (1951, part 3, 2126). See also Foot (1991, 45–46).

104. Quoted in Stueck (1995, 216).

105. Quoted in Zhang (1995, 157).

106. Stueck (1995, 216–17). At least as late as March 1951, Mao was planning military operations to prevent a stalemate at the 38th parallel (Zhang 1995, 144–45).

107. Stueck (1995, 208).

108. Ibid.

109. Ibid., 244.

110. Ibid.

111. U.S. Congress, Senate, *Military Situation in the Far East* (1951, part 5, 3605).

112. *Foreign Relations of the United States, 1951* (1983, vol. 7, 1293).

113. Longhand personal notes of Truman, January 27, 1952, "Longhand Notes File, 1930–1955," PSF, Box 282, Truman Library.

114. Longhand personal notes of Truman, May 18, 1952, "Longhand Notes File, 1930–1955," PSF, Box 282, Truman Library.

115. Quoted in Weathersby (1998, 109).

116. Robert A. Lovett to Senator Francis Case, October 30, 1952; OF 471-B: Prisoners of War (Koran Action), Truman Papers, Student Research File: "The Korean War: The Prisoner of War Issue and the Search for Peace," Truman Library; Wallace Carroll to Gordon Gray, December 28, 1951; 383.6: Report on Situation with Respect to Repatriation of Prisoners of War; Class 300—Adminis-

tration, 1951–53, PSB Files, Truman Papers, Student Research File: "The Korean War: The Prisoner of War Issue and the Search for Peace," Truman Library; JCS Chair Omar N. Bradley to George C. Marshall, August 8, 1951, 383.6, Report on Situation with Respect to Repatriation of Prisoners of War; Class 300—Administration, 1951–53, PSB Files, Truman Papers, Student Research File: "The Korean War: The Prisoner of War Issue and the Search for Peace," Truman Library.

117. Quoted in Gaddis (1987, 176). See also Reiter and Stam (2002, chapter 3).

118. Stueck (2002, 149–50).

119. Records of discussions at Princeton Seminars, February 13–14, 1954, folder 1 of 2, Reel 3, Track 1, p9, Box 81, Acheson Papers, Truman Library.

120. Christensen (1996, 151–52).

121. First quote from Chai (2001, 188). General Chai led the Chinese military mission to North Korea from August 1950 through 1955. The second quote is from Rear Admiral Arleigh Burke, quoted in Stueck (1995, 241). Interestingly, Stueck (242) takes issue with Burke's characterization.

122. Stueck (1995, 230–32).

123. Ibid., 279.

124. Jian (2001, 114).

125. Sale (1998, 160); LaFeber (1997, 117). Both these sources cite the documentation and analysis in Christensen (1995, esp. 268–69). Importantly, although Christensen argues that Truman by November recognized that the China threat helped boost support for the increase in defense spending, he does not argue that Truman approved NSC 81/1 or crossed the 38th parallel in order to increase defense spending.

126. Quoted in Christensen (1995, 268–69).

127. See, e.g., Foot (1985, 69–70).

128. Daily Opinion Summaries, Department of State, Nos. 1416-8, July 20, 21, and 24, 1950, Elsey Papers, Box 72, Truman Library.

129. Oshinsky (1983, 166–67).

130. Acheson (1969, 364–66); Reeves (1982, 328–29).

131. In his April 10, 1951 diary entry, Truman notes of the political fallout from MacArthur's dismissal, "Quite an explosion. Was expected but I had to act." Ferrell (1980, 251).

132. Oshinsky (1983, 194); Hamby (1995, 558).

133. Although some scholars have found in the Korean War a statistically significant relationship between the accumulation of casualties over time and the decline of support for the war, the actual relationship is more complex and nonlinear. Gartner and Segura (1998); Mueller (1985).

134. Christensen (1996, 152); Gaddis (1980, 111).

135. Mueller (1985, 50–51).

136. Ibid., 51. Italics in original.

137. Clodfelter (2002, 737).

138. Stueck (2002, 169).

139. Ambrose (1983, vol. 1).

140. Stueck (2002, 170–73).

141. Mueller (1985, 80).

142. Ambrose (1984, vol. 2, 30–35, 52); Gaddis (1997, 107–8).
143. Zhang (1995, 233–34); Ping (2001, 63).
144. Oshinsky (1983, 346).
145. Gaddis (1997, 109); Weathersby (1998, 108–10).
146. Stueck (1995, 2002).
147. Volkogonov (1991, 570). See also Chang and Halliday (2005, 390–91).
148. Jian (2001, 112–16).
149. Truman (1956, 332–33).
150. Quoted in Leffler (1992, 365–67).
151. Minutes of a cabinet meeting, July 14, 1950, "Memoranda of Conversations File, 1949–1953," box 67 Acheson papers, Truman Library.
152. Collins (1969, 83).
153. Quoted in Zhang (1992, 83, italics in original; also 83n).
154. *FRUS 1950* (1977, vol. 7, 506).
155. Quoted in Beisner (2006, 399).
156. Quoted in Beisner (2006, 399). See also Acheson (1969, 451).
157. Hughes (1963, 104–5).

CHAPTER SIX
THE ALLIES, 1940–42

1. Self (2006, 399).
2. Self (2005, 453–44).
3. May (2000, esp. 8–9, 205–9).
4. Self (2005, 446; see also 450–1).
5. Ibid., 456; Self (2006, 402–3).
6. Reynolds (1996, 202)
7. Self (2005, 445).
8. Ibid., 455.
9. Reynolds (1996, 202–3).
10. May (2000, 18).
11. Quoted in Self (2006, 400).
12. May (2000).
13. Roberts (1991, 211).
14. Lukacs (1999). Lukacs' remark relates to the title of the fourth volume of Churchill's six-volume history of World War II. Volume four was titled *The Hinge of Fate*, and covered the campaigns of 1942.
15. Colville (2004, 116); Self (2005, 533); Reynolds (1985, 157).
16. Reynolds (1985, 149).
17. Eden (1965, 123).
18. Nicolson (1967, 89).
19. Churchill (1949, vol. 2, 89). The report was written before the Dunkirk evacuation enjoyed success. It is not exactly clear whether or not the report presumes the successful evacuation of British troops from Dunkirk in its assessment of the weakness of British homeland defenses.

20. Gilbert (1995, vol. 2, 163–65); Roberts (1991, 218–19); Pimlott (1986, 27).

21. Quoted in Lukacs (1990, 95). This quotation from the report is not contained within the excerpt in Churchill (1949, vol. 1, 89), meaning that again Churchill provided an edited view of history in his own writings.

22. Churchill (1949, vol. 2, 89).

23. Reiter (2007).

24. Dalton (1957, 335); Reynolds (1985, 149).

25. Macleod and Kelly (1962, 343–44). "[Home]" inserted by Macleod and Kelly.

26. Ibid., 346.

27. Barnes and Nicholson (1988, 619). See also Eden (1965, 129).

28. Mcleod and Kelly (1962, 345). Undersecretary of State Alexander Cogan, a member of the War Cabinet, agreed, noting in his diary on May 28, "Prospects of B.E.F. look blacker than ever. Awful days!" Dilks (1971, 291).

29. Nicolson (1967, 89–90). Minister of Information Duff Cooper had similar thoughts, fearing surrender and seeing death as perhaps preferable in the event. Cooper (1953, 284).

30. Colville (2004, 113).

31. Gilbert (1995, vol. 2, 180).

32. Lukacs (1999, 176–77).

33. General Alfred Jodl diary entry for May 20, 1940, available at avalon .law.yale.edu/imt/1809-ps.asp (downloaded November 29, 2008).

34. Lukacs (1990, 80).

35. Costello (1991, 186).

36. Lukacs (1990, 98).

37. Pimlott (1986, 28n).

38. Gilbert (1983, vol. 6, 435–36).

39. Quoted in Jenkins (2001, 611).

40. Richard Austen Butler, an assistant to Halifax, may have put forth an unauthorized peace feeler on June 17, 1940. According to one report, he told the Swedish ambassador to Britain that "no opportunity for reaching a compromise would be neglected if the possibility were offered on reasonable conditions," and that Churchill might be replaced by Halifax on June 28, at which point negotiations with Germany might become possible. However, in the days that followed the Swedish ambassador told his government that he doubted that Butler's views were official, and the Swedish government was officially instructed that the British government had no interest in negotiations with Germany. Historians have concluded that it is doubtful that this feeler was authorized by Halifax, much less Churchill himself (Roberts 1991, 232; Munch-Peterson 1986).

41. Gilbert (1995, 169). Interestingly, in his postwar memoirs/history of World War II, Churchill denied that there was any consideration of terms, noting somewhat self-servingly that, "Future generations may deem it noteworthy that the supreme question of whether we should fight on alone never found a place upon the War Cabinet agenda. It was taken for granted and as a matter of course by these men of all parties in the State" (Churchill 1949, vol. 2, 177). This inaccuracy

has been called "the most breathtakingly bland piece of misinformation to appear in all these six volumes" (Jenkins 2001, 610).

42. Quoted in Roberts (1991, 227).

43. Ibid., 216–17. Relatedly, in a May 26 War Cabinet meeting, he remarked that "Herr Hitler thought that he had the whip hand. The only thing to do was to show him that he could not conquer this country." Gilbert (1995, vol. 2, 158).

44. Gilbert (1995, vol. 2, 180).

45. Ibid. This was a key point which Halifax did not grasp. Roberts (1991, 215–17).

46. Quoted in Gilbert (1983, vol. 6, 403).

47. Ibid., 444.

48. Gilbert (1995, vol. 2, 168).

49. Quoted in Jenkins (2001, 607).

50. Lukacs (1990, 96).

51. Gilbert (1995, vol. 2, 185).

52. Quoted in Roberts (1991, 236). See also note 48.

53. Gilbert (1995, vol. 2, 181).

54. Gilbert (1991, vol. 2, 157).

55. Reynolds (1985, 148–49).

56. Gilbert (1995, vol. 2, 181).

57. Pimlott (1986, 28).

58. Churchill (1949, vol. 2, 100).

59. Lukacs (1990, 38–39).

60. Gilbert (1991, 553–54).

61. Ibid., 588, 595–601.

62. Ibid., 615.

63. Ibid.

64. Dalton (1957, 335–36).

65. Gilbert (1995, vol. 2, 158).

66. Ibid., 153.

67. Ibid.

68. Quoted in Gilbert (1991, 646).

69. Mcleod and Kelly (1962, 386).

70. Quoted in Roberts (1991, 212).

71. Stevenson (1988).

72. Gilbert (1995, vol. 2, 158).

73. Ibid.

74. Ibid., 169.

75. Lord (1982, 272–73); Sebag-Montefiore (2006, esp. xi–xiv).

76. Lawlor (1994, 68–69); Mcleod and Kelly (1962, 362, 365).

77. Gilbert (1995, vol. 2, 202); Legro (1995, 163).

78. Quoted in Reynolds (1985, 154). Brackets in Reynolds.

79. Dilks (1971, 308).

80. Lawlor (1994, 65).

81. Ibid., 67.

82. Reynolds (1985, 167); Reynolds (1996, 206–7).

83. Reynolds (1996, 205–6); Gartner (1997, chapter 4).

84. Quoted in Jenkins (2001, 600).

85. Pimlott (1986, 27); Reynolds (1985, 162). Some at the time argued that with luck, even without American intervention, the German economy itself might collapse under the weight of mobilization as early as 1942 (Reynolds 1985, 157–58).

86. Quoted in Costello (1991, 99). Italics in original.

87. Ibid., 203–4.

88. Colville (2004, 113).

89. Gilbert (1995, vol. 2, 163).

90. Reiter and Stam (2002, 98).

91. Note that the portrayal here has emphasized British perceptions of the military outlook rather than the actual outlook; some historians have been highly critical of the accuracy of British judgments about the future course of the war at this stage (Reynolds 1985, esp. 167). Further, the interpretation here is consistent with the description of 1940 Anglo–German relations offered by Robert Powell (2006). Powell notes that incomplete information is an unsatisfactory explanation for Germany's decision to attack Britain in summer 1940. He notes that Germany attacked in the West not because of uncertainty about British intentions, but rather because it knew Britain would not make a separate peace, and hence Britain needed to be subdued in order to permit Germany a free hand to attack the Soviet Union. This chapter provides an explanation of why Britain would not make concessions, even believing Germany's intentions to be malign and its capabilities to be considerable: the British belief that any German commitment to abide by a war-ending agreement would not be credible, and that the only means of providing real peace was through military victory.

92. Sherwood (1950, 454–55, 491, 504).

93. Ibid., 465.

94. Roosevelt to Churchill, March 7, 1942, Kimball (1984, vol. 1, 390).

95. Dallek (1979, 331); www.presidency.ucsb.edu/ws/print.php?pid=16219 (downloaded October 15, 2007). See also Roosevelt (1950, vol. 2, 1298–99); Berinsky (2007, esp. 988).

96. Sherwood (1950, 498).

97. Gartner (1997, 97); Churchill (1950, vol. 4, 126).

98. Glantz and House (1995, 105–7); Israel (1966, 253–54).

99. Israel (1966, 252).

100. Quoted in Gilbert (1986, vol. 6, 78).

101. Israel (1966, 249).

102. Ibid., 255.

103. Reiter and Stam (2002, 35–37).

104. Roosevelt at some points incorrectly gave the impression that the idea of unconditional surrender emerged originally at the January 1943 Casablanca conference (Sherwood 1950, 695–97).

105. Armstrong (1961, 16).

106. Quoted in Armstrong (1961, 17). See also Roosevelt's statement just after Pearl Harbor (Beschloss 2002, 12), and the January 1, 1942 Allies' Joint Statement (Davis 2000, 371).

107. Eden (1965, 439).

108. Notter (1949, 124–33); O'Connor (1971, 37); Pogue (1973, 32). The security technical committee within the security committee met in May 1943 to discuss postwar plans for Japan in particular. Although an array of views was expressed, the common assumption was that the war had to end with the destruction of Japanese militarism and the Japanese empire (Iriye 1981, 122–28).

109. June 1, 1942, 10:30 a.m. meeting with President Roosevelt, Mr. Molotov, Mr. Litvinov, Mr. Hopkins, and Messrs. Pavlov and Cross, 3, in *The Papers of Cordell Hull* (Washington: Library of Congress, 1975), reel 22.

110. Dilks (1971, 506).

111. Feis (1967, 109n).

112. Dower (1986, 53–55); Security Technical Committee, May 7, 12, 1943, p. 10, 12, Harley Notter papers, National Archive, College Park, Maryland; Janssens (1995, 41).

113. Feis (1967, 108). On the effects of past experiences on foreign policy, see Reiter (1996).

114. "Minutes S-1, Meeting of April 15, 1942," 3, Notter papers; "Minutes S-2, Meeting of April 29, 1942," 1–2, Notter papers; Israel (1966, 264–65, 265n). Interestingly, although Davis supported unconditional surrender, he commented in a later meeting that the 1918 armistice had only limited applicability to the current circumstances because of different world conditions, such as the status of the British colonial empire. "Minutes S-3, Meeting of May 6, 1942," 4, Notter papers.

115. "Minutes S-4, Meeting of May 20, 1942," 1, Notter papers.

116. See the "Summary of Conclusions: The First Four Meetings of the Security Subcommittee," May 21, 1942, box 76, Notter papers. On Japan, see "Conditions for Japanese Surrender to the United Nations," May 27, 1942, prepared by General Strong, Notter papers.

117. "Minutes S-3, Meeting of May 6, 1942," 1, Notter papers.

118. "Minutes S-4, Meeting of May 20, 1942," 2, Notter papers. Records indicate that Norman Davis, a member of the committee, met with Roosevelt personally on May 18, 1942. "FDR: Day by Day—The Pare Larentz Chronology," May 18, 1942, Roosevelt Presidential Library, Hyde Park, New York.

119. Balfour (1979, 287–88).

120 Sherwood (1950, 227).

121. Quoted on Beschloss (2002, 12).

122. Quoted in Armstrong (1961, 18).

123. *Foreign Relations of the United States 1944* (1966, vol. 1, 501–2).

124. Armstrong (1961, 20); Janssens (1995, esp. 438).

125. Butcher (1946, 609–10).

126. Beschloss (2002, 115–16).

127. Quoted in Dower (1986, 56–57).

128. Churchill (1950 vol. 3, 606–7)

129. Pogue (1966, 160–61).

130. Sherwood (1950, 459).

131. Roosevelt (1950, vol. 1, 1304).

132. Beschloss (2002, 13).

133. Ibid., 13–15.

134. See, e.g., Förster (1997).

135. Erickson (1975, 222).

136. Braithwaite (2006, 214–25).

137. Glantz and House (1995, 82).

138. Braithwaite (2006, 240); Conquest (1991, 248).

139. Barros and Gregor (1995, 220); Volkogonov (1991, 412–13); Ronay (1989); Pavlenko (1989).

140. Watson (2005, 193). There are also bits of evidence indicating possible Soviet interest in negotiations with Germany later in the war, although this evidence is generally much more indirect and circumstantial than what is available concerning the October 1941 episode. See Mastny (1979, esp. 77–78, 83–84, 162).

141. There is also less reliable corroborative evidence, such as the September 5, 1941 message from Moscow to London hinting that the former was considering a separate peace with Germany, although this may of course have been posturing by Stalin to encourage Britain to put more pressure on Germany from the West. Welles (1950, 134).

142. Volkogonov (1991, 412–13).

143. Barber and Harrison (1991, 55n).

144. Ronay (1989).

145. Pavlenko (1989).

146. "The Beriya Case and 'Blank Spots' in Soviet History" (1988).

147. Chuev (1993, 14).

148. Sudoplatov and Sudoplatov (1994, 145).

149. Volgokonov (1991, 352–53).

150. MacKenzie (1994, esp. 510); Streim (1997, 295–97).

151. Quoted in Aspaturian (1963, 49).

152. Gorodetsky (1997, 347).

153. Sherwood (1950, 904).

154. Rosen (2005, chapter 4).

155. Braithwaite (2006).

156. Nove (1969, 270).

157. Barros and Gregor (1995, 220); Volgokonov (1991, 413).

CHAPTER SEVEN
THE LOGIC OF WAR: FINLAND AND THE USSR, 1939–44

1. Trotter (1991, 5–6).

2. Ibid., 14; Barros and Gregor (1995, 3–5).

3. Jakobsen (1961, 106); Edwards (2006, 69–73); Myllyniemi (1997).

4. Edwards (2006).

5. Van Dyke (1997, 13–14); Vehviläinen (2002, chapter 3).

6. Van Dyke (1997, 14); Spring (1986, 216).

7. Van Dyke (1997, 17–21); Jakobsen (1961).

8. Trotter (1991, 58–59).

9. "The Winter War" (1990, 203).

10. Khrushchev (1970, 152).

11. Van Dyke (1997, 40)

252 • Notes to Chapter Seven

12. Trotter (1991, esp. 35).
13. Viipuri is also known as Vyborg.
14. Van Dyke (1997, 77–81); Trotter (1991).
15. Khrushchev (1970, 153); Meretskov (1971, 112); Van Dyke (1997, 135).
16. Van Dyke (1997, 72).
17. Trotter (1991, 238–39).
18. Edwards (2006, 206–7); Tanner (1957, 219–20).
19. Edwards (2006, 203–4).
20. Trotter (1991, 135).
21. Ibid., 241.
22. Van Dyke (1997, 164–65).
23. Jakobson (1961, 236–41); Van Dyke (1997, 166).
24. Jakobson (1961, 248).
25. Van Dyke (1997, 176–78).
26. Jakobson (1961, 249); Tanner (1957, 212).
27. Van Dyke (1997, 175).
28. "The Winter War" (1990, 210).
29. Kollontai (1990, 197).
30. "The Winter War" (1990, 211; see also 205).
31. *Foreign Relations of the United States 1940* (1959, vol. 1, 299).
32. Quoted in Screen (2000, 153).
33. Jakobson (1961, 250).
34. Trotter (1991, 263); Condon (1972, 93); Khrushchev (1970, 155).
35. Screen (2000, 151).
36. Jakobson (1961, esp. 11).
37. Tanner (1957, 184).
38. Ibid., 227.
39. Ibid., 180. The Romanians made a similar argument, recalling their experience in World War I.
40. Jakobson (1961, 252); Tanner (1957, 183
41. Kulkov and Rzheshevsky (2002, 263–64).
42. On buffer states, see Fazal (2007)
43. Quoted in Vehviläinen (2002, 79).
44. Jokipii (1982, 86, 91); *Foreign Relations of the United States 1940* (1959, vol. 1, 340); Ziemke (1959, 115).
45. Vehviläinen (2002, 80–81).
46. Jokipii (1982, 89).
47. Mann and Jörgensen (2002, 67); Vehviläinen (2002, 78–83); Menger (1997, 527); Erfurth (1979, 3–5); Jokipii (1982, 92).
48. Menger (1997, 527–29); Vehviläinen (2002, 87–88); Mann and Jörgensen (2002, 67); Jokipii (1982, 87); Polvinen (1985); Ziemke (1959, 113–21). On the German warning to the Soviet Union, see Berezhkov (1969).
49. Menger (1997, 530–31); Jokipii (1982, 103).
50. Ziemke (1959, 204n). Some in Finland also sought territorial gains along with regime change, specifically the acquisition of Eastern Karelia, a portion of Soviet territory that contained Finnish speakers. Acquisition of this territory

would help build what was referred to as "Greater Finland." Vehviläinen (2002, 91–92).

51. Palm (1971, 15); Screen (2000, 172–73).

52. Quoted in Vehviläinen (2002, 89); Ziemke (1959, 204n). See also Menger (1997, 532).

53. *Foreign Relations of the United States 1941* (1958, vol. 1, 52, 59). Finland's faith in Germany may have been misplaced, since Hitler as early as July 1941 ordered that Finland become a tributary state within the Third Reich after the war (Palm 1971, 18n).

54. Screen (2000, 172).

55. Palm (1971, 15); *Foreign Relations of the United States 1941* (1958, vol. 1, 67).

56. *Foreign Relations of the United States 1941* (1958, vol. 1, 84).

57. Vehviläinen (2002, 90–97); Palm (1971, 20); *Foreign Relations of the United States 1941* (1958, vol. 1, 56, 67).

58. Vehviläinen (2002, 96–100).

59. Ibid., 120.

60. Ibid., 121.

61. Palm (1971, 24–25).

62. Ibid., 24.

63. Vehviläinen (2002, 121–22, 128).

64. Ibid., 123–24.

65. Ibid., 125.

66. Ibid., 1332); Churchill (1951, vol. 5, 399); Palm (1971, 81); Nevakivi (1996, 91).

67. Vehviläinen (2002, 132).

68. Ibid., chapter 7.

69. Ibid., 141; Glantz and House (1995, 202); Mawdsley (2005, 293–94).

70. Tuunainen (2006).

71. Vehviläinen (2002, 143–44).

72. Ibid., 145–46.

73. Ibid., 147–48.

74. Palm (1971, 22–23).

75. Ibid., 21.

76. Quoted in Palm (1971, 77–78).

77. Vehviläinen (2002, 151).

78. Quoted in Palm (1971, 75–76).

79. Ziemke (1959, 288).

80. Nevakivi (1996, 95–96); Ziemke (1959, chapter 14).

81. Nevakivi (1996, 93).

CHAPTER EIGHT
THE AMERICAN CIVIL WAR

1. Civil war scholars have previously applied some of the theoretical ideas in chapters 2 and 3 to civil wars. Walter (2002); Fearon (2004, 2007).

2. Quoted in McPherson (1988, 316–17).
3. Quoted in Goodwin (2005, 356; also 349)
4. Ibid., 371.
5. Thompson and Wainwright (1920, vol. 1, 4–5).
6. Livermore (1957).
7. See, e.g., McPherson (1988); Basler (1953), et al.
8. See Livermore (1957).
9. For example, the independent variable equates minor battles (like the Battle of Fort Wagner, which involved only 7,000 troops) with major clashes (like the Battles of Gettysburg involving 160,000 troops and Antietam involving 127,000 troops). Livermore (1957, 140–41)
10. McPherson (1988, 857–58).
11. Goodwin (2005, 445).
12. Oates (1977, 315).
13. McPherson (1988, 336).
14. Ibid., 535.
15. Ibid., 505.
16. Oates (1977, 315–16).
17. Pierce (1893, 33); Welles (1872).
18. Oates (1977, 299).
19. Ibid., 322.
20. Beale (1960, vol. 1, 143); Welles (1872, 847).
21. See Catton (1951, 316–21); Clodfelter (2002, 310).
22. Livermore (1957, 92–93).
23. Donald (1954, 150).
24. Beale (1960, vol. 1, 145).
25. Oates (1977, 253); Goodwin (2005, 404–5).
26. Goodwin (2005, 549).
27. Welles (1872, 841)
28. Oates (1977, 302).
29. Quoted in Oates (1977, 307).
30. Welles (1872, 844).
31. Basler (1953, vol. 5, 317–18).
32. Quoted in Nicolay and Hay (1890, vol. 6, 128).
33. Welles (1872, 873).
34. Beale (1960, vol. 1, 70). His public stance had not yet changed, however. As late as September 13, Lincoln expressed his doubts about the Emancipation Proclamation in a reply to Chicago Christians (Basler 1953, vol. 5, 419–25).
35. McElroy (1937, 358–62); Stroud (1959, vol. 2, 312–14); McPherson (1988, 567); Catton (1951, 322).
36. Donald (1954, 152); Beale (1960, vol. 1, 143); Catton (1951, 151–53).
37. See McPherson (1988, 558–63).
38. Carpenter (1866, 22, italics in original); Goodwin (2005, 468). See also Welles (1872, 845).
39. Smith (2002, 8).
40. Ibid., 52–64.
41. Quoted in McPherson 1988, (510; italics in original).

42. McPherson (1988, 526).
43. Ibid., 637.
44. Ibid., 664–65.
45. Ibid., 665.
46. Ibid., 670–71.
47. Ibid., 681.
48. McPherson (1988).
49. Rowland (1923, vol. 6, 145–46).
50. McPherson (1988, 742).
51. Oates (1977, 394); McPherson (1988, 757).
52. Quoted in (McPherson 1988, 771).
53. Basler (1953, vol. 7, 518n). Italics in original.
54. Oates (1977, 394).
55. Quoted in Goodwin (2005, 647).
56. Oates (1977, 395–96).
57. Basler (1960, vol. 7, 499–501, 506–8); McPherson (1988, 769).
58. Basler (1953, vol. 7, 506–7).
59. Beale (1953, vol. 7, 499–501).
60. Ibid., 451; Nicolay and Hay (1890, vol. 9, 221).
61. McPherson (1988, 770–71).
62. Nicolay and Hay (1890, vol. 9, 221).
63. Oates (1977, 388).
64. Stephens (1870, vol. 2, 619).
65. Quoted in McElroy (1937, 412, 414).
66. Callahan (1964, 246); Owsley (1931, 552–54).
67. Quoted in Gilmore (2007, 264); see also McElroy (1937, 414, 434).
68. Quoted in Saunders (1997, 163, 165). Italics in Saunders.
69. Stephens (1870, vol. 2, 610–14). In other statements at the time, both public and private, Lincoln took a different stance, holding fast to emancipation as a condition for peace. In a January 31 letter to Seward, Lincoln instructed that an "indispensable" condition of any settlement would be "No receding by the Executive of the United States on the Slavery question, from the position assumed thereon, in the late Annual Message to Congress, and on preceding documents" (Basler 1953, vol. 8, 279). A few days after the Hampton Roads meeting, Lincoln told General Grant privately that peace would require the end of CSA sovereignty and the abolition of slavery (Grant 1995, 405). It is possible that Lincoln was keeping his offer to the CSA secret to avoid damaging political repercussions. No one, including Stephens, kept written notes of the Hampton Roads meetings.
70. McPherson (1988, 822).
71. Note that this idea of war-termination diplomacy affecting the balance of power reverses the causal arrow of the bargaining model of war, which sees (perceptions of) the balance of power affecting war-termination diplomacy.
72. Davis (2001, 29).
73. Potter (1942, 1–6).
74. Quoted in Goodwin (2005, 294).
75. Basler (1953, vol. 4, 172).
76. Quoted in Gilmore (2007, 231–32).

77. Basler (1953, vol. 7, 500).
78. Weingast (1998). For a critique, see Carpenter (2002).
79. Rowland (1923, vol. 5, 409–10); McElroy (1937, 367–68).
80. Dirck (2001, 235).
81. Coulter (1950, 553)
82. *Official Records of the Union and Confederate Armies* (1899, series I, vol. 46, pt. 2, 1038).
83. Gilmore (2007, 267).
84. Foner (1988, 35–36).
85. Ibid., 60–61.
86. *Congressional Globe* (38th Congress, 1st Session 296).
87. Foner (1988, 61); manifesto quoted in Kirkland (1927, 98–99).
88. Kirkland (1927, 138).
89. Foner (1988, 61–71).
90. Hunter (1877, 176).
91. Quoted in Crist (2003, vol. 11, 381n)
92. Quoted in Kirkland (1927, 122–23).
93. Crist et al (2003, vol. 11, 3–18); Kirkland (1927, 204).
94. Quoted in McPherson (1988, 852).
95. Toft (2003); Walter (2006a, 2006b).
96. Quoted in McPherson (1988, 246).
97. Ibid., 247–48.
98. Basler (1953, vol. 4, 436). At least prior to war not all subscribed to this view, as some Unionist elements in the North suggested permitting secession peacefully (McPherson 1988, 250–52).
99. Pierce (1893, 106).
100. Quoted in McPherson (1988, 761).
101. Goodwin (2005, 645).
102. Quoted in Oates (1977, 395).

CHAPTER NINE
GERMANY, 1917–18

1. Stevenson (2004, 322).
2. There were only 176,000 American troops in France in December 1917 and 318,000 by March 1918, although by August 1918 there were 1.3 million Yanks in France to support the decisive final Allied offensive. Stibbe (2001, 164).
3. Van Evera (1999).
4. See Goemans (2000, 264).
5. See also Fischer (1967, 610–11).
6. Biddle (2004).
7. Ludendorff in particular was obsessed with preparing for the next war. For example, in May 1917 he fretted that diversion of nitrogen from German farmlands for munitions production would undermine agricultural production necessary during "the next war." Bailey (1966, 60n).

8. In the words of one historian, this goal was "among the most prominent and consistent of the Berlin government's war aims." Stevenson (1982, 505).

9. Quoted in Stibbe (2001, 15).

10. Zuber (2002, esp. 271). German operational plans grew in the latter half of August towards pursuing French armies into the French interior, but this was more aimed at preventing French reinforcement than in conquering France (esp. 275).

11. Herwig (1972, 212).

12. Fischer (1967, 103–4); Stevenson (1991).

13. Gatzke (1950, 13–14).

14. Quoted in Gatzke (1950, 15).

15. Stevenson (1982, 505).

16. Quoted in Fischer (1967, 113). See also Herwig (1972, 213).

17. Quoted in Herwig (1972, 215).

18. Gatzke (1950, 153); Herwig (1972, 214).

19. Herwig (1972, 217).

20. Stibbe (2001, 123).

21. Stevenson (1988, 162).

22. Ritter (1973, vol. 4, 45–46).

23. Scherer and Grunewald (1966, vol. 2, 429–30).

24. Quoted in Zabecki (2006, 76).

25. Quoted in Gatzke (1950, 240).

26. Lutz (1934, 88–89).

27. Gatzke (1950, 248). The December 1917 decision overruled the September 1917 Council of Bellevue decision, which leaned towards allowing German negotiators to give up Belgium in exchange for peace. Bailey (1966, 71–79).

28. Quoted in Gatzke (1950, 244). Brackets in Gatzke.

29. Quoted in Calder and Sutton (1928, vol. 1, 260).

30. Scherer and Grunewald (1974, vol. 3, 341–48); Zabecki (2006, 96).

31. Hindenburg (1920, 357).

32. Fischer (1967, 113).

33. Ritter (1973, vol. 4, 200, also 203); Calder and Sutton (1928, vol. 1, 259).

34. Quoted in Gatzke (1950, 254).

35. Stevenson (1988, 35).

36. On the Franco–Belgian agreement, see Reiter (1996). On 1940, see May (2000).

37. Parkinson (1978, 144).

38. Fischer (1967, 609).

39. Quoted in Herwig (1997, 394).

40. Herwig (1997, 394); Ludendorff (1919, vol. 2, 163).

41. Stevenson (1988, 170).

42. Quoted in Zabecki (2006, 95).

43. Fest (1972, 301, 304); Haig quoted in Lloyd George (1934, vol. 4, 315; see also 313, 318–19); Rothwell (1971, 148); French (1995, 146).

44. Ritter (1973, vol. 4, 206); Parkinson (1978, 148).

45. French (1995, 157).

46. Goemans (2000).

47. The only other such moderately exclusionary, semirepressive regime in Goemans' World War I study is Russia, although he notes (312) that the evidence regarding whether Russian behavior conforms with the expectations of his theory is thin and mixed.

48. Goemans (2000, 89–92).

49. Ibid., 98–105.

50. Asprey (1991, 291); Ritter (1972, vol. 3, 288).

51. Stevenson (1991, 104).

52. Herwig (2000, 193).

53. Asprey (1991, 291).

54. Quoted in Herwig (1997, 315).

55. Herwig (2000, 193).

56. Ritter (1972, vol. 3, 306–7).

57. Stevenson (1988, 75).

58. Stibbe (2001, 167).

59. Herwig (2000, esp. 200–205) provides explanations for the failure of unrestricted submarine warfare to drive Britain from the war. See also Hull (2005).

60. Lloyd George (1934, vol. 3, 83–84). See also Halpern (1994).

61. See Newbolt (1928, vol. 4, 385); Herwig (2000, 192).

62. Fayle (1924, vol. 3, 93).

63. Gartner (1997, chapter 3).

64. Stevenson (1988, 76); Hull (2005, 224–25).

65. Snyder (1984, 1991).

66. Goemans (2000, 262).

67. Gatzke (1950, 5–6). Goemans (2000, 266–67) includes a reduced version of this quote from Gatzke, and offers a different interpretation.

68. Retallack (1988, 217).

69. Quoted in Peck (1978, 182).

70. Gatzke (1950, 147).

71. Quoted in Peck (1978, 181).

72. Stibbe (2001).

73. Quoted in Gatzke (1950, 29).

74. Ibid., 17.

75. Quoted in Herwig (1997, 378).

76. Quoted in Stibbe (2001, 185).

77. Herwig (1997, 378). But see also Peck (1978, 212–13).

78. Gatzke (1950, 261).

79. Parkinson (1978, 108).

80. Goemans (2000, 117–18).

81. Herwig (1997, 374–75).

82. Ritter (1973, vol. 3, 448, 457).

83. Lee (2005, 132).

84. Quoted in Herwig (1972, 219–20). Italics in original.

85. Quoted in Asprey (1991, 359–60).

86. Lee (2005, 147); Kitchen (1976, 167).

87. Herwig (1997, 381–82).

88. Goemans (2000, 267); Gatzke (1950, 228).

89. Gatzke (1950, 245).

90. Kitchen (1976, 29).

91. Feldman (1966, 138).

92. Herwig (1997, 195); Asprey (1991; 243–52); Parkinson (1978, 107–8); Feldman (1966, 138–41).

93. Kitchen (1976, 38–39). See also Asprey (1991, 249–50). Kitchen (1976, 39) notes that the extent of Bauer's ties to the industrialists is hard to gauge because potentially compromising documents in Bauer's personal papers have been destroyed. Although Feldman (1966, 141) notes that the Association of German Iron and Steel Industrialists wrote a memo in 1916 complaining about Falkenhayn, he argues that the "*coup de grâce*" that brought Falkenhayn down was the Romanian debacle.

94. Herwig (1997, 196); Asprey (1991, 246–47).

95. Bailey (1980).

96. Asprey (1991).

97. Gatzke (1950, 251) argued: "To avoid [democratization's] endless terror, Ludendorff put everything on one card, an all-out offensive against the west." The key piece of evidence for Gatzke is an excerpt from a letter Ludendorff wrote on January 1, 1918: "I always hope that the Prussian franchise falls through. If I didn't have that hope, I would advise the conclusion of any peace. With this franchise we cannot live. . . . Let the disturbances come. I would rather endure a terrible end than endless terror. Are there no more fighters left? Can the best among us be frightened by the bogie of 'internal unrest?' To look the danger straight in the eye and then at it! Only thus can we win; and if we should lose it would be better than acting against one's conviction" (quoted in Gatzke 1950, 250–51; for original, see Knesebeck 1927, 164). Gatkze argues that this statement is critical, because, "The constant stress on the strategic necessity as the only argument for western annexations is belied by his statement that once the Prussian franchise had been conceded, any peace would suit him" (Gatzke 1950, 251). However, the quote does not quite support this interpretation, that annexation is only meaningful because of its domestic political implications. Rather, it seems more like any Western gains would be meaningless if the franchise is granted because of the horrors the franchise would present. He does not make the argument that gains in the West will help stem the franchise.

98. Bailey (1980, 159).

99. Stibbe (2001, 168).

100. Bailey (1980, 172).

101. Herwig (1997, 381); Zabecki (2006, 92–93). Goemans (2000, 267–68) also proposes that individual states feared a shift in the balance of power if expansion in the West was abandoned, since Eastern states would capture the economic benefits of the territorial acquisitions from Russia, and other states would get little or nothing. Goemans provides evidence of individual states lobbying for various pieces of Western expansion, but missing is any evidence that these pressures ultimately had any effect on the decision to continue the war or to maintain high war aims. Feldman (1966, 444) claims that, "The right wing deputies believed that a great German military victory would obviate the need for social and political re-

form," but his citation in support of this claim is Rosenberg (1931, 210–11), and Rosenberg does not himself make the claim in the cited pages.

102. Herwig (1997, 376–81); Zabecki (2006, 92–93); Stibbe (2001, 166).

103. Herwig (1997, 305).

104. Zabecki (2006, 93–94); Ludendorff (1919, vol. 2, 161–65). Related to this point, Goemans (2000, 264) cites a critical February 19, 1918 statement by Ludendorff about the forthcoming offensives, in which Ludendorff stated that if the offensives fail, "In that case Germany must go under," to which Goemans draws the inference that Ludendorff knew that the offensive risked Germany's defeat. This quote comes from the memoirs of Prince Max of Baden, and notably Baden remarks that Ludendorff's remarks here have often been misinterpreted, and that Max thought Ludendorff's view was that "Our situation is such that we must either win or go under," which is more like the idea that Germany needed to win the war at all costs (Calder and Sutton 1928, vol. 1, 258, 258n). Ludendorff's statement ("Dann muss Deutschland eben zugrunde gehen!") is translated slightly differently elsewhere, such as, "Then Germany will just have to suffer annihilation" (Goodspeed 1966, 196).

105. Goodspeed (1966, 192). For dissent, see Chickering (1998, 178–79).

106. Biddle (2004, chapter 5); Kitchen (2001, 233); Zabeski (2006, esp. 311–13). However, Zabecki (312) wonders if even this outcome would have accomplished German strategic goals, as perhaps American forces would have streamed into Britain, and British and American forces might have prepared for an eventual counterattack, presaging the 1944 D-Day invasion.

107. Quoted in Tuchman (1962, 142).

108. Masefield (1916, 104).

109. Bailey (1966, 59–60) remarked: "Ludendorff's arguments for a *Hindenburgfriede*, or peace of conquest, were several. One, although he never formulated it systematically, was that the army ought to have some sort of reward for its sacrifices. Another argument was that annexation was the only alternative to revolution, for Ludendorff believed that the German people would overthrow their government if the war ended without material reward. Still another was dynastic, for Ludendorff thought the German monarchy would be strengthened if the war ended with several new provinces under the scepter of the House of Hohenzollern. But for Ludendorff the most compelling argument of all for a *Hindenburgfriede* was that only such a peace would prepare Germany for 'the next war.' It was virtually dogma in the German General Staff that the present war would be followed by one final holocaust in which all of Germany's neighbors would seek to deprive Germany of the spoils of the first war. Ludendorff insisted that Germany could only have a chance of winning 'the next war' if she shielded herself by annexing as much territory along her frontiers as possible."

CHAPTER TEN
JAPAN, 1944–45

1. Quoted in Ienaga (1978, 139).

2. Sagan (1988); Barnhart (1984, esp. 450–53).

3. Quoted in Agawa (1979, 243–44). Not all had faith that this strategy would work, however. One high-ranking naval officer declared at an October 6, 1941 meeting that he "had no confidence that Japan could win the war." Quoted in Ienaga (1978, 134).

4. Bix (2000, 446).

5. Krebs (2005); Hasegawa (2005).

6. Kido (1984, 327); Butow (1954, 13–14).

7. Butow (1954, 11n); On Toyoda, see *Interrogations of Japanese Officials* (vol. 2, 316). On Yonai, see *Interrogations of Japanese Officials* (vol. 2, 331). On Nagano, see *Interrogations of Japanese Officials* (vol. 2, 352). On Takata, see *Interrogations of Japanese Officials* (vol. 1, 262). On Nomura, see *Interrogations of Japanese Officials* (vol. 2, 393–94). Lieutenant Colonel Roji Tanaka agreed that Midway and Guadalcanal were the turning points. *Interrogations of Japanese Officials* (vol. 2, 530). Captain Toshikazu Ohmae, a staff officer, testified that after Guadalcanal he felt that Japan could not win but would not lose, that after the Marianas he had little hope, and that after Okinawa it was all over. *Interrogations of Japanese Officials* (vol. 1, 177).

8. Iriye (1981, 96–97).

9. Browne (1967, 163).

10. Quoted in Bix (2000, 458).

11. Ibid., 460.

12. *The Tokyo Major War Crimes Trial* (1998, 31069).

13. Bix (2000, 450, 454); Coox (1988, 355).

14. Bix (2000, 469–70); Coox (1988, 358).

15. Quoted in Bix (2000, 469).

16. Butow (1954, 22n).

17. Hastings (2007, 44).

18. Bix (2000, 478); *The Tokyo Major War Crimes Trial* (1998, vol. 65, 31074); Coox (1988, 363).

19. However, these changes did not indicate an increased Japanese willingness to offer concessions to the Allies. Iriye (1981, 97–98).

20. Butow (1954, 25n).

21. See Drea (1998, 194, 199).

22. Hasegawa (2005, 121).

23. Frank (1999, 89).

24. Drea (1998, 189).

25. Bix (2000, 453–66)

26. Quoted in Bix (2000, 476).

27. Ibid., 481. For a slightly different translation, see Drea (1998, 197).

28. Kido (1984, 374).

29. Drea (1998, 196); Butow (1954, 43n); Sigal (1988, 33–37).

30. Drea (1998, 39).

31. Frank (2007, 69).

32. Bix (2000, 489).

33. Ibid., 488; Reiter (2007). Others, like retired foreign minister Shidehara Kijuro, agreed that Japan must fight on (Bix 2000, 492).

34. Drea (1998, 199).

35. Hasegawa (2005, 38).

36. Quoted in Frank (1999, 99). See also Frank (2007, 259n).

37. Hata (2007, 52).

38. Quoted in Coox (1970, 88).

39. Quoted in Frank (2007, 80).

40. Hata (2007, 55).

41. Bix (2000, 503).

42. Quoted in Frank (1999, 89).

43. Quoted in Coox (1970, 87).

44. Hasegawa (2005, 79).

45. Kido (1984, 435).

46. Hata (2007, 57).

47. Bix (2000, 493–94); Frank (1999, 102).

48. Hasegawa (2005, 215).

49. Frank (1999); Hasegawa (2005, 2007); Pape (1996).

50. Drea (1998, 208).

51. Coox (1970, 89).

52. Drea (1998, 213).

53. Slantchev (2003a) presents a complete information account of the Japanese decision to surrender. He is correct that Japanese decision-making was largely driven by their beliefs about their abilities to inflict costs on the U.S., but as described in this chapter, the Japanese beliefs about their abilities to inflict costs changed over time as they received new information.

54. Quoted in Hasegawa (2005, 219–20). The bracketed "no" is in Hasegawa.

55. In his quantitative tests, Goemans (2000, 56) declares that regimes receiving a score of −7 to 16 on the 0 to 20 Polity scale to be semirepressive and moderately exclusionary; World War II Japan is squarely in this range, receiving a coding of 11.

56. On Japan, see Ienaga (1978).

57. Shillony (1976). Jack Snyder (1991) categorized both World War I Germany and World War II Japan as cartelized regimes—regimes run by oligarchs that have limited but not fully democratic political institutions and leadership constraints. Notably, Goemans and Snyder offer loosely related hypotheses, since Snyder proposes that domestic political institutions in mixed regimes cause them to pursue imperial overexpansion, whereas Goemans proposes that domestic political institutions in mixed regimes cause them to pursue high war aims.

58. Shigemitsu (1958, 300).

59. Bix (2000, 473).

60. Hasegawa (2005, 29).

61. Magic intelligence decrypt, July 13, 1945, p. A5. Available at www.gwu.edu/~nsarchiv/NSAEBB/NSAEBB162/31.pdf (accessed October 11, 2007).

62. Magic intelligence decrypt, July 12, 1945. Available at www.gwu.edu/~nsarchiv/NSAEBB/NSAEBB162/29.pdf (accessed October 11, 2007).

63. Hasegawa (2005, 59).

64. Reiter (2007).

65. Evans and Peattie (1997, 501); Morison (1963, 479–80).

66. Warner and Warner (1982, 320–21); Hattori (1996, 21). See also Bix (2000, 482, 745n). Ohnuki-Tierney (2002, 161) is more skeptical of the effectiveness of the suicide operations, noting that of the 3,300 or so planes in the operation, only 11.6 percent hit their vessels. Saburo Ienaga (1978, 183) is even more skeptical, estimating a success rate of just 1–3 percent. However, it is difficult to calculate how effective such aircraft would have been if they had been employed in nonsuicide missions. One possible comparison is provided here in the text. Notably, pilots involved in these attacks were not Japan's best pilots but instead mostly student conscripts and training pilots, and by this point (1944–45) American forces enjoyed substantial superiority.

67. Brown (1958, vii).

68. Hattori (1996, 18).

69. Warner and Warner (1982, 320).

70. In late 1944 and early 1945, Japan did launch some 9,300 "balloon bombs" against North America, although these conventional munitions ultimately did very little damage (Bix 2000, 481–82). This campaign is a poor candidate as a gamble for resurrection. Japan had launched direct (although small) attacks on the American homeland throughout the war. Also, the balloon bomb attacks introduced little risk to Japan, since many belligerents had already launched widespread conventional attacks on civilian targets throughout the war, so the balloon bombs would not be viewed as especially barbaric war crimes, in contrast to the use of biological weapons.

71. Tanaka (1996, 139–45); Barenblatt (2004, 189–90).

72. *Tokyo Major War Crimes Trial* (1998, vol. 65, 31068).

73. Hasegawa (2005, 37).

74. Quoted in Drea (1998, 199).

75. Kido (1984, 424, 428).

76. Frank (1999, 96). See also Kido (1984, 435).

77. Magic intelligence decrypt, July 12, 1945. Available at www.gwu.edu/~nsarchiv/NSAEBB/NSAEBB162/29.pdf (accessed October 11, 2007).

78. Frank (1999, 345).

79. Quoted in Frank (1999, 293–94).

80. Quoted in Bix (2000, 509–10).

81. Ienaga (1978, 221).

82. Ibid., 221.

83. Snyder (1991).

84. See the testimony of Vice Admiral Paul H. Weneker, a German Naval Attaché serving in Japan during the war. *Interrogations of Japanese Officials* (N.d., vol. 1, 285). See also Hastings (2007, 40); Drea (1998, 187, 191–93, 197–98); Frank (2007). Some have argued that these false reports may have helped buoy the Emperor's hopes that a decisive battle sufficient to force American concessions remained possible.

85. Quoted in Shigemitsu (1958, 271).

86. Quoted in Browne (1967, 160).

87. Ibid., 174.

88. Ibid., 165–76.

89. Coox (1975, 125, 131–36).

90. Kido (1984, 336);
91. Bix (2000, 480–81); Drea (197–98).
92. Coox (1975, 142–43).
93. See the testimony of Lieutenant General Ija Kawabe in *Interrogations of Japanese Officials* (N.d., vol. 2, 424).
94. Butow (1954, 42).
95. Drea (1998, 198).
96. As early as late December 1941, Prince Higashikuni encouraged Tojo to initiate peace talks with China, Britain, and the U.S., remarking that "This war must be terminated as soon as possible." In February 1942, Kido thought that Japan could take advantage of the capture of Singapore to push for peace. He shared his thoughts with the Emperor, who in turn suggested to Tojo that Japan should seek peace as soon as possible. Tojo rejected both suggestions. Coox (1975, 142); Butow (1954, 14); Kido (1984, 328).
97. Coox (1975, 28–29).
98. Large (1992, 113).
99. Bix (2000, esp. 439); Hastings (2007, 41).
100. Kido (1984, 359); *The Tokyo Major War Crimes Trial* (1998, vol. 65, 31070–71).
101. Shillony (1981, 61).
102. Kido (1984, 428).
103. Drea (1998, 209). See also Hastings (2007, 42).
104. Coox (1970, 154).
105. Frank (1999, 315–19).
106. Drea (1998, 201–2).
107. Ibid., 202.
108. Large (1992, 117–18).
109. Shillony (1981, 35–36); Bix (2000, 447, 481, 484–85). Certainly, the Emperor's military strategy suggestions were sometimes ignored by the military, as when in the defense of the Solomon Islands a single lieutenant colonel blocked the Emperor's repeated recommendation that Army Air Force units be dispatched in support of the defensive effort. Hata (2007, 48).
110. Quoted in Frank (1999, 311).
111. Giangreco (1997); Frank (1999).
112. Frank (1999, 195).
113. Hastings (2007, 481).
114. Frank (2007, 80).

Chapter Eleven
Conclusions

1. Perhaps another case is Britain in 1917–18, when it refused to try to reach a limited settlement with Germany because of fear that Germany might reattack in the future.
2. Walt (1996).
3. Reiter and Stam (2002, chapter 6).

4. On elite cues and the casualty–public opinion relationship, see Berinsky (2007).

5. Mueller (1985); Gartner and Segura (1998).

6. Goodman (1978).

7. Reiter and Stam (2002); Slantchev (2004).

8. On war duration, see Slantchev (2004). The nine wars are Mexico in the U.S.–Mexican War; China in the Boxer Rebellion; Greece in its 1919–22 war with Turkey; China in the 1931–33 Manchurian War; Bolivia in the Chaco War; Japan in World War II; Germany in World War I; Turkey in World War I; Russia in World War I.

9. Goemans (2000, 312).

10. Jones (1968, 118).

11. Bauer (1974, 312–13).

12. Betts (1977); Gelpi and Feaver (2002). See also Snyder (1991).

13. Rosen (2005, esp. 106–10).

14. Israel (1966, 230, 259).

15. Loewenstein and Moore (2004).

16. Reiter and Stam (2002, chapter 6).

17. Smith and Stam (2004) present a model of updating beliefs about the balance of power which incorporates variance around, as well as the mean of, beliefs.

18. Johnson (2004).

19. Lo, Hashimoto, and Reiter (2008).

20. Walter (2002).

21. Available at www.whitehouse.gov/nsc/nss.pdf (downloaded September 5, 2007).

22. Werner (1999); Lo, Hashimoto, and Reiter (2008).

23. Bueno de Mesquita and Downs (2006).

24. Peic and Reiter (2008).

25. Reiter (2006b).

26. MacFie (1975).

27. Mark Mazetti, "U.S. Finding Says Iran Halted Nuclear Arms Effort in 2003," *The New York Times*, 4 December 2007, A1.

28. Glaser and Fetter (2005).

29. Reiter (2006a).

30. Reiter (2005).

31. Ginor and Remez (2007).

32. Reiter (2006a).

Bibliography

Acheson, Dean. 1969. *Present at the Creation: My Years in the State Department.* New York: Norton.

Admati, Anat R. and Motty Perry. 1987. Strategic Delay in Bargaining. *Review of Economic Studies* 54 (July): 345–64.

Agawa, Hiroyuki. *The Reluctant Admiral: Yamamoto and the Imperial.* John Bester, trans. New York: Harper and Row, 1979.

Ambrose, Stephen E. 1983–84. *Eisenhower.* 2 vols. New York: Simon and Schuster.

Armstrong, Anne. 1961. *Unconditional Surrender: The Impact of the Casablanca Policy upon World War II.* New Brunswick: Rutgers University Press.

Aspaturian, Vernon. 1963. Dialectics and Duplicity in Soviet Diplomacy. *Journal of International Affairs* 17.

Asprey, Robert B. 1991. *The German High Command at War: Hindenburg and Ludendorff Conduct World War I.* New York: William Morrow and Company.

Austin, Warren R. 1950. President Malik's Continued Obstruction Tactics in the Security Council. *Department of State Bulletin* 23 (August 28): 326–31.

Axelrod, Robert. 1984. *The Evolution of Cooperation.* New York: Basic Books.

Bailey, Stephen. 1966. Erich Ludendorff as Quartermaster General of the German Army 1916–1918. Unpublished Ph.D. Dissertation, Department of History, University of Chicago.

———. 1980. The Berlin Strike of January 1918. *Central European History* 13 (January): 158–74.

Baker, James A. III. 1995. *The Politics of Diplomacy: Revolution, War and Peace, 1989–1992.* With Thomas M. Defrank. New York: G. P. Putnam's Sons.

Balfour, Michael. 1979. The Origin of the Formula: "Unconditional Surrender" in World War II. *Armed Forces and Society* 5 (February): 281–301.

Barber, John and Mark Harrison. *The Soviet Home Front, 1941–1945: A Social and Economic History of the USSR in World War II.* London: Longman, 1991.

Barenblatt, Daniel. 2004. *A Plague Upon Humanity: The Secret Genocide of Axis Japan's Germ Warfare Operation.* New York: HarperCollins.

Barnes, John and David Nicholson, eds. 1988. *The Empire at Bay: The Leo Amery Diaries 1929–1945.* London: Hutchinson.

Barnhardt, Michael A. 1984. Japanese Intelligence Before the Second World War: "Best Case" Analysis. In Ernest May, ed., *Knowing One's Enemies: Intelligence Assessment Before the Two World Wars,* 424–55. Princeton: Princeton University Press.

Barros, James, and Richard Gregor. 1995. *Double Deception: Stalin, Hitler, and the Invasion of Russia.* DeKalb, IL: Northern Illinois University Press.

Basler, Roy P., ed. 1953. *The Collected Works of Abraham Lincoln.* 9 vols. New Brunswick, NJ: Rutgers University Press.

Bauer, K. Jack. 1974. *The Mexican War, 1846–1848.* New York: Macmillan.

Baum, Matthew A. 2002. The Constituent Foundations of the Rally-Round-the-Flag Phenomenon. *International Studies Quarterly* 46 (June): 263–98.

Beale, Howard K., ed. 1960. *Diary of Gideon Welles: Secretary of the Navy Under Lincoln and Johnson.* 3 vols. New York: Norton.

Bearce, David H., Kristen M. Flanagan, and Katharine M. Floros. 2006. Alliances, Internal Information, and Military Conflict Among Member-States. *International Organization* 60 (Summer): 595–625.

Beardsley, Kyle and Holger Schmidt. 2007. United Nations Intervention and Recurring Conflict: An Extension and Re-Assessment. Unpublished ms. Emory University.

Beisner, Robert L. 2006. *Dean Acheson: A Life in the Cold War.* Oxford: Oxford University Press.

Bennett, D. Scott. 1998. Integrating and Testing Models of Rivalry Termination. *American Journal of Political Science* 42 (October) 1200–1232.

Berezhkov, V. M. 1969. In Hitler's Chancellery. In Seweryn Bialer, ed., *Stalin and His Generals*, 122–28. New York: Pegasus.

Berger, Thomas U. 1998. *Cultures of Antimilitarism: National Security in Germany and Japan.* Baltimore: The Johns Hopkins University Press.

Berinsky, Adam. 2007. Assuming the Costs of War: Events, Elites, and American Public Support for Military Conflict. *Journal of Politics* 69 (November) 975–97.

The Beriya Case and "Blank Spots" in Soviet History. 1988. *Summary of World Broadcasts*, BBC, Part 1, USSR. May 2. SU/0140 B/4-B/5.

Berman, Larry. 1982. *Planning a Tragedy: The Americanization of the War in Vietnam.* New York: Norton.

Beschloss, Michael. 2002. *The Conquerors: Roosevelt, Truman and the Destruction of Hitler's Germany, 1941–1945.* New York: Simon and Schuster.

Betts, Richard K. 1977. *Soldiers, Statesmen, and Cold War Crises.* Cambridge: Harvard University Press.

Biddiscombe, Perry. 1998. *Werwolf! The History of the National Socialist Guerrilla Movement.* Toronto: University of Toronto Press.

Biddle, Stephen. 2004. *Military Power: Explaining Victory and Defeat in Modern Battle.* Princeton: Princeton University Press.

Biddle, Stephen and Stephen Long. 2004. Democracy and Military Effectiveness. *Journal of Conflict Resolution* 48 (August): 525–46.

Bix, Herbert P. 2000. *Hirohito and the Making of Modern Japan.* New York: HarperCollins.

Blainey, Geoffrey. 1988. *The Causes of War.* 3rd ed. Basingstoke, UK: Macmillan.

Blaydes, Lisa. 2004. Rewarding Impatience: A Bargaining and Enforcement Model of OPEC. *International Organization* 58 (Spring): 213–37.

Boehmer, Charles, Erik Gartzke, and Timothy Nordstrom. 2004. Do Intergovernmental Organizations Promote Peace? *World Politics* 54 (October): 1–38.

Bohlen, Charles E. 1973. *Witness to History, 1929–1969.* New York: Norton.

Bradley, Omar N. and Clay Blair. 1983. *A General's Life.* New York: Simon and Schuster.

Braithwaite, Rodric. 2006. *Moscow 1941: A City and Its People at War.* London: Profile Books.

Brodie, Bernard. 1973. *War and Politics*. New York: Macmillan.

Brooks, Risa. 2003. Making Military Might: Why Do States Fail and Succeed? A Review Essay. *International Security* 28 (Fall): 149–91.

Brown, C. R. 1958. Foreword. In Rikihei Inoguchi and Tadashi Nakajiima with Roger Pineau, *The Divine Wind: Japan's Kamikaze Force in World War II*. Annapolis, MD: United States Naval Institute.

Browne, Courtney. 1967. *Tojo: The Last Banzai*, New York: Holt, Rinehart, and Winston.

Bueno de Mesquita, Bruce and George W. Downs. 2006. Intervention and Democracy. *International Organization* 60 (Summer): 627–49.

Bueno de Mesquita, Bruce, Alastair Smith, Randolph M. Siverson, and James D. Morrow. 2003. *The Logic of Political Survival*. Cambridge, MA: MIT Press.

———. 2006. Selection Institutions and War Aims. *Economics of Governance* 7 (2006): 31–52.

Bundy, McGeorge. 1988. *Danger and Survival: Choices About the Bomb in the First Fifty Years*. New York: Vintage.

Bush, George and Brent Scowcroft. 1998. *A World Transformed*. New York: Vintage.

Butcher, Harry C. 1946. *My Three Years with Eisenhower*. New York: Simon and Schuster.

Butow, Robert J. C. 1954. *Japan's Decision to Surrender*. Stanford: Stanford University Press.

Byman, Daniel L. and Matthew C. Waxman. 2000. Kosovo and the Great Air Power Debate. *International Security* 24 (Spring): 5–38.

Cagle, Malcolm W. and Frank A. Manson. 1957. *The Sea War in Korea*. Annapolis, MD: United States Naval Institute.

Calder, W. M. and C.W.H. Sutton, trans. 1928. *The Memoirs of Prince Max of Baden*. New York: Charles Scribner's Sons.

Callahan, James Morton. 1964. *Diplomatic History of the Southern Confederacy*. New York: Frederick Ungar.

Carpenter, Daniel. 2000. What is the Marginal Value of *Analytic Narratives*? *Social Science History* 24(4) Winter: 653–67.

Carpenter, F. B. 1866. *Six Months at the White House with Abraham Lincoln*. New York: Hurd and Houghton.

Catton, Bruce. 1951. *Mr. Lincoln's Army*. New York: Anchor Books.

Chai, Chengwen. 2001. The Korean Truce Negotiations. In Xiaobing Li, Allan R. Millett, and Bin Yu, trans. and eds., *Mao's Generals Remember Korea*. Lawrence, KS: University Press of Kansas, 2001, 184–232.

Chang, Jung and Jon Holliday. 2005. *Mao: The Unknown Story*. London: Jonathan Cape.

Chapman, Terrence L. and Dan Reiter. 2004. The United Nations Security Council and the Rally 'Round the Flag Effect. *Journal of Conflict Resolution* 48 (December): 886–909.

Chickering, Roger. 1998. *Imperial Germany and the Great War, 1914–1918*. Cambridge: Cambridge University Press.

Chiozza, Giacomo and H. E. Goemans. 2004a. International Conflict and the Tenure of Leaders: Is War Still *Ex Post* Inefficient? *American Journal of Political Science* 48 (July): 604–19.

Chiozza, Giacomo and Henk E. Goemans. 2004b. Avoiding Diversionary Targets. *Journal of Peace Research* 41 (July): 423–43.

Christensen, Thomas J. 1995. A "Lost Chance" for What? Rethinking the Origins of U.S.–PRC Confrontation. *Journal of American–East Asian Relations* 4 (Fall): 249–78.

———. 1996. *Useful Adversaries: Grand Strategy, Domestic Mobilization, and Sino-American Conflict, 1947–1958.* Princeton: Princeton University Press.

Chuev, Feliks Ivanovich. 1993. *Molotov Remembers: Inside Kremlin Politics.* Albert Resis, ed. Chicago: Ivan R. Dee.

Churchill, Winston S. 1948–53. *The Second World War.* 6 vols. Boston: Houghton Mifflin.

Clausewitz, Carl von. 1976. *On War.* Michael Howard and Peter Paret, eds. Princeton: Princeton University Press.

Clodfelter, Micheal. 2002. *Warfare and Armed Conflicts: A Statistical Reference to Casualty and Other Figures, 1500–2000.* 2nd ed. Jefferson, NC: McFarland.

Collins, J. Lawton. 1969. *War in Peacetime: The History and Lessons of Korea.* Boston: Houghton Mifflin.

Collins, John M. 1998. *Military Geography for Professionals and the Public.* Washington: National Defense University.

Colville, John. 2004. *The Fringes of Power: Downing Street Diaries 1939–1955.* Revised ed. London: Weidenfeld and Nicolson.

Condon, Richard W. 1972. *The Winter War: Russia Against Finland.* New York: Ballantine Books.

Congressional Globe. 1864. 38th Congress, 1st Session (January 21, part 1), 296.

Conquest, Robert. 1991. *Stalin: Breaker of Nations.* New York: Viking.

Cooper, Duff. 1953. *Old Men Forget.* London: Rupert Hart-Davis.

Coox, Alvin D. 1970. *Japan: The Final Agony.* New York: Ballantine.

———. 1975. *Tojo.* New York: Ballantine.

———. 1988. The Pacific War. In Peter Duus, ed., *Cambridge History of Japan,* 315–82. 6 vols. Cambridge: Cambridge University Press.

Coser, Lewis A. 1961. The Termination of Conflict. *Journal of Conflict Resolution* 5 (December, no. 4), 347–53.

Costello, John. 1991. *Ten Days to Destiny: The Secret Story of the Hess Peace Initiative and British Efforts to Strike a Deal with Hitler.* New York: Morrow.

Coulter, E. Merton. 1950. *The Confederate States of America 1861–1865.* Baton Rouge, LA: Louisiana State University Press.

Cramton, Peter C. 1992. Strategic Delay in Bargaining with Two-Sided Uncertainty. *Review of Economic Studies* 59 (January): 205–25.

Crist, Lynda Lasswell, Barbara J. Rozek, and Kenneth H. Williams, eds. 2003. *The Papers of Jefferson Davis.* 11 vols. Baton Rouge, LA: Louisiana State University Press.

Croco, Sarah. 2007. Leadership Change, Settlement Costs and War Termination. Presented at the annual meeting of the Peace Science Society (International), Columbia, South Carolina, November 2–4.

Daily Korea Summaries. Truman Presidential Library.

Dallek, Robert. 1979. *Franklin D. Roosevelt and American Foreign Policy, 1932–1945*. Oxford: Oxford University Press.

Dalton, Hugh. 1957. *The Fateful Years, 1931–1945*. London: Muller.

Davis, Kenneth S. 2000. *FDR, The War President, 1940–1943: A History*. New York: Random House.

Davis, William C. 2001. *An Honorable Defeat: The Last Days of the Confederate Government*. New York: Harcourt.

Desch, Michael C. 2002. Democracy and Victory: Why Regime Type Hardly Matters. *International Security* 27 (Fall): 5–47.

Diehl, Paul, Jennifer Reifschneider, Paul R. Hensel. 1996. United Nations Intervention and Recurring Conflict. *International Organization* 50 (Autumn): 683–700.

Dilks, David, ed. 1971. *The Diaries of Sir Alexander Cadogan*. New York: G. P. Putnam's Sons.

Dirck, Brian R. 2001. *Lincoln and Davis: Imagining America, 1809–1865*. Lawrence, KS: University Press of Kansas.

Donald, David, ed. 1954. *Inside Lincoln's Cabinet: The Civil War Diaries of Salmon P. Chase*. New York: Longmans, Green and Co.

Dower, John W. 1986. *War Without Mercy: Race and Power in the Pacific War*. New York: Pantheon.

———. 1999. *Embracing Defeat: Japan in the Wake of World War II*. New York: Norton.

Downs, George W., David M. Rocke, and Peter N. Barsoom. 1996. Is the Good News About Compliance Good News About Cooperation? *International Organization* 50 (Summer): 379–406.

Drea, Edward J. 1998. *In the Service of the Emperor: Essays on the Imperial Japanese Army*. Lincoln: University of Nebraska Press.

Dunmore, Helen. 2001. *The Siege*. New York: Viking.

Eden, Anthony. 1965. *The Reckoning*. Boston: Houghton Mifflin.

Edwards, Robert. 2006. *White Death: Russia's War on Finland, 1939–40*. London: Weidenfeld and Nicolson.

Erfurth, Waldemar. 1979. *The Last Finnish War*. Washington: University Publications of America.

Erickson, John. 1975. *The Road to Stalingrad*. New York: Harper and Row.

Evans, David C. and Mark R. Peattie. 2007. *Kaigun: Strategy, Tactics, and Technology in the Imperial Japanese Navy, 1887–1941*. Annapolis, MD: U.S. Naval Institute Press.

Farrar, L. L., Jr. 1975. Opening to the West: German Efforts to Conclude a Separate Peace With England, July 1917–March 1918. *Canadian Journal of History* 10 (April): 73–90.

Fayle, C. Ernest. 1920–24. *Seaborne Trade*. New York: Longmans Green.

Fazal, Tanisha M. 2007. *State Death: The Politics and Geography of Conquest, Occupation, and Annexation*. Princeton, NJ: Princeton University Press.

FDR: Day by Day—The Pare Larentz Chronology. Roosevelt Presidential Library, Hyde Park, New York: Roosevelt Presidential Library.

Fearon, James D. 1994. Domestic Political Audiences and the Escalation of International Disputes. *American Political Science Review* 88 (September): 577–92.

———. 1995a. The Offense-Defense Balance and War Since 1648. Prepared for
presentation at the annual meeting of the International Studies Association,
Chicago, Illinois, February 21–25.

———. 1995b. Rationalist Explanations for War. *International Organization* 49
(Summer, no. 3): 379–414.

———. 1997. Bargaining Over Objects That Influence Future Bargaining Power.
Presented at the annual meeting of the American Political Science Association,
Washington, DC, August 28–31.

———. 1998. Bargaining, Enforcement, and International Cooperation. *International Organization* 52 (Spring): 269–305.

———. 2004. Why Do Some Civil Wars Last So Much Longer Than Others?
Journal of Peace Research 41 (3): 275–301.

———. 2007. Fighting rather than Bargaining. Presented at the annual meeting of
the American Political Science Association, Washington, DC, August 31, 2007.

Fearon, James D. and David D. Laitin. 2003. Ethnicity, Insurgency, and Civil War.
American Political Science Review 97 (February): 75–90.

Feaver, Peter D. and Christopher Gelpi. 2004. *Choosing Your Battles: American
Civil-Military Relations and the Use of Force.* Princeton: Princeton University
Press.

Feis, Herbert. 1967. *Churchill, Roosevelt, Stalin: The War They Waged and the
Peace They Sought.* Princeton: Princeton University Press.

Feldman, Gerald. 1966. *Army, Industry, and Labor in Germany, 1914–1918.*
Princeton: Princeton University Press.

Ferrell, Robert H., ed. 1980. *Off the Record: The Private Papers of Harry S.
Truman.* New York: Harper and Row.

Fest, W. B. 1972. British War Aims and German Peace Feelers During the First
World War (December 1916–November 1918). *Historical Journal* 15 (no. 2):
285–308.

Fey, Mark and Kristopher Ramsay. 2007. Mutual Optimism and War. *American
Journal of Political Science* 51 (October): 738–54.

Filson, Darren and Suzanne Werner. 2002. A Bargaining Model of War and Peace:
Anticipating the Onset, Duration, and Outcome of War. *American Journal of
Political Science* 46 (October): 819–38.

———. 2004. Bargaining and Fighting: The Impact of Regime Type on War
Onset, Duration, and Outcomes. *American Journal of Political Science* 48
(April): 296–313.

Fischer, Fritz. 1967. *Germany's Aims in the First World War.* New York: Norton.

Foner, Eric. 1988. *Reconstruction, 1863–1877.* New York: Harper and Row.

Foot, Rosemary. 1985. *The Wrong War: American Policy and the Dimensions of
the Korean Conflict, 1950–1953.* Ithaca: Cornell.

———. 1991. *A Substitute for Victory: The Politics of Peacemaking at the Korean
Armistice Talks.* Ithaca: Cornell.

Fordham, Benjamin O. 2002. Another Look at "Parties, Voters, and the Use of
Force Abroad." *Journal of Conflict Resolution* 46 (August): 572–96.

Foreign Relations of the United States. 1970–1983. Washington, D.C.: U.S. Government Printing Office.

Förster, Jurgen E. 1988. The Dynamics of *Volksgemeinschaft*: The Effectiveness of the German Military Establishment in the Second World War. In Allan R. Millett and Williamson Murray, eds., *Military Effectiveness*, vol. 3, 180–220. Boston: Allen and Unwin.

Fortna, Virginia Page. 2004a. Interstate Peacekeeping: Causal Mechanisms and Empirical Effects. *World Politics* 56 (July): 481–519.

———. 2004b. *Peace Time: Cease-Fire Agreements and the Durability of Peace*, Princeton: Princeton University Press.

———. 2005. Where Have All the Victories Gone? War Outcomes in Historical Perspective. Presented at the annual meeting of the International Studies Association, Honolulu, Hawaii, February.

Frank, Richard B. 1999. *Downfall: The End of the Imperial Japanese Empire*. New York: Random House.

———. 2007. Ketsu Go: Japanese Political and Military Strategy in 1945. In Tsuyoshi Hasegawa, ed., *The End of the Pacific War: Reappraisals*. Stanford: Stanford University Press, 65–94.

French, David. 1995. *The Strategy of the Lloyd George Coalition 1916–1918*. Oxford: Clarendon Press.

Fuller, John Douglas Pitts. 1936. *The Movement for the Acquisition of All Mexico*. Baltimore: Johns Hopkins Press.

Gaddis, John Lewis. 1980. The Strategic Perspective: The Rise and Fall of the "Defensive Perimeter" Concept, 1947–1951. In Dorothy Borg and Waldo Heinrichs, eds., *Uncertain Years: Chinese–American Relations, 1947–1950*, 61–118. New York: Columbia University Press.

———. 1987. *The Long Peace: Inquiries Into the History of the Cold War*. New York: Oxford University Press.

———. 1997. *We Now Know: Rethinking Cold War History*. Oxford: Oxford University Press.

———. 1982. *Strategies of Containment: A Critical Appraisal of Postwar American National Security Policy*. Oxford: Oxford University Press.

Garofano, John. 2002. Tragedy or Choice in Vietnam? Learning to Think Outside the Archival Box. *International Security* 26 (4): 143–65.

Gartner, Scott Sigmund. 1997. *Strategic Assessment in War*. New Haven: Yale University Press.

Gartner, Scott Sigmund and Marissa Edson Myers. 1995. Body Counts and "Success" in the Vietnam and Korean Wars. *Journal of Interdisciplinary History* 25 (Winter): 377–95.

Gartner, Scott Sigmund and Gary M. Segura. 1998. War, Casualties, and Public Opinion. *Journal of Conflict Resolution*. 42 (June): 278–300.

Gartzke, Erik and Kristian Skrede Gleditsch. 2004. Why Democracies May Actually Be Less Reliable Allies. *American Journal of Political Science* 48 (October): 775–95.

Gatzke, Hans W. 1950. *Germany's Drive to the West: A Study of Germany's Western War Aims During the First World War*. Baltimore: Johns Hopkins Press.

Gaubatz, Kurt Taylor. 1996. Democratic States and Commitment in International Relations. *International Organization* 50 (Winter): 109–39.

Gelpi, Christopher. 1997. Democratic Diversions: Governmental Structure and the Externalization of Domestic Conflict. *Journal of Conflict Resolution* 41 (April): 255–82.

———. 2003. *The Power of Legitimacy: Assessing the Role of Norms in Crisis Bargaining*. Princeton: Princeton University Press.

Gelpi, Christopher and Peter D. Feaver. 2002. Speak Softly and Carry a Big Stick? Veterans in the Political Elite and the American Use of Force. *American Political Science Review* 96 (December): 779–93.

Gelpi, Christopher, Peter D. Feaver, and Jason Reifler. 2005/06. Success Matters: Casualty Sensitivity and the War in Iraq. *International Security* 30 (Winter): 7–46.

George, Alexander L. and Andrew Bennett. 2005. *Case Studies and Theory Development in the Social Sciences*. Cambridge: MIT Press.

George, Alexander L. and Timothy J. McKeown. 1985. Case Studies and Theories of Organizational Decision Making. In Robert F. Coulam and Richard A. Smith, eds., *Advances in Information Processing in Organizations, Volume II, Research on Public Organizations*. Greenwich, CT: JAI Press, 21–58.

Giangreco, D. M. 1997. Casualty Projections for the U.S. Invasions of Japan, 1945–1946: Planning and Policy Implications. *Journal of Military History* 61 (July): 521–82.

Gilbert, Martin. 1983. *Winston S. Churchill*. 8 vols. London: Heinemann.

———. 1991. *Churchill: A Life*. London: Heinemann.

———, ed. 1995. *The Churchill War Papers*. 3 vols. New York: Norton.

Gilmore, James R. 2007. *Personal Recollections of Abraham Lincoln and the Civil War*. Mechanicsburg, Pennsylvania: Stackpole Books.

Ginor, Isabella and Gideon Remez. 2007. *Foxbats Over Dimona: The Soviets' Nuclear Gamble in the Six-Day War*. New Haven: Yale University Press.

Glantz, David M. and Jonathan M. House. 1997. *When Titans Clashed: How the Red Army Stopped Hitler*. Lawrence, KS: University Press of Kansas.

Glaser, Charles L. and Steve Fetter. 2005. Counterforce Revisited: Assessing the Nuclear Posture Review's New Missions. *International Security* 30 (Fall): 84–126.

Goddard, Stacie E. 2006. Uncommon Ground: Indivisible Territory and the Politics of Legitimacy. *International Organization* 60 (Winter): 35–68.

Goemans, H. E. 2000. *War and Punishment: The Causes of War Termination and the First World War*. Princeton: Princeton University Press.

Goldstein, Joshua S. 2001. *Gender and War: How Gender Shapes the War System and Vice Versa*. Cambridge: Cambridge University Press.

Goodman, Allan E. 1978. *The Lost Peace: America's Search for a Negotiated Settlement in the Vietnam War*. Stanford, CA: Hoover Institution Press.

Goodspeed, D. J. 1966. *Ludendorff: Soldier, Dictator, Revolutionary*. London: Rupert Hart-Davis.

Goodwin, Doris Kearns. 2005. *Team of Rivals: The Political Genius of Abraham Lincoln*. New York: Simon and Schuster.

Gordon, Michael R. and Bernard E. Trainor. 1995. *The Generals' War: The Inside Story of the Conflict in the Gulf*. Boston: Little, Brown.

Gorodetsky, Gabriel. 1997. Stalin and Hitler's Attack on the Soviet Union. In Bernd Wegner, ed., *From Peace to War: Germany, Soviet Russia and the World, 1939–1941*, 343–59. Providence: Berghahn Books.

Grant, Ulysses Simpson. 1995. *Personal Memoirs of U. S. Grant*. New York: Dover.

Guderian, Heinz. 1952. *Panzer Leader*. Constantine Fitzgibbon, trans. New York: E. P. Dutton & Co.

Halpern, Paul G. 1994. *A Naval History of World War I*. Annapolis, MD: Naval Institute Press.

Hamby, Alonzo L. 1995. *Man of the People: A Life of Harry S. Truman*. New York: Oxford University Press.

Hamza, Khidhir. 2000. *Saddam's Bombmaker: The Daring Escape of the Man Who Built Iraq's Secret Weapon*. With Jeff Stein. New York: Touchstone.

Harcave, Sidney. 2004. *Count Sergei Witte and the Twilight of Imperial Russia: A Biography*. Armonk, NY: M. E. Sharpe.

Harrison, Hope M. 2003. *Driving the Soviets Up the Wall: Soviet–East German Relations, 1953–1961*. Princeton: Princeton University Press.

Hasegawa, Tsuyoshi. 2005. *Racing the Enemy: Stalin, Truman, and the Surrender of Japan*. Cambridge: Harvard University Press.

———, ed. 2007. *The End of the Pacific War: Reappraisals*. Stanford: Stanford University Press.

Hassner, Ron E. 2003. "To Halve and To Hold": Conflicts Over Sacred Space and the Problem of Indivisibility. *Security Studies* 12 (Summer): 1–33.

Hastings, Max. 2007. *Nemesis: The Battle for Japan, 1944–45*. New York: HarperPress.

Hata, Ikuhiko. 2007. *Hirohito: The Shôwa Emperor in War and Peace*. Marius B. Jansen, ed. Folkestone, UK: Global Oriental, Ltd.

Hattori, Syogo. 1996. Kamikaze: Japan's Glorious Failure. *Air Power History* 43 (Spring).

Heller, Francis H., ed. 1977. *The Korean War: A 25-Year Perspective*. Lawrence, KS: The Regents Press of Kansas.

Herwig, Holger H. 1972. Admirals *versus* Generals: The War Aims of the Imperial German Navy, 1914–1918. *Central European History* 5 (September): 208–33.

———. 1987. Clio Deceived: Patriotic Self-Censorship in Germany after the Great War. *International Security* 12 (Fall): 5–36.

———. 1997. *The First World War: Germany and Austria-Hungary, 1914–1918*. London: Arnold.

———. 2000. Total Rhetoric, Limited War: Germany's U-Boat Campaign, 1917–1918. In Roger Chickering and Stig Förster, eds., *Great War, Total War: Combat and Mobilization on the Western Front, 1914–1918*, 189–206. Cambridge: Cambridge University Press.

Herzog, Chaim. 1998. *The War of Atonement: The Inside Story of the Yom Kippur War, 1973*. London: Greenhill Books.

Hickey, Michael. 1999. *The Korean War: The West Confronts Communism*. Woodstock, NY: Overlook Press.

Hindenburg, Marshal von. 1920. *Out of My Life*. F. A. Holt, trans. London: Cassell and Company.

Howard, Michael. 1961. *The Franco-Prussian War: The German Invasion of France, 1870–1871*. London: Rupert Hart-Davis.

Hughes, Emmet John. 1963. *The Ordeal of Power: A Political Memoir of the Eisenhower Years*. New York: Atheneum.

Hull, Isabel V. 2005. *Absolute Destruction: Military Culture and the Practices of War in Imperial Germany*. Ithaca, NY: Cornell University Press.

Hunter, R.M.T. 1877. The Peace Commission of 1865. *Southern Historical Society Papers* 3 (April): 168–76.

Huth, Paul K. 1988. *Extended Deterrence and the Prevention of War*. New Haven, CT: Yale University Press.

Ienaga, Saburo. 1978. *The Pacific War, 1931–1945*. New York: Pantheon.

Iklé, Fred Charles. 1964. *How Nations Negotiate*. New York: Harper and Row.

——. 2005. *Every War Must End*. Second revised ed. New York: Columbia University Press.

Interrogations of Japanese Officials. N.d. U.S. Strategic Bombing Survey. 2 vols.

Iriye, Akira. 1981. *Power and Culture: The Japanese–American War, 1941–1945*. Cambridge, Mass: Harvard University Press.

Israel, Fred L., ed. 1966. *The War Diary of Breckinridge Long: Selections from the Years 1939–1944*. Lincoln, Nebraska: University of Nebraska Press.

Jakobson, Max. 1961. *The Diplomacy of the Winter War: An Account of the Russo-Finnish War, 1939–1940*. Cambridge: Harvard University Press.

Janssens, Rudolf V. A. 1995. *"What Future for Japan?" U.S. Wartime Planning for the Postwar Era, 1942–1945*. Amsterdam: Rodopi.

Jenkins, Roy. 2001. *Churchill: A Biography*. New York: Farrar, Straus, and Giroux.

Jervis, Robert. 1978. Cooperation Under the Security Dilemma. *World Politics* 30 (January): 167–214.

——. 1980. The Impact of the Korean War on the Cold War. *Journal of Conflict Resolution* 24 (December): 563–92.

——. 1989. *The Meaning of the Nuclear Revolution*. Ithaca: Cornell University Press.

Jian, Chen. 1994. *China's Road to the Korean War: The Making of the Sino-American Confrontation*. New York: Columbia University Press.

——. 2001. *Mao's China and the Cold War*. Chapel Hill, NC: University of North Carolina Press.

Johnson, Dominic D. P. 2004. *Overconfidence and War: The Havoc and Glory of Positive Illusions*. Cambridge: Harvard University Press.

Jokipii, Mauno. 1982. Finland's Entrance Into the Continuation War. *Revue Internationale d'Histoire Militaire*. No. 53: 85–103.

Jones, Oakah L. 1968. *Santa Anna*. New York: Twayne.

Kahneman, Daniel, Paul Slovic, and Amos Tversky, eds. 1982. *Judgment Under Uncertainty: Heuristics and Biases*. Cambridge: Cambridge University Press.

Karig, Walter, Malcolm W. Cagle, and Frank A. Manson. 1952. *Battle Report: The War in Korea*. New York: Rinehart.

Kecskemeti, Paul. 1958. *Strategic Surrender: The Politics of Victory and Defeat.* Stanford: Stanford University Press.

Kennan, George F. 1967. *Memoirs 1925–1950.* New York: Pantheon.

Keohane, Robert O. Keohane. 1984. *After Hegemony: Collaboration and Discord in the World Political Economy.* Princeton, NJ: Princeton University Press.

Khrushchev, Nikita S. 1970. *Khrushchev Remembers.* Strobe Talbott, trans. and ed. New York: Little Brown.

Kido, Koichi. 1984. *The Diary of Marquis Kido, 1931–1945.* Frederick, MD: University Publications of America.

Kimball, Warren F., ed. 1984. *Churchill and Roosevelt: The Complete Correspondence.* 3 vols. Princeton: Princeton University Press.

Kirkland, Edward Chase. 1927. *The Peacemakers of 1864.* New York: MacMillan.

Kirshner, Jonathan. 2000. Rationalist Explanations for War? *Security Studies* 10 (1): 143–50.

Kitchen, Martin. 1976. *The Silent Dictatorship: The Politics of the German High Command under Hindenburg and Ludendorff, 1916–1918.* New York: Holmes and Meier.

———. 2001. *The German Offensives of 1918.* Charleston, SC: Tempus.

Knesebeck, Ludolf Gottschalk von dem. 1927. *Die Wahreit über den Propagandafeldzug und Deutschland Zusammenbruch: Der Kampf der Publizistik im Weltkrieg.* Berlin: Dr. von dem Knesebeck.

Kolb, Eberhard. 1989. *Der Weg aus dem Krieg. Bismarcks Politik im Krieg und die Friedensanbahnung 1870/1871.* Munich: R. Oldenbourg.

Kollontai, Alexandra. 1990. "Seven Shots" In the Winter of 1939. *International Affairs* (Moscow) (January): 180–201.

Koremenos, Barbara, Charles Lipson, and Duncan Snidal. 2001. The Rational Design of International Institutions. *International Organization* 55 (Autumn): 761–99.

Krebs, Gerhard. 2005. Operation Super Sunrise? Japanese–United States Peace Feelers in Switzerland, 1945. *Journal of Military History* 69 (October): 1081–120.

Kulkov, E. N. and O. A. Rzheshevsky, eds. 2002. *Stalin and the Soviet–Finnish War 1939–1940.* Tatyana Sokokina, trans. London: Frank Cass.

Kydd, Andrew H. 2005. *Trust and Mistrust in International Relations.* Princeton: Princeton University Press.

Labs, Eric J. 1997. Beyond Victory: Offensive Realism and the Expansion of War Aims. *Security Studies* 6 (Summer): 1–49.

LaFeber, Walter. 1974. Crossing the 38th: The Cold War in Microcosm. In Lynn H. Miller and Ronald W. Pruessen, eds., *Reflections on the Cold War: A Quarter Century of American Foreign Policy,* 71–90. Philadelphia: Temple University Press.

———. 1997. *America, Russia, and The Cold War.* 8th ed. New York: McGraw-Hill.

Lai, Brian. 2004. The Effects of Different Types of Military Mobilization on the Outcome of International Crises. *Journal of Conflict Resolution* 48 (April, no. 2): 211–29.

Lai, Brian and Dan Reiter. 2005. Rally 'Round the Union Jack? Public Opinion and the Use of Force in the United Kingdom, 1948–2001. *International Studies Quarterly* 49 (June): 255–72.

Lai, Brian and Dan Slater. 2006. Institutions of the Offensive: Domestic Sources of Dispute Initiation in Authoritarian Regimes, 1950–1992. *American Journal of Political Science* 50 (January): 113–26.

Large, Stephen S. 1992. *Emperor Hirohito and Shōwa Japan: A Political Biography*. London: Routledge.

Lawlor, Sheila. 1994. *Churchill and the Politics of War, 1940–1941*. Cambridge: Cambridge University Press.

Lebow, Richard Ned. 1981. *Between Peace and War: The Nature of International Crisis*. Baltimore: Johns Hopkins University Press, 1981.

Leckie, Robert. 1962. *Conflict: The History of the Korean War, 1950–53*. New York: G. P. Putnam's Sons.

Lee, John. 2005. *The Warlords: Hindenburg and Ludendorff*. London: Weidenfeld and Nicolson.

Leeds, Brett Ashley. 2003. Alliance Reliability in Times of War: Explaining State Decisions to Violate Treaties. *International Organization* 57 (Fall): 801–27.

Leeds, Brett Ashley and David R. Davis. 1997. Domestic Political Vulnerability and International Disputes. *Journal of Conflict Resolution* 41(6): 814–34.

Leffler, Melvyn S. 1992. *A Preponderance of Power: National Security, the Truman Administration, and the Cold War*. Stanford: Stanford University Press.

Legro, Jeffrey W. 1995. *Cooperation Under Fire: Anglo-German Restraint During World War II*. Ithaca: Cornell University Press.

Levontoğlu, Bahar and Branislav Slantchev. 2007. The Armed Peace: A Punctuated Equilibrium Theory of War. *American Journal of Political Science* 51 (October): 755–71.

Li, Xiaobing, Allan R. Millett, and Bin Yu, trans. and eds. 2001. *Mao's Generals Remember Korea*. Lawrence, KS: University Press of Kansas.

Liberman, Peter. 1996. *Does Conquest Pay? The Exploitation of Occupied Industrial Societies*. Princeton: Princeton University Press.

Lieber, Keir A. 2000. Grasping the Technological Peace: The Offense-Defense Balance and International Security. *International Security* 25 (Summer):

Lipson, Charles. 2003. *Reliable Partners: How Democracies Made a Separate Peace*. Princeton: Princeton University Press.

Livermore, Thomas L. 1957. *Numbers and Losses in the Civil War in America: 1861–65*. Bloomington, IN: Indiana University Press.

Lloyd George, David. 1933–37. *War Memoirs of David Lloyd George*. 6 vols. Boston: Little, Brown.

Lo, Nigel, Barry Hashimoto, and Dan Reiter. 2008. Ensuring Peace: Foreign Imposed Regime Change and Postwar Peace Duration, 1914–2001. *International Organization* 62 (Fall): 717–36.

Loewenstein, George and Don A. Moore. 2004. When Ignorance is Bliss: Information Exchange and Inefficiency in Bargaining. *Journal of Legal Studies* 33 (January): 37–58.

Long, Stephen B. 2007. Retaliatory Behavior and the Violation of Formal Cease-Fire Agreements, 1948–1998. Unpublished ms. Kansas State University.

Lord, Walter. 1982. *The Miracle of Dunkirk*. London: Allen Lane.

Ludendorff, Erich von. 1919. *Ludendorff's Own Story, August 1914–November 1918*. 2 vols. New York: Harper and Brothers.

Lukacs, John. 1990. *The Duel: 10 May–31 July 1940, The Eighty-Day Struggle Between Churchill and Hitler*. New York: Ticknor and Fields.

———. 1999. *Five Days in London: May 1940*. New Haven: Yale University Press.

Lutz, Ralph Haswell. 1934. *The Causes of the German Collapse in 1918*. W. L. Campbell, trans. Stanford, CA: Stanford University Press.

MacArthur, Douglas. 1964. *Reminiscences*. New York: McGraw-Hill.

MacFie, A. L. 1975. The British Decision Regarding the Future of Constantinople, November 1918–January 1920. *Historical Journal* 18 (2): 391–400.

MacKenzie, S. P. 1994. The Treatment of Prisoners of War in World War II. *Journal of Modern History* 66 (September): 487–520.

Macleod, Roderick, and Denis Kelly. 1962. *Time Unguarded: The Ironside Diaries, 1937–1940*. New York: David McKay Company.

Manchester, William. 1978. *American Caesar, Douglas MacArthur, 1880–1964*. Boston: Little Brown.

Mann, Chris and Christer Jörgensen. 2002. *Hitler's Arctic War: The German Campaigns in Norway, Finland, and the USSR 1940–1945*. London: Brown Partworks.

Mansfield, Edward D. and Jack Snyder. 2005. *Electing to Fight: Why Emerging Democracies Go to War*. Cambridge, MA: MIT Press.

Masefield, John. 1916. *Gallipoli*. New York: Macmillan.

Mastny, Vojtech. 1979. *Russia's Road to the Cold War: Diplomacy, Warfare, and the Politics of Communism, 1941–1945*. New York: Columbia University Press.

Mattes, Michaela. 2008. The Effect of Changing Conditions and Agreement Provisions on Conflict and Renegotiation Between States with Competing Claims. *International Studies Quarterly* 52 (June): 315–34.

Mawdsley, Evan. 2005. *Thunder in the East: The Nazi-Soviet War, 1941–1945*. London: Hodder Arnold.

May, Ernest R. 2000. *Strange Victory: Hitler's Conquest of France*. New York: Hill and Wang.

McElroy, Robert. 1937. *Jefferson Davis: The Unreal and the Real*. New York: Harper and Brothers Publishers.

McPherson, James M. 1988. *Battle Cry of Freedom: The Civil War Era*. New York: Ballentine.

Mearsheimer, John J. 1981. The Theory and Practice of Conventional Deterrence. Ph.D. diss., Cornell University. Ann Arbor, MI: University Microfilms, International.

Mearsheimer, John J. 1983. *Conventional Deterrence*. Ithaca: Cornell.

———. 2001. *The Tragedy of Great Power Politics*. New York: Norton.

Meernik, James. 2001. Domestic Politics and the Diversionary Use of Military Force by the United States. *Political Research Quarterly* 54 (December): 889–904.

Menger, Manfred. 1997. Germany and the Finnish 'Separate War' Against the Soviet Union. In Bernd Wegner, ed., *From Peace to War: Germany, Soviet Russia and the World, 1939–1941*. Providence, RI: Berghahn Books.

Meretskov, K. A. 1971. *Serving the People*. David Fidlon, trans. Moscow: Progress Publishers.

Merrill, Dennis, ed. 1997. *Documentary History of the Truman Presidency*. Vol. 18. University Publications of America.

Mitchell, Sara McLaughlin and Paul R. Hensel. 2007. International Institutions and Compliance with Agreements. *American Journal of Political Science* 51 (October): 721–37.

Morgenthau, Hans J. 1967. *Politics Among Nations: The Struggle for Power and Peace*. 4th ed. New York: Alfred A. Knopf.

Morison, Samuel Eliot. 1963. *The Two-Ocean War: A Short History of the United States Navy in the Second World War*. Boston: Little, Brown.

Mueller, John E. 1980. The Search for the "Breaking Point" in Vietnam: The Statistics of a Deadly Quarrel. *International Studies Quarterly* 24 (December): 497–519.

———. 1985. *War, Presidents, and Public Opinion*. Lanham, MD: University Press of America.

———. 1994. *Policy and Opinion in the Gulf War*. Chicago: University of Chicago Press.

Munch-Peterson, Thomas. 1986. "Common Sense not Bravado": The Butler-Prytz Interview of 17 June 1940. *Scandia* 52 (1): 73–114.

Murray, Williamson. 1984. *The Change in the European Balance of Power, 1938–1939: The Path to Ruin*. Princeton: Princeton University Press.

Muthoo, Abhinay. 1999. *Bargaining Theory with Applications*. Cambridge: Cambridge University Press.

Myllyniemi, Seppo. 1997. Consequences of the Hitler–Stalin Pact for the Baltic Republics and Finland. In Bernd Wegner, ed., *From Peace to War: Germany, Soviet Russia and the World, 1939–1941*, 79–94. Providence, RI: Berghahn Books.

National Security Council Records. College Park, Maryland: National Security Archive.

Nerhem, Steven William. 2000. NSC-81/1 and the Evolution of U.S. War Aims in Korea June–October 1950. Carlisle Barracks, PA: U.S. Army War College.

Newbolt, Henry. 1928. *Naval Operations*. Vol. 4. New York: Longmans Green.

Nicolay, John G. and John Hay. 1890. *Abraham Lincoln: A History*. 10 vols. New York: Century.

Nicolson, Harold. 1967. *The War Years, 1939–1945: Volume II of Diaries and Letters*. Nigel Nicolson, ed. New York: Atheneum

Nicolson, Nigel. 1985. *Napoleon 1812*. New York: Harper and Row.

Notter, Harley A. 1949. *Postwar Foreign Policy Preparation, 1939–1945*. Washington: Department of State.

Notter Papers. College Park, Maryland: National Security Archive.

Nove, Alec. 1969. *An Economic History of the U.S.S.R.* London: Allen Lane.

Oates, Stephen B. 1977. *With Malice Toward None: The Life of Abraham Lincoln*. New York: Harper and Row.

O'Connor, Raymond G. 1971. *Diplomacy for Victory: FDR and Unconditional Surrender*. New York: Norton.

Official Records of the Union and Confederate Armies. 1899. Washington: U.S. Government Printing Office.

Offner, Arnold A. 2002. *Another Such Victory: President Truman and the Cold War, 1945–1953*. Stanford: Stanford University Press.

Ohnuki-Tierney, Emiko. 2002. *Kamikaze, Cherry Blossoms, and Nationalisms: The Militarization of Aesthetics in Japanese History*. Chicago: University of Chicago Press.

Oneal, John R. and Jaroslav Tir. 2006. Does the Diversionary Use of Force Threaten the Democratic Peace? Assessing the Effect of Economic Growth on Interstate Conflict, 1921–2001. *International Studies Quarterly* 50 (December): 755–59.

Oren, Michael B. 2002. *Six Days of War: June 1967 and the Making of the Modern Middle East*. Oxford: Oxford University Press.

Oshinsky, David M. 1983. *A Conspiracy So Immense: The World of Joe McCarthy*. New York: Free Press.

Owsley, Frank Lawrence. 1931. *King Cotton Diplomacy: Foreign Relations of the Confederate States of America*. Chicago: University of Chicago Press.

Palm, Thede. 1971. *The Finnish-Soviet Armistice Negotiations of 1944*. Stockholm: Almqvist & Wiksell.

Pape, Robert A. 1996. *Bombing to Win: Air Power and Coercion in War*. Ithaca: Cornell.

The Papers of Cordell Hull. 1975. Washington: Library of Congress.

Parkinson, Roger. 1978. *Tormented Warrior: Ludendorff and the Supreme Command*. London: Hodder and Stoughton.

Pavlenko, Nikolay. 1989. Tragediya Krasnoi Armii. *Moscovkie Novosti*. May 7, no. 19, 9.

Peck, Abraham J. 1978. *Radicals and Reactionaries: The Crisis of Conservatism in Wilhelmine Germany*. Washington: University Press of America.

Peic, Goran and Dan Reiter. 2008. Foreign-Imposed Regime Change and Civil War Onset, 1920–2004. Presented at the annual meeting of the Peace Science Society (International), October 25, Claremont, California.

Pickering, Jeffrey and Emizet Kisangani. 2005. Democracy and Diversionary Military Intervention: Reassessing Regime Type and the Diversionary Hypothesis. *International Studies Quarterly* 49 (March): 23–43.

Pierce, Edward L., ed. 1893. *Memoirs and Letters of Charles Sumner. Vol. IV, 1860–1874*. Boston: Roberts Brothers.

Pillar, Paul R. 1983. *Negotiating Peace: War Termination as a Bargaining Process*. Princeton: Princeton University Press.

Pimlott, Ben, ed. 1986. *The Second World War Diary of Hugh Dalton*. London: Jonathan Cape.

Ping, Du. 2001. Political Mobilization and Control. In Xiaobing Li, Allan R. Millett, and Bin Yu, trans. and ed., *Mao's Generals Remember Korea*, 61–105. Lawrence, KS: University Press of Kansas.

Pletcher, David M. 1973. *The Diplomacy of Annexation: Texas, Oregon, and the Mexican War*. Columbia, Missouri: University of Missouri Press.

Pogue, Forrest C. 1966. *George C. Marshall: Ordeal and Hope, 1939–1942*. New York: Viking.

———. 1973. *George C. Marshall: Organizer of Victory, 1942–1945*. New York: Viking.

Pollack, Kenneth M. 2002a. *Arabs at War: Military Effectiveness, 1948–1991*. Lincoln, NE: University of Nebraska.

———. 2002b. *The Threatening Storm: The Case for Invading Iraq*. New York: Random House.

Polvinen, Tuomo. 1985. The Great Powers and Finland 1941–1944. *Revue Internationale d'Histoire Militaire* (no. 62): 133–52.

Potter, David M. 1942. *Lincoln and His Party in the Secession Crisis*. New Haven: Yale University Press.

Powell, Colin L. 1995. *My American Journey*. With Joseph E. Persico. New York: Random House.

Powell, Robert. 2002. Bargaining Theory and International Conflict. *Annual Review of Political Science* 5 (June): 1–30.

———. 2004. The Inefficient Use of Power: Costly Conflict with Complete Information. *American Political Science Review* 98 (May): 231–41.

———. 2006. War as a Commitment Problem. *International Organization* 60 (Winter): 169–203.

Press, Daryl G. 2005. *Calculating Credibility: How Leaders Assess Military Threats*. Ithaca: Cornell.

Reed, William. 2003. Information and Economic Interdependence. *Journal of Conflict Resolution* 47 (February): 54–71.

———. 2003. Information, Power, and War. *American Political Science Review* 97 (November): 633–41.

Reeves, Thomas C. 1982. *The Life and Times of Joe McCarthy: A Biography*. New York: Stein and Day.

Reiss, Hans, ed. 1970. *Kant's Political Writings*. H. B. Nisbet, trans. London: Cambridge University Press.

Reiter, Dan. 1995. Exploding the Power Keg Myth: Preemptive Wars Almost Never Happen. *International Security* 20 (Fall): 5–34.

———. 1996. *Crucible of Beliefs: Learning, Alliances, and World Wars*. Ithaca: Cornell University Press.

———. 2003. Exploring the Bargaining Model of War. *Perspectives on Politics* 1 (March): 27–43.

———. 2005. Preventive Attacks Against Nuclear Programs and the "Success" at Osiraq. *Nonproliferation Review* 12 (July): 355–71.

———. 2006a. Preventive Attacks Against Nuclear, Biological, and Chemical Weapons Programs: The Track Record. In William Keller and Gordon Mitchell, eds., *Hitting First: Preventive Force in U.S. Security Strategy*. Pittsburgh: University of Pittsburgh Press, 27–44.

———. 2006b. *Preventive War and Its Alternatives: The Lessons of History*. Carlisle, PA: Strategic Studies Institute, U.S. Army War College.

———. 2007. Nationalism and Military Effectiveness. In Elizabeth A. Stanley-Mitchell and Risa Brooks, eds., *Creating Military Power: The Sources of Military Effectiveness*, 27–54. Palo Alto: Stanford University Press.

Reiter, Dan and Allan C. Stam. 2002. *Democracies at War*. Princeton: Princeton University Press.

———. 2007. Democracies at War Revisited: Extensions and Controversies. Presented at the annual meeting of the International Studies Association, Chicago, Illinois, February 28–March 3.

Retallack, James N. 1988. *Notables of the Right: The Conservative Party and Political Mobilization in Germany, 1876–1918*. Boston: Unwin Hyman.

Reynolds, David. 1985. Churchill and the British 'Decision' to Fight on in 1940: Right Policy, Wrong Reasons. In Richard Langhorne, ed., *Diplomacy and Intelligence during the Second World War: Essays in Honour of F. H. Hinsley*, 147–67. Cambridge: Cambridge University Press.

———. 1996. Churchill the Appeaser? Between Hitler, Roosevelt, and Stalin in World War Two. In Michael Dockrill and Brian McKercher, eds., *Diplomacy and World Power: Studies in British Foreign Policy*, 197–220. Cambridge: Cambridge University Press.

Ricks, Thomas E. 2006. *Fiasco: The American Military Adventure in Iraq*. New York: Penguin.

Ridgway, Matthew B. 1988. *The Korean War*. 2nd ed. New York: Da Capo Press.

Risse-Kappen, Thomas. 1995. *Cooperation Among Democracies: The European Influence on U.S. Foreign Policy*. Princeton: Princeton University Press.

Ritter, Gerhard. 1969–1973. *The Sword and the Scepter: The Problem of Militarism in Germany*. 4 vols. Heinz Norden, trans. Coral Gables, FL: University of Miami Press.

Roberts, Andrew. 1991. *"The Holy Fox": A Biography of Lord Halifax*. London: Weidenfeld and Nicolson.

Ronay, Gabriel. 1989. Stalin "Offered Hitler a Deal." *Sunday Times* (London). May 28.

Roosevelt, Elliott, ed. 1950. *F.D.R. His Personal Letters: 1928–1945*. 2 vols. New York: Duell, Sloan, and Pearce.

Rose, Gideon Gregory. 1994. Victory and Its Substitutes: Foreign Policy Decisionmaking at the Ends of Wars. Ph.D. diss. Harvard University.

Rosen, Stephen Peter. 2005. *War and Human Nature*. Princeton: Princeton University Press.

Rosen, Steven. 1972. War Power and the Willingness to Suffer. In Bruce Russett, ed., *Peace, War, and Numbers*, pp. 167–83. Beverly Hills: Sage.

Rosenberg, Arthur. 1931. *The Birth of the German Republic, 1871–1918*. New York: Oxford University Press.

Rothwell, V. H. 1971. *British War Aims and Peace Diplomacy, 1914–1918*. Oxford: Clarendon Press.

Rowland, Dunbar, ed. 1923. *Jefferson Davis, Constitutionalist, His Letters, Papers, and Speeches*. 10 vols. Jackson, MS: Mississippi Department of Archives and History.

Sagan, Scott D. 1988. The Origins of the Pacific War. In Robert I. Rotberg and Theodore K. Rabb, eds., *The Origin and Prevention of Major Wars*, 323–52. Cambridge, UK: Cambridge University Press.

Sale, Sara L. 1998. *The Shaping of Containment: Harry S. Truman, The National Security Council, and the Cold War*. Saint James, NY: Brandywine Press.

Sanford, George. 2005. *Katyn and the Soviet Massacre of 1940: Truth, Justice, and Memory.* London: Routledge.

Sarkees, Meredith Reid. 1997. The Correlates of War Data on War: An Update to 1997. *Conflict Management and Peace Science* 18 (Fall): 123–44.

Sartori, Anne E. 2005. *Deterrence by Diplomacy.* Princeton: Princeton University Press.

Saunders, Robert, Jr. 2001. *John Archibald Campbell, Southern Moderate, 1811–1889.* Tuscaloosa, Alabama: University of Alabama Press.

Schelling, Thomas C. 1960. *The Strategy of Conflict.* Cambridge: Harvard.

———. 1966. *Arms and Influence.* New Haven: Yale University Press.

Scherer, André and Jacques Grunewald. 1962–78. *L'Allemagne et Les Problèmes de la Paix Pendant la Première Guerre Mondiale.* 4 vols. Paris: Presses Universitaires de France.

Schiff, Zeev. 1974. *A History of the Israeli Army (1870–1974).* Raphael Rothstein, trans. and ed. San Francisco: Straight Arrow Books.

Schnabel, James F. and Robert J. Watson. 1979. *The History of the Joint Chiefs of Staff. Volume III, The Korean War.* 2 parts. Wilmington, DE: Michael Glazier, Inc.

Schwartzkopf, H. Norman. 1992. *It Doesn't Take a Hero.* Written with Peter Petre. New York: Bantam.

Schweller, Randall L. 1998. *Deadly Imbalances: Tripolarity and Hitler's Strategy of World Conquest.* New York: Columbia University Press.

Screen, J.E.O. 2000. *Mannerheim: The Finnish Years.* London: Hurst & Company.

Sebag-Montefiore, Hugh. 2006. *Dunkirk: Fight to the Last Man.* Cambridge: Harvard University Press.

Segev, Tom. 2007. *1967: Israel, the War, and the Year That Transformed the Middle East.* Jessica Cohen, trans. New York: Metropolitan Books.

Self, Robert, ed. 2005. *The Neville Chamberlain Diary Letters. Volume 4: The Downing Street Years, 1934–1940.* Aldershot, UK: Ashgate.

———. 2006. *Neville Chamberlain: A Biography.* Aldershot, UK: Ashgate.

Selten, R. 1978. The Chain Store Paradox. *Theory and Decision,* 9, 127–59.

Sherman, William Tecumseh. 1990. *Memoirs of General W. T. Sherman.* New York: The Library of America.

Sherwood, Robert E. 1950. *Roosevelt and Hopkins: An Intimate History.* Revised ed. New York: Harper and Brothers.

Shigemitsu, Mamoru. 1958. *Japan and her Destiny: My Struggle for Peace.* Oswald White, trans. F.S.G. Piggott, ed. London: Hutchinson.

Shillony, Ben-Ami. 1976. Wartime Japan: A Military Dictatorship? In Harold Z. Schiffrin, ed., *Military and State in Modern Asia,* 61–88. Jerusalem: Jerusalem Academic Press.

———. 1981. *Politics and Culture in Wartime Japan.* Oxford: Clarendon Press.

Sigal, Leon V. 1988. *Fighting to a Finish: The Politics of War Termination in the United States and Japan, 1945.* Ithaca: Cornell University Press.

Simmel, Georg. 1904. The Sociology of Conflict, I. *American Journal of Sociology* 9 (January, no. 4): 490–525.

Simmons, Beth A. 2000. International Law and State Behavior: Commitment and Compliance in International Monetary Affairs. *American Political Science Review* 94 (December): 819–35.

———. 2002. Capacity, Commitment, and Compliance. *Journal of Conflict Resolution* 46 (December): 829–56.

Slantchev, Branislav L. 2003a. The Power to Hurt: Costly Conflict with Completely Informed States. *American Political Science Review* 97 (February): 123–33.

———. 2003b. The Principle of Convergence in Wartime Negotiations. *American Political Science Review* 97 (November): 621–32.

———. 2004. How Initiators End Their Wars: The Duration of Warfare and the Terms of Peace. *American Journal of Political Science* 48 (October): 813–29.

Smith, Alastair and Allan C. Stam. 2001. Issues, Stakes, and the Nature of War. Presented at the annual meeting of the American Political Science Association, August 30–September 2.

Smith, John David. 2002. Let Us All Be Grateful That We Have Colored Troops That Will Fight. In John David Smith, ed., *Black Soldiers in Blue: African American Troops in the Civil War Era*. Chapel Hill, NC: University of North Carolina Press.

Snyder, Jack. 1984. *The Ideology of the Offensive: Military Decision Making and the Disasters of 1914*. Ithaca, NY: Cornell University Press.

———. 1991. *Myths of Empire: Domestic Politics and International Ambition*. Ithaca, NY: Cornell University Press.

Spring, D. W. 1986. The Soviet Decision for War Against Finland, 30 November 1939. *Soviet Studies* 38 (April): 207–26.

Stam, Allan C. III. 1996. *Win, Lose, or Draw: Domestic Politics and the Crucible of War*. Ann Arbor, MI: University of Michigan Press.

Stanley-Mitchell, Elizabeth. 2002. Working Out the Inevitable: Domestic Coalitions in War Termination. Ph.D. diss, Harvard University.

Stephens, Alexander. 1870. *A Constitutional View of the Late War Between the States*. 2 vols. Philadelphia: National Publishing Company.

Stevenson, David. 1982. Belgium, Luxembourg, and the Defense of Western Europe, 1914–1920. *International History Review* 4 (November): 504–30.

———. 1988. *The First World War and International Politics*. Oxford: Oxford University Press.

———. 2004. *Cataclysm: The First World War as Political Tragedy*. New York: Basic Books.

Stibbe, Matthew. 2001. *German Anglophobia and the Great War, 1914–1918*. Cambridge: Cambridge University Press.

Stoddard, William O. 1890. *Inside the White House in War Times*. New York: Charles L. Webster.

Streim, Alfred. 1997. International Law and Soviet Prisoners of War. In Bernd Wegner, ed., *From Peace to War: Germany, Soviet Russia and the World, 1939–1941*. Providence, RI: Berghahn Books, pp. 293–308

Stroud, Hudson. 1959. *Jefferson Davis: Confederate President*. 2 vols. New York: Harcourt, Brace, and Company.

Stueck, William. 1983. The March to the Yalu: The Perspective from Washington. In *Child of Conflict: The Korean–American Relationship, 1943–1953*, Bruce Cumings, ed., 195–237. Seattle: University of Washington Press.

———. 1995. *The Korean War: An International History*. Princeton: Princeton University Press.

———. 2002. *Rethinking the Korean War: A New Diplomatic and Strategic History*. Princeton: Princeton University Press.

Sudoplatov, Pavel and Anatoli Sudoplatov. 1994. *Special Tasks: The Memoirs of an Unwanted Witness—A Soviet Spymaster*. With Jerrold L. Schecter and Leona P. Schecter. Boston: Little Brown.

Supplemental Appropriations for 1951. 1950. Hearings before the Committee on Appropriations, U.S. Senate. 81st cong, 2nd sess. Washington: U.S. Government Printing Office.

Tanaka, Toshiyuki. 1996. *Hidden Horrors: Japanese War Crimes in World War II*. Boulder: Westview Press.

Tanner, Fred. 1993. Postwar Arms Control. *Journal of Peace Research* 30 (February): 29–43.

Tanner, Väinö. 1957. *The Winter War: Finland Against Russia 1939–1940*. Stanford: Stanford University Press.

Tarar, Ahmer and Bahar Levontoğlu. 2006. Public Commitment in Crisis Bargaining. Working paper, Texas A&M University, August 25.

Thompson, Robert Means and Richard Wainwright, eds. 1920. *Confidential Correspondence of Gustavus Vasa Fox, Assistant Secretary of the Navy 1861–1865*. New York: Naval History Society.

Thucydides. 1998. *The Peloponnesian War*. Steven Lattimore trans. Indianapolis, IN: Hackett.

Toft, Monica Duffy. 2003. *The Geography of Ethnic Violence*. Princeton: Princeton University Press.

Tokyo Major War Crimes Trial: The Records of the International Military Tribunal for the Far East. 1998. R. John Pritchard, ed. 124 vols. Lewiston, NY: Edwin Mellen Press.

Trachtenberg, Marc. 1991. *History and Strategy*. Princeton: Princeton University Press.

Trotter, William R. 1991. *A Frozen Hell: The Russo-Finnish War of 1939–1940*. Chapel Hill, NC: Algonquin Books.

Truman, Harry S. 1956. *Memoirs*. 2 vols. Garden City, NJ: Doubleday.

Tuchman, Barbara W. 1962. *The Guns of August*. New York: Bantam.

Tuunainen, Pasi. 2006. The Battle of Encirclement at Ilomantsi in July–August 1944—An Example of the Application of the Idea of *Cannae* in the Finnish Art of War. *Journal of Slavic Military Studies* 19 (March): 107–22.

U.S. Congress, Senate. 1951. *Military Situation in the Far East*. Hearings before the Committee on Armed Services and the Committee on Foreign Relations, 82d Cong., 1st sess. Washington, DC: U.S. Government Printing Office.

Valentino, Benjamin, Paul Huth, and Dylan Balch-Lindsay. 2004. "Draining the Sea": Mass Killing and Guerrilla Warfare. *International Organization* 58 (Spring): 375–407.

Van Dyke, Carl. 1997. *The Soviet Invasion of Finland, 1939–1940*. London: Frank Cass.

Van Evera, Stephen. *The Causes of War: Power and the Roots of Conflict*. Ithaca, NY: Cornell University Press, 1999.

Vehviläinen, Olli. 2002. *Finland in the Second World War: Between Germany and Russia*. Gerard McAlester, trans. New York: Palgrave.

Volkogonov, Dmitrii. 1991. *Stalin: Triumph and Tragedy*. Harold Shukman, ed. and trans. London: Weidenfeld.

Wagner, R. Harrison. 2000. Bargaining and War. *American Journal of Political Science* 44 (July): 469–84.

———. 2007. *War and the State: The Theory of International Politics*. Ann Arbor, MI: University of Michigan Press.

Wainstock, Dennis D. 1999. *Truman, MacArthur, and the Korean War*. Westport, CT: Greenwood Press.

Walt, Stephen M. 1996. *Revolution and War*. Ithaca: Cornell University Press.

Walter, Barbara F. 2002. *Committing to Peace: The Successful Settlement of Civil Wars*. Princeton: Princeton University Press.

———. 2006a. Building Reputation: Why Governments Fight Some Separatists but Not Others. *American Journal of Political Science* 50 (April): 313–30.

———. 2006b. Information, Uncertainty, and the Decision to Secede. *International Organization* 60 (Winter): 105–35.

Waltz, Kenneth N. 1979. *Theory of International Politics*. New York: Random House.

Warner, Denis and Peggy Warner with Sadao Seno. 1982. *The Sacred Warriors: Japan's Suicide Legions*. With Sadao Seno. New York: Van Nostrand.

Watson, Derek. 2005. *Molotov: A Biography*. New York: Palgrave.

Wawro, Geoffrey. 2003. *The Franco-Prussian War: The German Conquest of France in 1870–1871*. Cambridge, UK: Cambridge University Press.

Weathersby, Kathryn. 1998. In Odd Arne Westad, ed., *Brothers in Arms: The Rise and Fall of the Sino–Soviet Alliance, 1945–1963*, 90–116. Stanford: Stanford University Press.

Weems, John Edward. 1974. *To Conquer a Peace: The War Between the United States and Mexico*. Garden City, NY: Doubleday.

Weingast, Barry R. 1998. Political Stability and Civil War: Institutions, Commitment, and American Democracy. In Robert H. Bates, Avner Grief, Margaret Levi, Jean-Laurent Rosenthal, and Barry R. Weingast, eds., *Analytic Narratives*, 148–93. Princeton: Princeton University Press.

Weisiger, Alex. 2008. From Small Wars to Armageddon: Explaining Variation in Interstate War Duration and Severity. Ph.D. diss, Columbia University.

Welles, Gideon. 1872. The History of Emancipation. *The Galaxy: A Magazine of Entertaining Reading* 14 (December): 838–51.

Welles, Sumner. 1950. *Seven Decisions that Shaped History*. New York: Harper.

Wendt, Alexander. 1999. *Social Theory of International Politics*. Cambridge: Cambridge University Press.

Werner, Suzanne. 1996. Absolute and Limited War: The Possibility of Foreign-Imposed Regime Change. *International Interactions* 22(1): 67–88.

Werner, Suzanne. 1998. Negotiating the Terms of Settlement: War Aims and Bargaining Leverage. *Journal of Conflict Resolution* 42 (June): 321–43.

———. 1999. The Precarious Nature of Peace: Resolving the Issues, Enforcing the Settlement, and Renegotiating the Terms. *American Journal of Political Science* 43 (July): 912–34.

———. 2000. Deterring Intervention: The Stakes of War and Third-Party Involvement. *American Journal of Political Science* 44 (October): 720–32.

Werner, Suzanne and Amy Yuen. 2005. Making and Keeping Peace. *International Organization* 59 (Spring): 261–92.

Whitney, Courtney. 1955. *MacArthur: His Rendezvous With History.* Westport, CT: Greenwood.

"The Winter War." *International Affairs* (Moscow) (January): 202–15, 149.

Wolford, Scott. 2007. The Turnover Trap: New Leaders, Reputation, and International Conflict. *American Journal of Political Science* 51 (October): 772–88.

Wolford, Scott, Dan Reiter, and Clifford Carrubba. 2008. Information, Commitment, and War. Unpublished manuscript. Emory University, Atlanta, Georgia.

Woodward, Bob. 1999. *Shadow: Five Presidents and the Legacy of Watergate.* New York: Simon and Schuster.

———. 2006. *State of Denial.* New York: Simon and Schuster.

Yuen, Amy T. 2007. Strategic Choices and Third-Party Intervention in Interstate Conflicts. Ph.D. diss., Emory University, Atlanta, Georgia.

Zabecki, David T. 2006. *The German 1918 Offensives: A Case Study in the Operational Level of War.* London: Routledge.

Zhang, Shu Guang. 1992. *Deterrence and Strategic Culture: Chinese-American Confrontations, 1949–1958.* Ithaca: Cornell University Press.

———. 1995. *Mao's Military Romanticism: China and the Korean War, 1950–1953.* Lawrence, KS: University Press of Kansas.

Ziemke, Earl F. 1959. *The German Northern Theater of Operations, 1940–1945.* Washington: U.S. Government Printing Office.

Zuber, Terence. 2002. *Inventing the Schlieffen Plan: German War Planning, 1871–1914.* Oxford: Oxford University Press.

Index

Radford, Arthur W., 72
rally round the flag effect, 9
Rangoon, 110
rationalism, 48, 50
Raymond, Henry, 152
Reagan, Ronald, 24
realism, 22–24, 234n3
regime change. *See* states
reputation effects: Churchill and, 101;
 Civil War and, 161; indivisibility effects
 and, 48; Japan and, 192, 198, 219; Korean War and, 90, 243n66; reputation
 as scarce goods, 8; Stalin and, 126;
 U.S. and, 89–90; war and, 11, 221;
 World War II and, 101, 192, 198, 219.
 See also political issues; resolve; war—
 termination
research: on bargaining models, 8, 14, 15;
 on commitments, 3; on information and
 war, 15; on war and use of force, 10–11;
 on war outcomes and termination, 1–2,
 5–6, 43. *See also* methods
research—specific projects: Civil War
 (U.S.), 143; democratization, 226; information models, 233n37; international institutions, 223; interstate wars, 224,
 225, 236n62; intrastate conflict, 224; Korean War, 68, 79, 88, 245n133; military
 preferences in war, 220
resistance and insurgencies: absolute war
 and, 30; characterization of, 59; Iraq
 War of 1991 and, 40; postwar activities
 of, 28, 30–31
resolve: Franco-Prussian War and, 33; Gulf
 War of 1991, 238n101; Korean War
 and, 78; misrepresentation of, 14; Vietnam War and, 13; war initiation and,
 167; war outcomes and, 2–3, 12–13, 17;
 war reinitiation and, 37; World War I
 and, 174, 176; World War II and, 97,
 117, 186, 187, 194–95, 196, 202. *See
 also* reputation effects
revolutions, 37, 175, 182, 217
Reynaud, Paul, 100
Rhee, Syngman, 66, 67
Ribot, Alexandre, 173
Robertson, William, 173
Roberts, William L., 69
Romania. *See* World Wars I and II; *individual countries*
Rome, 72

Rommell, Erwin, 109
Roosevelt, Franklin D.: Churchill and,
 101, 107; commitment dynamics and,
 54, 213, 223; confidence of, 222; Hali-
 fax telegram to, 104; Japan and, 109,
 111; leadership of, 222; Stalin and, 115,
 135; war aims and demands of, 110–11,
 112–13, 114, 115, 213, 223; World War
 II and, 26, 57, 107, 218
Rosecrans, William, 150
Rusk, Dean, 13, 78, 81, 90
Russia, 22, 61, 121. *See also* World War I
Russo-Japanese War (1904–5), 10, 192
Ryti, Risto, 133, 136

salami tactics, 48
Santa Anna, Antonio López, 219–20
Sato, Naotoke, 200
Scowcroft, Brent, 46
secession: in civil wars, 161; commitment
 dynamics and, 26; by the Confederacy,
 140, 141, 145–46, 157, 161–62, 163–
 64, 223, 256n98; by Ireland, 26
Second Punic War (218–201 BC), 72
Seizo, Arisue, 194
September 11, 2001, 224
Serbia, 12
Seven Years' War (1756–63), 72
Seward, William, 9, 142, 149, 155, 160
Sherman, Forrest, 72, 73, 75
Sherman, William, 154, 160
Shigemitsu, Mamoru, 192, 199
Shimada, Shigetarō, 193
Simmel, Georg, 15
Singapore, 108, 110
Sitting War (1939–40), 96
Sitzkrieg (1939–40), 96
Six-Day War (1967), 12, 14, 24, 45–46,
 228, 233n34
slaves and slavery: Civil War and, 146,
 147–48; Lincoln and, 140, 143, 145,
 146, 147–48, 149–50, 155; as a political
 issue, 158; Thirteenth Amendment and,
 155, 156; U.S.-Mexico War and, 40. *See
 also* Civil War (U.S.); Emancipation
 Proclamation
Smith, Walter Bedell, 113
Social Democratic Party (Germany), 179
South Africa, 228
South America, 109
South Carolina, 160